HERE IN AMERICA'S TEST KITCHEN

HERE IN
AMERICA'S TEST KITCHEN

BY THE EDITORS OF
COOK'S ILLUSTRATED

ILLUSTRATIONS
John Burgoyne

PHOTOGRAPHY
Keller + Keller
Bill Miles
Elisabeth O'Donnell
Carl Tremblay
Daniel Van Ackere

BOSTON COMMON PRESS BROOKLINE, MASSACHUSETTS

Boston Common Press
17 Station Street
Brookline, Massachusetts 02445

ISBN 0-936184-59-0
Library of Congress Cataloging-in-Publication Data
The Editors of Cook's Illustrated

Here in America's Test Kitchen: All-New Recipes, Quick Tips, Equipment Ratings, Food Tastings, and Science
Experiments from the Hit Public Television Show.
1st edition

ISBN 0-936184-59-0 (hardback): $29.95
I. Cooking. I. Title
2002

Manufactured in the United States of America

Distributed by Boston Common Press, 17 Station Street, Brookline, MA 02445

Designed by Amy Klee
Edited by Jack Bishop

CONTENTS

PREFACE

TELEVISION IS A POWERFUL AND CURIOUS MEDIUM. IT has the ability to make the ordinary extraordinary by lending a larger-than-life patina to what might, in real life, be considered quite ordinary. But I have seen a comforting trend in television lately. "Reality-based" shows are doing well, "how-to" shows with real experts rather than celebrities are popular, and ordinary citizens are popping up on television talk shows as experts. Their only claim to fame is that they know something about the topic at hand.

Of course, this is the essence of country life. One's expertise is at a premium rather than one's reputation. One of my Vermont neighbors, Ken, is not movie star—when he removes his cap, his forehead is as white as a trout's belly and his hair is a riot of straggly bits—but he knows a lot about stone walls. He built a 200-foot stone wall for us in 10 days, hauling the stone from up in the woods in his broken-down pickup. Each stone was perfectly placed, nestled into the curves of its immediate neighbors as if they were sleeping puppies. There is art to his craft, and he knows stone better than most people know their own children. Ken is an expert, but he doesn't brag about himself. He just shows up for work.

At America's Test Kitchen, we are not movie stars, either. The lights and cameras can't disguise the fact that we are just ordinary cooks, like you, our viewers. We just happen to have a lot of time on our hands to investigate what makes a recipe work. Each week, we invite you along for the ride as we try to solve the riddle of the perfect chicken Milanese or the best Texas chili (if there is a "best" chili recipe). America's Test Kitchen is indeed a real place, not a TV set, where the sinks really work and where our staff of cooks test and taste food every working day of the year. Simply put, we show up for work with a keen appetite for investigating recipes. That makes us, I suppose, a "reality-based" TV show, too. We try to show the good and the bad, the successes and the failures. We like to film our disasters rather than hide them because we have learned more from our mistakes than our successes.

Thanks for watching the show and for buying this book. We hope that we know as much about cooking as Ken does about stone walls. At the least, we are happy to share with you what we do know and perhaps we can learn something about cooking together as we test and retest in search of our idea of the "best" recipe.

Christopher Kimball
Founder and editor, *Cook's Illustrated* magazine
Boston, Massachusetts, 2002

ACKNOWLEDGMENTS

THIS BOOK BEGAN WITH THE RECIPES, EQUIPMENT ratings, food tastings, and science experiments conducted by the editors, writers, and cooks in America's Test Kitchen. Editor Jack Bishop shaped this information into a manuscript, and art director Amy Klee and graphic designer Nina Madjid gave these words form. John Burgoyne drew all of the illustrations and Amy Keller, Joe Keller, Elisabeth O'Donnell, Carl Tremblay, and Daniel Van Ackere took the photographs that fill the pages in this book. The photograph on the front cover was taken by Bill Miles.

India Koopman copyedited the manuscript, and Rebecca Hays and Jessica Quirk guided the book through the production process. The following individuals on the editorial, production, circulation, customer service, and office staffs also worked on the book: Ron Bilodeau, Barbara Bourassa, Rich Cassidy, Sharyn Chabot, Mary Connelly, Cathy Dorsey, Ruth Duncan, Jim McCormack, Jennifer McCreary, Amy Monaghan, Nicole Morris, Henrietta Murray, Sumantha Selvakumar, and Mandy Shito.

Without the work of the marketing, publicity, and sales staffs, readers would not find our books. Special thanks to Deborah Broide, Steven Browall, Shekinah Cohn, Connie Forbes, Julie Gardner, Jason Geller, Larisa Greiner, Robert Lee, David Mack, Steven Sussman, Jacqui Valerio, and Jonathan Venier, all of whom contributed to our marketing and distribution efforts.

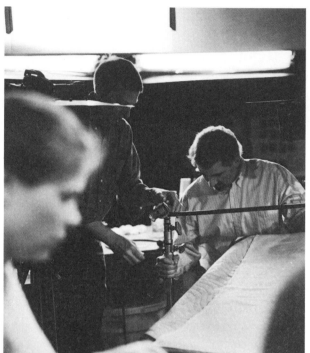

HERE IN AMERICA'S TEST KITCHEN

AMERICA'S TEST KITCHEN IS A 4,000-SQUARE-FOOT kitchen located in Brookline, Massachusetts, just outside Boston. It is a working kitchen that serves as the home for *Cook's Illustrated* magazine. Founded in 1980, *Cook's Illustrated* (formerly *Cook's Magazine*) is dedicated to finding the best methods for preparing favorite dishes. Every week our cooks test hundreds of recipes to find out which techniques work and which ones don't. Should you melt or cream butter when making chocolate cookies? What's the best way to peel and mince garlic? Which cheese is the best choice for macaroni and cheese? These are typical questions that we try to answer every day. How do we answer them? We answer all questions by performing comparison tests. We will make macaroni and cheese with a dozen kinds of cheese and then taste each one to figure out which cheese (or cheeses) are right for the recipe.

During the year, hundreds of pieces of equipment pass through America's Test Kitchen as we evaluate the basic tools most cooks need at home. Is that $120 German chef's knife better than a $30 knockoff? Which oven thermometers are most accurate and most stable? What's the best scrubber for removing scorched food from pots and pans? As with our recipe tests, we learn by doing. To find out which chef's knife is the sharpest and most comfortable, four editors and test cooks spent several weeks slicing tomatoes and bacon, chopping butternut squash and onions, mincing parsley and ginger, and butchering whole chickens. We went through cases of food before proclaiming one knife the winner. (It turns out that one of the cheap knives we tested is better than many of the expensive knives costing four times as much.)

We put popular food items through the same process. Can canned beef broth or bouillon cubes rival the flavor of homemade stock? Which tortilla chips make the best nachos? Is sea salt better than table salt? What about kosher salt? Can tasters tell the difference between pure vanilla extract and imitation products made from wood pulp? To answer these questions, we conduct dozens of blind taste tests every month. For instance, we tasted nine brands of salt in five different ways—in plain water, in chicken stock, in pasta cooking water, in biscuits, and sprinkled on beef tenderloin. In most cases, we found that regular table salt (costing just 36 cents per pound) was just as good as fancy sea salts (costing up to 100 times as much).

In addition to figuring out which cooking techniques, pieces of equipment, and ingredients are best, we want to know why they are the best. The science of food is an important element in every test we perform. Why is pie dough made with butter and shortening flakier than pie dough made with just butter? What makes rice sticky? How come evaporated milk makes a smoother sauce for macaroni and cheese than heavy cream? We talk to scientists, develop theories, and run tests to understand why certain techniques and ingredients succeed or fail in a particular recipe. We also rely on a food laboratory to test products. We learn just how much fat is in each brand of chocolate tested or how much bacteria is left in sponges that have been disinfected by various methods.

The Television Show

OUR TELEVISION SHOW BRINGS YOU THE VERY BEST FROM an entire year's work in America's Test Kitchen. We turn our favorite recipes, our most interesting equipment ratings, our most surprising food tastings, and our most unusual science experiments into lively, informative television segments. Christopher Kimball, the founder and editor of *Cook's Illustrated* magazine, is the host of the show and chief skeptic. He wants to know why, what, how, when, and where. He gets those answers from the test cooks and editors that appear on camera.

Julia Collin, Bridget Lancaster, and Matthew Card demonstrate recipes, explaining key points in our testing and development process. They show Chris (and the audience) which techniques and ingredients worked and which ones flopped. Julia, Bridget, and Matt demonstrate the right way to slice onions, sear steaks, bread chicken cutlets, drain pasta, grate cheese, and more. As you watch them cook, you'll learn the

Clockwise from upper left: Adam Ried, Julia Collin, Bridget Lancaster, Matt Card, Dawn Yanagihara, John "Doc" Willoughby, Erin McMurrer, Meg Suzuki, Jack Bishop, and Chris Kimball.

secrets to extra-crisp twice-baked potatoes, chewy molasses cookies, and smoky barbecued baby back ribs.

Adam Ried, our equipment expert, demonstrates the results of extensive kitchen tests. He shows Chris and the audience the pepper mills that received good ratings from our testers and those that failed miserably. Adam teaches us what to look for when shopping for steak knives, rice cookers, nonstick skillets, gas grills, and more. We learn that steak knives with straight (rather than serrated) edges are the best choice and that gas grills with lava rocks are prone to flare-ups and should be avoided. Kitchen equipment can be expensive and often involves a long-term commitment. With Adam's help, you will become a more informed shopper and will avoid those gadgets and tools that sound great but don't deliver.

Jack Bishop focuses on the ingredients that home cooks use every day. Is there even one decent brand of store-bought pie crust? Which brand of pasta tastes best and cooks up firm and chewy every time? What's the difference between mild, robust, and blackstrap molasses? To answer these questions, we assemble several dozen tasters in the test kitchen and have them rate the molasses, the pasta, and the pie crusts. Jack presents highlights of these tastings to Chris, who tastes the products for himself before the cameras. Can Chris pick out the losers and the winners? Just as important, Jack explains what makes one product better than another.

John "Doc" Willoughby is our science buff. He wants to know why something works and helps illustrate complex scientific principles with down-to-earth (and sometimes downright silly) demonstrations. Why does braising make smothered pork chops so tender? Why does buttermilk give quick breads such a good texture? With the help of some dolls, puppets, balloons, water pistols, toy fans, and more, Doc explains the science behind our recipes.

Behind the Scenes

AMERICA'S TEST KITCHEN IS MORE THAN JUST THE EDITORS and cooks you see on air. Recipes, food tastings, equipment tests, and science experiments result from the combined efforts of dozens of editors, cooks, researchers, and writers.

During filming, executive chefs Erin McMurrer and Dawn Yanagihara ran the "back kitchen," where all of the food that appeared on camera originated. Along with the on-air crew, Erin and Dawn also planned and organized the 26 television episodes shot in June 2002. Rebecca Hays and India Koopman helped develop science and equipment segments, and Julia Collin organized all of the tastings for the television show.

Every day chefs Matthew Card and Meg Suzuki were in the kitchen from early in the morning to late at night helping Erin and Dawn cook all of the food needed on set. Chefs Keith Dresser, Nancy Jordan, Kate Neave, Rajeev Samantrai, Merrill Stubbs, and Nina West and assistants Judy Davis, Pring Ram, and Shelley Rashotsky also worked long hours peeling potatoes, making pies, and baking cookies. Shannon Blaisdell and Rebecca Hays helped coordinate the efforts of the kitchen with the television set, readying props, equipment, and food, and Rebecca also made countless shopping trips to pick up ingredients.

Jim McCormack, vice president for operations and technology, and Rich Cassidy, our systems administrator, supervised the process that turned our test kitchen into a television studio. They made sure all of the wiring, computers, and ovens were ready to go.

The staff of A La Carte Communications turned our recipes, tastings, equipment tests, and science experiments into a lively television show. Special thanks to executive producer Geof Drummond; director/editor Herb Sevush; director of photography Dean Gaskill; coordinating producer Kimberly Nolan; production manager Rena Maliszewski; audio engineer Gilles Moran; technical engineer Eliat Goldman; script supervisor/makeup specialist Brenda Coffey; cameramen Tommy Hamilton, Steve Hussar, Michael McEachern, and Mark Rast; jib cameraman Mark Britt; production assistants Leland Drummond and Yale Miller; and grip/gaffers Aaron Frutman, Jack McPhee, and Patrick Ruth.

We hope this book captures the fun that takes place every day in America's Test Kitchen. When we come to work each morning, we never know quite what to expect. The day might begin with tasting 5 New York cheesecakes that were made the day before and have been chilling overnight. Next we might be testing kitchen torches on ramekins of crème brûlée. By lunch, four test recipes of chili might be ready for sampling, and the afternoon might include a tasting of store-bought barbecue sauces.

Although the food changes (almost hourly), our mission remains the same. We want to make your job in the kitchen easier and the food you make better. We hope our television show and this book will do just that. Contact us at www.americastestkitchen.com if you have comments or questions about the show or the book. Visit www.cooksillustrated.com for information about *Cook's Illustrated* magazine.

HERE IN AMERICA'S TEST KITCHEN

We taste-tested five brands of store-bought guacamole and found that none compare with the real thing, made with fresh avocados.

PARTY foods

Nachos, Buffalo wings, and sangría are too down-market, too much like junk food, to merit much attention from the "serious" food press. But let's face it—who doesn't like a plate of good nachos or Buffalo wings? The key is to use good ingredients and proper techniques to make this honest party food taste good.

With nachos, the solution turns out to be relatively simple. Rather than relying on processed cheese, jarred salsa, and packaged guacamole, choose fresh, wholesome ingredients. Follow the test kitchen's lead and you can turn out a plate of nachos good enough for company.

Buffalo wings also suffer from subpar ingredients—bottled blue cheese dressing and poor-quality hot sauces—as well as from poor—or nonexistent—technique on the part of the cook. More often than not, Buffalo wings are flabby and greasy, not perfectly crisp, as they should be.

Finally, sangría is not a serious drink—all you do is add sugar to wine, right? But there's a world of difference between a candy-sweet sangría made with 7UP and the real thing. We'll show you why.

NACHOS

WHAT WE WANTED: To free nachos from the suffo-cating grasp of packaged ingredients and make them taste good again.

Nachos are a simple, culinary pleasure many of us crave: crisp, warm tortilla chips mingling with melted cheese under a colorful banner of spicy salsa, luxurious guacamole, and a dollop of sour cream. Yet as elementary and popular as nachos are, finding a good plate of them can be hard. The worst examples appear at the snack counters of airports and large discount marts, where trays of chips that taste like cardboard are squirted with a few pumps of unnaturally fluid "cheese," doused with watery jarred salsa, and (if you're lucky) served with a miniscule portion of ready-made guacamole. But it doesn't have to be this way.

After sampling some local nacho fare and trying out a few recipes, we homed in on some key issues. First, the chips must be crisp and hot, not lukewarm, soggy, or charred. Second, there must be no shortage of cheese; a chip with-out cheese is just not a nacho. Third, there is no such thing as minimalist nachos. Good nachos require not only a hearty helping of cheese but also ample amounts of garnishes, such as salsa, guacamole, sour cream, jalapeños, and scallions. Finally, although it may seem blindingly obvious, we noted that fresh, quality ingredients make good nachos, while processed ingredients make airport nachos. With these insights in mind, we were ready to create a good plate of nachos, and tasters were already jockeying for position at the kitchen counter.

Finding that 8 ounces of chips made enough nachos for four to six people and fit easily into a 13 by 9-inch baking dish, we made batches with increasing amounts of shredded cheese until tasters cried uncle. Four cups was just right; lesser amounts left some chips neglected, and more just about drowned the chips. To ensure an even distribution, it was necessary to toss the cheese with the chips before cook-ing. But the act of tossing, we quickly discovered, was brutal on the delicate chips, and some of the cheese was lost to the bottom of the baking dish. Instead, we tried building the nachos in layers—two layers of chips topped with cheese—which ensured even distribution. Not surprisingly, these first few batches tasted far better than any nachos we had eaten elsewhere. The simple pairing of good-quality chips (see the Tasting Lab on page 8) with a generous amount of evenly distributed cheese had already made a huge difference.

Next we held a cheese tasting. Although most recipes call for cheddar or Monterey Jack, we wondered how tasters would react to other types of cheese, such as American, Havarti, Gouda, Muenster, or any of the jalapeño-studded varieties, such as pepper cheddar, pepper Jack, and pepper Havarti. Cheddar turned out to be tasters' overall favorite, with a potent and legitimate flavor, although Gouda was surprisingly good and garnered second place. To our great surprise, Monterey Jack was disappointingly bland and taste-less, while American and the peppered varieties of cheddar, Monterey Jack, and Havarti all tasted commercial and over-processed. The other oddball contestants, Muenster and reg-ular Havarti, had decent if unremarkable flavors but were quick to turn rubbery as they cooled. We tried using pre-shredded cheddar to save time but found the flavor dull and the texture dry. We got much better results by shredding a block of cheese in a food processor fitted with the shredding disk, which was easy enough and took little time. A greased box grater (see the illustrations on page 6) is another good way to accomplish this task quickly and easily.

We had been baking the nachos in a 350-degree oven for 20 minutes to melt the cheese and heat the chips through but wanted to experiment with speedier methods. The broiler caused the top layer of chips to burn before the inner layers of cheese had time to melt. Hot ovens set between 425 and 450 degrees produced chips with charred edges, but a 400-degree oven managed to both melt the cheese and warm the chips through to a lightly toasted crisp in a mere 10 minutes. Not only was this a time saver, but the nachos tasted more fresh and less dried out than those baked for a longer period of time in a cooler oven.

Chips and cheese may be the nacho plate's workhorses, but without salsa, guacamole, and sour cream, nachos look naked. And not just any old salsa or guacamole will do—they have to be fresh and lively tasting. Although salsa and guacamole are now conveniently sold in jars and tubs in the supermarket, most of these products are just about inedible (see the Tasting Labs on pages 10 and 7). Luckily, both can also be made at home in a few minutes, and the results are more than worth the effort. When and where they are placed on the chips and cheese are also crucial to success. As for when, they must be added after the chips emerge from the oven to provide contrast in temperature, texture, and flavor. As for where, while many recipes tell the cook to spread each topping evenly over each chip, this instruction is both silly and time-consuming. We found that it's easier to simply dump a few scoops of salsa and guacamole on a small portion of the chips, off to the side, so that most of the chips remain unencumbered and easy to pick up.

Tasters liked the spicy addition of thinly sliced jalapeños, preferring them fresh rather than canned. They tasted best when sprinkled into the layers along with the cheese, which, when melted, helped the peppers adhere to the chips. Fresh, sliced scallions and wedges of lime—both added when the nachos emerge from the oven—were also welcome additions. The issue of spicy, ground beef and refried beans—common additions to a nacho plate—provoked some controversy in the test kitchen. The result? We decided to use these ingredients in variations, as they quickly transform nachos into an indulgent, artery-clogging meal.

WHAT WE LEARNED: Layer shredded cheddar cheese and chips to ensure even coverage, use a hot oven rather than the broiler to melt the cheese, and add sliced, fresh jalapeños for some heat.

CHEESY NACHOS WITH GUACAMOLE AND SALSA serves 4 to 6

See our Tasting Labs on tortilla chips (page 8) and cheddar cheese (page 160) to see which brands we recommend.

- 8 ounces tortilla chips
- 16 ounces cheddar cheese, shredded (4 cups)
- 2 large jalapeño chiles (¾ ounce each), sliced thin (about ¼ cup)
- 2 scallions, sliced thin
- 1 recipe Fresh Guacamole (recipe follows)
- ½ cup (4 ounces) sour cream
- 1 recipe One-Minute Salsa (recipe follows)
- 1 lime, cut into 6 wedges

Adjust oven rack to middle position and heat oven to 400 degrees. Spread half of chips in even layer in 13 by 9-inch baking dish; sprinkle evenly with 2 cups cheese and half of jalapeño slices. Repeat with remaining chips, cheese, and jalapeños. Bake until cheese is melted, 7 to 10 minutes. Remove nachos from oven and sprinkle with scallions. Along edge of baking dish, drop scoops of guacamole, sour cream, and salsa. Serve immediately, passing lime wedges separately.

VARIATIONS

CHEESY NACHOS WITH REFRIED BEANS

Follow recipe for Cheesy Nachos with Guacamole and Salsa, dropping ¾ cup (about 6 ounces) refried beans in small spoonfuls on each chip layer before sprinkling with cheese.

CHEESY NACHOS WITH SPICY BEEF

A quickly made ground beef mixture turns nachos into a meal.

- 2 teaspoons corn or vegetable oil
- 1 small onion, chopped fine
- 1 large garlic clove, minced or pressed through garlic press (about 1½ teaspoons)
- 1 tablespoon chili powder

¼	teaspoon dried oregano
½	teaspoon ground cumin
½	teaspoon ground coriander
¼	teaspoon cayenne
⅛	teaspoon salt
½	pound 90 percent lean (or leaner) ground beef

1. Heat oil in medium skillet over medium heat until shimmering, but not smoking. Add onion and cook, stirring occasionally, until softened, about 4 minutes. Add garlic, spices, and salt; cook, stirring constantly, until fragrant and combined with onion, about 1 minute. Add ground beef and cook, breaking up meat with wooden spoon and scraping pan bottom to prevent scorching, until beef is no longer pink, about 5 minutes.

2. Follow recipe for Cheesy Nachos with Guacamole and Salsa, sprinkling half of beef mixture on each chip layer before sprinkling with cheese.

FRESH GUACAMOLE makes about 1½ cups

See the illustrations on page 7 for tips on dicing an avocado.

2	small, ripe avocados (preferably Hass)
1	tablespoon minced red onion
1	small garlic clove, minced or pressed through garlic press (about ½ teaspoon)
½	small jalapeño chile, stemmed, seeded, and minced (about 1½ teaspoons)
2	tablespoons fresh minced cilantro leaves
	Salt
1	tablespoon juice from 1 lime

1. Halve 1 avocado, remove pit, and scoop flesh into medium bowl. Using fork, mash lightly with onion, garlic, jalapeño, cilantro, and ⅛ teaspoon salt until just combined.

2. Halve and pit remaining avocado. Using a dinner knife, carefully make ½-inch crosshatch incisions in flesh, cutting

down to but not through skin. Using a soup spoon, gently scoop flesh from skin; transfer to bowl with mashed avocado mixture. Sprinkle lime juice over and mix lightly with fork until combined but still chunky. Adjust seasoning with salt, if necessary, and serve. (Can be covered with plastic wrap pressed directly onto surface of mixture, and refrigerated for up to 1 day. Return guacamole to room temperature, removing plastic wrap just before serving.)

TECHNIQUE: Shredding Soft Cheeses

Soft cheeses such as cheddar, Monterey Jack, and mozzarella can stick to a box grater and cause a real mess. Here's how to keep the holes on the grater from becoming clogged.

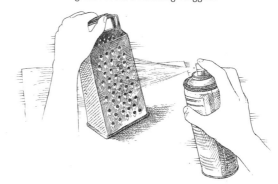

1. Lightly coat the side of the box grater with large holes with nonstick cooking spray.

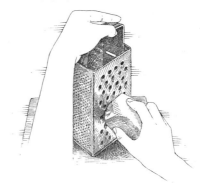

2. Shred the cheese as usual. The cooking spray will keep the cheese from sticking to the grater.

ONE-MINUTE SALSA makes about 1 cup

This quick salsa can be made with either fresh or canned tomatoes. If you like, replace the jalapeño with ½ chipotle chile in adobo sauce, minced.

½   small jalapeño chile, stemmed and seeded (about 1½ teaspoons)

¼   small red onion, peeled and root end removed

1   small garlic clove, minced or pressed through garlic press (about ½ teaspoon)

2   tablespoons fresh cilantro leaves

¼   teaspoon salt
     Pinch ground black pepper

2   teaspoons juice from 1 lime

2   small ripe tomatoes (about ¾ pound), each cored and cut into eighths, or one (14½-ounce) can diced tomatoes, drained

Pulse all ingredients except tomatoes in food processor until minced, about five 1-second pulses, scraping down sides of bowl as necessary. Add tomatoes and pulse until roughly chopped, about two 1-second pulses.

TASTING LAB: Store-Bought Guacamole

AT THE HEART OF ANY GOOD GUACAMOLE IS A RIPE, HASS avocado. These small, rough-skinned gems soften when left on the counter for a few days. But it can be hard to find fully ripened avocados for a spur-of-the-moment guacamole. Wondering if any of the ready-made tubs of guacamole at the supermarket would be an acceptable substitute, we tasted five brands to compare them with our own recipe.

At first glance, some of these guacamoles looked pretty good. But after sampling just a bite or two, tasters gagged, sealing the fate of these pretenders. The best of the lot, AvoClassic Guacamole, came out of a sealed plastic pouch and garnered comments such as "could be worse," and "not bad with some doctoring." The next best representative was

Goya's Guacamole Dip, which had a "thin and mealy" texture and tasted "like nothing." Voicing increasingly negative reactions, tasters found the Trader Joe's and Calavo brands to be harsh and acidic, with flavors that "burned the back of the throat." Ranked at the very bottom was La Mexicana Guacamole, which drew comments such as "What is in this?" By comparison, our freshly made guacamole tasted almost angelic, with a pure, honest avocado flavor. So if you think the mood might strike, buy some avocados a few days ahead.

TECHNIQUE: Dicing an Avocado

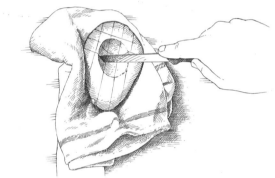

1. Use a dish towel to hold the avocado steady. Make ½-inch crosshatch incisions in the flesh of each avocado half with a dinner knife, cutting down to but not through the skin.

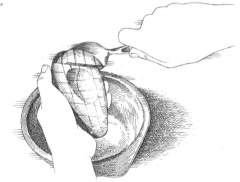

2. Separate the diced flesh from the skin using a soup spoon inserted between the skin and flesh, gently scooping out the avocado cubes.

TASTING LAB: Tortilla Chips

FOR OUR TASTING OF TORTILLA CHIPS, WE DECIDED TO keep things simple: We stuck to chips made from white or yellow corn in the basic triangular shape. In addition, all of the chips we tasted were salted and "full fat." We tasted the chips solo, with salsa (testing each chip for its "scoopability"), and in nachos (testing the chips for durability and texture after blanketing them with cheese and toppings).

Most tortilla chips are made from just three basic ingredients—corn, oil, and salt—and processed in similar fashion (explained below), yet our tasters found a wide range of textures and flavors in the 10 brands we sampled. How, we wondered, could such simple ingredients and a consistent manufacturing process yield such different results?

To understand what gave the chips we tasted such different flavors and textures, we began by examining the manufacturing process and the primary ingredient, corn. Tortilla chips begin with masa, or corn dough. Resembling cookie dough in texture, masa can be made from a number of different corn products, including corn flour, which has the texture of fine sand; stone-ground corn flour, which has a rougher, grittier texture; and stone-ground corn (made from softened whole corn kernels), which is very rough, like pebbly sand. Water is added to the corn product and the dough is mixed. The masa gets flattened into a strip and goes through a contraption that looks something like a giant rolling pin (sometimes called a sheeter) that cuts the dough into triangles. The triangles are baked for less than a minute at up to 800 degrees, which dries out the dough so that it doesn't absorb too much oil when it gets fried. After baking, the dough triangle looks, feels, and tastes like a corn tortilla. Next the chips get cooled on a multilevel conveyor belt. This prevents puffing during the next phase, frying. The baked and cooled chips are flash-fried in 350-degree oil for only 1 minute; then the chips get cooled again in a cooling tunnel, salted, and bagged.

Based on our tasting results, we concluded that a masa made with stone-ground whole corn kernels will result in a grittier, heartier chip than one made from a silky corn flour masa. Many manufacturers make a big deal out of their chips being made from stone-ground masa. A stone-ground corn chip, they say, has more texture, is stronger, and absorbs less oil. While that all sounds good on paper, in reality we found that tasters preferred finer and more fragile chips made with corn flour, like second-place Miguel's, described as "delicate," or third-place Newman's Own, called "crisp." (Frito-Lay, which manufactures our top-rated Doritos chips, would not comment on the ingredients in its masa. However, given the delicate texture of Doritos, it seems likely that corn flour is used here, too.) In contrast, two of the roughest, heartiest stone-ground chips, Nana's Cocina and Kettle Foods, ended up at the bottom of the scorecard. Their textures were described as "stale" and like "cardboard," respectively.

Another argument that enthusiasts of stone-ground corn flour make against the use of fine-ground corn flour is that it acts like a sponge, absorbing more oil. But in our tasting we didn't find that to be true. Both Miguel's and Newman's use fine flours, and neither was greasy. Yet the Nana's Cocina chips, which are made from whole corn kernels ground in lava stones, were called "slick" and "oily." In addition, despite differences in the texture of the masa and the chips, all of the chips we sampled contain similar amounts of fat, from 5.5 to 7 grams per 1-ounce serving.

Finally, we come to the flavor of the masa itself. We thought there might be a continental divide between those who preferred white or yellow corn tortilla chips, but we found that we liked both types. Our first-, third-, and fourth-place chips are all yellow corn varieties, while our second-, fifth-, and sixth-place picks are made with white corn. In general, we found white corn chips to be more subtly corn flavored, whereas yellow corn chips tasted "toasty" and "nutty."

In addition to the masa, salt has a big impact on tortilla chip flavor. Here the results of our tasting were quite clear. More salt makes a tastier chip. Among the top five brands, four have sodium levels between 110 and 120 milligrams

Rating Tortilla Chips

WE TASTED 10 BRANDS OF TORTILLA CHIPS, PLAIN, WITH SALSA, AND IN NACHOS. TASTERS JUDGED THE CHIPS FOR FLAVOR, texture, durability, and size. Chips are listed in order of preference. All brands are sold in supermarkets, and all are available nationally except for Doritos, which is distributed only in the West.

HIGHLY RECOMMENDED
1. Doritos Toasted Corn Tortilla Chips

$3.29 for 13.5 ounces

Tasters loved the "fresh," "toasted corn" flavor and "crisp," "perfect" texture.

HIGHLY RECOMMENDED
2. Miguel's Stowe Away White Corn Tortilla Chips

$2.95 for 7 ounces

These "thick" chips retained a "delicate crispness." Flavor was subtle, with tasters calling it "toasted" and "authentic."

HIGHLY RECOMMENDED
3. Newman's Own Organics Yellow Corn Tortilla Chips

$2.29 for 8 ounces

Chips tasted "home-fried" and "corny." These were the thinnest chips tested; packages had a higher-than-average number of broken chips.

HIGHLY RECOMMENDED
4. Bearitos Stoneground Organic Yellow Corn Tortilla Chips

$2.79 for 16 ounces

Many tasters believed these chips had the "best corn flavor" but complained that the chips were "too hard" and "broke apart" when eaten.

RECOMMENDED
5. Santitas White Corn Tortilla Chips

$1.99 for 18 ounces

This "durable" but "crisp" chip stood up to nachos and salsa. Some tasters commented that these chips "could use more corn flavor."

RECOMMENDED
6. Cape Cod White Corn Tortilla Chips

$1.99 for 9 ounces

Tasters liked the "crisp," "thick" texture but called the flavor "bland," "unremarkable," and reminiscent of "church communion."

RECOMMENDED
7. Tostitos Restaurant-Style White Corn Tortilla Chips

$2.29 for 13.5 ounces

"This is your basic Sunday football chip," said one taster. Others said they were "too flimsy" in flavor and texture and didn't "hold up to heavy dipping."

NOT RECOMMENDED
8. Nana's Cocina Traditional Stoneground Yellow Corn Tortilla Chips

$2.69 for 16 ounces

Chips had a "fatty" mouthfeel that was "slick and oily." Tasters also found these chips to be overly "thin" and somewhat "stale."

NOT RECOMMENDED
9. Old Dutch Original Restaurant-Style Tortilla Chips

$3.19 for 15 ounces

These "thin" chips were deemed "too large" and "fell apart easily" when dunked in salsa. Several tasters picked up on an unwelcome "smoky," "popcorn" flavor.

NOT RECOMMENDED
10. Kettle Foods Five Grain Organic Yellow Corn Tortilla Chips

$1.99 for 8 ounces

Tasters described these chips made with five sprouted grains as being "strangely sweet," with a "stale," "old cornmeal" flavor.

per ounce. The sodium level in the five lowest-ranked brands ranges from 40 to 90 milligrams per ounce.

Now that we understood more about the inner workings of masa and the effect of salt levels on flavor, we moved on to the oil. We thought that the success of our second favorite brand, Miguel's, might be due in part to the corn/oil combination. Miguel's pairs canola oil with its white corn masa chip. Because canola is a neutral-flavored oil, using it with the subtle-flavored masa works well, as the flavor of the oil doesn't overwhelm that of the chip.

But then we came to Cape Cod chips, which were something of an anomaly. Like Miguel's, they are made with white corn masa and fried in canola oil. So why were Miguel's chips described as having a "toasted," "authentic" flavor, whereas Cape Cod chips were deemed "bland" and "unremarkable?" The most obvious difference right off the bat was in the packaging. Miguel's tortilla chips are packaged in a "metallized" bag, meaning that the bag's surface has been lined with a very thin film of aluminum.

Craig Mooney, vice-president of sales for Miguel's, says that the metal lining helps to ward off oxidation of the oil by blocking light. "Light can oxidize the product and cause it to go bad," he explained; the foil-lined bag "also creates a moisture barrier to help the chips stay crunchy." In fact, we observed that all of our top three chips, Doritos, Miguel's, and Newman's Own, are packed in metallized bags. Could oxidation be a reason for the lack of flavor in Cape Cod and the "off" flavors in some of the other brands we tasted?

According to Theron Downes, a packaging professor with Michigan State University, "there are piles of evidence" that a metallized bag improves the shelf life of fried foods. In fact, Dr. Downes even refuses to purchase peanuts, a high-fat and light-susceptible food, packaged in clear bags because the oil in the peanuts goes rancid from oxidation within a couple of weeks.

In the end, the results of our tasting were unexpected. Doritos won over smaller, boutique brands like Nana's Cocina and Kettle Foods. Although many boutique brands make a big deal about the organically raised, stone-ground

corn they use, it seems that the secret to a great tortilla chip isn't all that complicated. Just use fine corn flour (not coarse stone-ground), add plenty of salt, and then pack the chips in a foil-lined bag to keep the oil from oxidizing.

TASTING LAB: Jarred Salsa

THERE ARE SO MANY JARRED SALSAS ON THE MARKET today that for the preliminary round of our tasting we sampled dozens of brands. We included the brands that dominate the category (Old El Paso, Tostitos, and Ortega), along with some smaller "gourmet" brands. We also included four refrigerated salsas. Unlike jarred salsas, these products, which are sold in plastic tubs, have a shelf life of a month or two. (Jarred salsas keep for a year or more unopened.) Manufacturers add preservatives to keep refrigerated salsas from becoming moldy, but there is little they can do to prevent the mushy texture and slimy mouthfeel. The refrigerated salsas we tasted ranged from possibly edible after many margaritas to inedible under any circumstances. We decided to omit this category from our final tasting.

Supermarket brands of jarred salsa come in three different styles: mild, medium, and hot. Mild salsas are generally quite bland (some would say insipid), and hot salsas can be so hot that they are hard to taste, especially one after another. We decided to test only medium salsas for our final tasting.

Of the 12 jarred salsas we ultimately sampled for our final round of tests, we could not recommend even one—not even in a pinch. All 12 were watery and sweet, with mushy vegetables and overprocessed flavors. None came close to the full, fresh flavors of our homemade salsa. Our advice is to make your own salsa, even if you have to use canned tomatoes.

BUFFALO WINGS

WHAT WE WANTED: Juicy meat with a crisp coating and a spicy, slightly sweet, and vinegary sauce.

First conceived of at the Anchor Bar in Buffalo, New York in the 1960s, Buffalo wings are now found throughout the country at any bar or Super Bowl party worth its salt. The odd combination of chicken wings slathered with hot sauce and dunked in blue cheese dressing may seem like a drunken concoction best forgotten about the next morning, but it is actually a harmonious union. The sauce's bright heat is tamed by the soothing, creamy dip. Under the right circumstances, even bad wings (and we have had our share of flabby, tough wings in greasy sauce) are pretty good. But we wanted to come up with a recipe for really good wings.

For Buffalo wings, the raw chicken wing itself is almost always cut in two segments, the relatively meatless wingtip removed. The wings come packaged as whole wings or as pre-cut segments affectionately referred to as drumettes. We found that pre-cut wings were often poorly cut and unevenly sized, so we chose to buy whole wings and butcher them ourselves, which was easy and economical.

While the wings were easy to butcher, cooking them proved a little trickier because of their high fat content. At the Anchor Bar, Buffalo wings are deep-fried, which renders the fat and leaves the skin crisp and golden. But deep-frying can be a daunting project in a home kitchen. We hoped that oven-roasting might be a viable alternative. We placed the wings on a rack resting on a rimmed baking sheet so that the chicken would not be sitting in fat. At 300 degrees, the wings cooked for an hour and were wan and dry. At 375 degrees, the chicken was still a little flabby after 45 minutes of cooking, and the meat was dry.

We decided to switch gears and try the stovetop. Sautéing the wings did little for their flavor or texture. And they were still greasy because the fat was not rendered. Pan-frying, or cooking the chicken partially submerged in fat, yielded much better results, but turning the chicken midway through cooking prompted hot fat to spatter about. We decided that if we were going to pan-fry, we might as well try deep-frying. Maybe there was something to tradition after all. We found that if we used a deep Dutch oven and kept the oil at a constant 360 degrees, spattering oil was minimal and cleanup easy.

We tossed the wings with salt, pepper, and cayenne and then fried them for about 12 minutes, or until golden. While these wings were juicy and crisp, most tasters wanted an even crispier exterior. We did not want to resort to a batter, so we tried dredging the wings, testing one batch dredged in flour and another in cornstarch. The cornstarch provided a thin and brittle coating, not unlike tempura, that was the tasters' favorite. We found that thoroughly drying the chicken with paper towels prior to tossing with the cornstarch and seasonings ensured crisp skin and no gumminess.

With the wings fried and placed in the oven to keep warm, we were ready to tackle the sauce. Most recipes we found agreed that authentic Buffalo wing sauce, as made at the Anchor Bar, is nothing but Frank's Louisiana Hot Sauce and butter or margarine, blended in a 2-to-1 ratio. Most recipes also suggest intensifying the sauce's heat with a bit of Tabasco or other hot pepper sauce because on its own, Frank's is not quite spicy enough. While we liked this simple sauce, most tasters wanted something a little more dynamic. We included brown sugar to round out the flavors. A little cider vinegar balanced out the sugar and added a pleasing sharpness.

WHAT WE LEARNED: Coat the wings with cornstarch for a supercrisp exterior and deep-fry (rather than roasting, sautéing, or pan-frying) the wings for the best texture. Then deepen the flavor of the traditional hot sauce by adding brown sugar and cider vinegar.

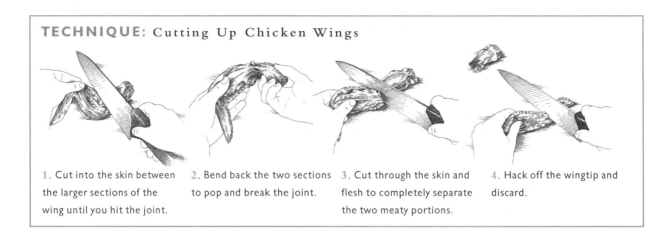

TECHNIQUE: Cutting Up Chicken Wings

1. Cut into the skin between the larger sections of the wing until you hit the joint.

2. Bend back the two sections to pop and break the joint.

3. Cut through the skin and flesh to completely separate the two meaty portions.

4. Hack off the wingtip and discard.

BUFFALO WINGS serves 6 to 8 as an appetizer

Frank's Louisiana Hot Sauce is not terribly spicy. We like to combine it with a more potent hot sauce, such as Tabasco, to bring up the heat. You will need to double the recipe for blue cheese dressing on page 62.

sauce

- 4   tablespoons unsalted butter
- ½   cup Frank's Louisiana Hot Sauce
- 2   tablespoons Tabasco or other hot sauce, plus more to taste
- 1   tablespoon dark brown sugar
- 2   teaspoons cider vinegar

wings

- 1–2 quarts peanut oil, for frying
- 1   teaspoon cayenne
- 1   teaspoon ground black pepper
- 1   teaspoon salt
- 3   tablespoons cornstarch
- 18 chicken wings (about 3 pounds), wingtips removed and remaining wings separated into 2 parts at joint (see illustrations above)

vegetables and dressing

- 4   medium stalks celery, cut into thin sticks
- 2   medium carrots, peeled and cut into thin sticks
- 1½ cups Rich and Creamy Blue Cheese Dressing (see page 62)

1. FOR THE SAUCE: Melt butter in small saucepan over low heat. Whisk in hot sauces, brown sugar, and vinegar until combined. Remove from heat and set aside.

2. FOR THE WINGS: Preheat oven to 200 degrees. Line baking sheet with paper towels. Heat 2½ inches of oil in large Dutch oven over medium-high heat to 360 degrees. While oil heats, mix together cayenne, black pepper, salt, and cornstarch in small bowl. Dry chicken with paper towels and place pieces in large mixing bowl. Sprinkle spice mixture over wings and toss with rubber spatula until evenly coated. Fry half of chicken wings until golden and crisp, 10 to 12 minutes. With slotted spoon, transfer fried chicken wings to baking sheet. Keep first batch of chicken warm in oven while frying remaining wings.

3. TO SERVE: Pour sauce mixture into large bowl, add chicken wings, and toss until wings are uniformly coated. Serve immediately with carrot and celery sticks and blue cheese dressing on the side.

EQUIPMENT CORNER: Kitchen Tongs

SOMETIMES THE MORE THOUGHT YOU GIVE SOMETHING the better, but sometimes good enough is best left alone. The latter seems to be the case with tongs. We found that the simplest design—your basic, lightweight, agile-yet-sturdy restaurant tongs—easily bested all of the new "improved" tongs we tested. Testers dismissed tricky self-locking mechanisms, curved handles, nylon pincers, tight springs, or excess heft.

Oversized tweezers, for example, are not a good substitute for tongs, and the heft you value in a saucepan or stockpot is not a good quality when it comes to tongs. Heavy tongs (one pair weighed 10 ounces, with our top-rated models weighing half that) became tiresome to use, as did tongs with too much tension built into their springs. Tongs that respond to a light touch are the easiest and most comfortable to use as well as the most effective. We also liked tongs with the widest span between the pincers (6 inches or more was ideal) since they could hold big items, such as a roast.

To test the effectiveness of the tongs (and the one pair of tweezers), we used them to pick up slim asparagus spears, to retrieve irregularly shaped corn on the cob from boiling water, to sauté slippery scallops, to pan-fry breaded chicken cutlets, to move ramekins filled with water and chocolate mousse from one spot to another, and to turn a 3-pound pot roast. One pair of lightweight restaurant-style stainless steel tongs passed every test, and another, similar pair came very close.

TECHNIQUE: Disposing of Oil Neatly

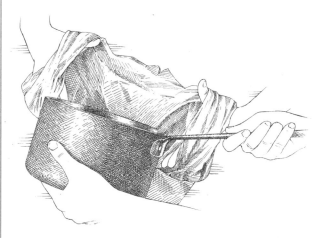

Deep-fried foods, such as Buffalo wings, are a real treat, but cleaning up after frying is not. Disposing of the spent oil neatly and safely is a particular challenge. Here's how we do it. We make a quadruple- or quintuple-layered bag using four or five leftover plastic grocery bags. With someone holding the layered bags open over a sink or in an outdoor area, we carefully pour the cooled frying oil from the pot into the innermost bag. We tie the bag handles shut and dispose of the oil in the garbage.

Rating Kitchen Tongs

WE TESTED NINE PAIRS OF TONGS, EACH AROUND 12 INCHES LONG. WE RAN EACH PAIR THROUGH SEVEN KITCHEN tests to assess ease of use as well as its ability to grasp slippery items, small items, and large items. The tongs are listed in order of preference. See www.cooksillustrated.com for up-to-date prices and mail-order sources for top-rated products.

HIGHLY RECOMMENDED
1. Edlund Locking 12-Inch Tongs
$9.95
These stainless steel tongs turned in a perfect score, excelling in each and every test. They're light, agile, and easy to use.

HIGHLY RECOMMENDED
2. Oxo Good Grips Locking 12-Inch Tongs
$9.99
These stainless steel tongs with rubber handles earned a perfect score in all tests but one—grasping a filled ramekin. Because most cooks are unlikely to use tongs for this purpose, we gave these tongs high marks anyway.

RECOMMENDED
3. Vollrath Stainless Steel Utility Tong
$3.20
These tongs are quite similar to the highly rated Edlund tongs, except they don't open quite as far—just 4 inches from tip to tip versus 6 inches for the Edlund tongs. As a result, it's difficult to grasp large items, such as a roast, with these tongs.

RECOMMENDED WITH RESERVATIONS
4. Chantal Locking Kitchen Tongs, Model KT-TG12
$14.99
These tongs got the job done in each of our tests but not without a fair amount of effort on the part of the cook. The tension built into these stainless steel tongs is too high.

RECOMMENDED WITH RESERVATIONS
5. Amco Stainless Steel and Nylon Locking Tongs
$10.99
These tongs were quite good at grasping solid foods such as corn on the cob, but their thick nylon tips ran into trouble when handling slippery foods.

NOT RECOMMENDED
6. Oneida Self-Locking Tongs
$7.99
These stainless steel tongs were unable to grasp a large pot roast because they did not open far enough. They also had too much built-in tension and a self-locking mechanism that sometimes came into play when you didn't expect it.

NOT RECOMMENDED
7. Calphalon Nylon Tongs
$8.00
These plastic tongs couldn't hold slippery foods. The narrow 2-inch span made it impossible to pick up large items.

NOT RECOMMENDED
8. All-Clad 12-Inch Locking Tongs
$20.00
These sturdy stainless steel tongs are built to last a lifetime, but their heft and the high degree of built-in tension made them somewhat challenging to use.

NOT RECOMMENDED
9. Endurance Sauté Tweezer
$6.99
These oversized stainless steel "tweezers" did a good job of picking up asparagus stalks, but they failed other tests.

SANGRÍA

WHAT WE WANTED: Many people mistake sangría for an unruly collection of fruit awash in a sea of overly sweetened red wine. But we were after a robust, sweet-tart punch, with the operative flavors of wine and citrus balanced against a simple, fruity background.

S angría may be a party drink consumed without much thought, but there's no reason why it can't be better than the sweet concoctions served in most punch bowls. Working to find the right ingredient proportions for a standard 750-milliliter bottle of wine, we started by testing the other building blocks of sangría: orange and lemon slices, juice, sugar, and orange-flavored liqueur.

After tinkering with various proportions of cut-up fruit, we settled on a ratio of two oranges to one lemon. We tried limes, too, but found them too bitter. We did note that two sliced oranges and one sliced lemon in the pitcher made it difficult to pour the sangría, so we opted to squeeze the juice from one of the oranges. We also tried peeling the fruit, on the theory that the zest and pith might be contributing some bitterness, but without them, the sangría tasted too winey and a bit flat. Last, we tried mashing the fruit and the sugar together gently in the pitcher before adding the liquids. This improved the sangría by releasing some juice from the fruit and oils from the zest.

We wondered whether the type of sugar was important, since granulated, superfine, and a simple syrup of sugar dissolved in water all appeared in recipes. The flavor difference turned out to be infinitesimal, as did any difference in the mouthfeel of the drink, as each one dissolved completely. What did matter was the amount of sugar—¼ cup gave the punch a pleasant, but not cloying, sweetness.

The orange liqueur that is part of all sangría recipes also provides some sweetness and fruitiness. We tried expensive brands such as Cointreau, Curaçao, and Grand Marnier, as well as the more pedestrian Triple Sec, which was the

surprise prize winner for its bold, sweet flavor. One-quarter cup of Triple Sec was just right; less, or none, made for a bland and one-dimensional sangría.

With the basic formula down, we turned to the choice of wine. Across the board, bartenders, wine merchants, and Spanish restaurateurs all advised us to keep it cheap. They argued that the addition of sugar and fruit would throw off the balance of the wine, so why spend a lot on something

carefully crafted and pricey? Our testing so far had been done with a discount liquor store's house-label Merlot, a medium-bodied wine that cost a whopping $4.49 a bottle. Other wines we had tried included Beaujolais-Villages, which tasters thought too fruity and light; Zinfandel, which tasted bright and acidic; jug Burgundy, which was somewhat richer and rounder; and Rioja, which tasters found a bit flat and dull. We tried a more expensive Merlot (priced at $16.99), but only 1 taster out of 5 preferred the sangría made from it. Our advice, then, is to use cheap wine whose character you know and can live with. Fruity, pleasant Merlot is a good choice.

Many of the recipes we consulted moved well beyond the basic ingredients. Some had long lists of fruits, including apples, grapes, peaches, kiwis, cherries, and berries; others called for nonalcoholic filler ingredients, such as mineral or sparkling water, ginger ale, cold tea, lemonade, pineapple juice, or cranberry juice. One by one, we sampled, and rejected, each of these. Consistently, we all preferred the straightforward flavor of citrus to the floating-fruit-salad approach, and everyone agreed that fillers, even in small amounts, diluted the wine, demoting it to a mere background flavor. Our reactions to more potent additions, including gin, sweet vermouth, port, and the traditional brandy, were similar. Even amounts as small as a tablespoon moved sangría away from our ideal of a light, refreshing, quaffable summer drink.

A number of recipes suggested preparing the sangría ahead of time and letting it rest in the refrigerator before serving. When all was said and done, we came to consider the resting time essential. After tasting an eight-hour-old sangría, a freshly made batch seemed harsh and edgy. Rest assured, though, if you can't stand the anticipation, two hours of refrigeration serves the purpose adequately.

WHAT WE LEARNED: **The best sangría is based on cheap wine and uses oranges and lemons as the only fruit. Let the flavors of the sangría blend in the refrigerator for at least two hours and preferably longer.**

SANGRÍA serves 4

The longer sangría sits before drinking, the more smooth and mellow it will taste. A full day is best, but if that's impossible, give it an absolute minimum of two hours to sit. Use large, heavy, juicy oranges and lemons for the best flavor. Doubling or tripling the recipe is fine, but you'll have to switch to a large punch bowl in place of the pitcher. We tried several inexpensive wines, and tasters thought most of them performed well in this recipe. A fruity Merlot is an especially good choice.

  2 **large juice oranges, washed; one orange sliced; remaining orange juiced**
  1 **large lemon, washed and sliced**
 ¼ **cup sugar**
 ¼ **cup Triple Sec**
  1 **(750-milliliter) bottle inexpensive, fruity, medium-bodied red wine, chilled (see note)**

1. Add sliced orange, lemon, and sugar to large pitcher; mash gently with wooden spoon until fruit releases some juice but is not totally crushed and sugar dissolves, about 1 minute. Stir in orange juice, Triple Sec, and wine; refrigerate for at least 2 hours and up to 8 hours.

2. Before serving, add 6 to 8 ice cubes and stir briskly to distribute settled fruit and pulp; serve immediately.

Matt and Dawn prepare the ingredients for soup making.

HEARTY soups

Everyone likes hearty soups, especially when the weather turns cold. And the notion of a meal in a bowl is certainly appealing. However, many cooks think more is better when it comes to hearty soups. Stick-to-your-ribs can be an appealing goal for stews, but too often we've found that hearty soups are heavy, starchy, gluey, or just downright tired.

Ham and split pea soup is not a light endeavor. That said, the texture should not be pasty. The peas should melt to form a creamy base for bits of ham and flavorful vegetables, such as onions and carrots. Of course, every spoonful should capture the smoky, sweet essence of ham. We set out to capture this flavor without using a huge bone from a roasted holiday ham.

When it comes to potato-leek soup, potatoes come first in name only. The sweet leek flavor should dominate here. The potatoes are a neutral foil for the leeks and provide the soup with body and heft. Of course, potatoes that fall apart and release their starch can turn this soup into a thick porridge reminiscent of cafeteria food. The trick is to cook the potatoes until tender without letting them dissolve into a starchy mess.

HAM AND SPLIT PEA SOUP

WHAT WE WANTED: Old-fashioned ham flavor from a readily available cut that would also provide enough meat for the soup. The texture must be creamy and thick but not heavy or gluey. Bits of aromatic vegetables (especially onions and carrots) should punctuate the soup.

Old-fashioned recipes for ham and split pea soup start with the bone from a large roast ham that has been nearly picked clean. The bone and some split peas are thrown into a pot with some water and cooked until the meat falls off the bone. By that time, the fat has discreetly melted into the liquid, and the peas have become creamy enough to thicken the soup.

We love split pea soup made this way, but times have changed. Except for the occasional holiday, most cooks rarely buy a bone-in ham, opting more often for the thin-sliced deli stuff. We wondered if we could duplicate this wonderful soup without buying a huge ham.

To test our belief that a ham stock is crucial to split pea soup, we made several pork stocks and pork-enhanced canned chicken broths. In addition to making stock the old-fashioned way from a meaty ham bone, we made stock from smoked pork necks, pork hocks (fresh and smoked), and smoked ham shanks. We also made cheater's stocks: kielbasa simmered in canned chicken broth, kielbasa simmered in water, bacon simmered in chicken broth, and bacon simmered in water.

The stocks based on hocks—fresh as well as smoked—were more greasy than flavorful. In addition, the hocks gave up very little meat, making it necessary to purchase an additional portion of ham to fortify the soup. Ham shanks, which include the hock, made a pleasant but lightweight stock that was a tad greasy and salty—both fixable problems had the stock been more stellar. Pork necks, which are not widely available, made a fairly flavorful but salty stock. All four cheater's stocks failed. Both the kielbasa- and bacon-enhanced chicken broths tasted strongly of overly processed meat, while the water-based versions tasted weak.

Not surprisingly, the stock made from the bone of a big ham was the winner. It was meaty and full-flavored, rich but not greasy, nicely seasoned without being overly salty, and smoky without tasting artificial. Unlike any of the other broths, this one sported bits of meat. And not just good meat—great meat. The tender pieces of ham that fell away from the bone during cooking were not just a nice byproduct of stock making. They were the glory of our split pea soup. But was there a way around buying half a ham (with an average weight of about 8 pounds) just to make a pot of soup?

After checking out the ham and smoked pork cases at several different stores, we discovered the picnic from the pork shoulder. Unlike what we generally refer to as ham, which comes from the back legs of the animal, the picnic comes from the shoulders and front legs. Smaller than a ham, the half-picnic weighs only 4½ pounds. After making a couple more pots of soup, we found that the picnic pork shoulder—with its bones, fat, rind, and meat—made outstanding stock, and, after two hours of simmering, the meat was meltingly tender yet still potently flavorful.

Because we did not need the entire picnic half for our pot of soup, we pulled off and roasted two of its meatier muscles and used the remaining meat, bone, fat, and rind to make the soup. At around 99 cents per pound, a picnic shoulder is usually cheaper than a ham and often cheaper than pork hocks, shanks, or neck bones as well. Here, we thought, was the modern solution. Rather than buy a ham for eating (and eating and eating) with a leftover bone for soup, purchase a picnic for soup, and roast the remaining couple of pounds for eating.

There are several ways to make ham and split pea soup. You can throw all of the ingredients—ham bone, peas, and diced vegetables—into a pot and simmer until everything is tender. Or you can sauté the vegetables, then add the remaining ingredients and cook the soup until the ham and peas are tender. Alternatively, you can cook the ham bone and peas (or give the ham bone a little bit of a head start) until ham and peas are tender and then add raw, sautéed, or caramelized vegetables to the pot, continuing to cook until the vegetables are tender and the flavors have blended.

Although we had hoped to keep the soup a straightforward, one-pot operation, we found out pretty quickly that dumping everything in at the same time resulted in gloppy, overcooked peas and tired mushy vegetables by the time the ham was tender. For textural contrast in this smooth, creamy soup, we ultimately preferred fully—though not overly—cooked vegetables.

Our best soups were those in which the vegetables spent enough time in the pot for their flavors to blend but not so long that they had lost all of their individual taste. Of the soups with vegetables added toward the end of cooking, we preferred the one with the caramelized vegetables. The sweeter vegetables gave this otherwise straightforward meat-and-starch soup a richness and depth of flavor that made the extra step and pan worth the trouble.

Many pea soup recipes call for an acidic ingredient—vinegar, lemon juice, fortified wines such as sherry or Madeira, Worcestershire sauce, or sour cream—to bring balance to an otherwise rich, heavy soup. After tasting all of the above, we found ourselves drawn to balsamic vinegar. Unlike any of the other ingredients, balsamic vinegar contributed a mildly sweet, mildly acidic flavor that complemented the soup perfectly.

WHAT WE LEARNED: Ham stock is essential for this soup, and you can get it with a picnic shoulder, a cut that adds great flavor and provides plenty of meat. For the best flavored and textured aromatic vegetables, sauté them in a separate pan. Finish the soup with a splash of mildly sweet balsamic vinegar.

HAM AND SPLIT PEA SOUP serves 6

Use an entire small 2½-pound smoked picnic portion ham if you can find one. Otherwise, buy a half-picnic ham and remove some meat (see illustrations on page 22), which you can roast and use in sandwiches, salads, or omelets.

- 1 piece (about 2½ pounds) smoked, bone-in picnic ham
- 4 bay leaves
- 1 pound (2½ cups) split peas, rinsed and picked through
- 1 teaspoon dried thyme
- 2 tablespoons extra-virgin olive oil
- 2 medium onions, chopped medium
- 2 medium carrots, chopped medium

TECHNIQUE: Drip-Free Ladling

Here's how we keep drips and spills to a minimum when ladling soups or stews. Before lifting the filled ladle up and out of the pot, dip the bottom back into the pot, so the liquid comes about halfway up the ladle. The tension on the surface of the soup grabs any drips and pulls them back into the pot.

<table>
<tr><td>2</td><td>medium stalks celery, chopped medium</td></tr>
<tr><td>1</td><td>tablespoon unsalted butter</td></tr>
<tr><td>2</td><td>medium garlic cloves, minced (about 2 teaspoons)</td></tr>
<tr><td></td><td>Pinch sugar</td></tr>
<tr><td>3</td><td>small red potatoes, scrubbed and cut into ½-inch dice (about ¾ cup)</td></tr>
<tr><td></td><td>Ground black pepper</td></tr>
<tr><td></td><td>Minced red onion (optional)</td></tr>
<tr><td></td><td>Balsamic vinegar</td></tr>
</table>

1. Place ham, bay leaves, and 3 quarts water in large stockpot or Dutch oven. Cover and bring to a boil over medium-high heat. Reduce heat to low and simmer until meat is tender and pulls away from bone, 2 to 2½ hours. Remove ham meat and bone from pot and set aside.

2. Add split peas and thyme to stock. Bring back to boil, reduce heat, and simmer, uncovered, until peas are tender but not dissolved, about 45 minutes. Meanwhile, when ham is cool enough to handle, shred meat into bite-sized pieces and set aside. Discard rind and bone.

3. While split peas are simmering, heat oil in large skillet over high heat until shimmering. Add onions, carrots, and celery and sauté, stirring frequently, until most of liquid evaporates and vegetables begin to brown, 5 to 6 minutes. Reduce heat to medium-low and add butter, garlic, and sugar. Cook vegetables, stirring frequently, until deeply browned, 30 to 35 minutes; set aside.

4. Add sautéed vegetables, potatoes, and shredded ham to pot with split peas. Simmer until potatoes are tender and peas dissolve and thicken soup to consistency of light cream, about 20 minutes more. Season with pepper to taste. (The soup can be refrigerated in an airtight container for 2 days. Warm soup over low heat until hot.) Ladle soup into bowls, sprinkle with red onion, if using, and serve, passing balsamic vinegar separately.

HAM AND SPLIT PEA SOUP WITH CARAWAY

Toast 1½ teaspoons caraway seeds in small skillet over medium-high heat, stirring frequently, until fragrant and browned, about 4 minutes. Follow recipe for Ham and Split Pea Soup, substituting toasted caraway seeds for dried thyme.

TECHNIQUE:
Handling a Half-Picnic Ham

A half-picnic ham is readily available in supermarkets but contains too much meat for a pot of soup. Our solution is to pull off several meaty sections of the ham and roast the meat for sandwiches, salads, and egg dishes.

1. With your fingers, loosen the large comma-shaped muscles on top of the picnic half.

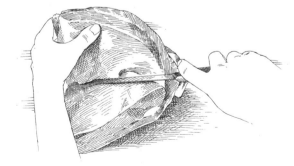

2. Use a knife to cut the membrane separating the comma-shaped muscles from the rest of the roast. The remaining meat and bone can be used to make soup.

RUSTIC POTATO-LEEK SOUP

WHAT WE WANTED: A chunky soup with bits of tender but not mushy potatoes and plenty of leek flavor.

We have always liked the classic creamy soup that French cooks make from potatoes and leeks. But sometimes this recipe seems a little too refined. At times we want these two ingredients at their most basic. So we decided to part company with the creamy French classic and take on the challenge of a more chunky, peasant-style French soup.

Ironically, the two ingredients that should make this soup great (potatoes and leeks) can also be its downfall. The potatoes should actually play only a supporting role; the leeks, gritty and time-consuming to clean though they are, are the real star of this soup. Cooking time is also crucial. Undercook the soup and the flavors will not meld; cook it too long and you will have a mixture of broken-down bits with little flavor or bite.

We tested the potatoes first. (See the Tasting Lab on page 25 for more information on the types of potatoes.) Quickly eliminating high-starch, low-moisture baking potatoes, which broke down immediately, we duly rejected the flavorful, medium-starch Yukon Gold as well. These potatoes broke down, too—just not as quickly. We settled on waxy, low-starch Red Bliss potatoes, which held their texture and did not become waterlogged during cooking. Then we reduced the proportion of potatoes altogether, giving the leeks the leading role.

Next we wanted to pump up the flavor of the soup. We decided to use not only the white part of the leek but also the light green part (the very dark green part is tough and should be discarded), and we left the chopped pieces large enough to create textural interest. A whopping 4 pounds of leeks used this way provided nonstop flavor. Water wasn't dynamic enough, so we used chicken stock instead.

But our real breakthrough came in the province of

technique. We knew that potatoes and leeks would need different simmering times. Stewing the leeks in some butter over a low flame to coax out as much flavor as possible, we added the potatoes later, with the chicken stock, then simmered them until almost tender. At that point we removed the pot from the heat, allowing the potatoes to finish cooking in the hot stock so they would not overcook and become mushy. The result: a soup with perfectly cooked potatoes, sweet and tender leeks, and an outspoken leek flavor. Because the potatoes were not cooked long enough to release their starch and thicken the broth, we added a little flour to cook with the leeks, giving the broth just the right amount of body to pull everything together.

WHAT WE LEARNED: For real leek flavor, use a lot of leeks and sweat them in a covered pot with butter. Don't overcook the potatoes or they will make the soup gluey. This is best accomplished by letting the potatoes finish cooking in the soup off heat.

RUSTIC POTATO-LEEK SOUP serves 6 to 8

This soup is hearty enough to serve as a main course, perhaps accompanied by crusty bread and preceded or followed by salad. Leeks differ. If yours have large desirable white and light green sections, use 4 pounds of leeks; if they're short on these parts, go with 5 pounds.

4–5 pounds leeks (see note)
6 tablespoons unsalted butter
1 tablespoon all-purpose flour
5¼ cups homemade chicken stock or canned low-sodium chicken broth
1 bay leaf
1¾ pounds red potatoes (about 5 medium), peeled and cut into ¾-inch dice
Salt and ground black pepper

1. Cut off roots and tough dark green portion of leeks, leaving white portion and about 3 inches of light green portion. Clean leeks following illustrations at right. Slice leeks in half lengthwise and chop into 1-inch pieces. (You should have about 11 cups.)

2. Heat butter in large stockpot or Dutch oven over medium-low heat until foaming. Stir in leeks, increase heat to medium, cover, and cook, stirring occasionally, until leeks are tender but not mushy, 15 to 20 minutes; do not brown the leeks. Sprinkle flour over leeks and stir to coat evenly. Cook until flour dissolves, about 2 minutes.

3. Increase heat to high; whisking constantly, gradually add stock. Add bay leaf and potatoes, cover, and bring to a boil. Reduce heat to medium-low and simmer, covered, until potatoes are almost tender, 5 to 7 minutes. Remove pot from heat and let stand, covered, until potatoes are tender and flavors meld, 10 to 15 minutes. Discard bay leaf and season with salt and pepper to taste. (Soup can be refrigerated in airtight container for a day or two. Warm over low heat until hot; do not boil.) Serve immediately.

TECHNIQUE:
Two Ways to Clean Leeks

Leeks are often quite dirty and gritty, so they require thorough cleaning. There are two ways to do this. Both methods require that you first cut the dark green portion into quarters lengthwise, leaving the root end intact.

1. Hold the leek under running water and shuffle the cut layers like a deck of cards.

2. An alternative is to slosh the cut end of the leek up and down in a bowl of water.

RUSTIC POTATO-LEEK SOUP WITH KIELBASA

Eight ounces of cooked ham, cut into 1/2-inch dice, can be substituted for the sausage, if desired. Whichever you choose, season the soup with care, since both ham and kielbasa are fully seasoned.

Follow recipe for Rustic Potato-Leek Soup, stirring in 8 ounces kielbasa sausage, cut into ½-inch slices, just before removing pot from heat in step 3. Proceed as directed.

RUSTIC POTATO-LEEK SOUP WITH WHITE BEANS

Follow recipe for Rustic Potato-Leek Soup, reducing potatoes to 2 medium (about ¾ pound). Just before removing pot from heat in step 3, stir in 1 cup hot water and 1 cup canned cannellini beans that have been drained and rinsed well. Proceed as directed.

TASTING LAB: Potatoes

ALTHOUGH ALL VEGETABLES VARY IN SIZE AND FRESHNESS, most markets carry only a single variety. Broccoli is broccoli, carrots are carrots. Even when there are several varieties (as with heirloom tomatoes), most can be used interchangeably in recipes. Yes, one tomato might look a bit different or be a bit sweeter than another, but they all will taste fine in salads.

With potatoes, this is not the case. Make French fries with Red Bliss potatoes and the fries will be greasy and heavy. Use russets in salad or corn chowder and they will fall apart in a soggy mess.

The fact that dozens of potato varieties are grown in this country makes the question of which potato is best for a specific recipe even more confusing. At any time you may see as many as five or six kinds of potatoes in your supermarket. Go to a farmers' market and you may see a dozen varieties. Some potatoes are sold by varietal name (such as Red Bliss or Yukon Gold), others by generic name (all-purpose, baking, etc.).

To make sense of this confusion, it is helpful to group potatoes into three major categories based on their ratio of solids (mostly starch) to water. The categories are high-starch/low-moisture potatoes, medium-starch potatoes, and low-starch/high-moisture potatoes.

High-starch/low-moisture potatoes, such as russets or Idahos, generally lose their shape when simmered in soups or stews. Because they have so little moisture, they tend to soak up liquid as they cook and eventually implode. In some cases, such as when you want the potatoes to thicken a soup, this can be desirable. Medium-starch potatoes, such as Yukon Golds and Yellow Finns, do a better job of holding their shape but share many traits in common with high-starch potatoes. Low-starch/high-moisture potatoes hold their shape better than other potatoes when simmered. This category includes all red-skinned potatoes, such as Red Bliss and Red Creamer, as well as freshly dug potatoes, which are often labeled "new" potatoes. Low-starch potatoes should be selected when potatoes are to hold their shape, as in Rustic Potato-Leek Soup.

Rating Vegetable Peelers

WE TESTED 10 PEELERS ON SIX DIFFERENT FRUITS AND VEGETABLES. WE WANTED THIN STRIPS OF PEEL WITH LITTLE FLESH from apples, carrots, potatoes, and lemon, which we considered a single category. In a second category were tough-skinned butternut squash and celery root, from which we wanted thicker, fleshier strips of peel. In a third category, maneuverability, we assessed each peeler's performance on items with curves, crevices, and rough skin. We also evaluated handle-grip comfort, hand strain, sharpness of the blade, and the downward pressure required to peel. Peelers are listed in order of preference. See www.cooksillustrated.com for up-to-date prices and mail-order sources for top-rated products.

RECOMMENDED

1. Oxo Good Grips Peeler

$6.00

Sharp blade, comfortable grip, great on curves, but bulky in small hands. The best overall peeler.

RECOMMENDED

2. Kuhn Rikon Peeler

$3.25

Takes off very wide, thick strips of peel, so it's especially good on butternut squash and celery root. We keep one around just for these tasks.

NOT RECOMMENDED

3. Kyocera P-1 Ceramic Yoke Peeler

$14.95

Some of the same strengths as the Kuhn Rikon peeler, but blade travel is less smooth and price is much higher.

NOT RECOMMENDED

4. Ekco Deluxe Peeler

$2.49

Familiar, cheap, and adequate for easy peeling, but almost useless on tough jobs like squash. Has stainless steel blade.

NOT RECOMMENDED

5. Ekco Peeler

$1.29

Same as Deluxe version but with carbon steel blade that is not appreciably sharper than stainless steel, and it rusts.

NOT RECOMMENDED

6. Henckels Swivel Peeler

$11.00

An expensive peeler that hugs curves but glides right over the skin on flat surfaces of squash and rough skin of celery root.

NOT RECOMMENDED

7. Farberware Stainless Soft Grip Euro Peeler

$5.99

Blade does not feel sharp, and it slides right over curved surfaces. Bulky in all but large hands.

NOT RECOMMENDED

8. Henckels Vegetable Peeler

$8.00

Exceptionally sturdy, but it feels like you're using a paring knife. Not for thin or delicate skins. Blade angle feels awkward.

NOT RECOMMENDED

9. Farberware Euro Peeler

$3.99

To get decent leverage with the blade, you must really choke up on the handle, which strains the hand. Blade is not particularly sharp.

NOT RECOMMENDED

10. Revereware Comfort Grip Permasharp Peeler

$4.99

The grip feels bulky even in large hands. The blade is recessed so far into the frame that often the blade can't reach the food.

EQUIPMENT CORNER: Vegetable Peelers

YOU MIGHT IMAGINE THAT ALL VEGETABLE PEELERS ARE pretty much the same. Not so. In our research, we turned up 25 peelers, many with quite novel features. The major differences were the fixture of the blade, either stationary or swiveling; the material of the blade, carbon stainless steel, stainless steel, or ceramic; and the orientation of the blade to the handle, either straight in line with the body or perpendicular to it. The last arrangement, with the blade perpendicular to the handle, is called a harp, or Y, peeler because the frame looks like the body of a harp or the letter Y. This type of peeler, which is popular in Europe, works with a pulling motion rather than the shucking motion of most American peelers.

For our tests we narrowed the number of peelers to 10 and then recruited several cooks to peel carrots, potatoes, lemons, butternut squash, and celery root. In most cases, testers preferred the Oxo Good Grips peeler with a sharp stainless steel blade that swivels. Peelers with stationary blades are fine for peeling carrots, but they have trouble hugging the curves on potatoes. As for blade material, we found peelers made from stainless steel, carbon steel, and ceramic that were both sharp and dull. We concluded that sharpness is a factor of quality control during the manufacturing process and not blade material.

The Y-shaped peelers tested well, although they removed more flesh along with the skin on potatoes, lemons, and carrots and therefore did not rate as well as the Oxo Good Grips. The one case where this liability turned into an asset was with butternut squash, where these Y shaped peelers took off the skin as well as the greenish-tinged flesh right below the skin in one pass. With the Oxo Good Grips, it was necessary to go over the peeled flesh once the skin had been removed. Among Y-shaped peelers, testers preferred the Kuhn Rikon. Because both the Oxo Good Grips and Kuhn Rikon peelers can be had for less than $10, we recommend that you purchase both.

TASTING LAB: Salt

THE FOOD PRESS HAS EXALTED EXOTIC SEA SALTS. WE wondered if a pinch here or a smidgen there is really worth as much as $36 per pound. Will your biscuits or steak taste better if you spend more money on salt?

And what about choosing an everyday salt for adding to pasta water or chicken stock? More home cooks are following the lead of chefs and keeping kosher salt (rather than table salt) next to the stove. Chefs have spread the word that these oversized grains of salt have a pure, clean flavor and that it's much easier to pick up the large crystals with your fingers. While the argument about crystal size is persuasive, we wondered if kosher salt really does taste better than table salt.

Salt is either mined from ancient seas that dried up millions of years ago or obtained by evaporating seawater. In their pure form, sodium chloride, salts from both sources taste the same. What distinguishes one salt from another in color and flavor are the type and amount of minerals (such as magnesium, calcium, and potassium) and/or clays attached to the crystals of sodium chloride. The size and texture of the crystals—whether big flakes, irregularly shaped large grains, or regularly shaped small grains—are largely determined by the way the salt is processed.

Sea salt is obtained from seawater held in large, shallow ponds or large pans. As the water evaporates, coarse crystals of salt fall to the bottom. The crystals are collected by raking. The white fleur de sel, or "flower of the salt," is harvested from salt that forms on the surface of the pans as a thin film and is quickly skimmed. It is extremely expensive. (The brand we tested costs $36 per pound.)

Table salt is usually obtained by pumping water into an underground salt deposit to dissolve the salt, pumping the brine to the surface, settling impurities, and vacuum-evaporating the clear brine. Rapid vacuum evaporation yields the tiny, regularly shaped grains that fit through the holes in a salt shaker. Some table salt is taken from the sea and then processed by vacuum evaporation to yield small crystals.

Kosher salt can be mined or taken from the sea. Processing is designed to produce coarse, irregular crystals that will cling to meat during koshering, in which the salt is applied to draw blood out of just-butchered meats.

Unlike kosher salt and sea salt, most table salts contain additives. Iodized table salt contains potassium iodide, which protects against thyroid disease. Dextrose may be added to help stabilize the iodine, and calcium silicate or one of several other drying agents are often added to prevent caking. Many experts claim these additives can impart an off flavor.

To make sense of all these claims, we tasted two kinds of table salt (one iodized, one not), two brands of kosher salt, and five widely available sea salts. The price per pound ranged from 36 cents to $36. Tests were divided into three categories: salt used at the table (we sprinkled each sample on roast beef), salt used in baking (we used a plain biscuit recipe), and salt dissolved in liquids (we tested each salt in spring water, chicken stock, and pasta cooking water).

Of the five tests run, we uncovered the most profound differences in our beef tenderloin test. Tasters loved the crunch of the large sea salt flakes or crystals when sprinkled over slices of roast tenderloin. Here, Maldon Sea Salt was the clear winner, followed by Fleur de Sel de Camargue and Light Grey Celtic Sea Salt.

Why did the sea salts win this test? According to Dr. Gary Beauchamp, director of the Monell Chemical Senses Center in Philadelphia and a leading expert on the science of taste and smell, flat crystals or crystals with holes cause a taste sensation different from that of regularly shaped small crystals. And, based on our test results, it's clear that large crystals provided a more pleasing sensory stimulation than fine table salt. In fact, tasters really objected to fine salts sprinkled on the beef, calling them "harsh" and "sharp." Tasters did like kosher salt on meat, but not as much as sea salt, which has larger crystals.

Does this mean that our tasters were reacting to the additives in table salt that the chefs had warned us about? It's possible, but given the results in our other tests, we are not convinced. In fact, the one fine sea salt in our tasting (La Baleine) finished next-to-last in this test, and it does not contain any additives. It's hard to sprinkle fine sea or table salt evenly over meat, and we think tasters may have been hitting pockets with a lot of salt and reacting negatively.

In the biscuit tests, Morton table salt was the winner, and most of the sea salts landed at the bottom of the ratings. The explanation here is simple. Small salt crystals are more evenly distributed in baked goods than large crystals, and tasters didn't like getting a big hit of crunchy salt as they nibbled on biscuits.

In the spring water, chicken stock, and pasta cooking water, tasters felt that all nine salts tasted pretty much the same. Why didn't the fancy sea salts beat the pants off plain table salt in these tests? The main reason is dilution. Yes, sea salts sampled right from the box (or sprinkled on meat at the table) did taste better than table salt. And while crystal size did undoubtedly affect flavor perception in the tenderloin test, we suspect that our tasters were also responding favorably to some of the trace minerals in these salts. But mineral content is so low in sea salt (by weight, less than 1 percent in all brands tested) that any effect these minerals might have on flavor was lost when a teaspoon of salt was stirred into a big pot of chicken stock or pasta cooking water.

One final (and very important) point. Our results should not be taken to mean that all salts behave in the same way in the kitchen. For example, salts with a fine texture may seem saltier than coarse salts because of the way the crystals pack down in a teaspoon when measured. For instance, a teaspoon of coarse Maldon Sea Salt contains just half as much salt as a teaspoon of fine table salt.

What, then, can we conclude from the results of these tests? For one, expensive sea salts are best saved for the table, where their delicate flavor and great crunch can be appreciated. Don't waste $36-a-pound sea salt by sprinkling it into a simmering stew. If you like to keep coarse salt in a ramekin next to the stove, choose a kosher salt, which costs just pennies per pound. If you measure salt by the teaspoon when cooking, you might as well use table salt, which is also the best choice for baking.

Rating Salts

NINE SALTS WERE PUT THROUGH A BATTERY OF TESTS. WE FOUND THAT FLAVOR DIFFERENCES WERE SUBTLE. TEXTURE was a consideration in only the biscuit and tenderloin tests. Salts are listed in order of preference based on all tests, but the difference between the first- and last-place brands was small. See www.cooksillustrated.com for up-to-date prices and mail-order sources for sea salts.

RECOMMENDED

1. Maldon Sea Salt, Maldon, England

$6.95 for 8.5 ounces ($13.08 per pound)

These light, airy, crunchy flakes resemble pyramids and are a perfect match with meat. Available in gourmet stores and by mail.

RECOMMENDED

2. Fleur de Sel de Camargue, Provence, France

$9.95 for 4.4 ounces ($36.18 per pound)

The "great crunch" of this hand-harvested salt propelled it to second place in the tenderloin test. "Gritty" in biscuits. Available in gourmet stores and by mail.

RECOMMENDED

3. Morton Kosher Salt, United States

$1.69 for 48 ounces ($0.56 per pound)

This "straightforward" salt finished third in the biscuit test. Tasters liked the crunch of these medium-sized grains on the tenderloin. Available in supermarkets.

RECOMMENDED

4. Diamond Crystal Kosher Salt, United States

$1.99 for 48 ounces ($0.66 per pound)

Tasters enjoyed this salt on the tenderloin. The biscuits were mild and buttery, though one taster detected "pockets of salt." Available in supermarkets.

RECOMMENDED

5. Light Grey Celtic Sea Salt, Brittany, France

$7.75 for 24 ounces ($5.17 per pound)

This hand-harvested salt has a unique grayish hue because of its high mineral content. Coarse "pebbles" were too large in the biscuits but better suited to tenderloin. Available in gourmet stores and by mail.

RECOMMENDED

6. La Baleine Sea Salt Fine Crystals, Provence, France

$4.89 for 26.5 ounces ($2.95 per pound)

This finely ground sea salt comes from the Mediterranean and was judged to have a clean, sweet, mild flavor, but tasters thought powdery grains were "inappropriate for garnishing roasts." Available in supermarkets.

RECOMMENDED

7. Morton Iodized Table Salt, United States

$0.59 for 26 ounces ($0.36 per pound)

This salt won first place in the biscuit test, but tasters disliked the way these small grains "dissolved into nothingness" on the meat. Available in supermarkets.

RECOMMENDED

8. Esprit du Sel de Île de Ré, Brittany, France

$9.00 for 8.8 ounces ($16.36 per pound)

Tasters thought the irregularly coarse grains were just right for tenderloin but resulted in an unappealing, crunchy texture in biscuits. Available in gourmet stores and by mail.

RECOMMENDED

9. Morton Non-Iodized Table Salt, United States

$0.59 for 26 ounces ($0.36 per pound)

This salt was described as "sharp and characterless" when sprinkled on tenderloin. However, these small grains were thought to be perfect for biscuits. Available in supermarkets.

DRESSING UP vegetables

You can't serve steamed broccoli every night. No matter how well executed, it's just too boring. Every cook needs foolproof recipes for dressing up everyday vegetables. Frozen vegetables (such as tired twice-baked potatoes and army-green stuffed bell peppers) are not the answer. You might as well stick with steamed broccoli. Our goal was simple. Rescue two favorite fancy vegetable dishes—twice-baked potatoes and stuffed bell peppers—from the clutches of cafeterias, bad steakhouses, and frozen food manufacturers.

A good twice-baked potato is a study in contrasts. The crisp potato shell nestles a creamy, smooth filling that is rich but not overwhelming. Although this vegetable side dish looks a lot more impressive than your average baked potato, it should not require much more work.

Stuffed bell peppers certainly sound like a good idea. But how many times have you bitten into a pepper that is crunchy or, worse still, slimy and soft? And the rice filling is often soggy, bland, or made sickly sweet with too much ketchup. How can something so classic go so wrong? We knew that the test kitchen could revive these dishes and still keep them simple and straightforward.

Garlic gets sliced, slivered, and minced in preparation for testing vegetable recipes.

TWICE-BAKED POTATOES

WHAT WE WANTED: Twice-baked potatoes are at the apex of American potato cookery. Although they are not difficult to make, the process can be time-consuming. We wanted to perfect the process—from baking the potatoes and readying the shells to preparing the filling and baking when filled.

This simple dish—essentially baked russet potatoes from which the flesh has been removed, mashed with dairy ingredients and seasonings, mounded back in the shells, and baked again—offers a good range of both texture and flavor in a single morsel. When done well, the skin is chewy and substantial without being tough, with just a hint of crispness to play off the smooth, creamy filling. In terms of flavor, cheese and other dairy ingredients make the filling rich and tangy, a contrast with the mild, slightly nutty potato shell.

Because twice-baked potatoes are put in the oven twice, we found it best to bake them for just an hour, rather than the usual 75 minutes we allocate for plain baked potatoes. Oiling the skins before baking promotes crispness, not something you necessarily want in plain baked potatoes but a trait we came to love in creamy twice-baked potatoes.

Our favorite baked potato recipe underscores the importance of opening the potatoes right after baking to release as much steam as possible. For twice-baked potatoes, it's advisable to wait a few minutes for the potatoes to cool before slicing them apart and emptying out the flesh.

Once we had emptied the potato halves of their flesh, we noticed they got a little flabby sitting on the counter waiting to be stuffed. Because the oven was still on and waiting for the return of the stuffed halves, we decided to put the skins back in while we prepared the filling. This worked beautifully, making the shells extra crisp.

Pleased with our chewy, slightly crunchy skins, we now had to develop a smooth, lush, flavorful filling that would hold up its end of the bargain. (Lumpy, sodden, and dull-tasting would not do.) Twice-baked potatoes are usually filled with a mixture of well-mashed potato, shredded cheese, and other dairy ingredients, including one or more of the usual suspects: butter, sour cream, cream cheese, yogurt, ricotta, cottage cheese, milk, cream, and buttermilk. Various herbs and spices also often show up, as do diced meats and sautéed vegetables.

To get an idea of how we wanted to flavor our filling, we prepared 10 different recipes with various ingredient combinations. In a rare display of accord, all tasters agreed on a few general observations. First, everyone preferred tangy dairy products, such as sour cream, yogurt, and buttermilk, to sweet ones, such as milk, cream, and ricotta. Second, the use of only one dairy ingredient produced a rather dull, one-dimensional filling. A second ingredient added depth of flavor and complexity. Third, nobody favored too fatty a mouthfeel, a preference that left the addition of large amounts of butter (some recipes use up to a full stick for four potatoes) and cream cheese out of the running. Dozens of further tests helped us refine our filling to a rich, but not killer, combination of sharp cheddar, sour cream, buttermilk, and just 2 tablespoons of butter.

With the filling mixed and mounded back into the shells, our last tests centered on the final baking. We wanted to do more than just heat the filling through; we were intent of forming an attractive brown crust on it as well. Broiling turned out to be the easiest and most effective method. After about 10 minutes, the potatoes emerged browned, crusted, and ready for the table.

WHAT WE LEARNED: Oil the potatoes before baking for a crisp skin, and bake the hollowed-out shells to prevent sogginess. Use a combination of sour cream, buttermilk, and just 2 tablespoons of butter for a tangy filling that's rich but not heavy. Broil the filled potato shells to create a crisp crust on top.

TWICE-BAKED POTATOES serves 6 to 8

To vary the flavor a bit, try substituting other types of cheese, such as Gruyère, fontina, or feta, for the cheddar. Yukon Gold potatoes, though slightly more moist than our ideal, gave our twice-baked potatoes a buttery flavor and mouthfeel that everyone liked, so we recommend them as a substitute for the russets.

    4   medium russet potatoes (7 to 8 ounces each),
        scrubbed, dried, and rubbed lightly with
        vegetable oil
    4   ounces sharp cheddar cheese, shredded
        (about 1 cup)
    ½   cup sour cream
    ½   cup buttermilk
    2   tablespoons unsalted butter, softened
    3   medium scallions, sliced thin
    ½   teaspoon salt
        Ground black pepper

1. Adjust oven rack to upper-middle position and heat oven to 400 degrees. Bake potatoes on foil-lined baking sheet until skin is crisp and deep brown and skewer easily pierces flesh, about 1 hour. Setting baking sheet aside, transfer potatoes to wire rack and let cool slightly, about 10 minutes.

2. Using oven mitt or folded kitchen towel to handle hot potatoes, cut each potato in half so that long, blunt sides rest on work surface (see photograph at right). Using small spoon, scoop flesh from each half into medium bowl, leaving ⅛ to ¼ inch thickness of flesh in each shell. Arrange shells on lined baking sheet and return to oven until dry and slightly crisp, about 10 minutes. Meanwhile, mash potato flesh with fork until smooth. Stir in remaining ingredients, including pepper to taste, until well combined.

3. Remove shells from oven and increase oven setting to broil. Holding shells steady on pan with oven mitt or towel-protected hand, spoon mixture into crisped shells, mounding it slightly at center, and return potatoes to oven. Broil until spotty brown and crisp on top, 10 to 15 minutes. Allow to cool for 10 minutes. Serve warm.

VARIATIONS

TWICE-BAKED POTATOES WITH PEPPERJACK CHEESE AND BACON

Fry 8 strips (about 8 ounces) bacon, cut crosswise into ¼-inch pieces, in medium skillet over medium heat until crisp, 5 to 7 minutes. With slotted spoon, transfer bacon to paper towel-lined plate to drain; set aside. Follow recipe for Twice-Baked Potatoes, substituting pepperjack cheese for cheddar and stirring reserved bacon into filling mixture.

TWICE-BAKED POTATOES WITH CHIPOTLE CHILE AND ONION

For a slightly smoky aftertaste with just a hint of heat, limit the chipotle to 1 tablespoon; for a little heat, increase the chipotle to 1 1/2 tablespoons.

Heat 2 tablespoons butter in medium skillet over medium heat; add 1 medium onion, chopped fine, and sauté until

GETTING IT RIGHT:
Halving Baked Potatoes

This way

NOT this way

Most potatoes have two relatively flat, blunt sides and two curved sides. Halve the baked potatoes lengthwise so the blunt sides are down once the shells are stuffed, making the potatoes much more stable in the pan during final baking.

taking care not to brown garlic or ginger. Off heat, stir in 1 cup thawed frozen peas; set aside. Follow recipe for Twice-Baked Potatoes, omitting cheese and butter and stirring spiced peas into filling mixture.

TWICE-BAKED POTATOES WITH SMOKED SALMON AND CHIVES

This variation makes a fine brunch dish.

Follow recipe for Twice-Baked Potatoes, omitting cheese and scallions and stirring 4 ounces smoked salmon, cut into ½-inch pieces, and 3 tablespoons minced fresh chives into filling mixture. Sprinkle finished potatoes with additional chopped chives as a garnish just before serving.

TASTING LAB: Black Pepper

AS THE LONG-REIGNING KING OF SPICES, ONCE EQUAL IN value to gold, black pepper has become a kitchen table constant. The hard, dry, blackish kernels we know as peppercorns are derived from long, thin spikes of ripe green berries that grow on a vine reaching up to 100 feet long. Once picked, the berries are typically spread out on concrete slabs or straw mats, where they are left to dry in the sun for a number of days, changing from taut green balls to dark, wrinkled, dense kernels.

Not to be confused with chile pepper (Capsicum annuum), black pepper (Piper nigrum) grows in warm, moist climates all over the world, typically within about 15 degrees of the equator. Although most of us tend to think that one jar of black pepper is the same as another, several varieties exist. The most readily available include Vietnamese pepper, Lampong (from the island of Sumatra), and Malabar and Tellicherry (both from India). Among spice experts, each has gained a reputation for its particular attributes.

Neither a supermarket brand nor sometimes even a gourmet store brand is likely to specify from what part of the world its pepper was sourced. The product is advertised

soft, 3 to 4 minutes. Follow recipe for Twice-Baked Potatoes, omitting butter and adding 1 to 1½ tablespoons minced canned chipotle chiles in adobo sauce, reserved sautéed onion, and 2 tablespoons chopped fresh cilantro leaves to filling mixture.

TWICE-BAKED POTATOES WITH MONTEREY JACK AND PESTO

Follow recipe for Twice-Baked Potatoes, substituting Monterey Jack cheese for cheddar, reducing buttermilk to ¼ cup, omitting butter, and adding ¼ cup prepared pesto to filling mixture.

TWICE-BAKED POTATOES WITH INDIAN SPICES AND PEAS

Heat 2 tablespoons butter in medium skillet over medium heat. Add 1 medium onion, chopped fine, and sauté until soft, 3 to 4 minutes. Add 1 teaspoon finely grated fresh ginger, 3 medium minced garlic cloves (about 1 tablespoon), 1 teaspoon each ground cumin and ground coriander, and ¼ teaspoon each ground cinnamon, ground turmeric, and ground cloves; cook until fragrant, about 30 seconds more,

Rating Black Peppers

WE EVALUATED 10 BRANDS OF BLACK PEPPERCORNS OR GROUND BLACK PEPPER. WHOLE PEPPERCORNS WERE CRACKED within a half hour before tasting. The peppers are listed in order of preference. All of those in the recommended category received relatively close score results. See www.cooksillustrated.com for up-to-date prices and mail-order sources for top-rated products.

RECOMMENDED

1. McCormick/Schilling Whole Black Peppercorns (sold in glass jar)

$4.19 for 1.87 ounces

This pepper imparted a robust, piney aroma with orange notes. This line consists of either Malabar or Lampong pepper. Available in supermarkets. Sold on the West Coast under the Schilling label.

RECOMMENDED

2. Kalustyan's Vietnam Whole Black Pepper Corn

$4.99 for 4 ounces

This sample tasted mild and was noticeably smoky, with a "very distinct woody flavor." Not fiery, but heat "catches up to you." Available by mail.

RECOMMENDED

3. Kalustyan's Lampong Whole Black Pepper Corn

$4.99 for 4 ounces

This Indonesia pepper delivered a pungent aroma described as "penetrating" and "fruity." Its flavor was not as pungent as its aroma. Available by mail.

RECOMMENDED

4. Penzeys Malabar Black Peppercorns

$2.99 for 2.5 ounces

This Indian pepper had a rich fragrance with elements of fresh pine and lemon. Its flavor was "woodsy" and "biting," with "lots of heat." Available by mail.

RECOMMENDED

5. Penzeys Tellicherry Black Peppercorns

$2.99 for 4 ounces

This Indian pepper is left to mature on the vine to develop more flavor. The sample we tasted was "quite pungent," with "intense heat at the end." Available by mail.

RECOMMENDED

6. McCormick/Schilling Whole Black Peppercorns (sold in plastic bottle)

$2.29 for 2.37 ounces

Considered the least premium peppercorn in the McCormick/Schilling line, this pepper nonetheless held up reasonably well. Its flavor was musty as well as biting and pungent. Available in supermarkets.

NOT RECOMMENDED

7. McCormick/Schilling Pure Ground Black Pepper (sold in tin)

$1.89 for 2 ounces

Of all the ground pepper samples, this familiar tin can carried the most flavor but was still deemed bland. Available in supermarkets.

NOT RECOMMENDED

8. Spice Islands Whole Black Pepper

$3.89 for 2.4 ounces

Penetratingly hot and very "bitter" and "dusty." Available in supermarkets.

NOT RECOMMENDED

9. Spice Islands Fine Grind Black Pepper

$4.68 for 2.3 ounces

This pepper was described as "weak," having "no complexity" and only a light, latent heat. Available in supermarkets.

NOT RECOMMENDED

10. McCormick/Schilling Ground Black Pepper (sold in glass jar)

$4.39 for 1.62 ounces

This pricey ground pepper had "no interesting flavor characteristics to speak of," one taster asserted. Available in supermarkets.

simply as "black pepper," leaving the consumer with the choice of whole or ground.

For a spice that we use just about every day, and with a wide variety of foods, it's hard not to wonder if we have taken pepper too much for granted and are missing out on a greater taste experience. Perhaps we should be seeking out black pepper from a particular region of a particular country. Or, at the other end of the spectrum, perhaps all this fuss over grinding fresh whole peppercorns is nonsense, not really providing any improved flavor. We decided to hold a blind tasting to sort it all out.

We included in our tasting the two preeminent national supermarket brands as well as the above-mentioned varieties, which were ordered from specialty spice and gourmet stores. We skipped some varieties of black pepper, such as Brazilian and Ponape, because they proved too difficult to find on the retail level. Even some of those we did include in the tasting can be hard to track down. We also left out white pepper, which comes from the same plant as black pepper but is harvested when the berries are further ripened; they are then soaked, rubbed to remove their shells, and dried. Also excluded from our tasting were green peppercorns, which are unripe pepper berries, and pink peppercorns, which are not true peppercorns at all but come from a tree.

All of the peppers were offered plain but with the option of being tasted on plain white rice. Overall, our tasting confirmed that freshly ground pepper is far superior to

pepper purchased already ground. The latter carried minimal aroma and tended to taste sharp and dull, lacking in complexity. Those whole peppercorns that were fresh ground just before the tasting contained bold as well as subtle flavors and aromas that were both lively and complex.

As for differences between the varieties of whole peppercorns that were tasted fresh-ground, we found them to be distinct yet subtle. All were appreciated for their particular characteristics (see the chart on page 35), receiving high scores within a close range of one another. Based on these results, we concluded that what is important is not so much which variety of pepper you buy but how you buy it.

Why did we find the most noticeable differences in pepper to be between fresh ground whole pepper and commercially ground pepper? When a peppercorn is cracked, the volatile chemical components that give pepper its bold aroma as well as its subtle characteristics immediately begin to disperse. These more subtle flavors often include pine and citrus. So with time (and cracking), what remains is the predominant nonvolatile compound in black pepper, piperine. Piperine is the source of black pepper's renowned pungency and is what gives it its characteristic hot, sharp, and stinging qualities. It is also said to stimulate saliva and gastric juices, creating the sensation of hunger.

Knowing this, one of the easiest ways for a home cook to improve his or her cooking is simply by buying whole peppercorns and grinding them fresh with each meal. That way, instead of merely experiencing the sharp sensation that ground pepper has to offer, you will unleash a spectrum of flavors from earthy to exotic.

There are a couple of tips for buying pepper. As with any spice, purchase it from a reputable source that has high product turnover, so that you know you are buying a fresh product. The appearance of the peppercorns can also be an indicator of quality. Peppercorns that were not dried quickly enough take on a white tint to their dark color (not to be confused with white peppercorns) and will not be as flavorful. Quality black pepper should have a dark, shiny appearance and not be sitting in a lot of dust.

STUFFED PEPPERS

WHAT WE WANTED: Tender peppers with enough structure to hold a well-seasoned filling.

Mention stuffed peppers to most people and they think of a U.S. Army green shell crammed with leftovers from the school cafeteria. Although the classic 1950s sweet pepper filled with aromatic rice and beef and topped with ketchup may sound mediocre, this recipe can be delicious if prepared properly.

To get going, we tried a few classic recipes. Although these trial runs produced nothing as bad as what we remembered from the school cafeteria, they were far from perfect. First off, the peppers themselves varied greatly in degree of doneness. Some were so thoroughly cooked that they slumped onto their sides, unable to support their stuffed weight. On the other end of the spectrum, barely cooked peppers added an unfriendly crunch and bitter flavor to the mix. To be a success, the peppers themselves would have to yield a tender bite yet retain enough structure to stand up proudly on the plate.

None of the fillings hit home, either. An all-rice version was uninteresting, while another stuffed with all meat was leaden and greasy. One recipe called for small amounts of so many varied ingredients that it made us think its creator just wanted to clean out her refrigerator. We came away from this first round of tests wanting a simple yet gratifying filling, neither humdrum nor packed with odd ingredients.

To start, we needed a solid pepper venue with minimal crunch. So we steamed, microwaved, roasted, and blanched a round of peppers and lined them up for everyone in the test kitchen to examine. The steamed and microwaved examples were bland in both color and flavor. We tried roasting in an uncovered dish filled with a little water, an uncovered dish with no water, and a covered dish. Each procedure produced a bitter, subpar pepper. We knew that if we allowed the peppers to roast a little longer, their sugars would

eventually caramelize and the peppers would turn sweet. But at that point their texture would also have disintegrated into that of an Italian sandwich ingredient. Tasters unanimously preferred the vibrant color, sturdiness, and overall sweeter flavor of the blanched peppers; the hot water actually seemed to have washed away some of their bitterness.

Usually, a freshly blanched vegetable is plunged immediately into an ice cold water bath in a process known as shocking. The point is to halt the cooking process at just the right moment while stabilizing the vegetable's brightened color. We find water baths to be a real pain, especially in a kitchen where counter space is prime property. Although the shocked peppers had a slightly brighter hue than those that had been blanched but not shocked, they took much longer to heat through in the oven. So we abandoned shocking and instead fussed with blanching times, being careful to remove the peppers a little early and then allow the residual heat to finish their cooking. We found that a three-minute dip in boiling water followed by a cooling period on the countertop yielded the perfect balance of structure and chew.

Even with a pepper that's cooked to perfection, everyone knows that in this dish the stuffing is the star of the show. The options for stuffing ingredients are many, including couscous, polenta, and a number of interesting and unusual grains. But we landed on rice. A universal pantry ingredient, it is a classic in American recipes for stuffed peppers.

Because we wanted these stuffed peppers to work as a quick midweek meal, our goal was to keep the rice-based filling simple and satisfying, with a streamlined ingredient list and preparation method. Tasters did not care much for sausage, heavy seasonings, or a mix of too many ingredients. To our surprise, they were big fans of the classic 1950s version of a pepper stuffed with rice and ground beef. Sautéed onions and garlic rounded out the flavors, while tomatoes added a fresh note and some color. Bound together with a little cheese and topped with ketchup, this retro pepper is a model of simplicity, but it can be easily updated by using different spices and seasonings. We found that Middle Eastern and Italian flavors are especially well suited to this dish.

Now we had a pepper, and we had a filling. All we had to do was figure out the best way to get them together. The first trick is to use the boiling water from the blanched peppers to cook the rice. While the peppers cool and the rice cooks, the onions, garlic, and beef can be sautéed quickly. Then filling and peppers can be assembled and heated through in the oven. The result? Stuffed peppers that take only 45 minutes from start to finish—and that are also truly worth eating.

WHAT WE LEARNED: **Blanch the peppers to improve their flavor, color, and texture before stuffing them. Cook the rice in the hot blanching water to save time. Flavor a classic rice-and-beef filling with tomatoes, cheddar cheese, onion, and garlic for a basic stuffed pepper, or get more adventurous with either Italian or Middle Eastern flavors.**

CLASSIC STUFFED BELL PEPPERS
serves 4 as a light main dish or side dish

When shopping for bell peppers to stuff, it's best to choose those with broad bases that will allow the peppers to stand up on their own. (See the Tasting Lab on page 40 for more guidelines on selecting peppers for this recipe.) It's easier to fill the peppers after they have been placed in the baking dish because the sides of the dish will hold the peppers steady.

Salt
4 medium red, yellow, or orange bell peppers (about 6 ounces each), ½ inch trimmed off tops, cores and seeds discarded
½ cup long-grain white rice
1½ tablespoons olive oil
1 medium onion, chopped fine (about 1 cup)
12 ounces ground beef, preferably ground chuck
3 medium garlic cloves, minced (about 1 tablespoon)
1 (14½-ounce) can diced tomatoes, drained, ¼ cup juice reserved
5 ounces Monterey Jack cheese, shredded (1¼ cups)
2 tablespoons chopped fresh parsley leaves
Ground black pepper
¼ cup ketchup

1. Bring 4 quarts water to a boil in large stockpot or Dutch oven over high heat. Add 1 tablespoon salt and bell peppers. Cook until peppers just begin to soften, about 3 minutes. Using slotted spoon, remove peppers from pot, drain off excess water, and place peppers cut-sides up on paper towels. Return water to a boil; add rice and boil until tender, about 13 minutes. Drain rice and transfer it to large bowl; set aside.

2. Adjust oven rack to middle position and heat oven to 350 degrees.

3. Meanwhile, heat oil in 12-inch heavy-bottomed skillet over medium-high heat until shimmering. Add onion and cook, stirring occasionally, until softened and beginning to brown, about 5 minutes. Add ground beef and cook, breaking beef into small pieces with spoon, until no longer pink, about 4 minutes. Stir in garlic and cook until fragrant, about 30 seconds. Transfer mixture to bowl with rice; stir in tomatoes, 1 cup cheese, parsley, and salt and pepper to taste.

4. Stir together ketchup and reserved tomato juice in small bowl.

5. Place peppers cut-sides up in 9-inch square baking dish. Using soup spoon, divide filling evenly among peppers. Spoon 2 tablespoons ketchup mixture over each filled pepper and sprinkle each with 1 tablespoon of remaining cheese. Bake until cheese is browned and filling is heated through, 25 to 30 minutes. Serve immediately.

VARIATIONS

STUFFED BELL PEPPERS WITH SPICED LAMB, CURRANTS, AND FETA CHEESE

Middle Eastern flavors—ground lamb, warm spices, currants, and feta cheese—are used in this variation.

Salt
4 medium red, yellow, or orange bell peppers (about 6 ounces each), ½ inch trimmed off tops, cores and seeds discarded
½ cup long-grain white rice
1½ tablespoons olive oil
1 medium onion, chopped fine (about 1 cup)
12 ounces ground lamb
1 tablespoon ground cumin
1 teaspoon ground cardamom
½ teaspoon ground cinnamon
½ teaspoon hot red pepper flakes
3 medium garlic cloves, minced (about 1 tablespoon)
1 (1-inch) piece fresh ginger, minced (about 1 tablespoon)
¼ cup currants
1 (14½-ounce) can diced tomatoes, drained
6 ounces feta cheese, crumbled (1 cup)
2 tablespoons chopped fresh cilantro leaves
 Ground black pepper
⅓ cup roughly chopped salted, toasted cashews

1. Follow recipe for Classic Stuffed Bell Peppers through step 2.

2. Meanwhile, heat oil in 12-inch heavy-bottomed skillet over medium-high heat until shimmering. Add onion and cook, stirring occasionally, until softened and beginning to brown, about 5 minutes. Add ground lamb, cumin, cardamom, cinnamon, and red pepper flakes; cook, breaking lamb into small pieces with spoon, until no longer pink, about 4 minutes. Stir in garlic, ginger, and currants; cook until fragrant, about 30 seconds. Transfer mixture to bowl with rice; stir in tomatoes, cheese, cilantro, and salt and pepper to taste.

3. Continue with recipe for Classic Stuffed Bell Peppers from step 5, substituting chopped cashews for ketchup mixture and cheese topping.

STUFFED BELL PEPPERS WITH CHICKEN, SMOKED MOZZARELLA, AND BASIL

Ground chicken is a neutral background for the Italian flavors in this variation.

    Salt
4   medium red, yellow, or orange bell peppers
    (about 6 ounces each), ½ inch trimmed off
    tops, cores and seeds discarded
½   cup long-grain white rice
1½ tablespoons olive oil
1   medium onion, chopped fine (about 1 cup)
12 ounces ground chicken
3   medium garlic cloves, minced (about 1
    tablespoon)
1   (14½-ounce) can diced tomatoes, drained
4   ounces smoked mozzarella,
    shredded (1 cup)
2   tablespoons chopped fresh basil leaves
    Ground black pepper
⅓   cup fresh bread crumbs

1. Follow recipe for Classic Stuffed Bell Peppers through step 2.

2. Meanwhile, heat oil in 12-inch heavy-bottomed skillet over medium-high heat until shimmering. Add onion and cook, stirring occasionally, until softened and beginning to brown, about 5 minutes. Add chicken and cook, breaking it into small pieces with spoon, until chicken becomes opaque, about 4 minutes. Stir in garlic and cook until fragrant, about

30 seconds. Transfer mixture to bowl with rice; stir in tomatoes, cheese, basil, and salt and pepper to taste.

3. Continue with recipe for Classic Stuffed Bell Peppers from step 5, substituting bread crumbs for ketchup mixture and cheese topping.

TASTING LAB: Bell Peppers

BELL PEPPERS SPANNING THE COLORS OF THE RAINBOW are now commonly found sitting side by side in the grocery store, no matter what the season. Wondering if these cheerfully colored peppers had different flavors or were simply cultivated for eye appeal, we conducted a blind tasting. After masking our colleagues' eyes with scarves, we lined them up to taste both raw and blanched examples of red, yellow, orange, green, and purple peppers fresh from the market.

No one guessed all of the colors correctly, but the differences in taste were dramatic. The favorite colors turned out to be red and orange. Without exhibiting much of a pungent pepper flavor, they were both pleasantly sweet. The yellow pepper, with its mildly sweet and slightly tannic flavor, was also well liked. The green pepper, the most easily recognized, was universally disliked for its unripe bitterness. The absolute worst entry, however, was the thin-skinned purple pepper. Its slimy texture when blanched and its singularly unpleasing flavor elicited comments such as "What we imagine a shoe tastes like" and "Did we just eat a slug?"

As it turned out, these comments weren't far off the mark. As a bell pepper ripens, it turns from green to yellow, orange, or red, depending on the variety. These bright peppers are sweeter simply because they are ripe, whereas the bitter green pepper is unripe. Purple peppers, too, are harvested when immature and would turn an uncommonly dark green if allowed to ripen fully. So unless you're fond of the tannic bitterness of the common green and the purple varieties, we suggest sticking with yellow, orange, or red.

TECHNIQUE: Keeping Stuffed Peppers Upright

Here are four neat ways to keep stuffed peppers from spilling their contents as they bake.

   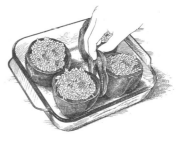

A. Instead of cooking peppers in the baking pan called for in most recipes, put them in a tube pan. The snug fit makes the peppers sit right up.

B. Place the peppers in the cups of a muffin tin.

C. Place each stuffed pepper in an individual ovenproof custard cup. This is a great system when you want to cook only a couple of peppers instead of a whole batch.

D. Reserve the tops of the peppers, which you have cut off to open the peppers for stuffing, and insert them between the stuffed peppers in the pan for added stability.

Rating Pepper Mills

WE RATED 12 PEPPER MILLS, EACH ONE AS CLOSE AS POSSIBLE TO 8 INCHES IN HEIGHT. WE EVALUATED THEM ACCORDING to grind quality, grind speed, ease of filling, and ease of use. The mills are listed in order of preference. See www.cooksillustrated.com for up-to-date prices and mail-order sources for top-rated products.

RECOMMENDED
1. Unicorn Magnum Plus Restaurant Use Peppermill

$45.00

Huge capacity, awesome speed, very easy to adjust the grind, and dazzlingly effective.

RECOMMENDED
2. East Hampton Industries (EHI) Peppermate Pepper Mill, Model 623

$40.00

Detachable cup captures pepper to make measuring easy. Huge opening makes this mill easiest to fill. Among the fastest grinders.

RECOMMENDED
3. Oxo Good Grips Grind It Pepper Mill, Model 41202

$19.99

Difficult to determine grind setting, but lightning-fast speed.

RECOMMENDED
4. Zyliss Large Pepper Mill

$27.50

Largest capacity, easy filling, and exemplary grind quality helps forgive its slower, but still acceptable, grind speed.

RECOMMENDED WITH RESERVATIONS
5. Oxo Good Grips Pepper Mill, Model 32180

$14.99

Excellent grind quality, but adjusting the grind can be a challenge. Comes with a coaster/base to catch spills.

RECOMMENDED WITH RESERVATIONS
6. Chef Specialties Windsor 8-Inch Pepper Mill

$22.99

Traditional design with good grind quality.

RECOMMENDED WITH RESERVATIONS
7. Peugeot Menton 20 cm Pepper Mill

$26.98

All grind adjustments seem to be on the fine side. Not great at producing coarse pepper.

RECOMMENDED WITH RESERVATIONS
8. Trudeau Iceberg Adjustable Pepper Mill, Model 071-7005

$16.98

Smallest capacity, but grind adjustment system uses lever and is well designed. Head with flat sides provides surer grip than round heads.

NOT RECOMMENDED
9. William Bounds Shake 'n Twist Salt and Pepper Grinder

$27.99

Fine grind is OK, but coarse and medium are uneven. Especially poor output.

NOT RECOMMENDED
10. Mr. Dudley Saturn Battery-Operated Peppermill, Model 6003W

$21.99

Gimmicky mill couldn't be easier to use, but how can you leave out something as basic as a grind adjustment? Medium grind only.

NOT RECOMMENDED
11. Zassenhaus Pepper Mill, Model 4

$34.95

Exceptionally difficult to crank. Finial has tiny spring that pops out the moment finial is unscrewed.

NOT RECOMMENDED
12. Chef 'n "The Pepper Ball," Model APG-66CBK

$14.99

Looks more comfortable to use than it actually is. Caused hand fatigue and has no settings between fine and coarse.

EQUIPMENT CORNER: Pepper Mills

PEPPER MILLS COME IN A VAST RANGE OF STYLES AND materials, but what really matters to us and other serious home cooks is performance. Is the fine-ground pepper truly fine? Is the medium grind really medium, or are there coarse particles mixed in? And how about output? Will you have to turn and turn and turn until your arm needs a brace to produce a teaspoon of ground pepper?

In this test we sought out top performers that would make great kitchen partners; appearance was pretty much beside the point. We rounded up 12 mills, each close to 8 inches high. Prices ranged from $14.99 to $45.

Most pepper mills work by similar means. Peppercorns are loaded into a central chamber, through which runs a metal shaft. Near the bottom of the mill, the shaft is connected to a grinding mechanism that consists of a rotating, grooved "male" head that fits into a stationary, grooved "female" ring. Near the top of the male piece, the large grooves crack the peppercorns and then feed the smaller pieces downward to be ground between the finer grooves, or teeth, of the male and female components.

The industry experts we queried explained that the specifics of the grinding mechanism are key to grind quality. Sharper teeth combined with a very tight tolerance between the pieces yield a better grind, which to us means finer fine-ground pepper. Unfortunately, none of these details are evident upon inspecting a pepper mill in a kitchen store.

In addition to having an excellent grind quality, Unicorn Magnum Plus managed an awesome output. In one minute of grinding, the Magnum produced an incredible average of 7.3 grams, or about 3½ teaspoons, of fine-ground pepper. By comparison, honors for the next highest average output went to the Oxo Grind It, at 5.1 grams, while about half the pack hovered around the two-grams-or-less mark (which, at roughly one teaspoon in volume, is perfectly acceptable).

Grind quality and speed are only half the battle—especially if most of your peppercorns land on the floor when you try to fill the mill. So we appreciated mills with wide, unobstructed filler doors that could accommodate the tip of a wide funnel or, better yet, the lip of a bag or jar so that we could dispense with the funnel altogether. The EHI Peppermate took high honors in this category, with a lid that snaps off to create a gaping 3-inch opening, followed by the Zyliss with a 2-inch opening and the Oxo Grind It with a wide-open 1⅜-inch mouth. With its sliding collar door, the Unicorn Magnum Plus was also easy to fill. Along the same lines, the more peppercorns a mill can hold, the less often it has to be filled. The Zyliss held a full cup, and the Unicorn Magnum Plus trailed behind by just 1 tablespoon.

The ease of adjusting the grind was another factor we considered. Changing the grind from fine to coarse involves changing the tolerances of, or distances between, the male and female grinding components. The more space between them, the larger the pepper particles and the coarser the grind. Traditionally, a knob at the top of the mill called the finial is used to adjust the grind. This was our least favorite design for two reasons. First, the finial must be screwed down very tight for a fine grind, which not only requires significant finger strength but also makes the head (or the crank) of the mill more difficult to turn. Second, the finial usually has to be removed entirely to fill the mill, which means you have to readjust the grind with each filling. We preferred mills like the Unicorn Magnum Plus, which use a screw or dial at the base of the grinding mechanism.

More than half of the mills tested did their jobs well, but the Unicorn Magnum Plus was the superstar. Its grind quality is exemplary, its output astounding, and its capacity huge. If that weren't enough, it's also easy to fill and comfortable to use. At $45, however, this mill was one of the two most expensive in the test (the second-place EHI Peppermate was $40). If your budget is a bit more restricted, we recommend both the Oxo Grind It ($19.99) and the Zyliss Large Pepper Mill ($27.50).

Straining the custard for crème brûlée removes the spent vanilla beans as well as any clumps of coagulated egg.

BISTRO *basics*

CHAPTER 4

Bistro classics, such as steak au poivre and crème brûlée, offer a taste of real French cooking without pretension and exhaustive preparation. Both dishes have short ingredient lists and are easily accomplished at home.

That said, there are plenty of bad versions of both dishes floating around. We've followed recipes that yielded overly peppery steaks that were nearly inedible. Often, some of the peppercorns fell off the steaks and burned in the pan, making the brandy-based sauce inedible as well. Talk about a waste of good meat.

Crème brûlée suffers from three main problems. First, too many chefs have tampered with its classic flavors (egg yolks, cream, and vanilla) to produce odd flavor pairings such as raspberry mocha crème brûlée. But even if you don't fiddle with the ingredients, it can be hard to get the texture just right. All too often the custard doesn't set up properly and sloshes around in the ramekin. At the opposite end of the spectrum, the custard can be too firm and rubbery. Finally, the burnt sugar topping, the hallmark of crème brûlée, can be hard to achieve. You don't want to set the sugar on fire, but a pale, thin, grainy crust won't do either.

The test kitchen has taken the guesswork out of these bistro favorites and made them foolproof in the American kitchen.

STEAK AU POIVRE

WHAT WE WANTED: Steak au poivre is often nothing more than uninspired skillet steak. We were after the real thing—a perfectly cooked steak with a well-seared crust of pungent, cracked peppercorns married to a silky sauce.

There's nothing complicated about steak au poivre. When well-executed, the slightly sweet, smooth sauce has more than a hint of shallot and brandy, the steak is well-browned on the outside and cherry-red on the interior, and the crust of cracked peppercorns provides a pungent, slow burn.

That's the good news. A third-rate steak au poivre has peppercorns that fall off the steak only to reveal underbrowned meat. What's more, the peppercorn coat prevents the steak from forming drippings in the skillet that are the foundation of a rich sauce, and few home cooks have beef or veal stock on hand to give the sauce the backbone it needs. Because most steak au poivre recipes make no attempt to solve these problems, the home cook is left aghast at the end result: wan, tasteless steaks covered by an insipid sauce.

Our first few tests were useful only in determining the best cut of steak for au poivre. Filets were tender but too mild-flavored. Rib-eyes, always a favorite in the test kitchen, have abundant fat pockets and pronounced veins of gristle that separate two differently textured muscles. A peppercorn crust obscures these imperfections, requiring scrutiny and maneuvering on the part of the diner to eat around these parts. Strip steaks, however, have external lines of gristle that are easily trimmed before cooking, and their neat, tight, even grain makes them particularly suited to steak au poivre.

We quickly determined peppercorn type. Among black, white, and a four-peppercorn blend of green, pink, black, and white, plain old black was the favorite in the test kitchen. Tasters extolled it for its sharp bite, rich and intense flavor, and elusive smokiness.

The steaks we cooked early on were crusted with a scant teaspoon of peppercorns on each side. Loose pepper fell off the steaks and scorched pitifully in the skillet. The pepper that did stick shielded the surface of the steaks, preventing browning and thereby the formation of a fond (the sticky browned bits left in a pan after sautéing) on which to build the sauce. In addition, most tasters thought we were far too liberal in our peppercorn allotment—the heat was vicious and incendiary. Our first thought was to cut back on the peppercorns, but then a light bulb went on. What if the steaks were coated on only one side? The unpeppered side would brown nicely, producing more fond for the sauce, and there would be no peppercorns on that side to singe.

Typically, steaks cook over intensely high heat. But for this new approach, we placed the skillet over medium heat until it was hot, and, after laying the steaks in the skillet—unpeppered-side down—turned up the heat to medium-high. This technique gave the steaks six minutes to brown on the first side and form a fond. Then the steaks were flipped onto their peppered side and given only three to five minutes (depending on desired doneness) to complete their cooking, this time without scorching the pepper.

All steak au poivre sauces contain beef or veal stock and brandy. Most contain cream, though some get their richness from butter only. The stock was the first problem. Most home cooks have only canned chicken and beef broth on hand, and the latter has long been considered either artificial tasting or weakly flavored in the test kitchen (see the Tasting Lab on page 139 for more information). Using chicken broth alone, we cooked down the liquid to concentrate its flavor, but the sauce still lacked meatiness and depth. We tried to doctor it with dried porcini mushrooms, but the mushroom flavor was too distinct. We tried commercial veal demi-glace (superconcentrated veal stock), but the tomato paste-laden demi-glace looked and tasted unnatural. Finally, we tried low-sodium beef broth straight from the can and reduced it. This sauce was beefier, more substantial, and deeper in color—but it was plagued by the tinny flavor characteristic of canned beef broth.

On the verge of giving up, we finally hit upon a solution. We reduced almost equal amounts of chicken and beef broths with sautéed shallots to about one-quarter of their original volume. Finally—a terrific, full-flavored sauce. But the long simmering time threw a wrench in the works. A typical pan sauce for steak is made by deglazing the skillet in which the steaks were cooked. This usually takes no longer than a few minutes and can be accomplished while the steaks repose. The sauce took well over 10 minutes, much longer than you'd want the meat to rest. The solution was straightforward: Reduce the broth mixture before cooking the steaks, then use the resulting liquid to deglaze the skillet.

Introducing brandy to the sauce was no trivial matter. We tried reducing it with the broth mixture to concentrate its flavor. This worked, but because we were also concentrating the sugar in the brandy, the resulting sauce tasted as sweet as butterscotch pudding, with no spirited bite. If we held off adding the brandy until much later in the sauce-making process, it tasted hot and raw. The time to add it was when the reduced broth mixture went into the skillet to deglaze it; the mixture simmers for about five minutes, just long enough for the brandy to reduce a bit, shake its alcoholic harshness, and meld with the broth.

Cream made the sauce luxurious and gave its texture substance. Only ¼ cup was needed, and, when added at the same time as the brandy, the cream had a chance to cook down and lend body to the sauce. To finish, butter whisked in at the end brought silkiness, a bit of raw brandy gave nice bite and fresh brandy flavor, and a teaspoon of lemon juice or champagne vinegar brightened things up.

WHAT WE LEARNED: Coat just one side of the steaks with peppercorns and then cook the steaks on the uncoated side as long as possible to promote browning and prevent scorching of the peppercorns. Make the sauce with a mixture of canned beef broth and canned chicken broth that has first been reduced, and then add brandy, cream, and butter.

STEAK AU POIVRE WITH BRANDIED CREAM SAUCE serves 4·

To save time, crush the peppercorns and trim the steaks while the broth mixture simmers. Many pepper mills do not have a sufficiently coarse setting. In that case, crush peppercorns with a sauté pan or rolling pin (see illustrations on page 48). See the Tasting Lab on page 35 for information about peppercorns and see the Equipment Corner on page 42 for information about pepper mills, including models capable of producing crushed peppercorns.

sauce

- 4 tablespoons unsalted butter
- 1 medium shallot, minced (about 3 tablespoons)
- 1 cup canned low-sodium beef broth
- ¾ cup canned low-sodium chicken broth
- ¼ cup heavy cream
- ¼ cup plus 1 tablespoon brandy
- 1 teaspoon juice from 1 lemon or 1 teaspoon champagne vinegar
  Salt

TECHNIQUE: Adhering the Pepper

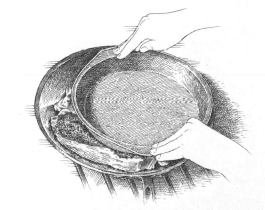

Pressing the steaks with a cake pan or flat pot lid once they have been placed in the hot skillet promotes browning and ensures that the peppercorns adhere.

steaks

> 4   strip steaks (8 to 10 ounces each), ¾ to 1 inch thick, trimmed of exterior gristle
>   Salt
> 1   tablespoon black peppercorns, crushed

1. Heat 1 tablespoon butter in 12-inch heavy-bottomed skillet over medium heat; when foaming subsides, add shallot and cook, stirring occasionally, until softened, about 2 minutes. Add beef and chicken broths, increase heat to high, and boil until reduced to about ½ cup, about 8 minutes. Set reduced broth mixture aside. Rinse and wipe out skillet.

2. Meanwhile, sprinkle both sides of steaks with salt; rub one side of each steak with 1 teaspoon crushed peppercorns, and, using fingers, press peppercorns into steaks.

3. Place now-empty skillet over medium heat until hot, about 4 minutes. Lay steaks unpeppered-side down in hot skillet, increase heat to medium-high, firmly press down on steaks with bottom of cake pan (see illustration on page 47), and cook steaks without moving them until well-browned, about 6 minutes. Using tongs, flip steaks, firmly press down on steaks with bottom of cake pan, and cook on peppered side, about 3 minutes for rare, about 4 minutes for medium-rare, or about 5 minutes for medium. Transfer steaks to large plate and tent loosely with foil to keep warm.

4. Pour reduced broth, cream, and ¼ cup brandy into now-empty skillet; increase heat to high and bring to boil, scraping pan bottom with wooden spoon to loosen browned bits. Simmer until deep golden brown and thick enough to heavily coat back of metal tablespoon or soup spoon, about 5 minutes. Off heat, whisk in remaining 3 tablespoons butter, remaining 1 tablespoon brandy, lemon juice or vinegar, and any accumulated meat juices. Adjust seasonings with salt.

5. Set steaks on individual dinner plates, spoon portion of sauce over steaks, and serve immediately.

TECHNIQUE: Crushing Peppercorns

If your pepper mill can't produce coarsely crushed peppercorns, you have two alternatives.

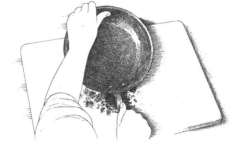

A. Use the back of a heavy pan and a rocking motion to grind peppercorns.

B. Spread the peppercorns in an even layer in a zipper-lock plastic bag and whack them with a rolling pin or meat pounder.

GETTING IT RIGHT:
Properly Ground Peppercorns

For steak au poivre, grind or crush whole peppercorns (left) to a very coarse texture (right). If your pepper mill cannot handle this task, see the alternate methods above. In any case, do not use finely ground pepper in this recipe.

CRÈME BRÛLÉE

WHAT WE WANTED: A proper crème brûlée should have a crackle-crisp bittersweet sugar crust over a chilly custard of balanced egginess, creaminess, and sweetness. Its light, silken, supple texture goes down easily, belying the dessert's richness; it's a masterful work of temperature, taste, and texture.

Beneath either a paltry sugar crust or one that requires a pickax, a majority of crème brûlées suffer from a trio of problems: The custard is tepid, not cold; the custard is leaden, not ethereal; and the flavors are sullen. We set out to fix these problems and create the perfect crème brûlée.

Crème brûlée is not complicated—it requires only six ingredients—and it can be made well in advance of serving. Despite this charming simplicity, however, it presents quite a few opportunities for things to go awry. A search of many recipes revealed standard ingredients, but ratios of eggs to cream varied, as did oven temperatures, so the devil was going to be in the details.

First we sought to settle the issue of eggs. Firmer custard, like that in crème caramel, is made with whole eggs, which help the custard to achieve a clean-cutting quality. Crème brûlée is richer and softer—with a pudding-like, spoon-clinging texture—in part because of the exclusive use of yolks. With 4 cups of heavy cream as the dairy for the moment, we went to work. The custard refused to set at all with as few as six yolks; with eight (a common number for the amount of cream) it was better, but still rather slurpy. With 12, however, a surprisingly large number of yolks, we struck gold. The custard had a lovely lilting texture, an elegant mouthfeel, a glossy, luminescent look, and the richest flavor.

We ventured to make crème brûlées with different kinds of cream. Half-and-half (with a fat content of about 10 percent) was far too lean, and the custard was watery and lightweight. With whipping cream (about 30 percent fat),

the custard was improved but still a bit loose. Heavy cream (about 36 percent fat) was the ticket. The custard was thick but not overbearing, luxurious but not death-defying.

We tested various sugar quantities, from ½ cup to ¾ cup. Two-thirds cup was the winner; with more sugar the crème brûlée was too saccharine, and with less the simple egg and cream flavors tasted muted and dull. We also found that a pinch of salt heightened flavors and that vanilla bean was superior to extract.

With proportions in place, we attempted to find the best cooking technique for the custard. Custard made with icebox-cold eggs and cream can go into the oven, but nearly all recipes instruct the cook to scald the cream before gradually whisking it into the yolks. When compared, a started-cold custard and scalded-cream custard displayed startling differences. The former had a silkier, smoother texture. Some research on custards told me that eggs respond favorably to cooking at a slow, gentle pace. If heated quickly, they set only just shortly before they enter the overcooked zone, leaving a very narrow window between just right and overdone. If heated gently, however, they begin to thicken the custard at a lower temperature and continue to do so gradually until it, too, eventually overcooks. In other words, the scalded-cream method is more likely to produce custard with an overcooked—hence, inferior—texture.

The downside to starting with cold ingredients is that unless the cream is heated, it is impossible to extract flavor from a vanilla bean. Also, if the cream is heated, the sugar can go into the pot for easy dissolution. Otherwise, the sugar must be vigorously beaten with the yolks to encourage it to dissolve. When we did this, the resulting custard was very frothy and baked up with a dry, soap-foam-like surface. Scalding cream and sugar, steeping with vanilla, then refrigerating until cold seemed an overwrought process, so we tested a hybrid technique. We heated only half the cream with the sugar and the vanilla bean. After a 15-minute off-heat steep to extract flavor from the vanilla bean, we added the remaining still cold cream to bring the temperature down before whisking it into the yolks. This hybrid technique created a custard with a fineness equal to the one started cold—and it baked in less time, too.

Next we investigated oven temperatures. At 325 degrees, the custards puffed and browned on the surface. Too hot. At 300 degrees, they fared beautifully. As for the water bath (or bain marie, which prevents the periphery of a custard from overcooking while the center saunters to the finish line), we used a large baking dish that held the ramekins comfortably. (The ramekins must not touch and should be at least ½ inch away from the sides of the dish.) We lined the bottom with a kitchen towel to protect the floors of the ramekins from the heat of the dish and to stabilize them.

The golden rule of custards is that they must not be overcooked lest they lose their smooth, silken texture and become grainy and curdled. Judging doneness by gently shaking the custards or by slipping a paring knife into them were not reliable techniques. An instant-read thermometer tells you exactly when the custards must come out of the oven: between 170 and 175 degrees. If you do not have a thermometer, look at the center of the custard. It should be barely set—shaky but not sloshy. The custard will continue to cook from residual heat once out of the oven. A deep chill then helps to solidify things. If your oven has a history of uneven heating, the custards may finish at different rates, so it is advisable to check each one separately rather than take out the whole lot at once.

For the crackly caramel crust we tried brown sugar, regular granulated sugar, and turbinado and Demerara sugars (the latter two are coarse light brown sugars). Because brown sugar is moist and lumpy, recipes often recommend drying it in a low oven and crushing it to break up lumps. We found that it just isn't worth the effort. Turbinado and Demerara sugars were superior to granulated only because their coarseness makes them easy to distribute evenly over the custards.

There are a few approaches to caramelizing the sugar. The broiler is almost guaranteed to fail; the heat is uneven

and inadequate. A salamander—a long-handled iron plate that is heated and held just above the sugar—is hardly practical because they are hard to come by. A torch accomplishes the task efficiently. A hardware-store propane torch is the tool of choice, but a small butane kitchen torch, available in cookware stores, can do the job, just at a more leisurely pace (see the Equipment Corner on page 53).

While being "brûléed," the custard is unavoidably warmed a bit. In standard round ramekins, usually only the upper third of the custard is affected. But in shallow dishes (our favorite for their higher ratio of crust to custard), the custard can be completely warmed through. In our opinion, a warm custard can ruin an otherwise perfect crème brûlée. To remedy this problem, we refrigerated the finished crème brûlées, and the crust maintained its crackly texture for up to 45 minutes. Beneath the shattering sugar crust lay an interplay of creamy, cold, sweet, bitter, smooth, and crackly . . . perfect crème brûlée.

WHAT WE LEARNED: Lots of yolks, turbinado sugar, an instant-read thermometer, and a final chill are the keys to perfect crème brûlée.

CLASSIC CRÈME BRÛLÉE Serves 8

Separate the eggs and whisk the yolks after the cream has finished steeping; if left to sit, the surface of the yolks will dry and form a film. A vanilla bean gives custard the deepest flavor, but 2 teaspoons of extract, whisked into the yolks in step 4, can be used instead. The best way to judge doneness is with a digital instant-read thermometer. The custards, especially if baked in shallow fluted dishes, will not be deep enough to provide an accurate reading with a dial-face thermometer. For the caramelized sugar crust, we recommend turbinado or Demerara sugar. Regular granulated sugar will work, too, but use only 1 scant teaspoon on each ramekin or 1 teaspoon on each shallow fluted dish. It's important to use ramekins that measure 4 to 5 ounces. To check the size of your ramekins, fill one to the rim with a measured amount of water.

    4   cups chilled heavy cream
    ⅔   cup (4⅔ ounces) granulated sugar
         Pinch salt
    1   vanilla bean, halved lengthwise
    12   large egg yolks
  8–12   teaspoons turbinado or Demerara sugar (see
         note)

1. Adjust oven rack to lower-middle position and heat oven to 300 degrees.

2. Combine 2 cups cream, sugar, and salt in medium saucepan; with paring knife, scrape seeds from vanilla bean into pan, submerge pod in cream, and bring mixture to boil over medium heat, stirring occasionally to ensure that sugar dissolves. Take pan off heat and let steep 15 minutes to infuse flavors.

3. Meanwhile, place kitchen towel in bottom of large baking dish or roasting pan and arrange eight 4- or 5-ounce ramekins (or shallow fluted dishes) on towel. Bring kettle or large saucepan of water to boil over high heat.

4. After bean has steeped, stir in remaining 2 cups cream to cool down mixture. Whisk yolks in large bowl until broken up and combined. Whisk about 1 cup cream mixture into yolks until loosened and combined; repeat with another 1 cup cream. Add remaining cream and whisk until evenly colored and thoroughly combined. Strain through fine-mesh strainer into 2-quart measuring cup or pitcher (or clean medium bowl); discard solids in strainer. Pour or ladle mixture into ramekins, dividing it evenly among them.

5. Carefully place baking dish with ramekins on oven rack; pour boiling water into dish, taking care not to splash water into ramekins, until water reaches two-thirds height of ramekins. Bake until centers of custards are just barely set and are no longer sloshy and digital instant-read thermometer inserted in centers registers 170 to 175 degrees, 30 to 35 minutes (25 to 30 minutes for shallow fluted dishes). Begin checking temperature about 5 minutes before recommended time.

6. Transfer ramekins to wire rack; cool to room temperature, about 2 hours. Set ramekins on rimmed baking sheet,

TECHNIQUE: Extra Grip for Tongs

We recommend the use of tongs to remove ramekins of custard from a water bath. Cooks who worry about the ramekins slipping in the tongs can try this tip. Slip rubber bands around each of the two tong pincers, and the sticky rubber provides a surer grip.

TECHNIQUE:
Improved Cushion for Water Bath

Many recipes for individual baked custard, including crème brûlée, recommend lining the bottom of the water bath pan with a kitchen towel to both insulate and cushion the ramekins. Of course, this leaves you with a sopping wet towel at the end of cooking. We've found that a nonstick baking mat (called a Silpat) can be used if you happen to own this handy kitchen item.

cover tightly with plastic wrap, and refrigerate until cold, at least 4 hours or up to 4 days.

7. Uncover ramekins; if condensation has collected on custards, blot moisture with paper towel. Sprinkle each with about 1 teaspoon turbinado sugar (1½ teaspoons for shallow fluted dishes); tilt and tap ramekin for even coverage. Ignite torch and caramelize sugar. Refrigerate ramekins, uncovered, to re-chill, 30 to 45 minutes (but no longer); serve.

VARIATIONS

ESPRESSO CRÈME BRÛLÉE

Place ¼ cup espresso beans in zipper-lock bag and crush lightly with rolling pin or meat pounder until coarsely cracked. Follow recipe for Classic Crème Brûlée, substituting cracked espresso beans for vanilla bean and whisking 1 teaspoon vanilla extract into yolks in step 4 before adding cream.

TEA-INFUSED CRÈME BRÛLÉE

Knot together the strings of 10 bags Irish Breakfast tea. Follow recipe for Classic Crème Brûlée, substituting tea bags for vanilla bean; after steeping, squeeze bags with tongs or press into mesh strainer to extract all liquid. Whisk 1 teaspoon vanilla extract into yolks in step 4 before adding cream.

SCIENCE DESK:
How Egg Yolks Thicken Custard

CUSTARDS LIKE CRÈME BRÛLÉE DEPEND ON THE THICKENING power of egg yolks. How do the yolks do it? A raw egg yolk is filled with tightly curled protein molecules, many of which contain sulfur atoms that are interspersed along their lengths. If given a chance to get together, these sulfur atoms can bond to one another, tying the protein molecules into clumps. That's what thickens a custard.

As long as the sulfur atoms are trapped within tightly wound protein molecules, however, they can't connect. When egg yolks are heated, the proteins unravel (in a process called denaturing) and the sulfur atoms are able to link up, in the process creating a tangled network of protein molecules that can hold water—in other words, a thickened custard.

But you can overdo it. If the protein molecules are heated too much, they straighten out completely, and so many sulfur atoms cross-link that the protein network tightens into tough clumps of curd, squeezing out some of the water. The result is a custard that has curdled or "weeps." That's why proper cooking creates a custard that is smooth and thick, while overcooking creates a custard that is tough and wet.

EQUIPMENT CORNER: Torches

A TORCH IS THE BEST WAY TO CARAMELIZE THE SUGAR ON your crème brûlée. We tested a hardware-store propane torch ($27) against four petite kitchen torches (prices ranged from $30 to $40) fueled by butane.

The propane torch, with its powerful flame, caramelized the sugar quickly and easily, but, admittedly, it's not for the faint-hearted. Although easy to wield, a propane torch puts out a lot of heat and works in just seconds, so you must work very carefully. (In contrast, the kitchen torches took about 1½ minutes to brûlée each custard.) If you opt for a propane torch, make sure to buy a model with a built-in trigger that does not need to be held in place for the torch to remain lit. The most widely available brand, Bernzomatic, worked well in our kitchen tests.

Among the four butane-powered kitchen torches we tested, only one is worth owning. The Bernzomatic Torch ST1100TS ($29.95) has a plastic flame adjuster that is clearly marked and stayed cool enough to handle without burning our fingers. This torch was also the easiest to operate.

The remaining models had flaws. The safety lock on the RSVP Culinary Butane Torch ($29.95) was difficult to engage and the air intake port became red-hot with use. The metal flame-width adjuster on the Bonjour Torch ($29.95) must be held in place during use, but it became very hot to the touch. Finally, although the Messermeister Chefflame Culinary Torch ($39.95) generated the most powerful flame of the kitchen torches tested, testers needed to use both hands to switch it on and found its large size awkward.

BEST TORCHES

With its powerful flame, the Bernzomatic propane torch (left) will brûlée a custard in seconds. If you don't want to use such a powerful torch, the Bernzomatic kitchen torch (right) is the best butane option. Just make sure to purchase a can of butane along with it—otherwise you'll have more luck "brûléeing" with a book of matches. See www.cooksillustrated.com for an up-to-date price and mail-order source for the kitchen torch. Most hardware stores stock the Bernzomatic propane torch.

STEAKHOUSE *dinner*

CHAPTER 5

What's America's favorite restaurant meal? Salad and filet mignon served steakhouse style is a top contender for the title. Crisp lettuce covered with a pungent, creamy dressing (we like blue cheese) starts things off. The main event is a thick, tender piece of filet mignon, perfectly cooked, so the center is rare and the exterior is well browned and crusted. The steak is napped with a thick, luxurious brown sauce, and every bite is worth the high price you are paying.

Of course, this vision is often a fantasy and the real thing closer to a nightmare. The lettuce is limp, the dressing gluey or watery, the steak overcooked or not properly browned, and the sauce characterless. When the check comes, it seems like all you're paying for is heartburn.

The logical solution is to make this meal at home. Although there are plenty of places where you can take a wrong turn, the test kitchen has worked out the kinks in these recipes, so you can rest assured that your money (and time) will be well spent.

We tested eight batches of dressing, each made with a different kind of blue cheese, before choosing our favorite.

FILET MIGNON

WHAT WE WANTED: A well-crusted steak that's perfectly cooked (to our way of thinking, rare or medium-rare) and served with a quick but luscious pan sauce.

When it comes to steak, Americans prize tenderness above all—and filet mignon is the most tender steak there is. It is also expensive, and both factors may drive its perennial popularity as a grand, splashy, celebratory restaurant meal. You've probably noticed that in a restaurant, filet mignon (also known as tenderloin steak or simply as filet) is usually served rare, with a deeply seared crust, and adorned with a rich, luxurious pan sauce or flavored butter.

Well, there is no reason to limit the fun to restaurants. Filets are available in any supermarket with a meat case, and they are not difficult to cook. We wanted to replicate the best restaurant filets at home, which meant developing a deeply browned, rich crust on both sides of each steak without overcooking the interior or scorching the drippings in the pan, which would go on to serve as the basis for a luscious sauce. To that end, we investigated the finer points of both the steaks themselves and the cooking process.

Filets are thick (usually 1¼ to 2 inches), boneless steaks cut from the slender, supertender, ultralean tenderloin muscle. We shopped for filets at six local supermarkets and were not satisfied with the butchering job from a single one. The steaks were usually cut unevenly, with one end noticeably thicker than the other (see Getting It Right on page 58). Beyond that, different steaks in the same package were different sizes and weights. This was far from ideal for expensive, premium steaks. Consistency of size and thickness was important for even cooking within each steak, as well as from steak to steak, in the pan. With that in mind, we purchased a small, roughly 2-pound section of the tenderloin, called a tenderloin roast, and cut our own steaks from it. The process was easy, taking less than two minutes, and our

hand-cut filets were uniform. Tenderloin roasts were available wherever we shopped, so if you can get them, too, we recommend this practice. Alternatively, ask the butcher to cut the steaks for you.

To determine the optimal thickness for filets, we cooked steaks cut 1 and 2 inches thick and at ¼-inch intervals in between. Tasters preferred the 1½-inch cut, which made for a generous (but not over-the-top) portion.

Grilling is a good option for filets, but because we also wanted to make a pan sauce, we decided to cook our filets in a pan. The recipes we looked at suggested a couple of alternatives, including broiling, high-roasting (oven-roasting at high heat), and pan-searing (stovetop cooking over high heat), all of which we tried. Pan-searing was our approach of choice because it developed the deep brown, caramelized crust critical to the flavor of both the meat and the sauce. Right off the bat we confirmed our suspicion that filets are best cooked rare to medium-rare. In our opinion, cooking them to medium begins to compromise their tenderness, which is, after all, their raison d'être.

Our next tests involved searing well-dried filets in a dry pan and in a pan filmed with oil. (Drying the steaks thoroughly with paper towels aids development of a crust.) Not surprisingly for such lean meat, the oil was necessary to produce a deep, dark, satisfying crust, and we found that rubbing the oil right into the steaks reduced the spattering a little.

In our tests of different heat levels, we found that a crust formed over a consistently high flame was better developed than one formed over a medium-high flame. But this approach also created a problem. Over such high heat, the fond (the browned bits left in the pan after the steaks were cooked) was often scorched by the time the meat reached medium-rare, giving the sauce a bitter flavor. We tried a couple of things to remedy the problem.

First, we switched from the 12-inch skillet we'd been using (for four steaks) to a smaller, 10-inch model. The decreased surface area between the steaks helped protect the fond. (A heavy-bottomed or cast-iron skillet is essential here; the All-Clad 10-inch skillets we use in the test kitchen weigh about 2½ pounds. Smaller or lighter pans, we found, overheat too easily.) Second, we revisited the high-roasting method, combining it with our searing method by finishing the seared steaks on a preheated rimmed baking sheet in a hot oven. This approach offered the double advantage of protecting the fond from the direct heat of the oven and giving us a head start on the pan sauce while the steaks finished cooking.

Throughout testing, the oven time needed to achieve a given degree of doneness varied continually, as did our thermometer readings. While internal temperature guidelines for varying stages of doneness certainly do exist, it can be difficult to achieve an accurate reading in such a small piece of meat. The reading can be way off depending on where the thermometer probe hits, and it's surprisingly easy to miss dead center when you're working fast and juggling tongs and a hot steak in one hand and a thermometer in the other. In some cases we had readings as low as 117 degrees and as high as 140 degrees in the same steak. It all depended on the position of the thermometer probe.

What's a cook to do? Just make a small nick in the steak with the tip of a paring knife and look inside. Be sure to remove the steaks from the heat just before they are done to your liking. They will continue to cook a little off the heat, which should give them a perfect finish. This method never failed to produce steaks cooked just the way we like them.

WHAT WE LEARNED: **Sear on the stovetop and finish in the oven. To keep the drippings from burning, choose a pan just large enough to hold four filets (10 inches is just right). Finally, because an instant-read thermometer doesn't work all that well in such small steaks, nick the exterior and take a peak inside to see if the steak is done.**

PAN-SEARED FILET MIGNON serves 4

See Getting It Right on page 58 for information on buying filets or cutting your own from a tenderloin roast. Determining when the meat is cooked to your liking is key to a good steak, so pay close attention to the visual cues in step 3. If you choose to serve the steaks with one of the sauces that follow, have all the sauce ingredients ready before searing the steaks. Begin the sauce while the steaks are in the oven. To cook six steaks instead of four, switch to a 12-inch pan and use 6 teaspoons of olive oil.

4   center-cut filets mignon, 1½ inches thick, 7 to 8 ounces each, dried thoroughly with paper towels
4   teaspoons olive oil
    Salt and ground black pepper

1. Adjust oven rack to lower-middle position, place rimmed baking sheet on oven rack, and heat oven to 450 degrees. When oven reaches 450 degrees, heat 10-inch heavy-bottomed skillet (not nonstick) over high heat on stovetop until very hot.

2. Meanwhile, rub each side of steaks with ½ teaspoon oil and sprinkle generously with salt and pepper. Place steaks in skillet and cook, without moving steaks, until well-browned and a nice crust has formed, about 3 minutes. Turn steaks with tongs and cook until well-browned and a nice crust has formed on second side, about 3 minutes longer. Remove pan from heat, and use tongs to transfer steaks to hot baking sheet in oven.

3. Roast 2 to 4 minutes for very rare (center of steaks will appear cherry red and feel very soft and loose when cut with tip of paring knife), 4 to 6 minutes for rare (centers will appear red and soft), 6 to 8 minutes for medium-rare (centers will appear pink and feel firm but juicy), or 8 to 10 minutes for medium (centers will appear light pink and feel firm and compact). (After transferring steaks to oven, proceed with pan sauce.) Transfer steaks to large plate; loosely tent with foil or cover with bowl (see illustration on page 60), and let rest about 5 minutes before serving.

VARIATION

BACON-WRAPPED FILET MIGNON

Wrap 1 slice bacon around circumference of each filet, overlapping ends and securing to meat with toothpick. Follow recipe for Pan-Seared Filet Mignon, holding the filets two or three at a time on their sides briefly with tongs in skillet to crisp bacon slightly before transferring filets to oven.

MADEIRA PAN SAUCE WITH MUSTARD AND ANCHOVIES makes ⅔ cup, enough for 4 steaks
This sauce was inspired by one served in a Paris bistro, where the menu includes steak frites and nothing else. If you do not have Madeira on hand, sherry makes a fine substitute.

  1   medium shallot, minced (about 3 tablespoons)
  1   cup Madeira
  2   anchovy fillets, minced to paste (about 1 teaspoon)
  1   tablespoon minced fresh parsley leaves
  1   tablespoon minced fresh thyme leaves
  1   tablespoon Dijon mustard
  1   tablespoon juice from 1 lemon
  3   tablespoons unsalted butter, softened
      Salt and ground black pepper

After transferring steaks to oven, set skillet over medium-low heat; add shallot and cook, stirring constantly, until softened, about 1 minute. Add Madeira; increase heat to high, and scrape pan bottom with wooden spoon to loosen browned bits. Simmer until liquid is reduced to about ⅓ cup, 6 to 8 minutes. (If steaks are not yet out of oven, set skillet off heat and wait for steaks to come out of oven and rest

for 2 minutes before proceeding.) Add accumulated juices from baking sheet and reduce liquid 1 minute longer. Off heat, whisk in anchovies, parsley, thyme, mustard, lemon juice, and butter until butter has melted and sauce is slightly thickened. Season with salt and pepper to taste, spoon sauce over steaks, and serve immediately.

ARGENTINIAN-STYLE FRESH PARSLEY AND GARLIC SAUCE (CHIMICHURRI)
makes 1 generous cup
Like a loose, fresh salsa in consistency, this mixture is a common accompaniment to sautéed, roasted, and grilled meats in South America. For best results, use flat-leaf parsley.

  1   cup (packed) fresh parsley leaves
  5   medium garlic cloves, peeled
  ½   cup extra-virgin olive oil
  ¼   cup red wine vinegar
  2   tablespoons water

¼ cup finely minced red onion

1   teaspoon salt

¼ teaspoon red pepper flakes

Process parsley and garlic in workbowl of food processor fitted with steel blade, stopping as necessary to scrape down sides of bowl with rubber spatula, until garlic and parsley are chopped fine (20 one-second pulses); transfer to medium bowl. Whisk in remaining ingredients until thoroughly blended. Spoon about 2 tablespoons over each steak and serve. (Sauce tastes best when used fresh but can be refrigerated, with plastic wrap pressed directly on surface, up to 3 days.)

TECHNIQUE:
Best Tent for Roasts and Steaks

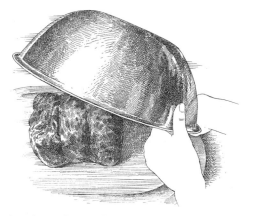

Roasts and steaks need to rest for several minutes before being carved or served to allow the juices to distribute themselves throughout the meat. Most recipes instruct the cook to cover the meat with foil while it rests to retain heat. An overturned bowl is easier to use and does a better job of retaining heat.

EQUIPMENT CORNER: Steak Knives

IF YOU'VE EVER SHOPPED FOR STEAK KNIVES, YOU MIGHT have noticed that sets of four can range in price from as little as $40 to as much as $150. We wondered if price really makes a difference when it comes to the performance of these knives, so we bought five sets of knives and cooked up some steaks to find out.

Our favorites were pricey. A set of four Henckels Four Star Steak Knives or Wüsthof-Trident Classic Steak Knives fetches between $140 and $150. Manufactured in the same manner as the other kitchen knives in their high-quality lines, these knives justly demand a high price. Fresh from their boxes, they had razor-sharp blades that sliced effortlessly through crusts and glided through meat, and their handles made them comfortable to use (Henckels got top honors here). But if you are lax in the upkeep of your knives, beware—these knives require regular honing and sharpening to be kept in tip-top shape.

Right behind these big shots were Chicago Cutlery Steak Knives, Walnut Tradition. At $40 for a set of four, it's easy to overlook their slightly less comfortable handles and somewhat flimsier feel and rank them right in with the best. These knives were also sharp, and the gently curved angle of the blades made for simple and smooth slicing. And they look like they belong in a butcher shop—or in the fist of a serious steak eater. Don't forget to steel these knives as well to keep them sharp.

Our least favorite knife sets contained knives with serrated blades. Henckels Gourmet Steak Knives, $40 for a set of four, and Dexter Russell Steakhouse Steak Knives, $30 for a set of four, required a good deal of sawing to cut through a steak and produced rather ragged pieces (not that your taste buds care). The cheaper set of Henckels steak knives felt insubstantial in their construction, whereas the Dexter Russell knives were of mammoth proportions. Neither requires steeling for upkeep.

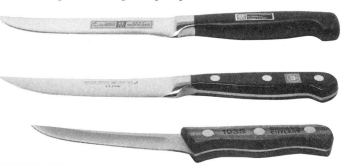

BEST STEAK KNIVES

The Henckels Four Star Steak Knives (top) were the top choice of testers, followed closely by the Wüsthof-Trident Classic Steak Knives (middle). At a fraction of the cost, the Chicago Cutlery Steak Knives, Walnut Tradition (bottom), are a great value with good (if not great) performance in our kitchen tests. See www.cooksillustrated.com for up-to-date prices and mail-order sources for these products.

BLUE CHEESE DRESSING

WHAT WE WANTED: **A dressing that boasts a complex mix of tart, sweet, and creamy.**

Pretty good blue cheese dressing, like that served in many steakhouses, is creamy and tangy, with a hint of sweetness and a few crumbles of blue cheese. It isn't as good as it could be because it isn't cheesy enough. But even at that, it is miles better than bottled blue cheese dressings from the grocery store. To us, those bottled brews are virtually inedible. Harsh, mayonnaise-like concoctions, they are either as sweet as candy or painfully vinegary and sour. In both cases, the result is a one-dimensional dressing completely lacking in that necessary blue cheese punch. We decided it was time to do a little research and development in the test kitchen.

We began by scouring cookbooks for blue cheese dressing recipes. They were all similar: no revelations, just a mixture of blue cheese with a creamy component, such as mayonnaise or sour cream or a combination of the two, thinned with either heavy cream or buttermilk or sometimes bulked up with cottage cheese.

We gathered our recipes and tried them one by one. In the initial tasting, a common complaint was that there wasn't enough blue cheese flavor. We found that the secret to the proper flavor and texture lay in the creamy components. Cottage cheese was the one entirely unwelcome ingredient. It watered down the dressing, and its flabby and bland curds did nothing for the flavor. After much tasting, we concluded that three creamy ingredients were necessary: mayonnaise to give the dressing body, sour cream to supply tang, and buttermilk to both thin out the dressing and support the role of the sour cream. Our challenge was to find the right balance of the three to achieve both good flavor and the right consistency. We tinkered around, and whereas some recipes called for as much as ½ cup of mayonnaise to ½ cup of crumbled blue cheese, we found only 2 tablespoons of

mayonnaise to be necessary. That amount, taken in combination with 3 tablespoons of sour cream and 3 tablespoons of buttermilk, gave our dressing a pleasant, creamy tang and enough fluidity to gently coat sturdy, leafy greens.

Realizing that buttermilk isn't often at hand in most households, we tried cream in place of it, but the flavor of the dressing fell flat under the weight of the cream. Milk is a better substitute, though it makes a somewhat lighter dressing.

At this point our dressing was good but just a bit dull. We added a smidgen of sugar for sweetness and white wine vinegar for a little zing. That was it. The dressing now had high and low notes that titillated the taste buds, was jam-packed with blue-cheesy flavor, and was delicious not just when eaten on a salad but on a chicken wing or even with a spoon.

Our next step was to investigate different kinds of blue cheese. We were surprised to find that a cheese that made a good dressing didn't necessarily make for good eating. A dressing made with an inexpensive domestic blue cheese—not a $17-per-pound French Roquefort—was our final choice. In general, we found that any rich, creamy blue cheese makes a good dressing. Really pungent cheeses, such as Spanish Cabrales, should be avoided (see the Tasting Lab on page 62 for details).

Finally, we had to decide on a mixing method. Some of the recipes we researched called for making the dressing in a blender or food processor, but we wanted to make our dressing in the simplest way possible with the fewest number of dirty dishes. We took to mashing the crumbled blue cheese and buttermilk together with a fork to break up the cheese a bit. This was an easy means of getting the texture we liked—creamy, with a few small crumbles of cheese, just enough to give the dressing some tooth.

WHAT WE LEARNED: **Use a mild blue cheese and combine it with buttermilk, sour cream, and mayonnaise for a dressing that is pleasantly tart and has plenty of body.**

RICH AND CREAMY BLUE CHEESE DRESSING makes about 3/4 cup

In a pinch, whole milk can be used in place of buttermilk. The dressing will be a bit lighter and milder in flavor, but will still taste good. Remember that aggressive seasoning with salt and pepper is necessary because the dressing will be dispersed over greens.

  2½ ounces blue cheese, crumbled (about ½ cup)
  3 tablespoons buttermilk
  3 tablespoons sour cream
  2 tablespoons mayonnaise
  2 teaspoons white wine vinegar
  ¼ teaspoon sugar
  ⅛ teaspoon garlic powder
     Salt and ground black pepper

Mash blue cheese and buttermilk in small bowl with fork until mixture resembles cottage cheese with small curds. Stir in remaining ingredients. Taste and adjust seasoning with salt and pepper. (Dressing can be refrigerated in airtight container for up to 2 weeks.)

LEAFY SALAD WITH BLUE CHEESE DRESSING serves 4

We dressed a variety of different salad greens and found that delicate ones, such as mesclun and butter lettuce, became soggy under the weight of this dressing. Sturdy romaine and curly leaf lettuce were our two favorites.

  10 cups loosely packed greens, such as Romaine or curly leaf lettuce
  ¾ cup Rich and Creamy Blue Cheese Dressing (recipe at left)

1. Wash and thoroughly dry greens. (Greens can be stored rolled in paper towels and refrigerated in salad spinner for 2 days or zipper-lock plastic bag for 1 week.)

2. Place greens in large bowl. If greens are too large to eat easily, tear them into manageable pieces with your hands. Pour dressing over greens and toss to coat evenly. Serve immediately.

TASTING LAB: Blue Cheese

USING OUR RECIPE, WE PREPARED EIGHT BATCHES OF blue cheese dressing, each containing a different blue cheese, and had our editorial staff engage in a blind taste test. While many tasters preferred the stronger cheeses when eaten alone, most preferred blue cheese dressing made with the milder, less pungent cheeses of the bunch.

Stella brand blue cheese (which is readily available in supermarkets) came out as our tasters' overall favorite for dressing because of its "nicely balanced flavor" and "nice

Rating Blue Cheeses

WE SAMPLED EIGHT BLUE CHEESES ON THEIR OWN AND IN A DRESSING POURED OVER GREENS. EATEN PLAIN, EACH cheese had its fans, but tasters agreed that the milder cheeses were better in the dressing. Cheeses are listed in order of preference based on the dressing test. Some of these cheeses are available in supermarkets, and all are sold in gourmet stores or cheese shops.

HIGHLY RECOMMENDED
1. Stella Blue, Wisconsin
$6.29 per pound

This supermarket brand was extremely crumbly and almost feta-like in texture. The simple flavor and "wet" texture that caused it to flounder as a table cheese made it an excellent addition to our dressing.

HIGHLY RECOMMENDED
2. Danish Blue, Denmark
$11.95 per pound

Danish Blue is straightforward and cheddar-like. It has a strong salty and tangy presence, is slightly crumbly in texture, and is spotted with silvery blue pockets.

RECOMMENDED
3. Maytag Blue, Iowa
$12.99 per pound

Creamy, fresh, and smooth, with a tangy bite of blue cheese flavor, Maytag Blue was very popular among our tasters. This fairly dense cheese is ivory-white in color (the palest of all), with minimal green-blue pockets of mold.

RECOMMENDED
4. Gorgonzola Naturale, Italy
$10.95 per pound

Gorgonzola Naturale was by far the creamiest and softest of all the cheeses included in the tasting. Described as "sweet" and "smooth," this cheese is fairly mild, with a distinguishing "musty" odor. Look for the Gorgonzola labeled Marca d'Oro, which means it is made with the highest quality milk. Be sure to eat it quickly, as it has a shelf life of only about two weeks.

RECOMMENDED
5. Blue Stilton, England
$13.95 per pound

Blue Stilton can be identified by its reddish-gold rind and butter-colored interior speckled with blue-green veins. It is a fairly firm cheese—sliceable, yet crumbly in texture—with a well-balanced, salty flavor that is buttery, nutty, and sweet.

RECOMMENDED
6. Bleu d'Auvergne, France
$9.95 per pound

This very approachable blue cheese was by described by one taster as "mellow" and "refreshing for blue cheese." It is rich, salty, slightly bitter, sweet, and buttery. A great cheese for about half the price of Roquefort.

RECOMMENDED
7. Roquefort, France
$16.95 per pound

This ivory-colored sheep's milk cheese is pocked throughout with dark green-blue mold, and it is very pungent. With a texture so creamy and buttery that it is almost spreadable, it tastes salty, sweet, and a bit tangy.

RECOMMENDED WITH RESERVATIONS
8. Cabrales, Spain
$14.99 per pound

Crumbly, chalky, and complex in flavor, delivering a spicy, peppery kick and a long finish. Deeper in color than the other cheeses we tasted, it is yellow-brown with a cast of gray and streaked with fine lines of gray-green mold. Good eating for those who like a very strong blue cheese flavor but overpowering in dressing.

sweetness." Danish Blue (also sold in many supermarkets) came in second; one taster described it as "bright," with a "good creamy and chunky balance." While pricier blue cheeses such as Stilton and Gorgonzola also did well, the lower-priced versions scored higher, making them the logical choice for our dressing. Stronger, more intense cheeses, such as Cabrales, did not fare well in our dressing taste tests.

Once greens have been washed and dried in a salad spinner, they can be stored until needed. Greens should be perfectly dry before being stored, so place them on paper towels to blot any remaining moisture. At this point, you have two storage options.

A. You can line the empty salad spinner with paper towels and then layer in the greens, covering each layer with additional towels. In this manner, the greens will keep in the refrigerator for about 2 days.

B. For longer storage (up to 1 week, if the greens are really fresh), loosely roll the greens in paper towels and then place the rolled greens inside a large zipper-lock plastic bag.

Cheesy Nachos with Guacamole and Salsa **page 5**

Rustic Potato-Leek Soup **page 24**

Kung Pao Shrimp **page 92**

Fried Rice with Shrimp, Pork, and Shiitakes **page 83**

Green Bean Casserole **page 229**

Pasta with Garlic and Oil **page 125**

70

Stuffed Bell Peppers with Spiced Lamb, Currants, and Feta Cheese **page 39**

Scalloped Potatoes **page 219**

Charcoal-Grilled Pork Chops **page 169**

Barbecued Baby Back Ribs **page 181**

Creamy Dill Cucumber Salad **page 199**

Pan-Seared Filet Mignon **page 57**

Stovetop Macaroni and Cheese **page 159**

Smothered Pork Chops **page 176**

Simple Lasagna with Hearty Tomato-Meat Sauce **page 130**

Great fried rice starts with chilled rice that is then piled high with ingredients that have been cooked in batches in a nonstick skillet rather than a wok.

CHINESE takeout

Few things are as seductive (and ultimately as disappointing) as Chinese takeout. The expectations are high—spicy, bold food ready in minutes. The reality is low—greasy, goopy food with way too much soy sauce and not nearly enough flavor.

The problem, of course, is not with the dishes themselves but with how they are prepared. Just as the best hamburger is made at home (not at McDonald's), we find that Chinese favorites taste better when made at home.

We've taken two classics—fried rice and kung pao shrimp—and made them better (a lot better) than just about any takeout version you've had before. We've kept the realities of American cooking in mind and relied on readily available ingredients as well as equipment you already have in your kitchen. Along the way, we hope you'll learn some easily mastered new techniques. So throw out those takeout menus and discover real Chinese cooking, the way it is meant to taste.

FRIED RICE

WHAT WE WANTED: Not the heavy, greasy, or soggy renditions we've eaten as takeout. To start, we wanted fried rice with firm, separate grains, and we wanted a finished dish so clean and light that we could distinguish its many different flavors in every bite.

Leftovers are an incredible boon to the busy cook—as long as you know what to do with them. Some are obvious, like using up that turkey or ham in sandwiches. Some are a bit more obtuse, like turning leftover mashed potatoes into potato pancakes. But when faced with the question of what to do with leftover rice, we say, "Fry it."

A sample from your local suburban Chinese restaurant, though, might give you pause. There the norm is often a heavy dish doused with so much soy sauce that you can hardly tell the mushrooms from the chicken. But this is no more representative of the virtues of this dish than a fast-food burger is of a great home-grilled version. We wanted a dish with both firm, distinct grains of rice and light, distinctive flavors. We also knew that the success of the dish would depend on the answers to four questions: what to add, how much to add, when to add it, and when to leave it alone.

Fried rice was created as a way to put leftover rice to good, tasty use. Unlike Chinese restaurants, however, most American cooks are unlikely to have leftover rice on hand, so we decided to experiment with making the dish from freshly cooked, still warm rice. It was a disaster. The grains gelled together in large clumps, and the whole dish was very wet. Rice freshly cooked and then allowed to cool to room temperature fared little better, still turning out wet and unappealing fried rice. What produced by far the best fried rice was rice that had been cooked and then chilled in the refrigerator overnight. The grains were more separate and evenly coated with oil, and the overall dish much drier.

But we wanted to see if we could avoid overnight refrigeration. We tried spreading the cooked rice on a sheet pan to cool it down to room temperature rapidly, then placed the pan in the refrigerator to chill completely. The resulting fried rice was drier and the clumps of rice much smaller than in versions prepared with fresh-cooked rice, making this method an option for cooks who want to make fried rice as quickly as possible from freshly cooked rice. But leftover rice is still the best option, as we found when we tried refrigerating cooked rice for different amounts of time. While rice kept in the refrigerator for four hours was acceptable, a whole night in the refrigerator produced the driest, most separate grains and therefore the best fried rice.

We tested various types of rice, including extra-long, long, medium, and short grain. All are suitable for fried rice after an overnight stay in the refrigerator. But don't try making fried rice with store-bought rice that has been pre-cooked, parboiled, or converted. These processed rices become soggy and wet, and the grains quickly begin to break down and disintegrate during frying.

Despite the preference of many Chinese-American restaurants for large quantities of soy sauce in their fried rice, a quick look through many Chinese cookbooks revealed salt as the preferred seasoning. When tested, this rice tasted very clean and light, but tasters longed for a more substantial flavor. We went back to the soy sauce, but the large amount (nearly six tablespoons) needed to fully season the dish caused the rice to turn soggy and ugly. We wanted to find a seasoning with enough flavor intensity to be used sparingly.

The answer was oyster sauce. More appropriately referred to as oyster-flavored sauce, this condiment is a highly concentrated combination of soy sauce, brine, and oyster extracts. It is very thick, salty, and potent. Fried rice made with this sauce was well seasoned but not soggy.

In the process of all this testing, we also figured out how best to add the usual egg and vegetables to the rice. To get the eggs to the right texture, we scrambled them lightly, then removed them from the pan, reserving them to be added back to the pan at the end of cooking for a quick warm-up. Similarly, we found that moisture from vegetables such as peas, mushrooms, green beans, and asparagus caused the rice to clump when added to the pan along with it. Sautéing the vegetables alone in oil first allows sufficient moisture to cook off, producing a drier dish with better-flavored vegetables. More tender vegetables, such as sprouts and scallions, along with herbs, hold their texture and flavor better if added at the end of the cooking process.

The odd thing about fried rice is that it's not truly fried. When food is fried, it is cooked in a large amount of fat, usually enough to cover the food (think of fried chicken). What we call fried rice is actually pan-fried or sautéed, which means it is cooked over relatively high heat in a much smaller amount of fat (in this case, oil). We needed to figure out exactly how much oil would be necessary, and we knew that the pan we used would determine the amount. Because we wanted to make a large quantity of fried rice we limited our testing to large (12-inch) skillets—nonstick and regular—and a 14-inch wok.

The wok held plenty of rice, but the sloped sides and small 6-inch bottom allowed only a small portion of the rice to cook at one time. The wok also required a great deal of oil. The rice on the bottom continually absorbed what was added. The flat surface of the skillet provided a larger cooking surface, and the rice sautéed more quickly and evenly. Choosing between regular and nonstick was easy. The regular skillet required much more oil to keep the rice from sticking, making the dish greasy. We preferred the nonstick skillet for the lighter rice it produced.

Even using a nonstick pan, we found that a moderate amount of oil was required to keep the rice grains separate. Too little oil caused the rice grains to clump together during sautéing.

WHAT WE LEARNED : For fried rice that is light and flavorful rather than sodden and greasy, cook the ingredients in batches in a large nonstick skillet rather than a wok. Start with chilled rice, and use oyster sauce to season the dish.

FRIED RICE WITH SHRIMP, PORK, AND SHIITAKES makes about 8 cups, serving 4 to 6

This classic combination can be served as a main course. See the Basic White Rice recipe on page 85 for tips on preparing and cooling rice.

½ ounce (5 to 6 medium) dried shiitake mushrooms

¼ cup oyster-flavored sauce

1 tablespoon soy sauce

3½ tablespoons peanut or vegetable oil

2 large eggs, beaten lightly

8 ounces small shrimp, peeled and deveined

1 cup frozen peas, preferably baby peas, thawed

8 ounces sliced smoked ham, cut into ½-inch pieces

2 medium garlic cloves, minced (about 2 teaspoons)

5 cups cold cooked white rice, large clumps broken up with fingers

1 cup bean sprouts

5 medium scallions, white and green parts, sliced thin (about ½ cup)

1. Cover dried shiitakes with 1 cup hot tap water in small microwave-safe bowl; cover with plastic wrap, cut several steam vents with paring knife, and microwave on high power for 30 seconds. Let stand until mushrooms soften, about 5 minutes. Lift mushrooms from liquid with fork, trim stems, and slice into ¼-inch strips; set mushrooms aside.

2. Combine oyster-flavored sauce and soy sauce in small bowl; set aside.

3. Heat 12-inch nonstick skillet over medium heat until hot. Add 1½ teaspoons oil and swirl to coat pan bottom. Add eggs and cook without stirring, until they just begin to set, about 20 seconds, then scramble and break into small pieces with wooden spoon; continue to cook, stirring

constantly, until eggs are cooked through but not browned, about 1 minute longer. Transfer eggs to small bowl and set aside.

4. Return skillet to medium heat and heat until hot; add 1½ teaspoons oil and swirl to coat pan bottom. Add shrimp and cook, stirring constantly, until opaque and just cooked through, about 30 seconds. Transfer to bowl with eggs and set aside.

5. Return skillet to burner, increase heat to high, and heat skillet until hot; add remaining 2½ tablespoons oil and swirl to coat pan bottom. Add peas, mushrooms, and ham; cook, stirring constantly, for 1 minute. Stir in garlic and cook until fragrant, about 30 seconds. Add rice and oyster sauce mixture; cook, stirring constantly and breaking up rice clumps, until mixture is heated through, about 3 minutes. Add eggs, shrimp, bean sprouts, and scallions; cook, stirring constantly, until heated through, about 1 minute. Serve immediately.

FRIED RICE WITH PEAS AND BEAN SPROUTS makes about 8 cups, serving 4 to 6

This lighter variation is best served as a side dish or for lunch. See the Basic White Rice recipe on page 85 for tips on preparing and cooling rice.

- ¼ cup oyster-flavored sauce
- 1 tablespoon soy sauce
- 3 tablespoons peanut or vegetable oil
- 2 large eggs, beaten lightly
- 1 cup frozen peas, preferably baby peas, thawed
- 2 medium garlic cloves, minced (about 2 teaspoons)
- 6 cups cold cooked white rice, large clumps broken up with fingers
- 1 cup bean sprouts
- 5 medium scallions, white and green parts, sliced thin (about ½ cup)

1. Combine oyster sauce and soy sauce in small bowl; set aside.

2. Heat 12-inch nonstick skillet over medium heat until hot; add 1½ teaspoons oil and swirl to coat pan bottom. Add eggs and cook without stirring, until they just begin to set, about 20 seconds, then scramble and break into small pieces with wooden spoon; continue to cook, stirring constantly, until eggs are cooked through but not browned, about 1 minute longer. Transfer eggs to small bowl and set aside.

3. Return skillet to burner, increase heat to high, and heat skillet until hot. Add remaining 2½ tablespoons oil and swirl to coat pan bottom. Add peas and cook, stirring constantly, 30 seconds; stir in garlic and cook until fragrant, about 30 seconds. Add rice and oyster-flavored sauce mixture; cook, stirring constantly and breaking up rice clumps, until mixture is heated through, about 3 minutes. Add eggs, bean sprouts, and scallions; cook, stirring constantly, until heated through, about 1 minute. Serve immediately.

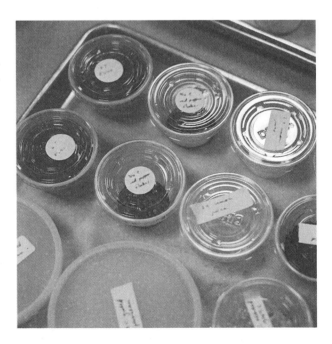

THAI-STYLE CURRIED CHICKEN FRIED RICE makes about 8 cups, serving 4 to 6

Curry powder, fish sauce, fresh chiles, and cilantro flavor this more exotic version of fried rice. See the Basic White Rice recipe at right for tips on preparing and cooling rice.

- 1 tablespoon dark brown sugar
- 3 tablespoons fish sauce
- 1 tablespoon soy sauce
- 2 small (about 8 ounces) boneless skinless chicken breasts, cut into 1-inch chunks
- ½ teaspoon salt
- 3½ tablespoons peanut or vegetable oil
- 2 large eggs, beaten lightly
- 1 teaspoon plus 1 tablespoon curry powder
- 1 large onion, sliced thin
- 2 medium garlic cloves, minced (2 teaspoons)
- 5 Thai green or 3 jalapeño chiles, seeded and minced (about 2 tablespoons)
- 6 cups cold cooked white rice, large clumps broken up with fingers
- 5 medium scallions, white and green parts, sliced thin (about ½ cup)
- 2 tablespoons minced fresh cilantro leaves
  Lime wedges for serving

1. Dissolve sugar in fish and soy sauces in small bowl; set aside. Season chicken with ½ teaspoon salt; set aside.

2. Heat 12-inch nonstick skillet over medium heat until hot. Add 1½ teaspoons oil and swirl to coat pan bottom. Add eggs and cook without stirring, until they just begin to set, about 20 seconds, then scramble and break into small pieces with wooden spoon; continue to cook, stirring constantly, until eggs are cooked through but not browned, about 1 minute longer. Transfer eggs to small bowl and set aside.

3. Return skillet to burner, increase heat to high, and heat skillet until hot; add 1½ teaspoons oil and swirl to coat pan bottom. Add 1 teaspoon curry powder and cook until fragrant, about 30 seconds; add chicken and cook, stirring constantly, until cooked through, about 2 minutes. Transfer to bowl with eggs and set aside.

4. Return skillet to high heat and heat until hot; add remaining 2½ tablespoons oil and swirl to coat pan bottom. Add onion and remaining 1 tablespoon curry powder and cook, stirring constantly, until onion is softened, about 3 minutes. Stir in garlic and chiles; cook until fragrant, about 30 seconds. Add rice and fish sauce mixture; cook, stirring constantly and breaking up rice clumps, until mixture is heated through, about 3 minutes. Add eggs, chicken, scallions, and cilantro; cook, stirring constantly, until heated through, about 1 minute. Serve immediately with lime wedges.

BASIC WHITE RICE makes about 6 cups

Serve this rice as is or chill the cooked rice as directed and use it for any fried rice recipe. Toasting the rice in a little oil makes the grains especially fluffy and separate.

- 2 teaspoons vegetable oil
- 1 cup long-grain white rice (not converted)
- 1½ cups water
- ½ teaspoon salt

1. Heat oil in medium saucepan over medium heat. Add rice and cook, stirring constantly, until transparent, 2 to 3 minutes. Add water and salt. Bring to boil, swirling pot to blend ingredients. Reduce heat to low, cover tightly, and cook until liquid is absorbed, about 15 minutes.

2. Turn off heat; let rice stand on burner, still covered, to finish cooking, about 15 minutes longer. Fluff with fork and serve immediately, or, for use in fried rice, spread cooked rice in even layer on parchment-lined baking sheet, cool to room temperature, about 30 minutes, then refrigerate, uncovered, until completely dry and grains are easily separated, at least 4 hours and up to 24 hours.

very sticky. This is why short-grain rice is perfect for sushi.

Long-grain rice, which is what we use for fried rice, has more amylose than amylopectin. Although the straight, bar-shaped amylose molecules are not as sticky as the amylopectin molecules, they are sticky enough to become tangled and cause individual grains of rice to clump when cooked. As a result, freshly cooked long-grain rice is still too sticky for use in fried rice.

When cooked long-grain rice is cooled, however, the grains go through a process called retrogradation. During this process, the amylose molecules realign within each single grain of rice. As this happens, you end up with separate grains, which is exactly what you want for fried rice.

TASTING LAB: Long-Grain Rice

ESSENTIALLY, WHITE RICE IS BROWN RICE MADE CONVENIENT. Developed thousands of years ago, the technique of stripping the germ and bran layers from brown rice to get white rice saves 30 minutes in cooking time. In today's busy world, that can make a big difference. Yet rice manufacturers have made cooking long-grain white rice even more of a snap with five-minute instant varieties and boil-in-bag options. We could not help but wonder whether so much convenience could still taste good. We decided to find out with a blind taste test.

To avoid comparing apples and oranges, we limited the candidates in our tasting to nationally distributed brands or major regional brands of plain, nonaromatic, long-grain white rice products. This gave us a lineup of eight products, including standard, instant, converted, and boil-in-bag.

To understand the differences in these products, it helps to know what they have in common. To begin with, all the rices in our tasting were long-grain, which means that each kernel is four to five times longer than it is wide when uncooked. Long-grain white rice is characteristically "fluffy" and is the least sticky of the white rices. In part, this is because it contains a high percentage of

SCIENCE DESK: What Makes Rice Sticky?

HOT, FRESHLY COOKED RICE MAKES STICKY, GLUEY FRIED rice, but cold rice fries up light and separate, making much better fried rice. Why? The answer has to do with the starches contained in rice.

Rice contains two types of starch: amylose and amylopectin. When you boil rice, these starches absorb water and swell up, which is why the grains of rice expand. Short-grain rice contains more amylopectin than amylose. Amylopectin molecules are branched, and when they expand the molecules clump together and make the rice

Rating Long-Grain Rices

WE TASTED EIGHT PLAIN, NONAROMATIC, LONG-GRAIN WHITE RICE PRODUCTS. WE PREPARED ALL RICES ACCORDING TO the package directions but omitted salt and butter or oil. Tasters rated the rices on flavor and texture. Rices are listed in order of preference. All brands are available in supermarkets.

RECOMMENDED

1. Uncle Ben's Boil-in-Bag Rice

$1.99 for 15.8 ounces

Startlingly simple if you are not averse to the plastic-pouch concept. Strong on looks but not as great on flavor; one taster best described it as "neutral." Notably moist but not watery, with only minor stickiness.

RECOMMENDED

2. Canilla Extra Long Grain Enriched Rice

$1.49 for 48 ounces

Tasters characterized the grains as stubby (yet slender). The flavor was nutty, somewhat buttery, and, in general, "good." The texture was firm, light, fluffy, and tender.

RECOMMENDED

3. Carolina/Mahatma Extra Long Grain Enriched Rice

$1.59 for 32 ounces

This rice was somewhere between clingy and separate. The grains were a bit pasty and dry, and there was some fraying at the tips, which one taster described as a "natural food appearance." Offsetting these characteristics were its pleasantly "al dente texture" and "clean flavor." This rice is also sold under the Mahatma label.

RECOMMENDED

4. Kraft Minute Brand Boil-in-Bag White Rice

$1.99 for 14 ounces

This rice was described as moist and fluffy but a little bit on the mushy side. Tasters' description of its flavor ranged from "mild," "sort of wheaty," and slightly buttery and nutty to "innocuous" and "boring." The grains were distinctly stubby.

RECOMMENDED

5. Uncle Ben's Converted Original Enriched Parboiled Long Grain Rice

$2.99 for 32 ounces

This rice was lauded for having a lot of flavor character and great potential for pilaf. The grains were very moist, firm, plump, separate, and "not chalky or mushy." The color was slightly off, which is typical of converted rices.

NOT RECOMMENDED

6. Success Enriched Precooked Natural Long Grain Rice

$3.99 for 32 ounces

This boil-in-bag variety was just a little too much of nothing. One taster described it as having "a weird, hollow flavor." Another described it as "flat." This rice was extremely light and fluffy, with very separate but dry grains.

NOT RECOMMENDED

7. Kraft Minute Brand Instant Enriched Long Grain White Rice

$3.49 for 28 ounces

The simplicity of this quick-cooking rice could not make up for its "complete lack of any rice flavor." This soggy, mushy, clumpy "Sno-Kone" white rice "tastes more like boiled rice water," said tasters. A chemical or metallic aftertaste was also criticized. The grains disintegrated in your mouth.

NOT RECOMMENDED

8. Uncle Ben's Enriched Long Grain Instant Rice

$1.99 for 14 ounces

"The strongest tasting rice I've ever eaten," commented one taster. Another described its flavor as "metallic" and "artificial." The rice was also mushy.

amylose, the less sticky of the two starches in rice, the other being amylopectin (see the Science Desk on page 86 for more information).

All of the rices were also milled using the standard process in which the hull is removed and the grains are then rubbed together by machine to remove the bran and germ. (Rice with bran and germ left intact is brown rice.) These two processes create standard white rice. Converted and instant rice are subjected to more processing.

The additional processing for converted rice is done before milling. The unmilled rice is soaked in hot water, then steamed and dried in the husk. This technique is far from modern, dating back about 1,500 years in India, where rice was put in large pots of water, soaked, steamed, and laid out in the sun to dry. Still practiced today in rural parts of India, this method makes it easier to remove the hull. For modern cooks the primary advantage of this processing is that the rice remains firmer and more separate when it's cooked. Some of the starch in the outer portion of the kernel becomes gelatinized when it's steamed in the husk. The rice kernel then dries harder than it is in its original state, and nutrients are retained as they seep from the bran into the kernel. The harder starch makes it more difficult for water to penetrate, so it takes about five minutes more time for converted rice to cook. The result is not only firmer, more separate rice but rice with a tan-yellow tint and a stronger flavor than standard rice.

On the opposite end of the spectrum is instant rice. To make it, milled rice is fully precooked and then dried very fast. This creates cracks or channels that facilitate the movement of water into the kernel as it cooks on the stove. You can see the cracks if you look closely at kernels of instant rice, which tend to be light and porous, like miniature puffed rice. This process makes cooking rice as effortless as making instant soup—stir into boiling water, cover, and let rest off heat for five minutes.

The compromise between the firm, separate kernels of converted rice and the convenience of instant rice seems to be boil-in-bag products. These modern innovations are made by precooking converted rice. In other words, these rices are parboiled prior to hulling, then precooked and dried after hulling and the removal of the bran and germ. The idea is that the parboiling will create rice grains with a firmer texture resistant to breaking down and turning mushy, so that even though they are also precooked they will remain firm and separate during their final 10 minutes of cooking.

When it came to tasting, our panel surprised us. As we expected, standard rices—that had not been subjected to any special processing to make them cook faster or end up with grains that were unusually separate—did well, finishing in second and third place. The surprise was the first-place finish of Uncle Ben's Boil-in-Bag, along with the fourth-place showing of Kraft's Boil-in-Bag. In both cases, the idea behind the dual processing of these rices really paid off. Tasters found the grains of Uncle Ben's, in particular, to be firm, perfectly unbroken, and nicely moist.

The converted rice garnered decent remarks but finished in the middle of the pack. As for instant rices, our tasters found these products unpalatably mushy, and they noted that the individual kernels tended to fall apart and fray. We also detected off flavors.

So if you aren't opposed to preparing your rice in a plastic pouch, a boil-in-bag rice might be the best option when you're looking for convenience. The trade-off, however, is that you get less rice for your dollar and you cannot cook these rices along with other seasonings or ingredients. Standard long-grain white rice takes a total of only 30 to 35 minutes to prepare (including resting time) and requires minimal attention. It also cooks up dry and fluffy, meaning that you can use it in fried rice, something we don't recommend you try with boil-in-a-bag rice, which tends to be moister and softer when cooked.

EQUIPMENT CORNER: RICE COOKERS

WITHOUT A DOUBT, THE EASIEST, MOST RELIABLE METHOD for preparing rice is the rice cooker. Besides turning out good rice (it's fluffy, separate, and still has a nice bite), rice cookers are easy to clean, especially models with a nonstick surface on the cooking pot. (When buying a rice cooker, we consider a nonstick finish a must.)

A rice cooker consists of a large chamber with an electric heating element on the bottom. A cooking pot slips into the holding chamber and is covered with a lid. The heating element brings the rice and water to a boil and maintains a constant temperature. When the temperature inside the cooking chamber rises above 212 degrees—a sign that there is no more steam and all the water has been absorbed—the rice cooker automatically shuts off. Most models actually switch to a "keep warm" mode, which holds rice for several hours without damage.

You can spend $20 for a bare-bones rice cooker or up to $180 for a high-tech fuzzy logic model with a small "electronic brain." We rounded up five rice cookers to see if more money bought a better machine. To put these rice cookers through their paces, we cooked 3 cups of long-grain rice, 3 cups of short-grain rice, and 1 cup of short-grain rice according to the manufacturers' specifications in each cooker. We kept the rice warm for three hours using the warming function, and we assessed cleanup.

We were looking for evenly cooked rice that was neither mushy nor overly firm. Burning on the bottom was considered unacceptable. The good news is that all three Japanese rice cookers passed this test. The Japanese invented rice cookers back in the 1950s and have clearly perfected this technology. The bad news is that the cheaper knock-offs from American companies did not perform as well.

Rice cooked in the Toastmaster Rice Cooker TR-5 ($19.99) was scorched every time. Rice did not burn in the Farberware Nutristeam Rice Cooker/Food Warmer FRA500 ($29.99), but it did come out dry and a bit hard, especially if the warming function was engaged.

Among the three Japanese models tested, we found minor differences in performance, but testers felt that it was best to recommend the least expensive model in this group, the National Rice Cooker/Steamer SR-W10NA, which costs just $37.99. Although some browning occurred on the bottom of the rice (especially if the warming function was used), this did not mar the texture or flavor of the rice. The Sanyo Electric Rice Cooker/Warmer ECJ-5104PF ($89.99) also produced a light brown layer of rice on the bottom.

Only the Zojirushi Neuro Fuzzy Rice Cooker and Warmer NS-JCC10 ($179.99) yielded pot after pot of rice without any browning of the bottom layer, even after several hours on the warming cycle. The dizzying array of options on this cooker include variable settings for "regular," "softer," and "harder" rice; settings for brown rice and rice porridge; and a special extended warming function that kicks in after eight hours. Although this ultrafancy model performed beautifully in tests, we are hard pressed to recommend spending so much money on a rice cooker, especially when the cheaper options perform basic tasks nearly as well.

BEST RICE COOKER
The National Rice Cooker/Steamer has a nonstick pan, an automatic warming feature, and a removable power cord for easy storage. This model turned out batch after batch of good rice and costs far less than high-end models with more bells and whistles. See www.cooksillustrated.com for an up-to-date price and mail-order source for this top-rated product.

KUNG PAO SHRIMP

WHAT WE WANTED: Tired of the sweet, gloppy restaurant renditions of this Sichuan classic, we wanted to take a few Asian pantry staples and just 30 minutes to make a spicy, sweet, salty, savory kung pao that would put most restaurant versions to shame.

This classic Sichuan stir-fry of shrimp, peanuts, and chiles in a rich brown sauce is a Chinese restaurant standard, yet the kung pao we sampled in a half dozen well-reputed spots around Boston was shocking. The first one was abysmal, with tough, tiny little shrimp drenched in a quart of pale, greasy, bland sauce, and things just got worse from there.

This sorry collection of kung pao renditions served as a not-so-subtle hint that we'd be better off making this dish at home. Like most stir-fries, kung pao cooks quickly, so it is well suited for a weeknight meal. Moreover, we thought that by carefully examining the key issues—those being the type and preparation of both the shrimp and the nuts along with the composition and texture of the sauce—we could come up with something much better than what we'd encountered in most restaurants.

Most Chinese stir-fries go heavy on the vegetables, but kung pao dishes are different. The quantity of vegetables is limited, with the emphasis instead on the shrimp and the nuts. The restaurant versions we tried often included green pepper, and some added bamboo shoots, carrots, celery, scallions, and zucchini. Tasters worked their way through these choices and more and settled on a modest amount of red pepper for sweetness and scallion for freshness, bite, and color. Kung pao needs nothing else from the vegetable kingdom.

Taking a step up the food chain, we looked at the shrimp next. Most restaurants use medium to small shrimp, which makes the dish seem skimpy and cheap. We felt that larger shrimp made a more satisfying kung pao, and large

shrimp were easier to peel, too. After checking out jumbo, extra-large, large, and medium (labels that are less helpful than the numbers assigned to shrimp to indicate size, such as 21/25, meaning that 21 to 25 shrimp make 1 pound), tasters selected extra-large (21/25 count) for their combination of succulence and generous appearance.

The best way to prepare the shrimp was a matter of some debate. Traditionally, they are "velveted"—coated with egg white, cornstarch, and seasonings—and then fried in a generous quantity of oil. The idea here is to create a softly crisp coating that will help the sauce adhere. Though velveting does have its supporters, we were not among them, for two reasons. First, the egg coating tended to cook up in unattractive clumps, which would later float about in the dish, and second, the two to three cups of oil required to deep-fry seemed both cumbersome and wasteful. Dealing with all that oil, from measuring it out to disposing of it later, edged the dish out of the realm of simple weeknight cooking. It would be much better, we felt, to quickly stir-fry the shrimp in a film of oil and to thicken the sauce slightly to help it coat the shrimp.

The nuts help define kung pao. In most of the restaurant dishes we tried, the flavor of the nuts was underdeveloped, so they acted more as a garnish than a key element. We wanted to better integrate the nuts into the dish and to deepen their flavor. One move accomplished both goals. Whereas most recipes add the nuts near the end of the cooking time, we stir-fried them right along with the shrimp at the beginning. This way, they toasted briefly in the pan, intensifying in flavor, which they then contributed to the sauce. Most kung pao recipes rely on either peanuts or cashews, and we appreciated the former for their savory flavor and crisp texture. By comparison, cashews seemed both sweet and a little soft.

The test kitchen has conducted extensive investigations into stir-frying technique, so we knew that a wide, heavy skillet, preheated until the oil smokes, is a better mate with the flat American stovetop burner than a deeply curved wok. With all that heat, though, it would be easy to over-cook, and therefore toughen, the shrimp and to burn the aromatic garlic and ginger that are part of the sauce. With a little care, both problems are easy to avoid. First, we learned not to cook shrimp all the way through at first because they will finish cooking in the sauce later; an initial stay in the pan of just under two minutes was ideal. With regard to the garlic and ginger, most stir-fry recipes add them near the beginning. We prefer to add them near the end of cook-ing to prevent burning and preserve their fresh flavors.

When it came to the sauce, we pictured it deep brown, syrupy in texture, and glistening, with balanced elements of sweet, savory, salty, garlicky, and hot. We tried both chicken broth and water as a base and preferred the broth for the savory underpinning it provided. For a bit of sweetness we added sugar in amounts from 1 tablespoon down to 1 tea-spoon, but even a mere teaspoon was overkill. Instead, we chose to add the classic trio of hoisin sauce, oyster-flavored sauce, and sesame oil, all available in the supermarket and all good sources of color, flavor depth, and subtle sweetness. An ample supply of garlic—three cloves—gave the sauce authority, and ginger and rice vinegar added brightness. We liked Chinese black rice vinegar (called Chinkiang vinegar) even better because it was more complex—smoky, salty, plum-like, and slightly sweet—but it is hard to come by in the supermarket. Cornstarch is the thickener of choice for Asian sauces, and 1½ teaspoons reliably gelled the sauce to a soft, glazey, shrimp-coating consistency.

Eager to see if we could streamline the recipe by omitting an ingredient (or maybe two?), we systemati-cally retested all of the sauce components. Alas, tasters agreed that each one brought a distinct flavor dimension to the party; without any one of them, the sauce suffered a bit, inching its way back toward the dreaded restaurant

kung pao we were determined to outdo.

Spicy chile heat may be kung pao's true calling card. (For details about the multitude of heat sources we tried, see the Tasting Lab on page 93.) Tasters unanimously chose whole dried chiles, which are traditional for this dish. We did alter the technique with which they are generally used, however, by stir-frying them with the shrimp and peanuts at the beginning of cooking. This extra bit of pan time toasted the chiles, deepening their flavor noticeably.

Now the next time the yen for kung pao hits, we'll leave the sweet, pasty, insipid stuff in the takeout box where it belongs. With fresh shrimp, a few Asian pantry ingredients, 20 minutes of prep time, and five minutes at the stove, we can rival the best that Chinatown has to offer.

WHAT WE LEARNED: Use extra-large shrimp, keep the amount of vegetables in check, add the chiles and nuts early so they toast and develop more flavor, and use a trio of Asian ingredients—hoisin sauce, oyster-flavored sauce, and sesame oil—to create a rich brown sauce.

KUNG PAO SHRIMP serves 4

We like the appearance of whole dried chiles as well as the toasty flavor they develop in the pan, but crushed red pepper flakes are a fine substitute. Feel free to increase the number of chiles to suit your taste. You can also substitute plain rice vinegar for the black rice vinegar (available in Asian markets), but we prefer the latter for its fruity, salty complexity. If you prefer roasted unsalted cashews over peanuts, substitute an equal amount. Unless you have a taste for the incendiary, do not eat the whole chiles in the finished dish. Serve kung pao shrimp with Basic White Rice (page 85). See page 93 for tips on deveining shrimp.

- 1 pound extra-large shrimp (21 to 25 count), peeled and deveined
- 1 tablespoon dry sherry or rice wine
- 2 teaspoons soy sauce
- 3 medium garlic cloves, minced (about 1 tablespoon)
- 1 piece (½-inch) fresh ginger, peeled and minced (about 2 teaspoons)
- 3 tablespoons peanut or vegetable oil
- ½ cup roasted unsalted peanuts
- 6 small whole dried red chiles (each about 1¾ to 2 inches long), 3 chiles roughly crumbled, or 1 teaspoon hot red pepper flakes
- ¾ cup canned low-sodium chicken broth
- 2 teaspoons black rice vinegar or plain rice vinegar
- 2 teaspoons Asian sesame oil
- 1 tablespoon oyster-flavored sauce
- 1 tablespoon hoisin sauce
- 1½ teaspoons cornstarch
- 1 medium red bell pepper, cut into ½-inch dice (about 1 cup)
- 3 medium scallions, white and green parts, sliced thin (about ¼ cup)

1. Toss shrimp with sherry and soy sauce in medium bowl; marinate for 10 minutes. Mix garlic, ginger, and 1 tablespoon oil in small bowl; set aside. Combine peanuts and chiles in small bowl; set aside. Mix chicken broth, vinegar, sesame oil, oyster-flavored sauce, hoisin sauce, and cornstarch in small bowl or measuring cup; set aside.

2. Heat 1 tablespoon oil in 12-inch skillet over high heat until just beginning to smoke. Add shrimp and cook, stirring

---

GETTING IT RIGHT: Shrimp Sizes

Shrimp are sold by size (small, medium, large, and so on) as well as by the number needed to make 1 pound, usually given in a range. Choosing shrimp by the numerical rating is more accurate than choosing by a size label, which varies from store to store. Here's how the two sizing systems generally line up.

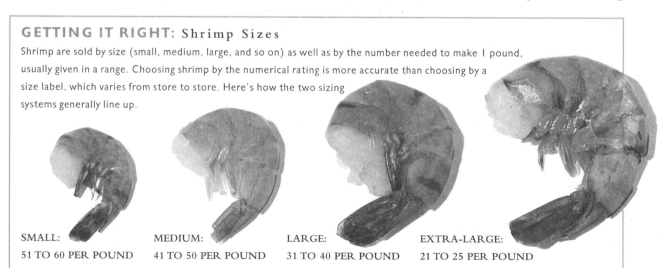

SMALL:
51 TO 60 PER POUND

MEDIUM:
41 TO 50 PER POUND

LARGE:
31 TO 40 PER POUND

EXTRA-LARGE:
21 TO 25 PER POUND

about once every 10 seconds, until barely opaque, 30 to 40 seconds; add peanuts and chiles, stir into shrimp, and continue cooking until shrimp are almost completely opaque and peanuts have darkened slightly, 30 to 40 seconds longer. Transfer shrimp, peanuts, and chiles to bowl; set aside. Return skillet to burner and reheat briefly, 15 to 30 seconds. Add remaining 1 tablespoon oil, swirl to coat pan, and add red bell pepper; cook, stirring occasionally, until slightly softened, about 45 seconds. Clear center of pan, add garlic-ginger mixture, mash into pan with spoon or spatula and cook until fragrant, 10 to 15 seconds; stir into pepper until combined. Stir broth mixture to recombine, then add to skillet along with reserved shrimp, peanuts, and chiles; cook, stirring and scraping up browned bits on bottom of pan, until sauce has thickened to syrupy consistency, about 45 seconds. Stir in scallions; transfer to serving plate and serve immediately.

TECHNIQUE: Deveining Shrimp

Once the shell has been removed, you should remove the black vein that runs along the curved outer side of the shrimp.

1. Slice along the back of the shrimp with a paring knife to expose the vein, then use the tip of the knife to lift it out.

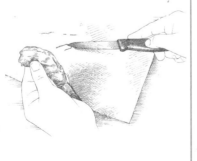

2. The vein may stick to the knife. Instead of struggling to remove it with your fingers, just wipe the blade against a paper towel. The vein will stick to the towel, which can be discarded once all of the shrimp have been deveined.

TASTING LAB: Chile Products

WITHOUT SPICY CHILE HEAT, IT'S NOT KUNG PAO. THE recipes we consulted, however, offered little agreement about the best source of that heat. We hit the supermarket down the street and picked up the most oft-repeated contenders, including several types of whole dried chiles (the traditional choice), crushed red pepper flakes, fresh chiles, chili oil, and two popular and widely available Asian chili sauces, Sambal and Sriracha. We returned to the test kitchen and conducted a side-by-side kung pao tasting.

The exact formula for Sambal, a chunky chili-garlic paste, varies from maker to maker. Ours was seasoned with salt, sugar, and rice vinegar. Smoother Sriracha is a popular Thai chili sauce, and ours was seasoned with salt, sugar, garlic, and fish extract. Both Sambal and Sriracha are common table condiments, but tasters gave them thumbs-down in the kung pao because they lacked depth and tended to taste too salty. Chili oil was also passed by because the one we used, actually a chili-flavored sesame oil, was judged too mild, and it made the sauce a bit greasy. The fresh chiles—jalapeños, to be exact—provided sharp heat, but the tasters did not appreciate the distinct green, vegetal notes. Crushed red pepper flakes provided a bright, direct heat that was utterly acceptable, but the tasters' favorite by a long shot were the whole dried chiles. They infused the kung pao with a round, even spiciness that gave the dish a deep, toasty, almost smoky dimension as well.

This finding, of course, begged the question of whether one particular type of dried chile would be best, since there are many varieties. With our sights set on relatively small chiles (large chiles simply looked wrong in the dish), we returned to the market and gathered six varieties, including an unnamed Asian specimen from the bulk bin, Japones, Arbol, Guajillo, Costeño, and Cascabel. Tasters strained to detect distinctions between them in the kung pao. We concluded that any small whole dried red chile will do quite nicely.

Stacks of pans ready for sautéing cutlets
or pan-roasting pieces of chicken.

CHICKEN in a flash

CHAPTER 7

While others might live by the mantra, "You can never be too rich or too thin," in the test kitchen our slogan goes something like this: "You can never have too many quick chicken dishes." Readers of the magazine and viewers of the television show tell us that chicken is their favorite weeknight entrée. As such, we are always looking for new dishes and new techniques to keep chicken fresh and interesting.

Italian cooking is always a good source of inspiration for simple but interesting recipes, and chicken is no exception. Chicken Milanese (pan-fried cutlets coated with bread crumbs and Parmesan) is a work-horse in our kitchen. Of course, if the coating fails to brown or falls off altogether, this dish isn't much good. Chicken piccata (with its bracing lemon and caper sauce) is another standby, but the sauce can be bland and pasty.

Another source of quick chicken recipes is restaurant cooking. We were intrigued by the notion of pan-roasting chicken parts—that is, starting them on the stovetop but finishing the cooking in the oven. Our goal was to make this chef's technique work at home.

CHICKEN MILANESE

WHAT WE WANTED: Juicy chicken cutlets covered with a crisp, evenly browned coating of bread crumbs and Parmesan. The coating must not peel away, as often happens, but remain firmly attached to the chicken.

Tender boneless chicken breast, pan-fried with a cloak of mild-flavored crumbs, has universal appeal. In Italy, grated Parmesan is added to the coating, and the dish is called chicken Milanese. Though simple, this dish can fall prey to a host of problems. The chicken itself may be rubbery and tasteless, and the coating—called a bound breading and arguably the best part of the dish—often ends up unevenly cooked, greasy, pale, or burnt.

For a breaded chicken cutlet to be great, the chicken itself must hold up its end of the bargain. Because the test kitchen is fiercely devoted to the benefits of brining poultry, we wondered what effect soaking the cutlets in a mixture of salt, sugar, and water would have. The brined cutlets were a hit, exceptionally juicy and seasoned all the way to the center. Brining takes just 30 minutes, during which time you can pull together other components of the recipe. It's not often that so little work yields such big benefits. (For cutlet recipes with a sauce, such as the piccata on page 104, the sauce adds moisture, and there's no need to brine the chicken.)

Throughout the first series of tests, we noticed that the thin tip of the cutlet and the opposite end, which was much more plump, cooked at different rates. This problem was a cinch to fix; all we had to do was pound the chicken breasts gently to an even ½ inch with a meat pounder (see the Equipment Corner on page 102). To promote even cooking, we also found it best to remove the floppy tenderloin from the underside of each cutlet before pounding.

The ideal breading should taste mild and comforting but not dull and certainly not greasy. To explore the possibilities, we pan-fried cutlets coated with fine, fresh bread crumbs (made from fresh sliced white sandwich bread ground fine in the food processor) and dry bread crumbs. The dry bread crumbs had an unmistakably stale flavor. The fresh bread crumbs swept the taste test, with their mild, subtly sweet flavor and light, crisp texture. We went on to test crumbs made from different kinds of white bread, including premium sliced sandwich bread, Italian, French, and country-style. The sandwich bread was the sweetest and appealed most to tasters in this recipe. That said, fresh crumbs made from all of these breads were good.

During the crumb testing, we made several important observations about the breading process. First, we learned that the cutlets must be thoroughly dried after brining. We also learned that we could not dispense with the coating of flour that went onto the chicken before the egg wash and crumbs. If the cutlets were even slightly moist, or if we skipped the flour coat, the breading would peel off the finished cutlets in sheets. In addition, we found it essential to press the crumbs onto the cutlets to ensure an even, thorough cover. Finally, we discovered that it was best to let the breaded cutlets rest for about five minutes before frying them; this step, too, helped to bind the breading to the meat.

Last, we explored the details of pan-frying. In any breaded preparation, the oil in the pan should reach one-third to one-half of the way up the food for thorough browning. Which fat should be used **for** sautéing the cutlets? Cutlets sautéed in olive oil were markedly better than those sautéed in vegetable oil.

WHAT WE LEARNED: For a crisp coating that won't fall off, dry the cutlets thoroughly and then flour them before dipping in egg wash and coating with fresh bread crumbs. Let the breaded cutlets rest for at least five minutes before frying them. Finally, use plenty of olive oil to pan-fry the cutlets.

CHICKEN MILANESE serves 4

Brining makes the cutlets juicier and more flavorful and is recommended. However, if you can find kosher cutlets (which have been soaked in saltwater during processing), skip this step and save yourself some time. When covering the cutlets with the bread crumb and cheese mixture, use your hands to pat a thorough, even coating onto the chicken to make sure the crumbs adhere. See the illustrations on page 98 for more tips on breading cutlets. The chicken is cooked in batches of two because the crust is noticeably more crisp if the pan is not overcrowded. Grind fresh or stale sandwich bread in a food processor to make homemade crumbs.

4	boneless, skinless chicken breasts (5 to 6 ounces each), tenderloins removed and reserved for another use, fat trimmed (see illustration at right)
½	cup kosher salt or ¼ cup table salt
½	cup sugar
	Ground black pepper
1¼	cups homemade bread crumbs
¼	cup finely grated Parmesan cheese
¾	cup unbleached all-purpose flour
2	large eggs
1	tablespoon plus ¾ cup olive oil
	Lemon wedges for serving

1. Use meat pounder, rubber mallet, or rolling pin to pound chicken breasts to even ½-inch thickness. Dissolve salt and sugar in 1 quart cold water in gallon-sized zipper-lock plastic bag. Add cutlets and seal bag, pressing out as much air as possible. Refrigerate until cutlets are fully seasoned, 30 minutes. Line baking sheet with triple layer of paper towels.

2. Remove cutlets and lay them in single layer on baking sheet. Cover with another triple layer of paper towels and press firmly to absorb moisture. Allow cutlets to dry for 10 minutes. Carefully peel paper towels off cutlets; sprinkle cutlets with pepper to taste and set them aside.

3. Adjust oven rack to lower-middle position, set large heat-proof plate on rack, and heat oven to 200 degrees. Combine bread crumbs and Parmesan cheese in shallow dish or pie plate. Spread flour in second shallow dish. Beat eggs with 1 tablespoon oil in third shallow dish.

4. Working with one at a time, dredge cutlets thoroughly in flour, shaking off excess. Using tongs, dip both sides of cutlets in egg mixture, taking care to coat them thoroughly and allowing excess to drip back into dish to ensure very thin coating. Dip both sides of cutlets in bread crumb mixture, pressing crumbs with your fingers to form an even, cohesive coat. Place breaded cutlets in single layer on wire rack set over baking sheet and allow coating to dry for about 5 minutes.

5. Meanwhile, heat 6 tablespoons of remaining oil in heavy-bottomed 10-inch nonstick skillet over medium-high heat until shimmering but not smoking, about 2 minutes. Lay two cutlets gently in skillet and cook until deep golden

---

TECHNIQUE: Trimming Cutlets

Most cutlets have a little yellow or white fat still attached to the breast meat. Lay each cutlet tenderloin-side down and smooth the top with your fingers. Any fat will slide to the edge of the cutlet, where it can be trimmed with a knife.

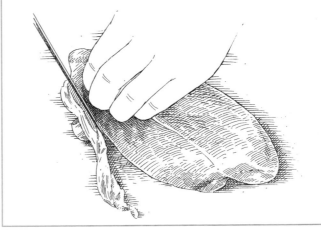

brown and crisp on first side, gently pressing down on cutlets with wide metal spatula to help ensure even browning, about 2½ minutes. Using tongs, flip cutlets, reduce heat to medium, and continue to cook until meat feels firm when pressed gently and second side is deep golden brown and crisp, 2½ to 3 minutes. Line warmed plate with double layer of paper towels and set cutlets on top; return plate to oven.

6. Discard oil in skillet and wipe skillet clean using tongs and large wad paper towels. Repeat step 5, using remaining 6 tablespoons oil and now-clean skillet to cook remaining cutlets. Serve immediately along with first batch and lemon wedges.

VARIATION

BREADED CHICKEN CUTLETS WITH GARLIC AND OREGANO

Follow recipe for Chicken Milanese, increasing bread crumbs to 1½ cups and omitting Parmesan cheese. Beat 3 tablespoons very finely minced fresh oregano leaves and 8 medium garlic cloves, minced to puree or pressed through garlic press (just under 3 tablespoons), into egg mixture in step 3.

EQUIPMENT CORNER: Inexpensive Nonstick Skillets

ALTHOUGH MOST HOME COOKS WOULD LIKE TO HAVE A battery of weighty, expensive, professional-grade pots and pans at their disposal, most of what gets used at home is a lot cheaper. Does lower-cost cookware necessarily mean a big performance trade-off? We examined that question recently by conducting a full set of cooking tests on eight inexpensive nonstick skillets, all purchased at hardware or discount stores for no more than $50 apiece.

Statistics reported by the Cookware Manufacturers Association indicate that 90 percent of all the aluminum cookware sold in the United States in 2001 was nonstick. The reasons to use nonstick are clear: Little or no fat is required to lubricate the food (and thereby prevent sticking), and cleanup is easy. Nonstick is terrific for extremely delicate, quick-cooking foods. Flaky white fish come to mind, as do certain egg dishes, like omelets and eggs sunny-side up, the integrity of which would be

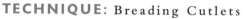

TECHNIQUE: Breading Cutlets

1. Dredge the cutlets thoroughly in flour, shaking off the excess.

2. Using tongs, dip both sides of the cutlets in the egg mixture, taking care to coat them thoroughly and allowing the excess to drip back into the dish to ensure a very thin coating. Tongs keep the breading from coating your fingers.

3. Dip both sides of the cutlets in the bread crumbs, pressing the crumbs with your fingers to form an even, cohesive coat.

destroyed were they to stick to the pan.

Those concerned with limiting their fat intake view the reduction of cooking fat as another significant benefit. This makes sense if you want a simply sautéed fish fillet or chicken cutlet garnished with a wedge of lemon or lime. It may mean trouble, however, if you prefer to garnish your food with a pan sauce. Pan sauces rely on fond, the tiny caramelized bits of food that stick to the pan as its contents cook. When liquid is added to the pan (in a process called deglazing), the bits of food dissolve to form the flavorful backbone of the sauce.

Because nonstick coatings prevent sticking, they also, in our experience, inhibit fond development. To test this notion, we sautéed chicken cutlets in each pan and then deglazed the fond left behind with 1 cup of water, which we then boiled hard for one minute. We were looking for rich, dark brown liquid shaded deeply by the dissolved fond. What we got, in each and every case, more closely resembled dirty bathwater. Not a single sample was dark enough to use in a sauce.

The chicken cutlet tests point to another drawback of nonstick cookware. Not only was the fond light, so was the chicken. The savory, caramelized crust that forms on the exterior of a piece of food as it sautés is the very reason to cook that way in the first place—the crust tastes great. None of the nonstick pans in our tests formed a crust on the lean chicken cutlets that would make us proud (or hungry). Nonstick pans are fine, however, when pan-frying in a significant amount of oil, as in our breaded chicken cutlet recipe on page 97. In fact, we like nonstick pans for this task because they are easier to clean than pans with conventional surfaces.

Here in the test kitchen we choose nonstick when we want to cook lightly, keep flavors fresh, or ensure easy cleanup. If browning or fond are important to the dish, we reach for a traditional pan.

The material used for nonstick coating—polytetrafluoroethylene, or PTFE—was developed by chemists at Dupont in the late 1930s. Trademarked originally as Teflon, the formula has evolved over the years, and now several companies in addition to Dupont sell PTFE to cookware manufacturers (many of which use individualized, proprietary, multicoat application processes to bond the coating to their pans). It is our understanding, however, that the majority of nonstick coatings today are made from the same basic substance.

The nonstick, nonreactive magic of PTFE is due, in large part, to one of the two types of atoms it contains—namely, fluorine. Every PTFE molecule contains two carbon atoms and four fluorine atoms. In the atomic world, fluorine is very highly resistant to bonding with other substances. That's why PTFE is so slippery.

And slippery it was. Every pan in our group received a good score in release ability and cleaning tests, the raisons d'être for nonstick. We tested both traits in a purposefully

TECHNIQUE:
Protecting Nonstick Surfaces

If you stack your cookware (as we do), you run the risk of scratching the nonstick surface. Some cooks slip each pan into a large zipper-lock bag before stacking it, while others place plastic lids (from sour cream, coffee, or yogurt containers) between pans to keep them from scratching each other. Our favorite way to protect nonstick cookware is to slide a doubled piece of paper towel between each pan as you stack them.

abusive manner by burning oatmeal into the pans over high heat for 45 minutes. That kind of treatment would trash a traditional pan, but the scorched cereal slid out of our nonstick pans with no fuss, and the pans practically wiped clean.

Most manufacturers recommend using plastic, rubber, coated, or wooden utensils to avoid scratching the nonstick coating (and all caution against using any sharp utensil such as a knife, fork, or beater). Makers of only three of our pans, the Farberware, Innova, and Bialetti, actually sanction the use of metal utensils.

In their new, off-the-shelf condition, all of our pans turned in a reasonable-to-good performance with foods best suited to nonstick cooking: eggs and fish. In fact, every pan but the Revere produced evenly cooked omelets and released them with ease. The omelet made in the Farberware pan was especially impressive. The Farberware also did a nice job searing salmon fillets to an even, crusty, medium

brown. (Salmon is much higher in fat than skinless chicken cutlets and so browns more easily, even in a nonstick pan.) Overall, however, our tests indicate that any of these pans could easily handle such light-duty tasks as cooking eggs. Low cost does not mean a big trade-off here.

Sauté speed is also an important measure of a pan's performance. We tested this by sautéing 1½ cups of hand-chopped onions over medium heat for 10 minutes in the hope of ending up with pale gold onions that bore no trace of burning. And you know what? For the most part, we did. The Wearever, T-Fal, Innova, and Revere pans, which were all on the light side in terms of weight, turned out the darkest onions, but they were still well within an acceptable color range. Onions sautéed in the Farberware, Meyer, Calphalon, and Bialetti were a shade lighter, indicating a slightly slower sauté speed. The Farberware onions, however, took top honors based on how evenly all the pieces colored.

TECHNIQUE: Cleaning Up Spilled Oil

Anyone who has ever dropped a glass bottle of oil on the floor knows how hard it can be to clean up. Here's how to clean an oil-slicked floor and avoid cuts from broken glass shards.

1. Sprinkle a thick layer of flour over the spilled oil and wait a few minutes for the flour to absorb the oil.

2. With a paper towel, or brush if there's any glass, move the flour around until it absorbs all the oil, and sweep it up with a dustpan and broom.

3. Spray the area with window cleaner and wipe away the last traces of oil and flour.

Rating Inexpensive Nonstick Skillets

WE SAUTÉED CHICKEN CUTLETS, SEARED SALMON FILLETS, AND MADE OMELETS IN EIGHT LARGE NONSTICK SKILLETS. WE tested sauté speed by cooking onions in oil over medium heat for 10 minutes. Pans were also evaluated for cleanup and release ability and are listed in ascending order of price within each category. See www.cooksillustrated.com for up-to-date prices and mail-order sources for top-rated products.

RECOMMENDED
1. Farberware Millennium 18/10 Stainless Steel 12" Nonstick Skillet

$29.99

Heaviest pan of the bunch, with the most solid construction. Fantastic omelets, golden brown fish, and evenly sautéed onions. Only with chicken did this pan falter—and not much at that.

RECOMMENDED WITH RESERVATIONS
2. T-Fal Ultrabase Royale Gala 12¼" Sauté Pan

$22.99

Great job on omelets and salmon, but only decent job on chicken and onions. Cool, comfortable, ergonomic handle.

RECOMMENDED WITH RESERVATIONS
3. Wearever Concentric Air Collection Super Slick Nonstick 12" Sauté Pan

$29.99

Comfortable handle came loose during testing. Sauté speed was a slightly slow medium. A little extra effort necessary to clean shiny rim thoroughly.

RECOMMENDED WITH RESERVATIONS
4. Innova Classicor Stainless Steel Excalibur 12" Nonstick Frypan

$39.99

Decent performance but didn't brown foods as evenly as top pans did, and channel around rim made it difficult to remove omelets neatly.

NOT RECOMMENDED
5. Revere Polished Nonstick Open Skillet-12"

$19.99

High sides make omelets a bit tricky. Browning on fish and chicken was unimpressive, and the handle loosened during testing. Our least favorite pan.

NOT RECOMMENDED
6. Bialetti Casa Italia Hi-Base 11"

$19.99

Slow sauté speed means food does not brown well. Handle loosened slightly during testing. Textured pan bottom was of no particular advantage.

NOT RECOMMENDED
7. Meyer Commercial Weight II 12" Nonstick Sauté Pan

$27.99

Solid and heavy, but produces sub-par browning when sautéing. Extra-thick, shiny rim requires extra elbow grease to clean.

NOT RECOMMENDED
8. Simply Calphalon Nonstick 12" Omelette Pan

$49.99

Most expensive pan in the group did not sauté to impress. Neither chicken nor onions browned sufficiently; fish was more successful.

That does not bode well for their future.

Of the pans we tested, the $30 Farberware Millennium offered the best combination of good nonstick performance (in suitable applications), pleasing heft at almost 3½ pounds, and solid construction. It even beat out the priciest pan in the test, the Calphalon.

EQUIPMENT CORNER: Meat Pounders

WHEN DEVELOPING OUR RECIPE FOR CHICKEN MILANESE, we tried several pounding gadgets—makeshift as well as purchased—and found that the best chicken breast pounders were relatively lightweight, with large flat surfaces. A disk-style pounder with a handle in the center was our favorite. As long as we pounded lightly, its relatively large, round surface quickly and efficiently transformed breasts into cutlets. If you don't have this kind of pounder, we suggest pounding gently with what you have on hand, which is likely heavier than our disk-style pounder. A rubber mallet or rolling pin would be our second choice, but the bottom of a small saucepan will work in a pinch.

BEST MEAT POUNDER
We tested several styles of meat pounder and found that a disk-style pounder with a handle in the center is the easiest on delicate chicken cutlets. It is our top choice.

Of course, construction quality is a concern with any piece of cookware, but especially with inexpensive models. Will the thing hold up, or will you have to replace it in six months? Based on our experience, you may well sacrifice a measure of construction quality with a budget pan. Pans with handles that were welded or riveted on to the pan body, including the Farberware, Innova, Meyer, and Calphalon, all felt solid and permanent. But the heat-resistant plastic (called phenolic) handles on the T-Fal, Revere, Bialetti, and Wearever pans were not riveted in place, and all three of them came loose during testing.

CHICKEN PICCATA

WHAT WE WANTED : **A classic chicken piccata with perfectly cooked cutlets and a lemony sauce punctuated with plenty of capers.**

Chicken piccata—sautéed cutlets with a lemon-caper sauce—is a restaurant classic that translates easily to the home kitchen. We imagined that piccata would be easy to perfect—and it was, after we realized that most recipes miss the point. To begin with, many cookbook authors add extraneous ingredients and thereby ruin the pure simplicity of the dish. The other major problem is blandness. Many recipes contain just a tablespoon of lemon juice and a teaspoon of capers, neither of which provides much flavor. Our goals were simple: to cook the chicken properly and to make a streamlined sauce that really tasted of lemons and capers.

Many piccata recipes call for flouring or breading the cutlets. As in past tests conducted, we found that floured cutlets browned better and were less likely to stick to the pan. Tasters did not like breaded cutlets—what's the point of developing a crisp crust only to douse it with sauce? We also tried dipping the cutlets in milk as well as beaten eggs before flouring them. Although the crust was a bit thicker when cooked, tasters felt that there was little advantage to this extra step.

With our chicken tests completed, we turned our attention to the sauce. We wanted a strong lemon flavor that wasn't harsh or overly acidic. We also wanted a sauce that was thick enough to nap the sautéed cutlets. We knew we wanted to deglaze the empty skillet used to cook the chicken with some liquid to loosen the flavorful browned bits on the pan bottom, then reduce the liquid and thicken it.

Most of the recipes we uncovered in our research called for 1 or 2 tablespoons of lemon juice. All of our tasters agreed that these sauces weren't lemony enough. We found that ¼ cup delivered a nice lemon punch. Recipes that

instructed the cook to deglaze the hot pan with lemon juice and then simmer the sauce for several minutes tasted flat. Adding the lemon juice toward the end of the cooking time helped to keep it fresh-tasting.

Our caper testing led us to a similar conclusion. You need to use a lot of capers—2 tablespoons is just right—and they should be added when the sauce is nearly done so they retain their structural integrity. (For more information on capers, see the Tasting Lab on page 105.)

We next focused on the liquid for deglazing the pan. Chicken broth and white wine were the most obvious candidates. The wine seemed like a good idea, but it contributed more acid to the sauce, which it did not need.

Broth proved a more neutral base for the lemon juice and capers.

Before deglazing the pan, we sautéed some aromatics in the pan drippings. We tested shallots, onions, scallions, and garlic separately. All were fine, although tasters preferred the shallots and garlic (one or the other). Just make sure to watch the pan carefully so that the aromatics don't burn. Add the broth to the pan as soon as the garlic or shallots start to color.

At this point, our sauce was quite good, but we wondered if there was another way to add lemon flavor. In our research, we uncovered several recipes that called for lemon slices. We halved a lemon, then cut it into very thin half-circles. We tried adding the lemon slices with the lemon juice, but the slices were too crunchy and numerous. For the next test, we used just half a lemon and added the slices with the broth. They simmered for five minutes and softened considerably. The longer simmering time also allowed oils from the peel to flavor the sauce. We tried replacing the sliced lemons with grated zest but found the sliced lemons more appealing and less work.

The last remaining issue for testing was thickening the sauce. Some recipes called for a roux (stirring flour into fat before adding the liquid), while others added either softened butter or softened butter mixed with flour once the sauce was cooked. A roux made the sauce too thick. Thickening the sauce at the end seemed more practical. The butter-flour paste gave the sauce a floury taste that dulled the flavors of lemon and capers. Plain butter proved best. Parsley, added with the butter, gave the sauce some color.

WHAT WE LEARNED: **Flour the chicken cutlets (they will brown better), but don't bother breading them (the sauce will just make the coating soggy). For fresh lemon flavor, use both juice and sliced lemons in the sauce. To keep the acidity under control, use chicken broth but not white wine. Finally, adding flour to the sauce to thicken it makes it too heavy; but butter gives the sauce some body without overthickening and is the right choice.**

CHICKEN PICCATA serves 4

Because this sauce is so light, we find that each person should be served 1 1/2 small cutlets. Serve the cutlets and sauce on a single platter and let each person help himself. For tips on juicing lemons, see page 283.

2   large lemons
6   boneless, skinless chicken breasts (5 to 6 ounces each), tenderloins removed and reserved for another use, fat trimmed (see illustration on page 97)
    Salt and ground black pepper
1/2 cup unbleached all-purpose flour
4   tablespoons vegetable oil
1   small shallot, minced (about 2 tablespoons), or 1 medium clove garlic, minced or pressed through garlic press (about 1 teaspoon)
1   cup canned low-sodium chicken broth
2   tablespoons drained small capers
3   tablespoons cold unsalted butter
2   tablespoons minced fresh parsley leaves

1. Adjust oven rack to lower-middle position, set large heat-proof plate on rack, and heat oven to 200 degrees.

2. Halve one lemon pole to pole. Trim ends from one half and cut it crosswise into slices 1/8 to 1/4 inch thick; set aside. Juice remaining half and whole lemon to obtain 1/4 cup juice; reserve.

3. Use meat pounder, rubber mallet, or rolling pin to pound chicken breasts to even 1/2-inch thickness. Sprinkle both sides of cutlets generously with salt and pepper. Measure flour into shallow baking dish or pie plate. Working with one cutlet at a time, coat with flour and shake to remove excess.

4. Heat 2 tablespoons oil in heavy-bottomed 12-inch skillet over medium-high heat until shimmering. Lay three chicken cutlets in skillet. Sauté cutlets until lightly browned on first side, 2 to 2½ minutes. Turn cutlets and cook until second side is lightly browned, 2 to 2½ minutes longer. Remove pan from heat and transfer cutlets to plate in oven. Add remaining 2 tablespoons oil to now-empty skillet and heat until shimmering. Add remaining chicken cutlets and repeat.

5. Add shallot or garlic to now-empty skillet and return skillet to medium heat. Sauté until fragrant, about 30 seconds for shallot or 10 seconds for garlic. Add stock and lemon slices, increase heat to high, and scrape pan bottom with wooden spoon or spatula to loosen browned bits. Simmer until liquid reduces to about ⅓ cup, about 4 minutes. Add lemon juice and capers and simmer until sauce reduces again to ⅓ cup, about 1 minute. Remove pan from heat and swirl in butter until butter melts and thickens sauce. Stir in parsley and season with salt and pepper to taste. Spoon sauce over chicken and serve immediately.

VARIATIONS

PEPPERY CHICKEN PICCATA

Follow recipe for Chicken Piccata, adding ½ teaspoon coarsely ground black peppercorns along with lemon juice and capers.

CHICKEN PICCATA WITH BLACK OLIVES

Follow recipe for Chicken Piccata, adding ¼ cup pitted and chopped black olives along with lemon juice and capers.

TASTING LAB: Capers

MANY PEOPLE ASSOCIATE CAPERS WITH ANCHOVIES AND assume that they come from the sea. Others assume that they must be related to peas or beans because of their shape. Capers are actually pickles made from the unopened flower buds of the caper shrub, which grows in the Mediterranean region. These briny morsels are used in countless Italian, Spanish, and Greek recipes.

Capers can be preserved in two ways. More often, the flower buds are soaked in saltwater, then packed in brine or a mixture of brine and vinegar. This is how capers are sold in most supermarkets. The other option is to cure them with salt. This kind of caper costs more and is available only in specialty markets.

In addition to differences in preservation technique, capers vary in size. The smallest capers—no larger than small peas—are called nonpareils. There are several more grades, the largest being the size of small olives and called gruesas. If you drink martinis, you may also have seen caperberries. These oval berries form if the flower buds are allowed to open and set fruit. Caperberries are pickled in brine, just like capers.

To make sense of these variables, we purchased six brands of capers and held a small tasting. We tasted small and large capers packed in brine and vinegar as well as one brand of salted capers. For cooking, tasters agreed that small capers are best because they can be used as is; larger capers are too potent to eat whole and should be chopped. Besides adding an extra step, chopped capers disintegrate when added to sauces.

The taste differences from brand to brand were subtle, although most tasters felt that the brand packed in wine vinegar was the least harsh and therefore the most flavorful. (Labels on the other bottles just said "vinegar.")

Capers packed in salt were unbearably salty straight from the bottle. Rinsing didn't do much to lessen their sting. Soaking in cool water for at least 20 minutes (preferably an hour) washed out enough of the salt to reveal the flavor of the capers. Without the salt (and because there's no vinegar), we picked up hints of herbs (especially oregano) and mustard that we never tasted in the brined capers. These salted capers were delicious, but once we used them in piccata, their subtle traits faded behind the flavors of the other ingredients.

Many sources suggest rinsing brined capers, too. We think you can skip this step. Drain the capers well and taste one. If they seem very salty or vinegary, you can rinse them. In most cases, this step won't be necessary.

PAN-ROASTED CHICKEN

WHAT WE WANTED: Superbly crisp skin on perfectly roasted chicken—all with just 20 minutes of cooking time.

To make a good basic roast chicken, some planning is required, and even then it can be a challenge to cook. For a moist, well-seasoned bird, you brine it; for the crispiest skin, you air-dry it; to coordinate the doneness of the thigh and breast, you flip the bird as it roasts. An hour or so later, the roast chicken emerges from the oven along with some drippings that, if not burnt, can be turned into a gravy or sauce before you dismantle the bird for serving.

In an effort to make roast chicken easier, we decided to investigate a technique found in several recent restaurant cookbooks: pan-roasting. This technique is used to cook cuts of meat, poultry, and fish that for reasons of size or thickness cannot be cooked exclusively on the stovetop without scorching the exterior. For pan-roasted chicken, the chicken is cut up (a slight variation, or cheat, if you must, on the roast chicken concept), browned on both sides on the stovetop, and then slid, skillet and all, into a hot oven to complete cooking. Pan-roasting means no iconic roast chicken to bring to the table, but we were hoping that it would deliver superior skin, shorter preparation time, and a rich, savory pan sauce to boot. The question was whether this technique was as simple and reliable as promised.

We began by cutting a 3½- to 4-pounder into eight pieces, two each of drumsticks and thighs and four breast pieces. This arrangement meant that each serving could consist of a portion of both white and dark meat. The wings we discarded because they are the least favorite sections to eat and the 12-inch skillet was already full without them.

Brining (soaking in a solution of salt and sometimes sugar) has become customary in our test kitchen. Tasting pan-roasted chickens side-by-side, we preferred brined birds for their moistness (which can act as a cushion against the effects of overcooking, if it happens) and for the agreeable saltiness that permeated the meat. However, we were forced to modify our all-purpose brine recipe, ousting the sugar because it led to uneven browning and burnt drippings. Because we were using a cut-up chicken, brining was expedited—just 30 minutes did the trick. (You can eliminate this step if you purchase a Kosher chicken. They are salted during processing, which has the same net effect as brining.) Air-drying, which we have found necessary to produce ultracrisp skin on roasted poultry, was not necessary. The hot skillet was crisping the skin quite well without adding hours to this weeknight recipe.

The next step was browning. A hot ovenproof skillet was key for achieving deep browning. Medium-high heat was optimal for even, controlled browning. High heat was a tad furious and sometimes resulted in burnt pan drippings (called fond). The chicken could be browned in a skillet without any oil (it had sufficient fat that rendered as it cooked and prevented sticking), but the browning was spotty and not ideal. However, even a mere tablespoon of oil was too much; when the excess fat was poured off before sauce making, the drippings woefully went with it. A teaspoon of oil, the barest coating on the skillet's surface, did the job well.

We browned the chicken parts on both sides before sliding them into the oven to roast. The burning question now was: When the chicken pieces go in the oven, should they be skin-side up or skin-side down? Compared side-by-side, skin-side up chicken was brown but mottled and crisped in some spots, soft in others. Skin-side down chicken was superior. The contact between the chicken skin and the hot metal of the pan clearly fostered a crackling crisp, darker, russet-toned skin. Both cast-iron and heavy-duty heat-conductive skillets performed well.

Suggested oven temperatures ranged from 375 all the way to 500 degrees. Four hundred fifty degrees was the winner; 500 sometimes singed the drippings, and lower temperatures simply took longer to cook the chicken through. The lowest rack setting was best as it seemed better suited to maintaining even heat.

Pan-roasted chicken recipes recommend removing the breast pieces before the leg pieces because the breast is done when it reaches 160 degrees and the leg 175 degrees (the identical problem that plagues whole roasted poultry). However, the digital thermometer told us that the breast pieces—despite being cut into quarters—and the leg pieces were finishing at about the same time. It appeared that the thickness of the breast pieces made them cook more slowly than the flat, thin thigh pieces and slim drumsticks.

Once the chicken was removed from the skillet, the fond (browned bits in the pan bottom) was crusty and plentiful, so we needed only a handful of ingredients to turn it into a sauce, keeping the flavors honest and simple. Using a potholder and utmost caution because the skillet handle was burning hot, we discarded most of the fat, sautéed minced shallots, and, in a step called deglazing, poured in chicken broth and white wine (vermouth, for more interesting flavor), scraping the skillet to loosen the fond. A couple sprigs of thyme added a herbaceous note. The liquid simmered to about half its original volume as the chicken reposed. With the flavors of the sauce concentrated and its consistency slightly thickened, we added juices that the resting chicken released and whisked in knobs of butter along with seasonings. A quick return to the skillet brought the chicken back up to serving temperature (skin-side up, of course, to keep the skin crisp).

Judging from the enthusiasm with which a plateful of pan-roasted chicken (and sauce) met, it was clear that this roast chicken was receiving high marks. Crisp-skinned roast chicken with an impressive sauce is possible on a weeknight.

WHAT WE LEARNED: **Brown the chicken parts in the barest film of oil on top of the stove, then put the chicken (still in the pan) into the oven, skin-side down, and roast until cooked through, about 10 minutes. As the chicken rests on a plate, add chicken broth and vermouth to turn the pan drippings into a flavorful sauce.**

PAN-ROASTED CHICKEN WITH SHALLOT AND VERMOUTH SAUCE serves 4

Brining the chicken is optional but highly recommended. If you opt not to brine, use a kosher chicken if one is available (kosher chickens are salted during processing and have the moistness and flavor of brined chickens). This recipe requires a 12-inch ovenproof skillet. The skillet handle will be blisteringly hot after being in the oven, so be sure to use a potholder or oven mitt to remove the skillet from the oven and when handling the skillet as you make the sauce. Dry white wine can be substituted for the vermouth.

chicken

1½ cups kosher salt or ¾ cup table salt
1 chicken (3½ to 4 pounds), cut into 8 pieces (4 breast pieces, 2 thighs, and 2 drumsticks, wings discarded) and trimmed of excess fat
   Ground black pepper
1 teaspoon vegetable oil

shallot and vermouth sauce

1 large shallot, minced (about 4 tablespoons)
¾ cup canned low-sodium chicken broth
½ cup dry vermouth
2 sprigs fresh thyme
3 tablespoons cold unsalted butter, cut into 3 pieces
   Salt and ground black pepper

1. Dissolve salt in 2½ quarts cold tap water in large container or bowl; submerge chicken pieces in brine and refrigerate until fully seasoned, about 30 minutes. Rinse chicken pieces under running water and pat dry with paper towels. Season chicken with pepper.

2. Adjust oven rack to lowest position and heat oven to 450 degrees.

3. Heat oil in heavy-bottomed 12-inch ovenproof skillet

over medium-high heat until beginning to smoke, about 3 minutes; swirl skillet to coat evenly with oil. Brown chicken pieces skin-side down until deep golden, about 5 minutes; turn chicken pieces, and brown until golden on second side, about 4 minutes longer. Turn chicken skin-side down and place skillet in oven. Roast until juices run clear when chicken is cut with paring knife, or thickest part of breast registers about 160 degrees on instant-read thermometer and thickest part of thighs and drumsticks registers about 175 degrees, about 10 minutes longer. Using potholder or oven mitt to protect hands from hot skillet handle, remove skillet from oven. Transfer chicken skin-side up to platter,

and let rest while making sauce. (If not making sauce, let chicken rest 5 minutes before serving.)

4. Still using potholder or oven mitt, pour off most of fat from skillet, add shallots, then set skillet over medium-high heat; cook, stirring frequently, until shallots are softened, about 1½ minutes. Add chicken broth, vermouth, and thyme; increase heat to high and simmer rapidly, scraping skillet bottom with wooden spoon to loosen browned bits. Simmer until slightly thickened and reduced to about ⅔ cup, about 6 minutes. Pour accumulated chicken juices into skillet, discard thyme, and whisk in butter one piece at a time. Season sauce to taste with salt and pepper. Return chicken pieces skin-side up to skillet; simmer to heat through, about 1 minute. Serve immediately.

VARIATIONS

PAN-ROASTED CHICKEN WITH SHERRY-ROSEMARY SAUCE

Follow recipe for Pan-Roasted Chicken with Shallot and Vermouth Sauce, substituting dry sherry for vermouth and 2 sprigs fresh rosemary for thyme.

PAN-ROASTED CHICKEN WITH COGNAC-MUSTARD SAUCE

Follow recipe for Pan-Roasted Chicken with Shallot and Vermouth Sauce, substituting ¼ cup each white wine and Cognac or brandy for vermouth and 1 tablespoon Dijon mustard for an equal amount of butter.

SCIENCE DESK: Is the Pan Hot Yet?

MOST HOME COOKS DO NOT PROPERLY PREHEAT THEIR skillets, which results in a lack of both crust and flavor development. This may be due in part to the advice of high-quality cookware manufacturers, who often suggest preheating a pan with a film of oil over low heat for only one to two minutes. Overheating, they warn, can cause discoloration. We followed their recommendations and were appalled at the sorry state of the food: pale, crustless, and with feeble browning. In our opinion, richly browned foods are worth risking discoloration, which, by the way, is easily removed with a little elbow grease.

How do you know when your skillet is properly preheated? We began with the common cookbook advice of sprinkling water in the preheated pan. If the droplets immediately bead up and dance on the skillet's surface, the pan is hot enough. Not exactly. Beading and dancing occur even when the skillet is too cool. We held outstretched palms a few inches above the surface of the skillet, but this proved to be a very inaccurate measure. We put bread crumbs, bread slices, sugar, popcorn kernels, rice, salt, ice cubes, and measured amounts of water into cold skillets, turned on the heat, and waited for some sort of sign. Bread crumbs and slices charred and smoked much too soon. Sugar melted, began to caramelize, and made a mess. Popcorn and rice browned unevenly and erratically after a few minutes, before the skillet was hot enough. Salt was lame. It showed no visible changes, even after the skillet was hotter than we cared for. Heated until every trace of water evaporated, ice cubes and measured amounts of water showed some promise, but given that boiling points vary with elevation, we thought the method a bit unreliable.

It was oil—smoking oil, to be exact—that held the answer. Measured into a cold skillet and heated for a few minutes, oil gives off wisps of smoke that serve as a visual alarm that the skillet is hot and ready. We tested our theory with beef steaks, chicken (skin-on), fish fillets, and steaks. In each case, oil that had just begun to smoke was a good indicator that the skillet was hot enough to produce well-crusted, good-tasting, and good-looking food without overcooking.

That said, not every kind of oil is suitable for high-heat browning and searing. Unrefined oils, such as extra-virgin olive oil, should not be used because their smoke points are low. Refined oils like vegetable, canola, corn, and peanut (be careful of the unrefined peanut oil carried in some grocery stores) work well because their smoke points are high (above

400 degrees). A word to the wise: Using just-smoking oil as a heat indicator is good only for browning and searing in very little oil, no more than a couple tablespoons. Smoking oil is simply too hot for pan-frying and deep-frying.

A few final words on browning and searing in a white-hot skillet. To minimize splattering and maximize browning, wick away excess moisture on the surface of the food with paper towels. For more serious splatter containment, use a splatter screen. And be prepared to turn on your exhaust fan or crack open a window. The light smoke that will waft from the skillet will dissipate more quickly with some ventilation.

Our favorite graters are modeled after a wood rasp, and they quickly turn a hunk of Parmesan into a fluffy mountain of cheese.

PASTA *classics*

Even cooks who don't know much about Italian cooking have probably heard of puttanesca and Bolognese. These two classic Italian pasta sauces appear in countless menus and nearly every Italian cookbook. Many gourmet markets sell their own "homemade" renditions.

But as with most ethnic dishes that obtain a certain level of popularity, these Italian sauces have been bastardized. Puttanesca should be a lively, fresh-tasting tomato sauce with garlic, anchovies, capers, and hot red pepper flakes. All too often the sauce is thick and gloppy, and the ingredients have dissolved into a stew-like mess.

Bolognese, the classic meat sauce from the city of Bologna in central Italy, is subjected to even worse treatment. Real Bolognese is all about the meat, with tomatoes, dairy, and wine adding supporting flavor but definitely kept in the background. Many American versions of this sauce are nearly all tomato with tiny flecks of meat.

The test kitchen has restored these classics to their full glory. Neither recipe is complicated, but the difference between the real thing and the offering at your local Italian restaurant might surprise you.

PASTA WITH PUTTANESCA SAUCE

WHAT WE WANTED: A balanced, lively tomato sauce in which each ingredient—the garlic, anchovies, olives, and capers—remains distinct.

Said to have been created by Neapolitan ladies of the night, puttanesca is a pasta sauce with attitude. Most home cooks buy this lusty sauce by the jar or know it as restaurant fare: a slow-cooked tomato sauce with garlic, hot red pepper flakes, anchovies, capers, and black olives tossed with spaghetti. But those of us who have once sampled the real thing are often disappointed with these efforts. Chock-full of high-impact ingredients, puttanesca is often overpowered by one flavor; it is too fishy, too garlicky, too briny, or just plain salty and acidic. It can also be unduly heavy and stew-like or dull and monochromatic. We were searching for a simple, satisfying sauce with aggressive but well-balanced flavors.

We started our testing by tossing all of the ingredients—minced garlic, minced olives, whole capers, minced anchovies, and hot red pepper flakes—into a base of canned tomatoes and simmering the lot for 25 minutes. The result was a dull sauce with undeveloped flavors. Our first revision began with sautéing the garlic in olive oil to deepen the garlic flavor. We soon found out that the garlic should not be allowed to brown; when it did, the sauce quickly became bitter. To rectify the problem, we mixed a bit of water with the garlic before it went into the pan. The water slowed the cooking, making the garlic less likely to brown and burn.

Deciding how to prepare and cook the olives was the next task. After several tests, we decided to toss coarsely chopped olives into the sauce at the very last minute, allowing the residual heat of the tomatoes to warm them. This preserved their flavor, their texture, and their independence. As for which olives worked best, we started with Neapolitan gaeta olives—small, black, earthy, and herbaceous. For good measure, we also tested alfonso, kalamata, and canned black olives in place of the gaetas. Tasters unanimously rejected the "insipid," "springy" canned olives but liked both the alfonso and kalamata olives for their "soft," "melting" qualities.

Capers were the least of our worries. Of all the ingredients, they were the most resilient, well able to retain their shape, texture, and flavor. Rinsing them thoroughly and adding them at the end of cooking along with the olives proved best.

Up to this point, the anchovies in the sauce, added along with the tomatoes to simmer, tasted flat and salty and gave the sauce a funky, fishy taste. We tried mashing whole fillets into the oil with a fork and found the process tedious and ineffective; stray chunks were left behind and inevitably ended up offending anchovy-sensitive tasters. What worked best was mincing the anchovies to a fine paste and then

adding them to the oil in the pan with the garlic. In two or three minutes, the anchovies melted into the oil on their own (no fork necessary), and their characteristically full, rich flavor blossomed.

Blooming an ingredient in oil is a technique often used to develop flavor. Because it worked so well with the garlic and anchovies, we decided to try it with the hot red pepper flakes instead of simmering them with the tomatoes, as we had in the original test. As they cooked with the garlic and anchovies, their flavor permeated the oil.

As for the tomatoes, we tested crushed tomatoes, canned whole tomatoes (chopped by hand), canned diced tomatoes, and fresh. The canned diced tomatoes were the winner. They had a sweet flavor and clung nicely to the pasta. But we still weren't sure whether we should use the diced tomatoes along with their juices or not. Testing the two options head to head made the choice easy. When cooked with tomatoes and their juices, the sauce took 25 minutes to cook down to the right consistency; when cooked with the diced tomatoes alone, it reached the optimum consistency in a mere eight minutes. Tasters were also unanimously in favor of the lightly cooked sauce, finding its flavor fresh and "less stewed" as well as "sweet." They also liked the "meaty texture" and firm bite of the tomatoes in this version of the sauce.

One last discovery improved the sauce still further. In the test kitchen, we are in the habit of reserving a little pasta cooking water to toss with the finished pasta to keep the sauce from drying out. On a whim, we decided to substitute some of the drained tomato juice for the water, which gave the sauce a brighter, livelier flavor.

WHAT WE LEARNED: **For a sauce with the best tomato flavor and a slightly clingy consistency, use canned diced tomatoes, and hold the cooking time to a minimum to keep the flavor fresh. Cook the garlic, anchovies, and hot red pepper flakes before adding the tomatoes so their flavors bloom. Add the olives and capers when the sauce is done to keep them intact.**

SPAGHETTI PUTTANESCA serves 4

The pasta and sauce cook in just about the same amount of time. If you like the fruitiness of extra-virgin olive oil, toss 1 tablespoon into the sauced pasta before serving.

- 3 medium cloves garlic, minced to paste or pressed through garlic press (about 1 tablespoon)
  Salt
- 1 pound spaghetti
- 2 tablespoons olive oil
- 1 teaspoon hot red pepper flakes
- 4 teaspoons minced anchovies (about 8 fillets)
- 1 (28-ounce) can diced tomatoes, drained, ½ cup juice reserved
- 3 tablespoons capers, rinsed
- ½ cup black olives (such as gaeta, alfonso, or kalamata), pitted and chopped coarse
- ¼ cup minced fresh parsley leaves

1. Bring 4 quarts water to rolling boil in large pot. Meanwhile, mix garlic with 1 tablespoon water in small bowl; set aside. When water is boiling, add 1 tablespoon salt and pasta; stir to separate noodles. Immediately heat oil,

GETTING IT RIGHT: Chopping Olives

Minced olives (left) produced a muddy sauce and purple spaghetti. Coarsely chopped olives (right) won't color the pasta and taste better.

garlic mixture, hot red pepper flakes, and anchovies in large sauté pan or skillet over medium heat. Cook, stirring frequently, until garlic is fragrant but not browned, 2 to 3 minutes. Stir in tomatoes and simmer until slightly thickened, about 8 minutes.

2. Cook pasta until al dente. Drain, then return pasta to pot. Add ¼ cup reserved tomato juice and toss to combine.

3. Stir capers, olives, and parsley into sauce. Pour sauce over pasta and toss to combine, adding more tomato juice to moisten if necessary. Adjust seasonings with salt to taste and serve immediately.

TASTING LAB: Anchovies

TO SOME, ANCHOVIES ARE THOSE "STINKY LITTLE FISH" that adorn (or despoil) the top of a pizza. But to us, those little fish are a pantry mainstay, contributing flavor to many sauces, salads, and sautés. But are all anchovies the same? A glance at the supermarket aisle revealed there were plenty of choices, and we set out to find the best one.

All preserved anchovies—small silver-skinned fish usually caught in warm Mediterranean waters—have been cured in salt, but they come to the market in two forms, packed in olive oil (we've all seen those flat, little tins), and packed in salt. Of the two kinds, the salt-packed variety are the least processed, having only their heads and some entrails removed, leaving the filleting and rinsing to the home cook. Oil-packed anchovies have been filleted at the factory and are ready-to-use. We purchased four brands of oil-packed anchovies along with one brand of salt-packed. Also included in the tasting was an anchovy paste sold in a tube.

We tasted the anchovies in our Caesar salad dressing and straight up and found ourselves liking best an expensive oil-packed brand from Spain. Tasters commented on the good flavor and firm texture of Ortiz oil-packed anchovies, which cost about $6 for a 3-ounce jar. The salt-packed

anchovies were a very close second, but they can be hard to find. The remaining brands of oil-packed anchovies did not fare as well, and tasters hated the anchovy paste. Although food snobs may insist that salt-packed anchovies are the only way to go, our tasters found that the right oil-packed anchovies can be just as good.

BEST ANCHOVIES

Ortiz oil-packed anchovies from Spain won our tasting of six leading brands. Tasters liked the salty and pleasantly fishy flavor as well as the firm, "meaty" texture of this expensive brand. See www.cooksillustrated.com for up-to-date prices and mail-order sources.

TASTING LAB: Dried Pasta

IN THE NOT-SO-DISTANT PAST, AMERICAN PASTA HAD A poor reputation, and rightly so. It cooked up gummy and starchy, and experts usually touted the superiority of Italian brands. We wondered if this was still the case. To find out, we tasted eight leading brands of spaghetti—four American and four Italian. Each brand was cooked in salted water until we judged the pasta to be al dente, then drained and served unadorned so we could really taste the pasta.

The results of the tasting—which was done in two rounds, one with our usual staff of test cooks and editors and another with a panel of Italian cookbook authors and chefs—were shocking. In both cases, American brands took two of the three top spots, while two Italian brands landed

Rating Dried Pastas

WE TASTED EIGHT LEADING BRANDS OF SPAGHETTI STRAIGHT FROM THE POT, UNSEASONED, UNSAUCED, AND AL DENTE. Tasters evaluated the pastas on both flavor and texture. All brands are available in supermarkets or gourmet stores.

HIGHLY RECOMMENDED

1. Ronzoni Spaghetti **$.99 for 16 ounces**

Won tasters over with its firm "rockin'" texture and its "nutty," "buttery," "classic" flavor. "Tastes most like pure pasta," said one taster.

RECOMMENDED

2. DeCecco Spaghetti **$1.79 for 16 ounces**

"Chewy" came to mind for more than a couple of tasters when sampling this pasta. Some tasters detected a distinctive wheat flavor, though others found it a bit "bland."

RECOMMENDED

3. Mueller's Spaghetti **$.89 for 16 ounces**

Several tasters remarked on this pasta's "clean" and "wheaty" flavor. Most agreed that its texture was firm, but some found it "a little rubbery."

RECOMMENDED

4. Barilla Spaghetti **$.99 for 16 ounces**

Several tasters complained about the lack of chew in this pasta, calling it "soft" and "yielding." A few complained about bland flavor, but others noted a "wheaty" and "toasted" flavor.

NOT RECOMMENDED

5. Rienzi Spaghetti **$.75 for 16 ounces**

While a few tasters picked up on a favorable egg flavor, most characterized this pasta as "bland." "Gummy" was another word that kept popping up.

NOT RECOMMENDED

6. 365 Brand Whole Foods Market Spaghetti **$.79 for 16 ounces**

Tasters faulted this pasta for having too much flavor, with complaints such as "strong egg flavor," "smoky flavor," and "a little bitter—like burnt toast." Some described its texture as thick and firm, but others found it grainy and rubbery.

NOT RECOMMENDED

7. Martelli Spaghetti **$3.00 for 17.5 ounces**

This pasta was repeatedly called "bland," and a few tasters noted an artificial flavor. The texture didn't win many fans either, with tasters labeling it "mealy," "gritty," "starchy," and "mushy."

NOT RECOMMENDED

8. Delverde Spaghetti **$.79 for 16 ounces**

Several tasters described this pasta as having a "raw" and "artificial" flavor. Comments on texture ranged from "not cooked" to "spongy" and "gummy."

at the bottom. It seems that American companies have mastered the art of making pasta.

American-made Ronzoni was the top finisher, with tasters praising its "nutty, buttery" flavor and superb texture. Mueller's, another American brand, took third place.

DeCecco was the highest-scoring Italian brand, finishing second in the tasting. It cooked up "very al dente" (with a good bite) and was almost chewy. Other Italian brands did not fare quite so well. Martelli, an artisanal pasta that costs three times as much as the winner, finished in next-to-last place, with comments like "gritty" and "mushy" predominating on tasters' score sheets. Another Italian brand, Delverde, sank to the bottom of the ratings.

Our conclusion: Save your money and don't bother with most imported pasta—American brands are just fine. If you want to serve Italian pasta in your home, stick with DeCecco.

EQUIPMENT CORNER: Sauté Pans

WITH SOME KITCHEN EQUIPMENT, THE DIFFERENCE between pricey and inexpensive models just isn't that big a deal—either will get the job done. But sauté pans are another story, primarily because of the nature of sautéing. When you sauté, you cook food quickly, with minimal fat, in a very hot pan. As it cooks, the food develops a nice, dark, flavorful crust, which is the glory of sautéing.

But there is a thin line between crusty and burnt—and it's a line that you definitely don't want to cross. To sauté successfully, you need a pan that distributes heat evenly, without hot spots that can cause food to scorch or burn outright. Additional factors to consider include browning performance, ovenworthiness (can the pan be used in the oven?), heft (does it feel substantial without being too heavy?), and construction (does it feel solid, with the handles attached firmly?). A number of pans on the market claim to fit the bill, but, at well over $100, many of them are also quite expensive. We opened our wallet and chose eight popular models in the 3-quart size, then headed off to the test kitchen for a two-week sauté-a-thon.

The popularity of nonstick pans compelled us to consider several in our tests. By and large, the nonstick pans performed on a par with the other pans in our tests. Yet for all of their virtues, the nonsticks had, in our opinion at least, what amounted to a serious flaw: They resist the development of a fond, the sticky, brown, caramelized film and bits that form on the pan bottom as the food cooks. When released from the pan bottom with the addition of liquid, which is then boiled to dissolve those bits (in a process called deglazing), the fond provides the savory underpinnings of sauces, stews, and braises. Fond develops because the drippings from the food stick to the pan—no sticking, no fond. As a result, when we used nonstick pans to make the sauce for a braised chicken dish, the sauce looked light and tasted weak. We advise you to stick with a traditional cooking surface.

Differences in the pans' sautéing and browning performance were not as significant as we had imagined they would be. All of the pans in our price range were thick enough to allow good conduction with no significant hot spots that could cause food to burn. Beyond that, each metal has a thermoconductivity coefficient; this refers to the amount of heat it can transfer over a centimeter of length in one second. Honors for best conductivity go to copper, at 0.94, and pure aluminum, at 0.53. At the other end of the spectrum is cast iron, which has a thermoconductivity coefficient of 0.12. This is the reason our enamel-covered cast-iron Le Creuset pan was so slow to heat, especially when compared with the copper Mauviel.

To our surprise, though, we discovered that the superconductivity of copper was not for us, especially in light of its high price. In our view, pans that sauté reliably at a medium pace—meaning that they hedge the threat of burning by heating neither too hot nor too fast—are preferred. In our tests, the copper did its work a bit too fast. It cooled quickly when we turned the flame down, but we would just as soon avoid the need to adjust the heat in the first place.

While variations in the sautéing and browning performance of the pans turned out to be relatively undramatic,

Rating Sauté Pans

WE EVALUATED EIGHT SAUTÉ PANS, EACH SOLD INDIVIDUALLY, WITH A CAPACITY OF 3 QUARTS (OR AS CLOSE to it as we could find in that manufacturer's line), and rated them according to a battery of kitchen tests. The pans are listed in order of preference. See www.cooksillustrated.com for up-to-date prices and mail-order sources for top-rated products.

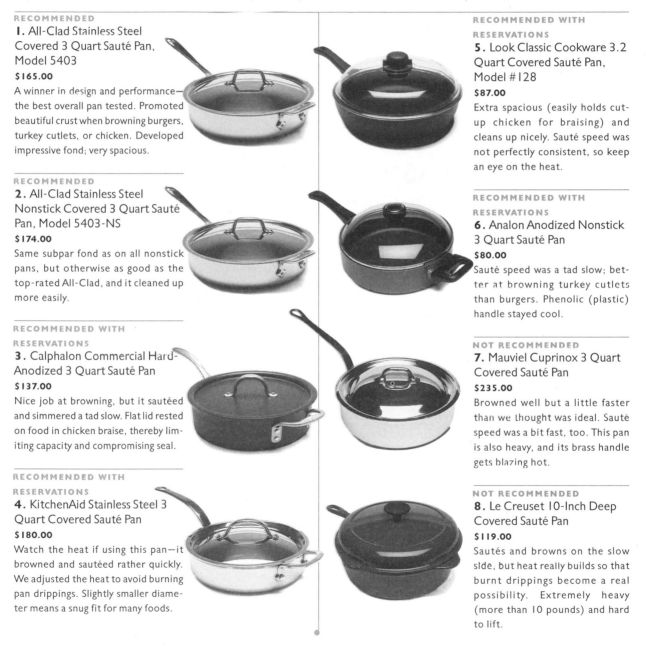

RECOMMENDED

1. All-Clad Stainless Steel Covered 3 Quart Sauté Pan, Model 5403

$165.00

A winner in design and performance—the best overall pan tested. Promoted beautiful crust when browning burgers, turkey cutlets, or chicken. Developed impressive fond; very spacious.

RECOMMENDED

2. All-Clad Stainless Steel Nonstick Covered 3 Quart Sauté Pan, Model 5403-NS

$174.00

Same subpar fond as on all nonstick pans, but otherwise as good as the top-rated All-Clad, and it cleaned up more easily.

RECOMMENDED WITH RESERVATIONS

3. Calphalon Commercial Hard-Anodized 3 Quart Sauté Pan

$137.00

Nice job at browning, but it sautéed and simmered a tad slow. Flat lid rested on food in chicken braise, thereby limiting capacity and compromising seal.

RECOMMENDED WITH RESERVATIONS

4. KitchenAid Stainless Steel 3 Quart Covered Sauté Pan

$180.00

Watch the heat if using this pan—it browned and sautéed rather quickly. We adjusted the heat to avoid burning pan drippings. Slightly smaller diameter means a snug fit for many foods.

RECOMMENDED WITH RESERVATIONS

5. Look Classic Cookware 3.2 Quart Covered Sauté Pan, Model #128

$87.00

Extra spacious (easily holds cut-up chicken for braising) and cleans up nicely. Sauté speed was not perfectly consistent, so keep an eye on the heat.

RECOMMENDED WITH RESERVATIONS

6. Analon Anodized Nonstick 3 Quart Sauté Pan

$80.00

Sauté speed was a tad slow; better at browning turkey cutlets than burgers. Phenolic (plastic) handle stayed cool.

NOT RECOMMENDED

7. Mauviel Cuprinox 3 Quart Covered Sauté Pan

$235.00

Browned well but a little faster than we thought was ideal. Sauté speed was a bit fast, too. This pan is also heavy, and its brass handle gets blazing hot.

NOT RECOMMENDED

8. Le Creuset 10-Inch Deep Covered Sauté Pan

$119.00

Sautés and browns on the slow side, but heat really builds so that burnt drippings become a real possibility. Extremely heavy (more than 10 pounds) and hard to lift.

certain aspects of pan design made a much bigger difference to us than we had anticipated. For example, each pan was rated at or very close to 3 quarts, but the pan diameters varied by more than an inch, from about 10 inches for the KitchenAid, Analon, and Mauviel to about 11 inches for the Look and All-Clad pans. A little larger diameter was a big advantage for the cook. For instance, the 11-inch All-Clad accommodated the chicken in our braised chicken test more comfortably than the smaller KitchenAid, Analon, and Mauviel, which were snug. This meant it was easier to slide tongs or a spatula into the All-Clad to move the chicken pieces without accidentally gouging or damaging them or splashing the sauce. It also meant more favorable conditions for sautéing turkey cutlets, which are wide and flat and need space around them to brown properly.

Handles were another important difference. If we're removing a dish from the oven, we always remember to don oven mitts, but we are not always so careful before grabbing the handle of a hot pan on the stove. If that handle is hot, we're in for a rude surprise. Hot handles turned out to be a problem with only two of the pans, the Le Creuset and the Mauviel copper. The stainless-steel handles of the All-Clad and KitchenAid pans and the cast-steel handle of the Calphalon stayed cool (though the KitchenAid tended to heat near the base), as did the phenolic (heat-resistant plastic) handles of the Look and Analon pans. Incidentally, the handles on all of the pans were ovenworthy, though up to only 350 degrees for the Analon and 500 degrees for the Look because of the phenolic material. All of the pans except for the Look and Mauviel have a helper handle, usually consisting of a small loop opposite the long handle so that the cook can use two hands to lift the pan when desired. We find the helper handle especially useful when we're hoisting full pans in and out of the oven.

What, at the conclusion of testing, do we recommend? Though none of these pans come cheap, the notoriously expensive copper (and our pan was not even the most expensive copper on the market) was not worth the extra money for the kind of cooking we do. Likewise, we did not like the Le Creuset pan, which was too slow to heat up and heavy to carry. For our money, the All-Clad pan, with a traditional cooking surface, provided the best combination of great design, ample proportions, and reliable performance. The Calphalon, KitchenAid, Analon, and Look pans all performed well, too, and some cost a few dollars less, but each had a design flaw that caused it to fall behind the All-Clad.

SCIENCE DESK: What Makes Some Pasta So Sticky?

IN REPEATED TESTS, WE'VE FOUND THAT YOU MUST COOK pasta in abundant water (4 quarts for 1 pound of pasta) to keep the strands from sticking together. When cooked in less water, the strands stick together, but why?

As the pasta cooks, various starches dissolve into the water. If there's plenty of water in the pot, the starches don't cause a problem. If there's not much water in the pot, however, the starches find each other—and the pasta—and form a sticky, starchy tangle. Keeping the water at a strong boil—the bubbles in the water move the pasta around—also helps to keep the dissolved starches and pasta from sticking together.

PASTA WITH BOLOGNESE SAUCE

WHAT WE WANTED: A complex sauce for pasta, with a good balance of flavors. The meat should be first and foremost, but sweet, salty, and acidic flavors should be present in the background.

Scores of delicious meat-based sauces are made in Italy and elsewhere, but slow-simmering Bolognese (it comes from the city of Bologna, hence the name) is perhaps the best. Unlike meat sauces in which tomatoes dominate (think jars of spaghetti sauce with flecks of meat in a sea of tomato puree), Bolognese sauce is about the meat, with the tomatoes in a supporting role. Bolognese also differs from many tomato-based meat sauces in that it contains dairy—butter, milk, and/or cream. The dairy gives the meat an especially sweet, appealing flavor.

Bolognese sauce is not hard to prepare (the hands-on work is less than 30 minutes), but it does require hours of slow simmering. The result must be worth the time. All Bolognese recipes can be broken down into three steps. First, vegetables are sautéed in fat. Ground meat is then browned in the pan. The final step is the addition of liquids and slow simmering over very low heat.

After an initial round of testing in which we made five styles of Bolognese, we had a recipe we liked pretty well. We preferred using only onions, carrots, and celery as the vegetables, and we liked them sautéed in butter rather than oil. We also discovered that a combination of ground beef, veal, and pork made this sauce especially complex and rich-tasting. The veal adds finesse and delicacy to the sauce, while the pork makes it sweet. Settling on the liquid element of the recipe proved more difficult.

The secret to a great Bolognese sauce is the sequential reduction of various liquids over the sautéed meat and vegetables. The idea is to build flavor and tenderize the meat, which toughens during the browning phase. Many recipes insist on a particular order for adding these liquids. The most common liquid choices we uncovered in our research were milk, cream, stock, wine (both red and white), and tomatoes (fresh, canned whole, crushed, or paste). We ended up testing numerous combinations to find the perfect balance.

Liquids are treated in two ways. In the earlier part of the cooking process, liquids are added to the pan and simmered briskly until fully evaporated, the point being to impart flavor rather than to cook the meat and vegetables. Wine is always treated this way; if the wine is not evaporated, the sauce will be too alcoholic. Milk and cream are often but not always treated this way. Later, either stock and/or tomatoes are added in greater quantity and allowed to cook off very slowly. These liquids add flavor, to be sure, but they also serve as the cooking medium for the sauce during the slow simmering phase.

We tested pouring wine over the browned meat first, followed by milk. We also tried them in the opposite order—milk, then wine. We found that the meat cooked in milk first was softer and sweeter. As the bits of meat cook, they develop a hard crust that makes it more difficult for them to absorb liquid. Adding the milk first, when the meat is just barely cooked, works better. The milk penetrates more easily, tenderizing the meat and making it especially sweet. We tried using cream instead of milk but felt that the sauce was too rich. Some recipes add a bit of cream at the end of cooking to finish the sauce, but we found even this addition overpowering. Milk provides just enough dairy flavor to complement the meat flavor. Wine, then, became the second liquid. While we liked both white and red, white wine was a bit more delicate and is our choice for the basic recipe.

Then we moved on to the final element in most recipes, the cooking liquid. We did not like any of the recipes we tested with stock. As for tomato paste, we felt that it had little to offer; with none of the bright acidity of canned whole tomatoes and no fresh tomato flavor, it produced a dull sauce.

We tried tomatoes three more ways—fresh, canned diced, and canned crushed. Fresh tomatoes did nothing for the sauce and were a lot of work, as we found it necessary to peel them. (If not peeled, the skins would separate during the long cooking process and mar the texture of the sauce.) Crushed tomatoes were fine, but they did not taste as good as the canned whole tomatoes that we chopped. Diced tomatoes have an additional benefit—the packing juice. Because Bolognese sauce simmers for quite a while, it's nice to have all that juice to keep the pot from scorching.

Our recipe was finally taking shape, with all the ingredients in place. But we still wanted to know if it was necessary to cook Bolognese sauce over low heat and, if so, how long the sauce must simmer. When we tried to hurry the process by cooking over medium heat to evaporate the tomato juice more quickly, the meat became too firm and the flavors failed to meld. Low simmering over the lowest possible heat—a few bubbles may rise to the surface of the sauce one at a time, but it should not be simmering all over—is the only method that allows enough time for flavor to develop and for the meat to become tender.

As for the timing, we found that the sauce was too soupy after two hours on low heat, and the meat was still pretty firm. At three hours, the meat was much softer, with a melt-in-the-mouth consistency. The sauce was dense and smooth at this point. We tried simmering the sauce for four hours but found no benefit. In fact, some batches cooked this long overreduced and scorched a bit.

WHAT WE LEARNED: For the most tender texture, cook the meat just until it loses its pink color and don't let it brown. For the best flavor, keep the vegetables to a minimum, add the milk before the wine, and use diced canned tomatoes. Finally, there are no shortcuts to great Bolognese— the sauce must simmer at the lowest possible heat for about three hours.

FETTUCCINE WITH BOLOGNESE SAUCE
serves 4

Don't drain the pasta of its cooking water too meticulously when using this sauce; a little water left clinging to the noodles will help distribute the very thick sauce evenly over the noodles, as will the addition of 2 tablespoons of butter along with the sauce. If doubling this recipe, increase the simmering times for the milk and the wine to 30 minutes each, and increase the simmering time once the tomatoes are added to 4 hours.

5 tablespoons unsalted butter
2 tablespoons minced onion
2 tablespoons minced carrot
2 tablespoons minced celery
¾ pound meatloaf mix or ¼ pound each ground beef chuck, ground veal, and ground pork
   Salt
1 cup whole milk
1 cup dry white wine
1 (28-ounce) can diced tomatoes with their juice
1 pound fresh or dried fettuccine
   Freshly grated Parmesan cheese

1. Heat 3 tablespoons butter in large, heavy-bottomed Dutch oven over medium heat. Add onion, carrot, and celery and sauté until softened but not browned, about 6 minutes. Add ground meat and ½ teaspoon salt; crumble meat into tiny pieces with edge of wooden spoon. Cook, continuing to crumble meat, just until it loses its raw color but has not yet browned, about 3 minutes.

2. Add milk and bring to a simmer; continue to simmer until milk evaporates and only clear fat remains, 10 to 15 minutes. Add wine and bring to a simmer; continue to simmer until wine evaporates, 10 to 15 minutes longer. Add tomatoes and their juice and bring to a simmer. Reduce heat to low so that sauce continues to simmer just barely, with occasional bubble or two at surface, until liquid has evaporated, about 3 hours (if lowest burner setting is too high to allow very low simmer, use flame tamer—see right). Adjust seasonings with salt to taste. Keep sauce warm. (The sauce can be refrigerated in an airtight container for several days or frozen for several months. Warm over low heat before serving.)

3. Bring 4 quarts water to rolling boil in large pot. Add 1 tablespoon salt and pasta. Cook until al dente. Drain pasta, leaving some water dripping from noodles. Toss with sauce and remaining 2 tablespoons butter. Distribute among individual bowls and serve immediately, passing Parmesan cheese separately.

VARIATIONS

FETTUCCINE WITH BEEF BOLOGNESE SAUCE

There is something very appealing about the simplicity of an all-beef sauce. While it may lack some of the finesse and sweetness of the master recipe, its pure beef flavor is uniquely satisfying.

Follow recipe for Fettuccine with Bolognese Sauce, substituting ¾ pound ground beef chuck for meatloaf mix.

FETTUCCINE WITH BEEF, PANCETTA, AND RED WINE BOLOGNESE SAUCE

All ground beef (rather than meatloaf mix) works best with the pancetta in this sauce. If you can't find pancetta, use prosciutto, but don't use American bacon, which is smoked and will overwhelm the beef. We found that red wine stands up to the more robust flavors in this sauce better than white wine.

Follow recipe for Fettuccine with Bolognese Sauce, adding 2 ounces minced pancetta to butter along with vegetables, substituting ¾ pound ground beef chuck for meatloaf mix, and substituting an equal amount of red wine for white wine.

TECHNIQUE: Improvised Flame Tamer

A flame tamer (or heat diffuser) is a metal disk that can be fitted over an electric or a gas burner to reduce the heat output. This device is especially useful when trying to keep a pot at the barest simmer. If you don't own a flame tamer (it costs less than $10 and is stocked at most kitchenware stores), you can improvise with tools you have on hand, as shown below. Another option (which might work on some gas stoves) is to stack two burner grates on top of each other.

A. A foil ring elevates the pot slightly above the flame or electric coil, allowing you to keep a pot of Bolognese sauce at the merest simmer. To make one, take a long sheet of heavy-duty aluminum foil and shape it into a 1-inch-thick ring that will fit on your burner. Make sure that the ring is of an even thickness so that a pot will rest flat on it.

B. A cast-iron skillet can absorb some of the heat from the burner and protect another pot from direct heat. Place the Dutch oven with the sauce inside a cast-iron skillet set on the burner.

PASTA quick and easy

Every cook needs quick pasta recipes in his or her repertoire. Pasta with garlic and oil is perhaps the most famous quick pasta dish. It starts with ingredients on hand—garlic, good olive oil, hot red pepper flakes—and turns them into something special, something uncommonly good. Of course, details make or break such a simple recipe. If the garlic is burned or the pasta sticks together, this dish is ruined. We've examined every aspect of this recipe in the test kitchen and finally perfected it.

Almost no one thinks of lasagna as quick or easy. Most recipes require a day's worth of labor. Although the results usually justify the effort, we wondered if there was another way. Starting with no-boil noodles (a convenience product that has become widely available in the past decade), we set out to make a great meat lasagna that could be in the oven in just 40 minutes. The surprise was that we succeeded and surpassed our expectations of just how good a "quick" lasagna could be.

Garlic ready for its starring role in pasta with garlic and olive oil.

PASTA WITH GARLIC AND OIL

WHAT WE WANTED: A flawless version of this quick classic, with bright, deep garlic flavor and no trace of bitterness or harshness.

Pasta with garlic and oil, or *aglio e olio* in Italian, looks guileless. It reads: "tangle of spaghetti flecked with parsley." But its subtext shouts garlic in every register, in every pitch. Twirled hot on a fork, this is among the most satisfying (and simple) dishes on earth. It has the texture of innocence and a tyrant's bite.

At first, we wondered why anyone would need a recipe for this dish. You take spaghetti or capellini, perfume it straight from its bath with high-quality olive oil and as much fresh garlic as decency allows, add a dusting of hot red pepper flakes, a little fistful of parsley, and there it is, pasta aglio e olio. And yet, and yet. Who hasn't ordered it in a restaurant to find its fresh scent tormented by burnt garlic or its noodles gripped in a starchy skein dripping with oil? Clearly, there was much to learn.

Diving into Italian cookbooks, we found general agreement on ingredients: all those mentioned above, along with a splash of hot pasta cooking water to keep the components in motion. Beyond the basics were regional variations that included a selection of fresh herbs, savory accents such as capers and anchovies, and bread crumbs. We first pursued the perfect garlic flavor, working down the list of possibilities from whole crushed cloves to grated raw garlic and using a pound of pasta for each test. We didn't care for sautéed whole or slivered garlic, whether ultimately removed from the dish or left in. In fact, no one cared for browned garlic at all—it was acrid and one-dimensional. Raw minced or grated garlic alone was zingy and metallic. We needed a third way.

We knew of a technique associated with Mexican cookery in which a large amount of minced garlic is sautéed slowly until it turns golden and mellow, thus producing a garlic flavor far more complex than does a simple sauté. We tried this with a full head of garlic (about ¼ cup minced) and were delighted to discover that the garlic, given low heat and constant stirring, became sticky and straw-colored, with a flavor that was butter-nutty and rich, adding a pronounced depth to the dish. But alone, this slow-sautéed garlic lacked brightness. We decided to combine the forces of cooked and raw by reserving a tablespoon of raw garlic, then stirring it into the fully cooked, candied garlic off the heat to release its perfume and spicy sharpness. The effect of this one-two garlic punch was outstanding, causing waves of flavor to resonate within the dish.

While conducting garlic experiments, it became obvious that other ingredient ratios—for example, the amount of oil—had to be established contiguously. Too much oil removed the silky mouthfeel we wanted for the pasta, but too little left the garlic mute. The amount of oil necessary varied with the diameter of the pasta as well—thicker strands, such as spaghetti, required more oil, even when the total weight of each batch of pasta was the same. In fact, the diameter of the pasta strands altered the behavior of the recipe to such a degree that we decided to work with just one type of pasta—spaghetti, which, unlike some thinner pastas, is available in every grocery store.

Olive oil contributes much of the freshness and verve to this dish; extra-virgin is a must. We settled on 6 tablespoons: 3 to sauté the garlic, 3 tossed into the pasta at the end for flavor.

Parmesan cheese is not conventional in this dish, but, heathens that we are, we liked the nutty depth of flavor it added. Resist, by all means, an urge to pour the contents of a little green cylinder on this dish—it will be forever ruined. A very modest sprinkle of coarsely grated Parmigiano-Reggiano, on the other hand, improves it. (Be sure to do your grating on the larger holes of a box grater; this will discourage the cheese from getting into a sticking contest with the pasta.)

We liked parsley for its freshness but didn't want it slipping around on the noodles like mower clippings; 3 tablespoons did the trick. Gentle seasoning improvements were effected with a touch of lemon juice and sea salt flakes—the bright citrus notes and wee crunch made a big difference.

Finally, sequence and timing matter greatly with this dish. Perhaps to a larger degree than other pastas, pasta aglio e olio suffers from being dumped into cold serving bowls or waiting around for diners to make their way to the table. The most familiar pasta tool, a set of tongs, cannot be recommended for tossing; bits of garlic get stuck in its craw, right where you don't want them. We recommend that you toss the hot strands with a heatproof spatula and use tongs only to transfer the pasta to bowls.

WHAT WE LEARNED: Cook most of the garlic over low heat until sticky and straw-colored for a mellow flavor, but add some raw garlic at the end for a complementary bite. A splash of lemon juice and a sprinkle of Parmesan may not be traditional, but they add finesse to this simple recipe.

PASTA WITH GARLIC AND OIL serves 4 to 6

For a twist on pasta with garlic and oil, try sprinkling toasted fresh bread crumbs over individual bowls, but prepare them before proceeding with the pasta recipe. We like the crunch of Maldon sea salt flakes (see the Tasting Lab on page 27) for this dish, but ordinary table salt is fine as well. Given the large amount of garlic in this recipe, you may want to mince it in a food processor. A garlic press or chef's knife are other options.

Salt (see note)
1 pound spaghetti
6 tablespoons extra-virgin olive oil
¼ cup minced garlic (about 30 small, 20 medium, 10 large, or 5 extra-large cloves) from 1 or 2 heads
¾ teaspoon hot red pepper flakes
3 tablespoons chopped fresh parsley leaves
2 teaspoons juice from 1 lemon
½ cup coarsely grated Parmesan cheese (optional)

TECHNIQUE:
Reserving Pasta Water to Thin a Sauce

In that last flurry of activity before saucing the pasta, it's easy to forget to save a bit of the pasta cooking water. To make sure you always have some pasta cooking water when you need it, set up the colander in the sink and place a measuring cup inside the colander. The cup will nudge your memory to scoop out some cooking water before draining the pasta.

1. Adjust oven rack to lower-middle position, set large heat-proof serving bowl on rack, and heat oven to 200 degrees. Bring 4 quarts water to rolling boil in large pot. Add 1 tablespoon salt and pasta to boiling water, stir to separate noodles, and cook until al dente; reserve ⅓ cup pasta cooking water and drain pasta.

2. While water is heating, combine 3 tablespoons oil, 3 tablespoons garlic, and ½ teaspoon salt in heavy-bottomed nonstick 10-inch skillet. Cook over low heat, stirring constantly, until garlic foams and is sticky and straw-colored, 10 to 12 minutes. Off heat, add remaining tablespoon raw garlic along with hot red pepper flakes, parsley, lemon juice, and 2 tablespoons pasta cooking water and stir well to keep garlic from clumping.

3. Transfer drained pasta to warm serving bowl; add remaining 3 tablespoons olive oil and remaining reserved pasta

cooking water and toss to coat. Add garlic mixture and ¾ teaspoon salt; toss well to combine. Serve immediately, sprinkling individual bowls with portion of Parmesan cheese, if desired.

EQUIPMENT CORNER:
Pasta Paraphernalia

NOWADAYS, COOKWARE STORES AND CATALOGS CONTAIN a mind-boggling array of pots, utensils, and gadgets for cooking pasta. They fall into two basic categories—tools intended to make it easier to drain pasta and tools intended to make it easier to handle cooked pasta. We tested a wide variety; here are our results.

Pot with Perforated Insert: We have to confess that we don't understand the growing popularity of these pasta pots. We tried both the 8-quart Multi Pot, which goes for about $45, and the All-Clad 7-quart Pasta Pentola, which sells for a steep $269. To get 4 quarts of water (the amount we recommended for cooking 1 pound of pasta) into the Multi-Pot insert, you must fill the pan with 6 quarts of water. If you do that, we found, the pot is prone to boiling over. The All-Clad insert is an inch smaller in diameter than the 8½-inch-diameter pot and sits 6 inches below the pot edge. It has a deceptive 2½-inch lip that sits above the pot edge, making it look as if it has a much greater capacity. In fact, as it turns out, the insert to this expensive 7-quart pot has a capacity of just 3 quarts; add any more and the water begins to boil over.

Mesh Inserts: The inexpensive mesh inserts sold in cookware stores proved much too small to be useful. They also tend to bob out of the water, which creates a suction at the bottom of the pan. When the suction releases, gurgles of boiling water are hurled from the pan.

Pasta Pronto: This pan takes a different approach to the issue of straining pasta. It has a perforated strainer lid with handles that swivel to hold the lid in place. It seems clever, but the handles do not actually lock the lid in place—your

---

TECHNIQUE:
Combating Odoriferous Ingredients

After working with pungent ingredients such as garlic, onions, or fish, many cooks use a little lemon juice to wash away any lingering odors from their hands. But sometimes the smell is stronger than the citrus. When that's the case, try washing your hands with a couple of tablespoons of mouthwash. Any inexpensive brand is fine.

grip does. Once you tilt the pan to strain, the grip can become awkward. We lost our grip once, and the sink was not so clean that we dared try to salvage the fallen noodles.

Strainer Plate: Just as it is to the Pasta Pronto pan, the risk of losing your noodles is inherent to the strainer plate, a crescent-shaped perforated stainless-steel plate meant to fit around the pot edge for straining. We found that it fits comfortably only with pans of certain sizes—and, again, sureness of grip was essential.

Pasta Rakes: The tines on the wooden versions of these rakes, designed to retrieve pasta, tend to fall out over time. The tines on the stainless-steel variety are welded in. But why spend $24 on a single-purpose utensil when a $5 pair of tongs works just fine?

Pasta Tongs: Again, why pay $14 for a pasta-particular utensil when an inexpensive pair of all-purpose tongs will toss and serve just as well? In addition, the handle on this utensil is too short for fetching noodles out of hot cooking water. (See page 13 for information on basic kitchen tongs.)

Pasta Forks: This is the only pasta-specific tool that we found useful. It effectively combs through long, sticky strands of noodles to separate them. The wood variety tends to be clunky and is prone to splitting with use, but both the plastic and stainless-steel versions work fine.

BEST PASTA TOOL

We tried a variety of devices for cooking, straining, and stirring pasta. Only one, a plastic pasta fork, is worth owning. Avoid wood forks, which we found tend to crack over time.

STREAMLINED LASAGNA

WHAT WE WANTED: Traditional lasagna takes the better part of a day to make. We wanted a really good meat lasagna that could be on the table in just 90 minutes.

Most families have homemade lasagna once, maybe twice a year, on holidays (especially if you are Italian) or birthdays. Lasagna is not enjoyed more frequently because it takes the better part of a day to boil the noodles, slow-cook the sauce, prepare and layer the ingredients, and then finally bake it off. Although this traditional method does produce a superior dish, we were interested in an Americanized version, one that could be made in two hours or less from start to finish. We would have to sacrifice some of the rich flavors of a traditional recipe, but we were hoping to produce a lasagna good enough for a family gathering. A bland, watery casserole just wouldn't do.

We knew from the start that to expedite the lasagna-making process we would have to use no-boil lasagna noodles (see the Tasting Lab on page 131). For those unfamiliar with or wary of them, relax. After a few initial tests, we discovered that the secret of no-boil noodles is to leave your tomato sauce a little on the watery side. The noodles can then absorb liquid without drying out the dish overall. With all this in mind, we got to work on the other components of the lasagna.

Italian cooks build the sauce from the meaty browned bits left in the pan from the meatballs and Italian sausages they cook and later layer into the lasagna. By combining top-quality tomato products with a four-hour simmer, they make a rich, thick, and complex-tasting sauce. We were after the same depth of flavor, but, as time was of the essence, meatballs and a slow simmer were out of the question. We began by concentrating on different kinds of ground meat.

Working with a base of sautéed aromatics (onions and garlic), an all-beef sauce turned out to be one-dimensional and dull. Adding ground pork was an improvement and certainly more interesting. Although the combination of beef and sweet Italian sausage (removed from its casing and browned with the beef) was even better, tasters were still left wanting. Finally, we turned to meatloaf mix, a combination of equal parts ground beef, pork, and veal sold in one package at most supermarkets. The flavor of the sauce this trio produced was robust and sweet. The texture wasn't right, though; it was still too loose and taco-like. We wanted something richer, creamier, and more cohesive, so our thoughts turned to Bolognese (see page 119), the classic three-hour meat sauce enriched with dairy. Borrowing the notion of combining meat and dairy, we reduced a quarter cup of cream with the meat before adding the tomatoes. The ground meat soaked up the sweet cream, and the final product was rich and decadent. Even better, at this point we had been at the stove for only 12 minutes.

Because no-boil noodles rely primarily on the liquid in the sauce to rehydrate and soften, we had to get the moisture content just right. If the sauce was too thick, the noodles would be dry and crunchy; too loose and they would turn flaccid, limp, and lifeless. We started building the sauce with two 28-ounce cans of pureed tomatoes, but tasters found this sauce too heavy for the lasagna, overwhelming the other flavors. Two 28-ounce cans of diced tomatoes yielded too thin a sauce. We settled on one 28-ounce can of each. The combination of pureed and diced tomatoes yielded a luxurious sauce, with soft but substantial chunks of tomatoes. We added the tomatoes to the meat mixture, warmed it through (no reduction necessary), and in just 15 minutes on the stove the meat sauce was rich, creamy, ultra-meaty, and ready to go.

Most Americans like their lasagna to be cheesy. It was a given that we would sprinkle each layer with mozzarella cheese—the classic lasagna cheese—and, after a test of whole versus part-skim, we found that whole milk mozzarella

was the best for the job. It had a more intense flavor than its part-skim counterpart and nicer melting qualities, which are crucial to this dish. We also tested shredded, bagged mozzarella, but because it has a very low moisture content, it melted oddly and was somewhat dry, not to mention unappetizing. Shredding a 1-pound block of whole milk mozzarella on a box grater or in the food processor is the ticket.

Ricotta was the next cheese up for scrutiny. As it turned out, it made little difference whether we used whole milk or part-skim ricotta. They were characteristically creamy and rich, and tasters gave them both a thumbs-up.

For added sharpness, we tested the ricotta mixture with Parmesan and Pecorino Romano cheeses. Tasters unanimously rejected the Pecorino for giving the lasagna a "sheepy" and "gamey" flavor. Grated Parmesan added a nice little kick to the mild, milky ricotta. An egg helped to thicken and bind this mixture, and some chopped basil added

flavor and freshness. Tucked neatly between the layers of lasagna, this ricotta mixture was just what we were after.

With all of the components of the lasagna decided, it was time to concentrate on the layering procedure. Smearing the entire bottom of a 13 by 9-inch glass dish with some of the sauce was the starting point. Next came the first layer of no-boil noodles, which we topped with ricotta, then mozzarella, and, finally, more meat sauce. We built two more layers using this same process. For the fourth and final layer, we covered the pasta with the remaining meat sauce and remaining mozzarella and then sprinkled the top with grated Parmesan.

In our tests, we found that covering the lasagna with foil from the outset of baking prevented the loss of moisture and helped soften the noodles properly. Removing the foil for the last 25 minutes of baking ensured that the top layer of cheese turned golden brown. An oven temperature of 375 degrees proved ideal. By the time the top was browned, the noodles had softened.

We found that lasagna made with no-boil noodles takes a little longer in the oven than conventional lasagna. The real time savings is in the preparation. Start to finish, the meat and tomato lasagna took about an hour and a half to make: 40 minutes prep time, 40 minutes in the oven, and 10 minutes to rest. Measuring the final product against an authentic Italian lasagna may not be entirely fair, but having the time to make it on a weeknight, or whenever the craving strikes, is satisfying beyond compare.

WHAT WE LEARNED: **Meatloaf mix (a combination of ground beef, veal, and pork) adds complexity to a quick meat sauce, while cream adds richness. No-boil noodles work fine as long as you don't reduce the sauce too much (the noodles need some liquid to soften) and you cover the baking dish during its first 15 minutes in the oven (to build up some steam).**

SIMPLE LASAGNA WITH HEARTY TOMATO-MEAT SAUCE serves 6 to 8

If you can't find meatloaf mixture for the sauce, or if you choose not to eat veal, substitute 1/2 pound ground beef and 1/2 pound sweet Italian sausage, casings removed, for the meatloaf mixture. The assembled, unbaked lasagna, if wrapped tightly in plastic wrap and then in foil, will keep in the freezer for up to 2 months. To bake, defrost it in the refrigerator for a day or two and bake as directed, extending the baking time by about 5 minutes.

tomato-meat sauce

- 1 tablespoon olive oil
- 1 medium onion, chopped fine (about 1 cup)
- 6 medium garlic cloves, minced or pressed through garlic press (about 2 tablespoons)
- 1 pound meatloaf mix or 1/3 pound each ground beef chuck, ground veal, and ground pork (see note)
- 1/2 teaspoon salt
- 1/2 teaspoon ground black pepper
- 1/4 cup heavy cream
- 1 (28-ounce) can pureed tomatoes
- 1 (28-ounce) can diced tomatoes, drained

ricotta, mozzarella, and pasta layers

- 15 ounces whole milk or part-skim ricotta cheese (1 3/4 cups)
- 2 1/2 ounces grated Parmesan cheese (1 1/4 cups)
- 1/2 cup chopped fresh basil leaves
- 1 large egg, lightly beaten
- 1/2 teaspoon salt
- 1/2 teaspoon ground black pepper
- 12 no-boil lasagna noodles from one 8- or 9-ounce package (for brand preferences, see the Tasting Lab on page 131)
- 16 ounces whole-milk mozzarella cheese, shredded (4 cups)

1. Adjust oven rack to middle position and heat oven to 375 degrees.

2. Heat oil in large Dutch oven over medium heat until shimmering, about 2 minutes; add onions and cook, stirring occasionally, until softened but not browned, about 2 minutes. Add garlic and cook until fragrant, about 2 minutes. Increase heat to medium-high and add ground meats, salt, and pepper; cook, breaking meat into small pieces with wooden spoon, until meat loses its raw color but has not browned, about 4 minutes. Add cream and simmer, stirring occasionally, until liquid evaporates and only fat remains, about 4 minutes. Add pureed and drained diced tomatoes and bring to simmer; reduce heat to low and simmer slowly until flavors are blended, about 3 minutes; set sauce aside. (Sauce can be cooled, covered, and refrigerated for 2 days; reheat before assembling lasagna.)

3. Mix ricotta, 1 cup Parmesan, basil, egg, salt, and pepper in medium bowl with fork until creamy; set aside.

4. Smear entire bottom of 13 by 9-inch baking dish with 1/4 cup meat sauce (avoiding large chunks of meat). Place 3 noodles in baking dish to create first layer. Drop 3 tablespoons ricotta mixture down center of each noodle and level domed mounds by pressing with back side of measuring spoon. Sprinkle layer evenly with 1 cup shredded mozzarella cheese. Spoon 1 1/2 cups meat sauce evenly over cheese. Repeat layering of noodles, ricotta, mozzarella, and sauce two more times. Place 3 remaining noodles on top of sauce, spread remaining sauce over noodles, sprinkle with remaining 1 cup mozzarella, then with remaining 1/4 cup Parmesan. Lightly spray a large sheet of foil with nonstick cooking spray and cover lasagna.

5. Bake 15 minutes, then remove foil. Return lasagna to oven and continue to bake until cheese is spotty brown and sauce is bubbling, about 25 minutes longer. Cool lasagna about 10 minutes; cut into pieces and serve.

TASTING LAB: No-Boil Lasagna Noodles

OVER THE PAST FEW YEARS, NO-BOIL (ALSO CALLED OVEN-ready) lasagna noodles have become a permanent fixture on supermarket shelves. Much like instant rice, no-boil noodles are precooked at the factory. The extruded noodles are run through a water bath and then dehydrated mechanically. During baking, the moisture from the sauce softens, or rehydrates, the noodles, especially when the pan is covered as the lasagna bakes. Most no-boil noodles are rippled, and the accordion-like pleats relax as the pasta rehydrates in the oven, allowing the noodles to elongate.

No-boil lasagna noodles come in two shapes. The most common is a rectangle measuring 7 inches long and 3½ inches wide. Three such noodles make a single layer in a conventional 13 by 9-inch lasagna pan when they swell in the oven. In local markets, we found three brands of this type of no-boil lasagna noodle: Ronzoni (made by New World Pasta, which sells the same product under the American Beauty, Skinner, and San Giorgio labels in certain parts of the country), Pasta DeFino (made in the United States), and Barilla (imported from Italy). Italian noodles made by Delverde came in 7-inch squares. We made lasagnas with each of the four noodles to see how they would compare.

Ronzoni and DeFino are both thin and rippled, and although tasters preferred the Ronzoni for their flavor and the DeFino for their sturdiness, both brands worked well. Barilla noodles tasted great but their texture was subpar. Two squares of Delverde noodles butted very closely together fit into a 13 by 9-inch pan, but, when baked, the noodles expanded and the edges jumped out of the pan and became unpleasantly dry and tough. The only way to avoid this is to soak these noodles in hot water until tender. You then can cut them with scissors to fit the measurements of the pan. These noodles were no timesaver.

In the end, we rejected the Italian noodles in favor of the two American brands tested. At least when it comes to convenience, American pasta companies are the leaders.

Rating No-Boil Lasagna Noodles

WE TESTED FOUR BRANDS OF NO-BOIL NOODLES IN our lasagna recipe. Tasters evaluated the noodles for flavor and texture. All brands are available in supermarkets.

RECOMMENDED
1. Ronzoni Oven Ready Lasagne
$.99 for 8 ounces
With its "lightly eggy" and "wheaty" flavor, and "tender," "perfectly al dente" texture, Ronzoni was the tasters' favorite.

RECOMMENDED
2. Pasta DeFino No Boil Lasagna
$2.29 for 8 ounces
These "fairly thick" noodles were praised for their "firm," "toothsome" texture and "mild" flavor.

RECOMMENDED WITH RESERVATIONS
3. Barilla Oven-Ready No-Boil Lasagna
$1.59 for 9 ounces
These flat noodles were the most "like fresh pasta" in the bunch. However, they were "a little too thin" and "slightly limp."

NOT RECOMMENDED
4. Delverde Instant No-Boil Lasagna
$4.59 for 17.5 ounces
These noodles were "unevenly cooked" with "hard, dry edges" and a "tender interior." They did have a "good, clean" flavor.

France's greatest beef stew starts with basic ingredients such as mushrooms, thyme, and butter.

BEEF
burgundy

If the Louvre were just a museum, then boeuf à la bourguignonne might be just beef stew. Both are French and utterly extraordinary, but only one can be enjoyed at home.

We liken beef Burgundy more to a fabulous prime steak napped with a rich red wine reduction sauce than to a mundane beef stew. The beef in beef Burgundy is cut into satisfyingly large chunks that become utterly tender. The braising liquid, brimming with voluptuous wine and infused with aromatic vegetables, garlic, and herbs, is finessed into a sauce of burgundy velvet studded with mushrooms and pearl onions. Beef Burgundy is earthy, big, robust, warm, and welcoming in a brooding sort of way.

At least that's what it is at its best. We have had versions that fell far short of this, with tough meat or a dull sauce with no flavor complexity. We wanted to find a way to bring this classic dish to its full potential in a home kitchen.

BEEF BURGUNDY

WHAT WE WANTED: A stew with satisfyingly large chunks of tender meat. A velvety sauce brimming with the flavor of good Burgundy wine and studded with caramelized mushrooms and pearl onions.

Recipes for beef Burgundy are very much alike. Aromatic vegetables (onions, garlic, and carrots), red wine, stock, herbs, mushrooms, and pearl onions are all requisite ingredients; their combinations and proportions and the variations in preparation and technique are where the recipes diverge.

We started by completing four recipes, and from these four we deduced a couple of things. First, marinating the beef in the red wine and herbs that will later go into the braise—a common recommendation in recipes—does not improve the flavor of the cooked meat. Second, the braising liquid requires straining to rid it of bits of aromatic vegetables and herbs so that it may become flawlessly smooth. We found that bundling in cheesecloth all the goods that must eventually come out of the pot made their extraction possible in one easy step. When wrapped in cheesecloth, however, the aromatic vegetables cannot first be sautéed—a customary step, the omission of which we feared would adversely affect the flavors of the braise. Remarkably, it did not. But perhaps this is why it took such generous amounts of chopped onions, carrots, and garlic as well as parsley, thyme, peppercorns, and bay leaves to create a balanced mélange of flavors.

The cut of beef best suited to the long braise of beef Burgundy is a chuck roast. It's the cut that almost every recipe calls for and the one we prefer in regular beef stew because of its rich, meaty flavor. Because the beef in a beef Burgundy is cut into chunks larger than those in a beef stew—a good 1½ to 2 inches—we found it necessary to take extra care to trim off as much fat and silver skin as possible; larger pieces of beef also mean larger,

more detectable bites of these undesirables.

Each and every beef Burgundy begins with either salt pork or bacon cut into lardons, or small strips, and fried to a crisp; the fat that results is used to brown the beef chunks. The crisped pork is added to the pot to simmer alongside the beef so that it can relinquish its flavors to the braise, providing a subtle, sweet underpinning and lending the sauce roundness and depth. We tried both bacon and salt pork and favored the cleaner, purer, more honest flavor of salt pork. Moreover, the thicker, more toothsome strips of salt pork had better texture than the thin, lifeless pieces of bacon. Salt pork can be a challenge to find in grocery stores, so we reasoned that just as blanching salt pork removes excess salt that would otherwise crystallize on the surface during frying, blanching thick-cut bacon ought to calm the smoke and sugar and make it appropriate for beef Burgundy. This worked well. The thick-cut bacon had more textural appeal than regular bacon and was an acceptable substitute for salt pork.

As for the stock that goes into the braise, most recipes call for beef, preferably homemade. Because making beef stock is so time-consuming, we wanted to try canned broth. Based on our tasting, we knew that canned beef broth does not make an acceptable substitute homemade beef stock (see the Tasting Lab on page 138 for details). Therefore, in all subsequent tests, we used what we have found to be the next best option—canned chicken broth—with excellent results. Still, beef Burgundy necessitates a good amount of liquid for braising, and too much chicken broth tasted too chickeny. Water was a fine filler, especially since the braising liquid is later reduced to create the sauce. We then tried something a bit unorthodox to boost flavor. Just a small amount of dried porcini mushrooms wrapped into the cheesecloth package brought the meatiness and savory quality that homemade beef stock would conceivably have added. A modicum of tomato paste added color and sprightliness.

Wine was the next issue. Beef Burgundy does not exist

without a healthy dose of it. We concluded after several batches that anything less than a whole bottle left the sauce lacking and unremarkable. After numerous experiments, we had determined that a Burgundy, or at least a decent Pinot Noir, is indeed the wine of choice (see the Tasting Lab on page 140 for more details). Though most recipes indicate that all of the wine should be added at the outset, one recipe, as well as one wine expert, recommended saving just a bit of the wine to add at the very end, just before serving. This late embellishment of raw wine vastly improved the sauce, brightening its flavor and giving it resonance.

Midway through testing, we decided we needed an alternative to browning the meat in a Dutch oven, where it would eventually be braised. Browning in batches took too long, and the drippings, or fond, that are essential flavor providers frequently burned. Evidently, the small cooking surface of even a large Dutch oven was a liability. We took to browning the beef in two batches in a heavy, large 12-inch skillet. To keep the fond from going to waste, we deglazed the pan with a bit of water and poured it directly

into the braising pot, where it would eventually marry with the broth and wine.

Next we went to work to find the best means of adding flour to thicken the braising liquid that must blossom into a velvety sauce. Tossing the beef in flour before browning interfered with the color the beef could attain and ultimately affected its flavor. We found it preferable to make a roux in the skillet and add broth and water to it, then have it join the beef, wine, and vegetable and herb bouquet in the braising pot. This afforded us the opportunity to cook the roux until it achieved a light brown color, which made a favorable impact on the flavor of the dish.

With everything assembled in the Dutch oven, into the oven it went, where the constant, all-encompassing heat produced an even simmer that required little attention. This was the time to prepare the mushrooms and pearl onions, both of which would later join the sauce. Peeling fresh pearl onions is a nuisance, but opening a bag isn't. We embraced peeled frozen pearl onions; contrary to expectations, when browned, the frozen onions are not inferior in flavor or texture to fresh, as they are when boiled. A brisk simmer in a skillet with some water, butter, and sugar, and then a quick sauté with the mushrooms, created glazed beauties that were ready to grace the sauce. The final flourish was a swish of brandy that added richness and warmth to an already magnificent boeuf à la bourguignonne.

WHAT WE LEARNED: **Start with a chuck roast cut into large chunks. Don't marinate the meat in wine but do brown it in a large skillet, using the rendered fat from salt pork to cook the meat. Make a roux (with butter and flour) to thicken the sauce, and wrap the aromatic vegetables in cheesecloth so they can be easily removed before building the sauce from the braising liquid. Finally, braise the meat in a combination of canned chicken broth and good red wine but save a little wine to add just before serving.**

BEEF BURGUNDY serves 6

If you cannot find salt pork, thick-cut bacon can be substituted. Cut it crosswise into 1/4-inch pieces and treat it just as you would the salt pork, but note that you will have no rind to include in the vegetable and herb bouquet. Boiled potatoes are the traditional accompaniment, but mashed potatoes or buttered noodles are nice as well.

beef braise

6	ounces salt pork, trimmed of rind (see illustration on page 141), rind reserved, and salt pork cut into 1/4 inch by 1/4 inch by 1-inch pieces
10	sprigs fresh parsley, torn into quarters
6	sprigs fresh thyme
2	medium onions, chopped coarse
2	medium carrots, chopped coarse
1	medium head garlic, cloves separated and crushed but unpeeled
2	bay leaves, crumbled
1/2	teaspoon black peppercorns
1/2	ounce dried porcini mushrooms, rinsed (optional)
4–4 1/4	pounds beef chuck roast, trimmed and cut into 2-inch chunks (see illustrations on page 137)
	Salt and ground black pepper
4	tablespoons unsalted butter, cut into 4 pieces
1/3	cup all-purpose flour
1 3/4	cups canned low-sodium chicken broth
1	bottle (750 ml) wine, red Burgundy or Pinot Noir
1	teaspoon tomato paste

onion and mushroom garnish

36	frozen pearl onions (about 7 ounces)
1	tablespoon unsalted butter
1	tablespoon sugar
1/2	teaspoon salt
10	ounces white button mushrooms, whole if small, halved if medium, quartered if large
2	tablespoons brandy
3	tablespoons minced fresh parsley leaves

1. Bring salt pork, reserved salt pork rind, and 3 cups water to a boil in medium saucepan over high heat. Boil 2 minutes, then drain well.

2. Cut two 22-inch lengths of cheesecloth. Following illustrations on page 138, wrap parsley, thyme, onions, carrots, garlic, bay leaves, peppercorns, porcini mushrooms, and blanched salt pork rind in cheesecloth and set in large oven-proof Dutch oven. Adjust oven rack to lower-middle position and heat oven to 300 degrees.

3. Set 12-inch skillet with salt pork over medium heat; sauté until lightly brown and crisp, about 12 minutes. With slotted spoon, transfer salt pork to Dutch oven. Pour off all but 2 teaspoons fat and reserve. Dry beef thoroughly on paper towels, then season it generously with salt and pepper. Increase heat to high and brown half of beef in single layer, turning once or twice, until deep brown, about 7 minutes; transfer browned beef to Dutch oven. Pour 1/2 cup water into skillet and scrape pan with wooden spoon to loosen browned bits. When pan bottom is clean, pour liquid into Dutch oven.

4. Return skillet to high heat and add 2 teaspoons reserved pork fat; swirl to coat pan bottom. When fat begins to smoke, brown remaining beef in single layer, turning once or twice, until deep brown, about 7 minutes; transfer browned beef to Dutch oven. Pour 1/2 cup water into skillet and scrape pan with wooden spoon to loosen browned bits. When pan bottom is clean, pour liquid into Dutch oven.

5. Set now-empty skillet over medium heat and add butter. When foaming subsides, whisk in flour until evenly moistened and pasty. Cook, whisking constantly, until mixture has toasty aroma and resembles light-colored peanut butter, about 5 minutes. Gradually whisk in chicken broth and 1 1/2 cups water. Increase heat to medium-high and bring to a simmer, stirring frequently, until thickened. Pour mixture into Dutch oven. Add 3 cups wine, tomato paste, and salt and pepper to taste to Dutch oven and stir to combine. Set Dutch oven over high heat and bring to a boil. Cover and place pot in oven. Cook until meat is tender, 2½ to 3 hours.

6. Remove Dutch oven from oven and, using tongs, transfer vegetable and herb bouquet to mesh strainer set over pot. Press liquid back into pot and discard bouquet. With slotted spoon, transfer beef to medium bowl; set aside. Allow braising liquid to settle about 15 minutes, then, with wide shallow spoon, skim fat off surface and discard.

7. Bring liquid in Dutch oven to boil over medium-high heat. Simmer briskly, stirring occasionally to ensure that bottom is not burning, until sauce is reduced to about 3 cups and thickened to consistency of heavy cream, 15 to 25 minutes.

8. While sauce is reducing, bring pearl onions, butter, sugar, ¼ teaspoon salt, and ½ cup water to a boil in medium skillet over high heat. Cover, reduce heat to medium-low, and simmer, shaking pan occasionally, until onions are tender, about 5 minutes. Uncover, increase heat to high, and simmer until all liquid evaporates, about 3 minutes. Add mushrooms and remaining ¼ teaspoon salt. Cook, stirring occasionally, until liquid released by mushrooms evaporates and vegetables are browned and glazed, about 5 minutes. Transfer vegetables to large plate and set aside. Add ¼ cup water to skillet and stir with wooden spoon to loosen browned bits. When pan bottom and sides are clean, add liquid to reducing sauce.

9. When sauce has reduced to about 3 cups and thickened to consistency of heavy cream, reduce heat to medium-low. Stir beef, mushrooms, and onions (and any accumulated juices), remaining wine from bottle, and brandy into Dutch oven. Cover pot and cook until just heated through, 5 to 8 minutes. Adjust seasonings with salt and pepper and serve, sprinkling individual servings with minced parsley.

TECHNIQUE: Cutting Stew Meat

Packages of stew meat usually contain misshapen pieces of various sizes, often from undesirable parts of the cow. To get stew meat pieces that are cut from the right part of the animal and regularly shaped, we suggest buying a boneless roast and cutting the meat yourself. This way you also ensure that all the pieces are the same size and will cook at the same rate.

1. Pull apart the roast at its major seams (delineated by lines of fat and silver skin). Use a knife as necessary.

2. With a paring knife, trim off excess fat and silver skin.

3. Cut the meat into 2-inch chunks for beef burgundy or 1-inch cubes for chili.

DO-AHEAD BEEF BURGUNDY

The braise can be made a day or two ahead, and the sauce, along with the onion and mushroom garnish, can be completed the day you intend to serve.

TECHNIQUE:
Making the Vegetable and Herb Bouquet

If you don't have cheesecloth, you can use a cloth stuffing bag, which is readily available in most supermarkets.

1. Cut two 22-inch lengths of cheesecloth and unfold each piece once lengthwise so that each forms a 2-ply, 22 by 8-inch piece. Lay the cheesecloth in a medium bowl, placing sheets perpendicular to each other. Place the designated ingredients in the cheesecloth-lined bowl.

2. Gather the edges of the cheesecloth securely and fasten with kitchen twine. Trim excess cheesecloth with scissors if necessary.

---

1. Follow recipe for Beef Burgundy through step 5. Using tongs, transfer vegetable and herb bouquet to mesh strainer set over Dutch oven. Press liquid back into pot and discard bouquet. Let beef cool to room temperature in braising liquid in Dutch oven. The braise can be kept covered in the refrigerator for 1 to 2 days.

2. To complete the dish, use slotted spoon to skim congealed fat off top and discard. Set pot over medium-high heat and bring to a simmer. With slotted spoon, transfer beef to medium bowl and set aside. Simmer sauce briskly, stirring occasionally to ensure that bottom is not burning, until reduced to about 3 cups and thickened to consistency of heavy cream.

3. Continue with recipe from step 8.

TASTING LAB: Beef Broth

BEEF BROTH IS A TRADITIONAL EUROPEAN AND AMERICAN staple, a key ingredient in many classic sauces as well as the basis for popular beef soups. Over the past few years, however, sales of beef broth have lagged. The most recent statistics for annual sales show that canned chicken broth outsells canned beef broth by 4 cans to 1.

When we tasted commercial beef broths, the reason for their slack sales became obvious: Most beef broths simply do not deliver full-bodied, beefy flavor. There might be subtle beef suggestions, but after tasting nearly all of the selected broths—bouillon-based, canned, gourmet, and organic— there remained one nagging question: "Where's the beef?"

As things stand, U.S. regulations for beef broth do not require much beef. A commercial beef broth need contain only 1 part protein to 135 parts moisture, according to the U.S. Department of Agriculture's standards. That translates to less than about an ounce of meat (or about one-quarter of a hamburger) to 1 gallon of water. To contain costs, most commercial producers stay very close to that limit. Generally, manufactured beef broth derives its flavor from

Rating Beef Broths

WE TASTED 10 BRANDS OF BEEF BROTH SOLD IN SUPERMARKETS. WE ALSO INCLUDED OUR HOMEMADE BEEF BROTH, which was picked out by every single taster as the best choice by far. Broths are listed in order of preference, although differences between "not recommended" products were more about how awful one was relative to another rather than any positive attributes.

RECOMMENDED IN A PINCH
1. Superior Touch Better Than Bouillon Beef Base

$4.00 for 8-ounce jar, which makes 10 quarts

This product actually includes beef and concentrated beef stock at the top of its ingredient list. More beef flavor than other choices, but can't compare with homemade. Many tasters complained about too much salt.

NOT RECOMMENDED
2. Herb Ox Beef Bouillon Cubes

$2.29 for 25 cubes, which makes about 6 quarts

"Tastes like it was produced in a lab, not a kitchen." Better than other bouillon products but still deemed "watery." One taster quipped, "Almost no beef flavor—a cow walked by the pot?"

NOT RECOMMENDED
3. Health Valley Beef Flavored Broth

$1.29 for 14.25 ounces

Lower in salt than other canned broths and "less offensive."

NOT RECOMMENDED
4. Campbell's Beef Broth

$1.25 for 10.5 ounces

Dark, coffee-like appearance and extreme saltiness. Its acidic (and salty) flavor was repeatedly compared with soy sauce.

NOT RECOMMENDED
5. Wyler's Bouillon Granules

$1.69 for 2½-ounce jar, which makes 4½ quarts

More like vegetable broth than beef broth. "Beef is elusive."

NOT RECOMMENDED
6. Knorr Beef Bouillon

$1.49 for 12 cubes, which makes 6 quarts

"Where's the beef?" asked one taster. Perhaps lingering somewhere behind the salt? Broth made from these bouillon cubes was very salty and greasy. Tasters complained of "commercial" and "industrial" flavors.

NOT RECOMMENDED
7. Bovril Concentrated Beef Flavored Liquid Bouillon

$3.69 for 4.2-ounce jar, which makes 6 quarts

Rich-colored broth "looks better than it tastes." Like too many other products we sampled, tasters rejected this one for its "blah flavor."

NOT RECOMMENDED
8. Swanson's Beef Broth

$.89 for 14.5 ounces

"Tastes extremely fake," wrote one taster. The consensus was that this broth was too greasy as well. The artificial taste of this major brand was a big turn-off.

NOT RECOMMENDED
9. College Inn Beef Broth

$.99 for 14.5 ounces

"Off" flavors were described by some tasters as being similar to "burnt plastic" or "metallic." Several tasters called this broth "horrific."

NOT RECOMMENDED
10. Walnut Acres Beef Broth

$2.99 for 15.5 ounces

This organic broth was the greasiest one tested. No beef flavor. As one taster said, "I thought it could not get any worse."

bare beef bones and a boost of various additives. A glance at the label on the side of any canned broth or boxed bouillon cubes will confirm this.

We wanted to talk to the manufacturers of beef broths to verify our impressions of the way they make their products, but calls to broth giants Hormel Foods and Campbell Soup Company were dead ends. Both declined to answer questions about the way they make their beef broths. But beef bones plus additives would certainly explain why none of the 10 commercial broths we tasted came even close to the full-bodied, beefy flavor of our homemade stock—made with 6 pounds of meat and bones in 2 quarts of water. Nearly all of the commercial broths were thin and flavorless except for their "off" or artificial flavors.

What seems to distinguish most supermarket broths from homemade, gourmet, or natural foods store broths is a riddling of flavor additives. Monosodium glutamate (MSG) can be found in nearly all supermarket beef broths (see the Science Desk on page 141). Disodium guanylate and disodium isonate, which are both yeast-based, hydrolyzed soy protein, are also typically added to commercial broths. Yeast extracts find their way into most of these broths as well. All approved by the U.S. Food and Drug Administration (FDA), these additives are intended to "enhance" flavor. As one FDA spokesperson explained, "You've got something that's kind of 'blah,' so to give it a little more taste they add these things."

Salt—and lots of it—also adds to the flavor of these broths. Most beef broth products contain about 35 percent of the daily allowance for sodium per serving. Salt is also added to help extract the needed protein from the bones.

The preferred product in our commercial broth tasting was a jarred beef base, Superior Touch Better Than Bouillon, but even this "winner" had an unflattering score of 4.6 on a scale of 0 to 10. Herb Ox Beef Bouillon Cubes lagged not too far behind but weren't good enough to recommend, even in a pinch. Even if you can get your hands on one of the "top finishers," however, we don't recommend their use in a recipe where the flavor of beef broth predominates, as it does in beef soup or stew.

BEEF BURGUNDY IS RIGHTFULLY MADE WITH TRUE Burgundy wine. This means a red wine made from the Pinot Noir grape grown in the French province of Burgundy. Characteristically, these wines are medium-bodied but also deep, rich, and complex, with earthy tones and a reticent fruitiness. They are also expensive. Throughout our testing, we emptied a $12 bottle of Burgundy—the least expensive we could find—into each batch of beef Burgundy. Quite frankly, it was making outstanding beef Burgundies.

Nonetheless, we wanted to try more costly, higher-quality Burgundies and found that they bettered the dish—a $30 bottle gave a stellar, rousing performance. We thought it worth exploring other wines, but, wanting to remain faithful to the spirit of the dish, we limited ourselves to Pinot Noirs made on the West Coast of the United States, which are slightly less expensive than Burgundies. We made beef Burgundies with domestic Pinot Noirs at three different price points, and even the least expensive wine—a $9 bottle—was perfectly acceptable, although its flavors were simpler and less intriguing than those of its Burgundian counterpart.

Both the Burgundies and the Pinot Noirs exhibited the same pattern—that is, as the price of the wine increased, so did the depth, complexity, and roundness of the sauce. We can advise with some confidence to set your price, then seek out a wine—either Burgundy or Pinot Noir—that matches it. But if your allegiance is to a true Burgundy, be warned that they can be difficult to find because production is relatively limited. We also caution you to beware of several very inexpensive mass-produced wines from California of questionable constitutions that are sold as "Burgundy." They are usually made from a blend of grape varieties, and whether or not they actually contain so much as a drop of Pinot Noir is a mystery. We made a beef burgundy with one of these wines, and it resulted in a fleeting, one-dimensional, fruity, sweet sauce.

BECAUSE MOST OF THE COMMERCIAL BEEF BROTHS IN our tasting (see the Tasting Lab on page 138) use monosodium glutamate (MSG) as a flavor enhancer, we decided to find out just how this product affects flavor. To provide the most dramatic illustration, we cooked up a batch of classic French beef stock, a practically flavorless liquid made with bones (without meat) and vegetables. We then tasted it plain and with ½ teaspoon of MSG per quart.

The difference was more distinct than we had expected. The plain stock was characterized by excessive vegetable and sweet flavors, while beef flavors were indiscernible. In contrast, the stock with MSG had, as one taster described, "higher flavor notes" that included beefy and more savory flavors and a subdued sweetness. What's more, it tasted nothing like the lowest-rated commercial broths we had sampled.

Just how that half-teaspoon of MSG can make such a difference is something scientists cannot fully explain, says food science professor F. Jack Francis of the University of Massachusetts at Amherst. MSG, like many other flavor enhancers, does not change the flavor of the substance to which it is added. Instead, it is believed to enhance the response of a person's taste buds, especially to meats and proteins, says Francis. Exactly how this happens scientists have yet to learn. Some describe it not only as a taste enhancer but also as a stimulator of a fifth taste perception in addition to sweet, sour, salty, and bitter. The Japanese call this taste perception umami, and it is best described as meaty or mushroom-like.

Popular as MSG is with commercial broth makers, it has not been especially popular with the American public. In the 1980s, people began to associate it with "Chinese restaurant syndrome," which has been reported to include symptoms such as headache, digestive upset, and chest pain. Even though numerous studies have failed to turn up an association between such symptoms and MSG, the reputation has stuck. It has been speculated that a type of bacteria quick to grow on cooked rice left at room temperature and able to cause food poisoning is the real source of trouble for those diners with "Chinese restaurant syndrome."

Nowadays most Chinese restaurants tout "No MSG" on their menus. Yet many people do not realize that it's still lurking in their hot-and-sour soup as well as many other non-Chinese dishes. That's because MSG is the salt form of glutamate, a naturally occurring substance found in such foods as peanut butter, rice, flour, and mushrooms.

TECHNIQUE:
Trimming Rind from Salt Pork

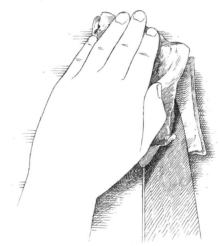

Salt pork is usually sold with the rind attached, and you must remove the tough rind before slicing or chopping it. Steady the salt pork with one hand, and with the other hand slide the blade of a sharp chef's knife between the rind and the fat, using a wide sawing motion to cut away the rind in one piece. Save the rind—it is added to the cheesecloth bundle with the vegetables and herbs.

EQUIPMENT CORNER:
Oven Thermometers

HAVE YOU EVER BAKED A CAKE OR PIE THAT WAS ONLY half-done after the suggested cooking time? We have, and often the reason was a poorly calibrated oven. The accuracy of your oven can spell the difference between disaster and culinary triumph. Just how bad is this problem? To find out, we tested 16 different ovens in the homes of friends and colleagues, setting each oven to 350 degrees. We then measured the temperature inside each oven and found that the actual temperatures ranged from 300 to 390 degrees. In fact, only two of 16 ovens tested registered within 10 degrees of the 350-degree mark.

Even the ovens here in our test kitchen often stray from reliability in between service calls from the professionals who recalibrate them. Recently, for example, we found that the ovens in our double wall-oven unit differed from each other by 30 degrees when set to the same temperature. That's why we often use an oven thermometer to tell us what's really going on. In fact, we consider the oven thermometer such an important tool that we rounded up eight popular models to test. With our ovens freshly calibrated and a computerized, supersensitive thermometer (the ChartScan Portable Data Recorder) in hand to accurately monitor oven temperatures, we set out to assess the various models based on readability, accuracy, and stability.

Cooking in an oven is not as straightforward a process as you might think. In fact, three different dynamics of heat transfer are simultaneously in play. Radiation is the heat energy (generated by the heating element) carried through the air inside the oven cavity. Convection is the movement of the hot air itself; think of the fan inside a convection oven. Last is conduction, which is the transfer of energy from one hot surface to another; think of a piece of meat browning while in contact with the surface of a hot pan. Of these three dynamics, radiation from the heating element is responsible for the lion's share of browning that occurs when you bake or roast in the oven.

Conversations with David Anderson, senior product manager at Whirlpool, revealed that the average oven designed for home use does not simply heat up to the temperature set on the dial and then stay there. Anderson noted that an oven's heating elements are either on at full power or off—with no middle ground. To maintain the desired temperature, the heating elements cycle within a manufacturer-determined tolerance, heating up and cooling down to temperatures just above and below the desired temperature. The precise temperature tolerances and timing of the cycles vary from manufacturer to manufacturer. For instance, Anderson said that Whirlpool uses one-minute intervals, so the elements will be on for one minute, then off for the next, then on again, and so forth as necessary. This cycling process is regulated by an internal temperature sensor located in the oven cavity.

We wanted to put this information to the test, so we hooked up our ChartScan Portable Data Recorder to an electric oven in the test kitchen and programmed it to record the temperature once every 10 seconds for $1\frac{1}{2}$ hours. We placed 15 temperature sensors, called thermocouples, at different locations up and down and side to side in the oven cavity and set the dial to 350 degrees. At the dead-center location in the oven, we found the temperature cycled within a range of roughly 25 degrees, from a low of about 335 degrees to a high of about 361 degrees. We analyzed a gas oven in the same manner and found the temperature spread to be somewhat narrower, between 343 and 359 degrees.

A careful look at the numbers generated by our ChartScan tests also confirmed the common assertion that the heat within an oven cavity is not consistent; that, in effect, there are hot and cold spots. Though we might have expected otherwise, we found that the bottom of our electric test oven tended to run hotter than the top, usually by 5 to 15 degrees. We also found that the rear of our oven ran hotter than the front by roughly 5 to 10 degrees. There was

Rating Oven Thermometers

WE RATED EIGHT OVEN THERMOMETERS AND EVALUATED THEM ACCORDING TO READABILITY, ACCURACY (IF THE temperature was off by more than 8 degrees the thermometer was downgraded slightly; if the temperature was off by more than 17 degrees the thermometer was downgraded more seriously), and temperature increments (10-degree increments proved more precise than 25-degree increments). Tests were performed in the same freshly calibrated electric oven in the test kitchen. The thermometers are listed in order of preference. See www.cooksillustrated.com for up-to-date prices and mail-order sources for top rated products.

HIGHLY RECOMMENDED
1. Taylor Classic Oven Guide Thermometer, Model 5921
$12.99

Temperature readings were spot on, and this Taylor passed our knock-over test with flying colors. The most stable thermometer of the group, in part because of its 4-inch length.

RECOMMENDED
2. Component Design Magnet Mounted Oven Thermometer, Model MOT1
$7.99

The magnet mounted on the back of the dial is a boon to stability. That, and the uncluttered dial graphics, earned the Component Design a second-place rating.

RECOMMENDED WITH RESERVATIONS
3. Cooper Oven Thermometer, Model 24HP
$7.95

The bold numbers on its compact face provide average readability. Not as stable as the top models.

RECOMMENDED WITH RESERVATIONS
4. Pyrex Accessories Oven Thermometer, #16416
$4.99

Excellent readability owing to its large, uncluttered, stark white dial face with clear, simple graphics. No Celsius scale and seems a bit flimsy.

RECOMMENDED WITH RESERVATIONS
5. Hoan Stainless Steel Oven Thermometer, Style No. 43460
$6.99

Bold numbers with red markers every 50 degrees make this thermometer easy to read despite its small dial face. No Celsius scale. Falls through oven rack easily.

RECOMMENDED WITH RESERVATIONS
6. Taylor Serviceman's Folding Oven Test Thermometer, Model 5903
$31.50

Arrived with neither instructions nor a hook, so we could not hang it from the rack. Very easy to read, and it's stable if you place it diagonally on the oven rack. No Celsius scale. The only thermometer tested that uses mercury.

RECOMMENDED WITH RESERVATIONS
7. Taylor Classic Oven Dial Thermometer, Model 5931
$5.99

Bold-face numbers help readability, but the poor design of the hanger hinders readability because it causes the dial face to tilt downward. No Celsius scale.

NOT RECOMMENDED
8. Polder Oven Thermometer
$7.95

Get out your reading glasses—you'll need them to decipher the crowded dial face. Two complete scales for Fahrenheit and Celsius are the culprits.

also a stunning difference from right to left in our oven, with the right side sometimes running up to 50 degrees hotter than the left!

The uneven heat is the reason why many cookbook authors suggest rotating pans in the oven when you bake. We ran a simple test of baking sugar cookies to confirm this advice. Sure enough, the cookies were browned a little less evenly from one side of the pan to the other when we failed to turn the cookie sheet partway through the baking time (see page 271 for details).

Curious as to whether there was any truth to the common kitchen wisdom that electric ovens heat more evenly than gas ovens, we repeated the ChartScan tests on a gas range in the test kitchen. The temperatures recorded in our tests bore out some validity in this axiom. For instance, the temperature differential between the bottom and top of the cavity was closer to 50 degrees, where it had been just 5 to 15 degrees in the electric oven.

An oven thermometer will give you a fighting chance in the guessing game of temperatures inside your oven. Widely available in stores from the local supermarket right up to fancy kitchenware emporia, we wondered if price—which ranged from a low of about $5 for the Pyrex model to a high of almost $32 for a mercury-based Taylor model—really mattered.

As awareness of mercury's toxic properties has increased, the mercury-based thermometers that were once common have become rare. In fact, the Taylor Serviceman's Folding Oven Test Thermometer was the only mercury-based model in our group of eight. In another Taylor model, the Classic Oven Guide Thermometer, blue-dyed alcohol took the place of mercury, but all of the other models were based on a bimetal coil. Engineers from Taylor Environmental Instruments explained that the bimetal coil, mounted inside the thermometer and attached at one end to the pointer on the dial, is made from two types of metal, bonded together, which have different rates of expansion and contraction when subjected to changes in temperature. When the temperature increases or decreases, the coil changes length, which causes the pointer on the dial face to rotate to indicate the temperature.

According to our tests at moderate to high oven temperatures, most of the thermometers were pretty accurate, but only one model, the Taylor Classic Oven Guide Thermometer, was spot-on at all the temperatures we tested. On the other hand, only three models—the Taylor Serviceman's Folding Oven Test Thermometer (with the mercury), the Taylor Classic Oven Dial Thermometer, and the Polder—produced readings that were more than 17 degrees off, which was the limit of our tolerance (see chart on page 143 for details).

During the testing, we also noted that two models in particular, the Cooper and the Polder, could be difficult to read owing to small dial faces that are overstuffed with graphics. When you shop, look for an uncluttered thermometer face with bold numbers for good readability. A large dial face (of 2 inches or more) is also preferred.

The last issue that affects everyday use is stability. All of the thermometers we tested can either sit on the oven shelf or hang from it. Either way, unfortunately, it is easy to knock over the thermometer while maneuvering a pan in or out of the oven. Even more irritating is when the thermometer falls through the wires of the rack to the bottom of the cavity. Both instances occasion a clumsy retrieval process with a hand shod in a bulky oven mitt. Two of the thermometers, the Taylor Classic Oven Guide, with its extrawide, 4-inch base, and the Component Design, with its built-in magnet, minimized such antics; they were exceptionally stable in our knock-over tests. At the same time, the Taylor Oven Guide and the Component Design are each only 2 inches tall, so it was easy to maneuver pans up and over without disturbing them.

All in all, most of the thermometers performed acceptably, but one, the moderately priced Taylor Classic Oven Guide, shone especially bright in every test. Though it is not the least expensive of the contestants, its readability, stability, and accuracy represent a good value as far as we're concerned.

Chris tries to spray Doc with water after a heated demonstration on the appeal of chiles.

TEXAS chili

CHAPTER 11

A strictly Texan chili, known as chili con carne, depends on either pureed or powdered ancho chiles, uses beef, excludes tomato, onion, and beans, and features a high proportion of meat to chiles. We wanted a chili that would be hearty, heavy on the meat, and spicy but not overwhelmingly hot. In other words, we wanted the real thing. We wanted a creamy consistency somewhere between soup and stew. The flavors would be balanced so that no single spice or seasoning competed with the chile or beef.

We traveled to chili country, cooked with various experts in their kitchens, and tried out dozens of recipes in the test kitchen. In the end, we think our chili is good enough to compete in any chili cook-off, even in Texas.

CHILI CON CARNE

WHAT WE WANTED: The real deal, with big chunks of meat, plenty of chile flavor but not searing heat, and a smooth, rich sauce that could be ladled over rice or soaked up with cornbread.

Because chiles are the heart of chili con carne, we decided to begin our research by learning about the different types. After considerable testing and tasting, we settled on a combination of ancho and New Mexico for the dried chiles (see the Tasting Lab on page 151 for more information), with a few jalapeños added for their fresh flavor and bite. Chilis made with toasted and ground whole dried chiles tasted noticeably fuller and warmer than those made with chili powder. The two main toasting methods are oven and skillet, and after trying both, we went to the oven simply because it required less attention and effort than skillet toasting. The chiles will puff in the oven, become fragrant, and dry out sufficiently after five to six minutes. One caveat, though: Overtoasted chiles can take on a distinctly bitter flavor, so don't let them go too long.

With the chiles chosen and toasted, the next big question was how best to prepare them. The two options here are to rehydrate the toasted chiles in liquid and process them into a puree or to grind them into a powder. It didn't take long for us to select grinding as the preferred method. It was easier, faster, and much less messy than making the puree, which tasters felt produced a chili that was too rich, more like a Mexican enchilada sauce than a bowl of chili.

This felt like the right time to determine the best ratio of chile to meat. Many of the recipes we looked at in our research suggested that a tablespoon of ground chile per pound of meat was sufficient, but we found these chilis to be bland and watery. Three tablespoons per pound of meat, on the other hand, produced chili with too much punch and richness. Two tablespoons per pound was the way to go.

There was little agreement in the recipes we had col-lected as to when the chile powder should be added. After running several tests, we found that sautéing the spices, including the chiles, is key to unlocking their flavor. We also discovered that blending the chile powder with water to make a paste keeps it from scorching in the pot; this step is advised.

Since chuck is our favorite meat for stewing, we knew it would work best in chili. Still, there were some aspects of the meat question that had to be settled. Should the chuck be standard hamburger grind, coarser chili grind, hand-cut into tiny cubes, or a combination? The chili made from cubes of beef was far more appealing than those made from either type of ground beef; they both had a grainy, extruded texture. Most of the recipes we looked at specified that the meat should be cut into ¼-inch cubes. However, we found that larger 1-inch chunks gave the chili a satisfying chew. In addition, cutting a chuck roast into larger chunks was much, much faster and easier than breaking it down into a fussy, ¼-inch dice.

Next we set out to determine the best type, or types, of liquid for the chili. The main contenders were water, chicken stock, beef stock, beer, black coffee, and red wine. We tried each one on its own, as well as in any combination we felt made sense. The surprise result was that we liked plain water best because it allowed the flavor of the chiles to come through in full force. Both stocks, whether on their own, combined in equal parts with each other, or with water, muddied the chile flavors. All of the other liquids, used either alone or mixed with an equal part of chicken stock or water, competed with the chile flavor.

Another basic factor to determine was the garlic. Tasters agreed that three cloves were too few and eight were too many, so we settled on five. We found many recipes that called for powdered garlic rather than fresh. Out of obligation, we tested powdered versus fresh garlic and found fresh to be far superior.

Though common in modern recipes, Texas chili lore leaves tomatoes and onions out of the original formula. These two ingredients may break with tradition, but we found both to be essential. The acidity of the tomato and the sweetness of the onion, both used in small amounts, add interest and dimension to the chili. The batches we tested without them were decidedly dull. We tested various amounts and types of tomato products and determined that more than one cup pushed the flavor of the chili toward that of spaghetti sauce. Products with a smooth consistency, such as canned crushed tomatoes or plain tomato sauce, helped create the smooth sauce we wanted.

We found that bacon gave the chili a subtly sweet, smoky essence that is most welcome. Other "secret" ingredients fell by the wayside. Coke imparted a sourish, off taste. Brown sugar cut the heat of the chiles too much. An ounce of unsweetened chocolate gave the chili a rounder, deeper flavor, and 2 tablespoons of peanut butter made the sauce creamier and earthy tasting. Much as we liked both peanut butter and chocolate, however, we decided they were not essential.

Chili is generally thickened to tighten the sauce and make it smoother. Flour, roux (a paste of flour and melted butter), cornstarch, and masa harina (a flour ground from corn treated with lime, or calcium oxide) are the most common options. Dredging the meat in flour before browning and adding a roux along with the liquid were both effective, but these approaches made it more difficult to finesse the consistency of the finished product because both were introduced early in the cooking process. Roux added at the end of the cooking left a faint taste of raw flour. We did prefer thickening at the end of cooking, though, because we could control the consistency by adding thickener gradually until the chili reached the right consistency. We like chili thick enough to coat the back of a wooden spoon, like the custard base of homemade ice cream.

Our first choice for thickening was masa harina, added at the end of cooking. Masa both thickened the chili and gave it a slightly sweet, earthy corn flavor. If masa harina is not available in your grocery store and you'd rather not mail-order it, use a cornstarch and water slurry. It brings no flavor to the chili, but it is predictable, easy to use, and gives the gravy a silky consistency and attractive sheen.

One last note. Time and time again, tasters observed that chili, like many stews, always improved after an overnight rest because the flavors blended and mellowed. If you can, cook your chili a day ahead. The result will be worth the wait.

WHAT WE LEARNED: Make your own chili powder by toasting and grinding two kinds of dried chiles. Cut a chuck roast into 1-inch cubes for a hearty texture, and add bacon for a subtle smokiness. Stock, beer, and wine compete with the chili flavor, so use water. Just before serving, thicken the chili with masa harina for a silky consistency and a hint of corn flavor.

CHILI CON CARNE serves 6

To ensure the best chile flavor, we recommend toasting whole dried chiles and grinding them in a minichopper or spice-dedicated coffee grinder, all of which takes only 10 (very well-spent) minutes. Select dried chiles that are moist and pliant, like dried fruit.

To toast and grind dried chiles: Place chiles on baking sheet in 350-degree oven until fragrant and puffed, about 6 minutes. Cool, stem, and seed, tearing pods into pieces. Place pieces of the pods in a spice grinder and process until powdery, 30 to 45 seconds.

For hotter chili, boost the heat with a pinch of cayenne, a dash of hot pepper sauce, or crumbled pequin chiles near the end of cooking.

Serve the chili with any of the following side dishes: warm pinto or kidney beans, corn bread or chips, corn tortillas or tamales, rice, biscuits, or just plain crackers. Top with any of the following garnishes: chopped fresh cilantro leaves, minced white onion, diced avocado, shredded cheddar or Jack cheese, or sour cream.

- 3 tablespoons ancho chili powder, or 3 medium pods (about ½ ounce), toasted and ground (see note)
- 3 tablespoons New Mexico chili powder, or 3 medium pods (about ¾ ounce), toasted and ground (see note)
- 2 tablespoons cumin seeds, toasted in dry skillet over medium heat until fragrant, about 4 minutes, and ground
- 2 teaspoons dried oregano, preferably Mexican
- 4 pounds beef chuck roast, trimmed of excess fat and cut into 1-inch cubes (see illustrations on page 137)
  Salt
- 7–8 slices bacon (about 8 ounces), cut into ¼-inch pieces
- 1 medium onion, minced
- 5 medium garlic cloves, minced (about 5 teaspoons)
- 4–5 small jalapeño chile peppers, stemmed, seeded, and minced
- 1 cup canned crushed tomatoes or plain tomato sauce
- 2 tablespoons lime juice
- 5 tablespoons masa harina or 3 tablespoons cornstarch
  Ground black pepper

1. Mix chili powders, cumin, and oregano in small bowl and stir in ½ cup water to form thick paste; set aside. Toss beef cubes with 2 teaspoons salt in large bowl; set aside.

2. Fry bacon in large Dutch oven over medium-low heat until fat renders and bacon crisps, about 10 minutes. Remove bacon with slotted spoon to paper towel–lined plate; pour all but 2 teaspoons fat from pot into small bowl; set aside. Increase heat to medium-high; sauté meat in four batches until well-browned on all sides, about 5 minutes per batch, adding 2 teaspoons bacon fat to pot each time as necessary. Set browned meat aside in large bowl.

3. Reduce heat to medium and add 3 tablespoons bacon fat to now-empty pan. Add onion and sauté until softened, 5 to 6 minutes. Add garlic and jalapeños and sauté until fragrant, about 1 minute. Add chili powder mixture and sauté until fragrant, 2 to 3 minutes. Add reserved bacon and browned beef, crushed tomatoes or tomato sauce, lime juice, and 7 cups water. Bring to simmer. Continue to cook at steady simmer (lowering heat as necessary) until meat is tender and juices are dark, rich, and starting to thicken, about 2 hours.

4. Mix masa harina with ⅔ cup water (or cornstarch with 3 tablespoons water) in small bowl to form smooth paste. Increase heat to medium, stir in paste, and simmer until thickened, 5 to 10 minutes. Adjust seasonings generously with salt and ground black pepper to taste. Serve immediately or, for best flavor, cool slightly, cover, and refrigerate overnight or for up to 5 days. Reheat before serving.

SMOKY CHIPOTLE CHILI CON CARNE

Grill-smoking the meat in combination with chipotle chiles gives this chili a distinct, but not overwhelming, smoky flavor. Make sure you start with a chuck roast that is at least 3 inches thick. The grilling is meant to flavor the meat by searing the surface and smoking it lightly, not to cook it.

1. TO SMOKE THE MEAT: Mince 4 medium garlic cloves with 2 teaspoons salt on cutting board to form smooth puree. Rub intact chuck roast with puree, and sprinkle evenly with 2 to 3 tablespoons New Mexico chili powder; cover and set aside. Meanwhile, build hot fire in grill. When you can hold your hand 5 inches above grill surface for no more than 3 seconds, spread hot coals to area about size of roast. Open bottom grill vents, scatter 1 cup soaked mesquite or hickory wood chips over hot coals, and set grill rack in place. Place meat over hot coals and grill-roast, opening lid vents three-quarters of way and covering so that vents are over roast. Sear meat until all sides are dark and richly colored, about 12 minutes per side. Remove roast to bowl; when cool to touch, trim and cut into 1-inch cubes, reserving juices.

2. TO MAKE THE CHILI: Follow recipe for Chili Con Carne, omitting the browning of beef cubes and substituting 5 minced canned chipotle peppers in adobo sauce for jalapeños. Add grilled meat and juices with cooked bacon.

TASTING LAB: Dried Chiles

FOR THE MOST PART, CHILI CON CARNE IS BASED ON FAIRLY mild dried chiles. The most common of these are dark, mahogany red, wrinkly skinned ancho chiles, which have a deep, sweet, raisiny flavor; New Mexico Reds, which have a smooth, shiny, brick-red skin and a crisp, slightly acidic, earthy flavor; California chiles, which are very similar to New Mexico Reds in appearance but have a slightly milder flavor; and long, shiny, smooth, dark brown pasilla chiles. Pasillas, which are a little hotter than the other three varieties, have grapey, herby flavor notes, and, depending on the region of the country, are often packaged and sold as either ancho or mulato chiles.

We sampled each of these types, as well as a selection of preblended commercial powders, alone and in various combinations in batches of chili. Though the chilis made with individual chiles tasted much more pure and fresh than any of the premixed powders, they nonetheless seemed one-dimensional on their own. When all was said and done, the two-chile combination we favored was equal parts ancho, for its earthy, fruity sweetness and the stunning deep red color it imparted to the chili, and New Mexico, for its lighter flavor and crisp acidity.

Chile heat was another factor to consider. Hotter dried chiles that appear regularly in chili include guajillo, de árbol, pequin, japonés, and cayenne. Though we did not want to develop a fiery, overly hot chili, we did want a subtle bite to give the dish some oomph. We found that minced jalapeños, added with the garlic to the chili pot, supplied some heat and a fresh vegetal flavor.

TASTING LAB: Chili Powder

ALTHOUGH WE PREFER TO MAKE OUR OWN CHILI POWDER for chili con carne, we know that many cooks will use commercial chili powder. Chili powder is a curious product, often misunderstood. For one thing, the kind you find in the supermarket on the A-to-Z shelf of single herbs and spices is not itself a single spice, made only from powdered dried chiles. While there is no established formula for making chili powder, it typically consists of about 80 percent chile pepper blended with garlic powder, oregano, ground cumin seed, sometimes salt, and occasionally monosodium glutamate. Some blends even include traces of clove, allspice, anise, and coriander. Although a number of powders made solely from chiles can now be found in ethnic and specialty

Rating Chili Powders

WE TASTED NINE BRANDS OF CHILI POWDER IN A BARE-BONES RECIPE CONSISTING OF ONION, GROUND BEEF, crushed tomatoes, salt, and chili powder. The chili powders were rated for their aroma, depth of flavor, freshness, and spiciness. The products are listed in order of preference. See www.cooksillustrated.com for up-to-date prices and mail-order sources for top-rated products.

HIGHLY RECOMMENDED
1. Spice Islands Chili Powder
$2.77 for 2.4 ounces

This well-known supermarket brand was the clear winner. "It's got a big flavor that stands out compared to the others." Some tasters noted a smoky character likened to chocolate and molasses. Available in supermarkets, primarily on the West Coast.

RECOMMENDED
2. The El Paso Chile Company's Chili Spices and Fixin's
$2.95 for 2.5 ounces

Tasters liked this sample for its decent depth of flavor, freshness, and "pizazz." It was described as "deep yet sweet and complex," "smoky," and "earthy." This blend was deep red in color and contained no salt. Available by mail.

RECOMMENDED
3. Pendery's Top Hat Chile Blend
$4.73 for 2.56 ounces

This blend had many fans, who cheered it on for its warmth, depth of flavor, and "definite character." One taster put it simply: "Very nice punch. Makes me sweat." Contains MSG. Available by mail.

RECOMMENDED WITH RESERVATIONS
4. McCormick/Schilling Chili Powder (sold in glass bottle)
$4.49 for 2.12 ounces

Tasters' comments on this chili powder were brief owing to the overwhelming consensus that there just was not much flavor to discuss. "Uninteresting, but not offensive." Available in supermarkets. Sold under the Schilling label on the West Coast.

RECOMMENDED WITH RESERVATIONS
5. McCormick/Schilling Chili Powder (sold in plastic bottle)
$2.99 for 2.5 ounces

This chili powder was recommended by one taster as "good for people who don't like very spicy food." For many other tasters, this meant "bland" and "boring." Available in supermarkets.

NOT RECOMMENDED
6. Tone's Mild Chili Powder
$1.08 for .65 ounces

This product was deemed the spiciest but for all the wrong reasons, or, actually, just one reason—an excess of oregano. Available in Midwest supermarkets.

NOT RECOMMENDED
7. Gebhardt Chili Powder
$4.00 for 3 ounces

This brand, which can be hard to find outside of Texas, is extremely popular among chili cook-off competitors. Our tasters were not as enamored. It was remarkably bland but did give the chili a "nice, bright red color." Available in Texas supermarkets and by mail.

NOT RECOMMENDED
8. Pendery's Original Chile Blend
$4.14 for 2.24 ounces

This blend was noticeably sweet, with an assertive cumin flavor. Available by mail.

NOT RECOMMENDED
9. Durkee Chili Powder
$1.99 for .87 ounces

This chili powder offered "nothing exciting and nothing off-putting." In sum: "Needs oomph." Available in supermarkets.

markets, we stuck to blends because they are what most Americans cook with.

Another curious thing about chili powder is that it is usually not the source of the fiery heat for which much chili con carne is so beloved. Fresh chiles or additional dried chiles are typically added to drive up the heat.

Before we held our tasting, we spoke to a number of chili experts—chefs, cookbook authors, manufacturers, and other aficionados—to gain a better understanding of the flavor profile we might be seeking from the ideal chili powder. We learned that the key to a successful chili powder is a careful blending of the chiles, spices, and seasonings. No one component is meant to stand out boldly. In other words, a successful chili powder should contribute a complexity of flavors that can be hard to pinpoint and that work on different levels. Our idea of success was also an "independent" chili powder, capable of making a bowl of chili tasty with little or no help from other spices and seasonings. In other words, while we appreciated the idea of complexity of flavor, we also wanted some bravado.

For the most part, the results reinforced this estimation of an ideal chili powder. Those chili powders that delivered the most depth and assertiveness of flavor, otherwise described as "oomph," were the most highly rated. Unfortunately, only a few products were up to the task. Most were too subtle, leaving tasters wanting more spice and heat. A few tasters preferred the milder samples simply because they do not care for strong-flavored chili.

First and foremost, "Fresh is flavor," said Park Kerr, founder of the El Paso Chili Co., whose chili powder took second place in the tasting. Because, like most spices, chili powder contains volatile flavor components, it is important to purchase it from a source that has steady turnover. A busy supermarket or specialty spice store is probably where you'll find the freshest product.

Our panel of experts also emphasized that good chili powder depends less on the type of chile or chiles used in the blend than on their quality. Manufacturers of the three top-ranked products in the tasting credited their product's success to careful selection of quality chiles. Pat Haggerty, president of Pendery's, likened chili powder to sausage making: the ingredients can be carefully selected or they can be mixed in with "scraps." Unfortunately, none of the manufacturers we contacted were willing to give us more information about the types of chiles they use in their powder or about how the chiles are treated, since they consider this proprietary information.

There is really no great secret, however, as to the general kind of chiles used to make chili powders. The most common are large pod-type red chiles, such as New Mexico, California, and pasilla chiles. On the heat level scale, these are at the dead bottom. (Most of the chiles used in chili powder average about 1,000 to 2,000 Scoville units, the standard measure for chile pepper heat. To compare, jalapeño chiles, which are not typically used in commercial chili powders, are rated at an average of 10,000 Scoville units.)

Most chili powder manufacturers buy the chiles for their chili powders dried and roasted to their specifications. Some manufacturers will have the chile seeds included in the grind, which is said to contribute a more nutty flavor. Others, such as Pendery's, insist that the seeds be removed, claiming that they dilute the chile flavor and act as mere filler. The ground chiles are then blended with spices according to a specific formula and technique the manufacturer develops.

A third aspect of quality concerned salt content. Most of the less expensive chili powders in the tasting contained twice as much sodium as the more expensive brands. While this didn't seem to make them taste salty, the potency of their flavor was decidedly less assertive.

Finally, serious chili cooks rate a chili powder for its ability to contribute to the famed rich, bright color of a "bowl of red." This may explain why Gebhardt, which is a startlingly bright red, is a popular choice with chili cook-off competitors nationwide. While we found it lacking in flavor, this very lack may appeal to cooks who want to use it as a base on which to begin building a unique flavor profile. Ironically, the top-scoring product, by Spice Islands, had a much deeper color, more like a rich rust. According to

Donna Tainter, director of quality control and research and development for Spice Islands, the rich color is attributed not so much to the blend of spices but to a caramelization process that occurs as the chiles and spices are blended. This not only deepens the color but imparts a distinct, complex flavor that won over tasters.

EQUIPMENT CORNER: Pot Scrubbers

AT THE END OF EVERY MEAL COMES THE CHORE NO COOK likes: cleaning the pots and pans. Even perfectly cooked food often leaves behind a trail of pots with caked-on grease and grime. And if you've burned something, the job is that much more difficult.

There are a number of pot scrubbers on the market—everything from traditional steel wool pads to scouring pads made of copper wires—and all are designed to handle heavy-duty cleanup jobs. We rounded up eight types of scrubber and put them to work.

We tested each one by cleaning stainless steel pots and pans that had been used to cook rice, ground beef, jam, oatmeal, and a white sauce. In each case, we overcooked the food so that some stuck to the bottom of the pan. We used a small amount of liquid soap with each scrubber. We also tested durability by using the same scrubber to clean four pots with burned rice on the bottom. After the oatmeal test, we measured the ease with which food could be removed from the scrubbers themselves.

In the end, tasters liked the scouring pads with copper wires. They handled the dirtiest pans and were extremely durable. Regular-old steel wool pads were fine for finishing up pans, but they are not the best choice for pots with burned, stuck-on food. (We put S.O.S pads through the complete battery of kitchen tests, but other steel wool pads with soap, including Brillo, showed similar strengths and weaknesses in tests.) We also like Dobie pads, sponges covered with soft nylon. These pads were good for easy-to-moderate jobs and were especially easy on testers' hands.

SCIENCE DESK: Why Do We Eat Chiles?

CHILES ARE MYSTERIOUS IN MANY WAYS. WHY DO WE SAY they are "hot" when they are not hot in temperature? Why do people in hot climates tend to eat more chiles than people in cold climates? And, perhaps oddest of all, why do people enjoy eating something that causes pain?

There are several interesting theories about this last question. A psychologist named Paul Rozin came up with a theory years ago that still makes sense to us. He says that eating chiles is an example of what he calls "benign masochism." What's that?

Riding a rollercoaster is an example of benign masochism. As the rollercoaster goes up and down, your heart pounds faster and you have an adrenaline rush. Although it can feel dangerous, you know the ride will end safely. That's also what happens when you eat chiles—your body reacts to the physical sensation of danger, including the release of those chemicals called endorphins that give you a sense of well-being once you realize the danger has passed. So you get the thrill that follows the experience of danger without experiencing real danger. Other people have called chile eating "mouth surfing" for the same reason.

And why do you suppose people in hot climates eat more chiles? Two reasons. One, that's where chiles are grown. Two, eating chiles produces sweat, and when sweat evaporates you feel cooler, which is a good thing in hot tropical weather.

Rating Pot Scrubbers

WE TESTED EIGHT WIDELY AVAILABLE POT SCRUBBERS, CLEANING PANS WITH BURNT RICE, GROUND BEEF, JAM, oatmeal, and white sauce. The scrubbers are listed in order of preference and top-rated brands are sold in supermarkets.

RECOMMENDED

1. Chore Boy Copper Scouring Pads **$1.59 for 2 pads**

The king of scouring pads—very tough on sticky, tough jobs, cleans up pretty well, and has good durability. The copper wires are very abrasive and are good for stubborn messes that nothing else will remove.

RECOMMENDED

2. S.O.S Steel Wool Soap Pads **$1.89 for 10 pads**

After repeated uses, these pads began to fall apart. But given that 10 pads come in each box, we consider these pads disposable after 2 or 3 uses. Perfect for "finishing" pans once most of the big mess has been removed.

RECOMMENDED

3. Scotch-Brite Dobie Cleaning Pad **$1.19 for 1 pad**

This pad—a conventional sponge covered with nylon mesh—was good for easy-to-moderate cleaning jobs. Comfortable nylon won't irritate hands. Easy to clean and durable.

RECOMMENDED WITH RESERVATIONS

4. S.O.S. Heavy Duty Extra Thick Scrubber Sponge **$.99 for 1 sponge**

This conventional sponge comes with a coarse scrubber pad attached to one side. The sponge provided a comfortable grip and is great for finishing the job once the heavy scrubbing is complete. However, the scrubber only performed adequately. Good if you don't have lots of tough cleaning jobs and don't want a separate scrubber.

RECOMMENDED WITH RESERVATIONS

5. Lifetime Hoan Corp. Nylon Scrubber Set **$1.49 for 3 scrubbers**

These round nylon scrubbers were easy to grab and fit nicely into the corners of pots. They didn't show any wear and tear after repeated use, but performance was a notch below top choices.

RECOMMENDED WITH RESERVATIONS

6. Scotch-Brite Heavy Duty Scour Pads **$.79 for 2 pads**

These thin, coarse green pads look like artificial turf and worked best if folded in half—the flat design doesn't provide anything to hold onto. These pads lost their "oomph" over time and are difficult to clean thoroughly.

NOT RECOMMENDED

7. S.O.S. Clean Rinse Scrubber Sponge **$.89 for 1 sponge**

This conventional sponge with soft, plastic bristles on one side didn't remove much food from pans. Barely passable only for the lightest of jobs.

NOT RECOMMENDED

8. Williams-Sonoma Brass Brush **$3.50 for 1 brush**

This brush has a long wooden handle and coarse brass bristles. Unfortunately, we couldn't get the brush into pan corners. Our hands didn't get wet, but the pans didn't get clean, either. Available at Williams-Sonoma stores.

AMERICAN casseroles

Americans love casseroles. We serve them at potluck dinners, church suppers, and family meals. The challenge when making a good casserole is keeping the ingredients as fresh-tasting as possible. Too many casseroles are overcooked and dull, reminiscent of the worst cafeteria food.

Macaroni and cheese and turkey Tetrazzini are two classic casseroles, but they are rarely as good as they can be. Macaroni and cheese from a box is horrid. Frozen versions aren't much better. The real thing boasts a cream sauce loaded with real cheese flavor. The sauce should be smooth (no lumps) and easy to make. Recipes for turkey Tetrazzini often start with canned cream of mushroom soup and bake so long that the noodles turn to mush. We knew we could do better—much better—in the test kitchen.

Turkey Tetrazzini starts
with spaghetti cooked
on top of the stove.

MACARONI AND CHEESE

WHAT WE WANTED: A rich, creamy casserole with plenty of cheese flavor, properly cooked noodles, and a flawlessly smooth sauce.

There are two distinct styles of macaroni and cheese. In the more common béchamel-based style, macaroni is blanketed with a cheese-flavored white sauce, usually topped with crumbs, and baked. In the less common custard-based style, a mixture of eggs and milk is poured over layers of grated cheese and noodles. As the dish bakes, the eggs, milk, and cheese set into a custard. This macaroni and cheese is also topped with bread crumbs and baked.

Even though macaroni and cheese can be a wonderful, satisfying dish, many of the recipes we tested were tired, leaden, and uninspired. Others attempted to perk up the dish with canned green chiles, scallions, or olives. And, of course, there were attempts to lighten it. No one seemed to really love the dish enough to give it the care it deserves.

Then we ran across a recipe in John Thorne's *Simple Cooking* (Penguin, 1989). "As it happens," he begins, "I'm very fond of macaroni and cheese, and keep a special spot in my heart for cooks who genuinely love it: they are not that many." After reading his four-page essay, we suspected that his recipe for macaroni and cheese would be the real thing, the others mere shadows.

Making the dish confirmed suspicions. Thorne's macaroni and cheese was the best. His recipe starts with macaroni cooked just shy of al dente. The hot, drained macaroni is then tossed with butter in a heatproof pan or bowl. Evaporated milk, hot red pepper sauce, dry mustard, eggs, and a large quantity of cheese are stirred into the noodles. The combination is baked for 20 minutes, with the addition of more cheese and milk and a thorough stir every 5 minutes. Frequent stirrings allow the eggs to thicken without setting, which results in an incredibly silky sauce. During cooking, the sauce settles into the tubular openings of the pasta, offering a burst of cheese with each bite.

Out of curiosity, we baked the two styles of macaroni and cheese defined earlier: one with a cheese-flavored béchamel sauce, the other thickened with eggs, milk, and cheese. The béchamel-based version was grainy and tasted exactly as Thorne predicted: not like macaroni and cheese but like "macaroni with cheese sauce." In terms of texture, Thorne's macaroni and cheese was smooth silk, while the béchamel dish was thick velvet. The custard-based macaroni and cheese, really a baked version of Thorne's recipe, held more promise, and we thought we might offer it as an alternative to his stirred version. A side-by-side tasting proved the two dishes to be very different, however. The stirred version had a luxuriously silky cheese sauce, while the baked egg, milk, and cheese formed an unappealingly dry custard that set around the noodles.

With the competition ruled out, we moved forward to study Thorne's recipe a little more closely. We wondered if the dish really required evaporated milk or if this was a carryover from the late 1930s, when the recipe was first published in *The Home Comfort Cook Book* (Wrought Iron Range Company, 1937). Wouldn't regular milk or half-and-half work equally well and taste better? What cheeses besides sharp cheddar would taste good?

After testing the recipe with whole and low-fat milks and half-and-half, we realized that evaporated milk was indeed an important ingredient. All the macaroni and cheese dishes made with fresh dairy curdled a bit, resulting in a chalky, grainy texture. The dish made with evaporated milk remained flawlessly smooth. We learned that the evaporation and sterilization process used to produce evaporated milk stabilizes the milk; this in turn stabilizes the macaroni and cheese. (See the Science Desk on page 162 for details on how this works.)

As for the cheese, we tried several sharp and extra-sharp cheddars and preferred the former. Because the recipe calls for such a large quantity, a slightly milder cheese is preferable. Further testing confirmed this point. Macaroni and cheese made with Gruyère was so strong we couldn't even eat it. To our surprise, highly processed cheeses like American performed quite well. Similar to the case of the evaporated milk, the processing stabilizes the cheese and makes for a more creamy dish. For flavor, use cheddar; for texture, buy American. We also found the dish did not suffer when prepared with only 12 ounces of cheese as opposed to the pound called for in the original recipe.

Our one final problem to solve concerned the temperature of the macaroni and cheese when served. We found that at the end of the 20 minutes of baking recommended by Thorne, the dish was hot but hardly piping. By the time tasters had consumed their portions, the cheese sauce had cooled and set a bit. This problem, we learned, could not be remedied by leaving the dish in the oven much longer than the suggested 20 minutes. To do so meant running the risk of curdling the eggs, and the dish would develop a subtle grainy texture.

We wondered if we could cook the macaroni and cheese on top of the stove instead of in the oven. We found that by using a heavy-bottomed pot and cooking over low heat, it was possible to make the macaroni and cheese on top of the stove in less than five minutes. Not only was this method quicker, it kept the macaroni and cheese piping hot. If you like macaroni and cheese baked in a casserole dish, simply put the finished macaroni and cheese in a dish, cover with crumbs, and broil to toast the crumbs.

WHAT WE LEARNED: **Don't use a flour-thickened béchamel or baked custard for this dish. For the best texture and flavor, make macaroni and cheese on the stovetop (not in the oven) and use evaporated milk in the sauce. For some crunch, sprinkle with toasted buttered bread crumbs just before serving.**

STOVETOP MACARONI AND CHEESE

serves 4 as a main course or 6 to 8 as a side dish

If you're in a hurry or prefer to sprinkle the dish with crumbled crackers (saltines aren't bad), you can skip the bread crumb step. To make fresh bread crumbs, trim crusts from about 5 slices of good-quality white bread (we like Pepperidge Farm Toasting White) and grind them in the food processor until evenly fine-textured, 20 to 30 seconds.

toasted bread crumbs

- 2   tablespoons unsalted butter
- 1   cup fresh bread crumbs (see note)
    Pinch salt

creamy macaroni and cheese

- 2   large eggs
- 1   (12-ounce) can evaporated milk
- ¼   teaspoon hot red pepper sauce
- 2   teaspoons salt
- ¼   teaspoon ground black pepper
- 1   teaspoon dry mustard, dissolved in 1 teaspoon water
- ½   pound elbow macaroni
- 4   tablespoons unsalted butter
- 12 ounces sharp cheddar, American, or Monterey Jack cheese, grated (about 3 cups)

1. FOR THE BREAD CRUMBS: Heat butter in large skillet over medium heat until foam subsides. Add bread crumbs; cook, tossing to coat with butter, until crumbs just begin to color, about 10 minutes. Season to taste with salt; set aside.

2. FOR THE MACARONI AND CHEESE: Mix eggs, 1 cup evaporated milk, pepper sauce, ½ teaspoon salt, pepper, and mustard mixture in small bowl; set aside.

3. Meanwhile, bring 2 quarts water to a boil in large heavy-bottomed saucepan or Dutch oven. Add remaining 1½ teaspoons salt and macaroni; cook until almost tender but still a little firm to the bite. Drain and return to pan over low heat. Add butter; toss to melt.

4. Pour egg mixture over buttered noodles along with three-quarters of cheese; stir until thoroughly combined and the cheese starts to melt. Gradually add remaining milk and cheese, stirring constantly, until mixture is hot and creamy, about 5 minutes. Serve immediately, topped with toasted bread crumbs.

VARIATION

"BAKED" MACARONI AND CHEESE

This dish is for those who prefer their macaroni and cheese served out of a baking dish. Smooth and creamy like the stovetop version, this version is broiled just long enough to brown the crumb topping.

Follow recipe for Stovetop Macaroni and Cheese, pouring cooked macaroni and cheese into 9-inch-square gratin dish (or another heatproof baking dish of similar dimensions). Spread crumbs evenly over top. Broil until crumbs turn deep brown, 1 to 2 minutes. Let stand to set a bit, about 5 minutes, and serve immediately.

TASTING LAB: Cheddar Cheese

A GREAT FARMHOUSE CHEDDAR CHEESE IS HARD, FINE-textured, and flaky, with a sharp, tangy edge that's a little sweet, nutty, slightly bitter, and herbaceous. These various flavors come together to create a well-balanced, complex, and rewarding taste experience. The bad news is that farmhouse cheddars are expensive ($11 to $19 per pound) and often hard to find. Because supermarket cheddars are so easy to find and afford, we were interested in exploring their merits. We organized a blind tasting of eight common brands to find out which ones were best fresh out of the package and which fared best in a grilled cheese sandwich.

Before conducting the tasting, we were keen to find out what sort of cheese qualifies as cheddar. Unlike other great cheeses, such as Parmigiano-Reggiano and Stilton, cheddar is not name-protected. Anyone can make cheddar cheese anywhere and in any way. Although the U.S. government has set standards for the final product (the cheese must have no less than 50 percent milk fat solids and no more than 39 percent moisture), the means by which manufacturers produce cheddar are ungoverned. This is why there is so much variation in flavor and why even within the "sharp" category we found some cheeses as mild as mozzarella and others as robust as Parmesan.

The traditional method for making cheddar cheese is called cheddaring. During cheddaring, the curd (made by adding acid-producing cultures and clotting agents to unpasteurized whole milk) is cut into slabs, then stacked, cut, pressed, and stacked again. Along the way a large amount of liquid, called whey, is extracted from the curd base. The remaining compacted curd is what gives farmhouse cheddars their hard and fine-grained characteristics.

The quicker, safer, more cost-effective way to make cheddar, which is employed by most manufacturers to meet the ever-increasing demand of the mass market for cheese, is called the stirred-curd method. Instead of being stacked and weighted, as in the cheddaring process, the curd is

Rating Cheddar Cheeses

WE TASTED EIGHT CHEDDAR CHEESES AVAILABLE IN SUPERMARKETS AND NATURAL FOODS STORES. WE LIMITED THE TASTING to "sharp" cheddars, which are aged from 60 days up to one year. Cheeses were tasted cubed and in grilled cheese sandwiches. Cheeses are listed in order of preference based on their combined scores when sampled raw and in sandwiches.

RECOMMENDED

1. Cabot Sharp Vermont Cheddar Cheese **$2.99 for 8 ounces; aged 5 to 8 months**

This cheese won both the grilled cheese and the raw tastings. Tasters liked its approachable flavor, described as "sharp," "clean," and "tangy." In a grilled cheese sandwich, it was "buttery" and "mellow" without being even the slightest bit greasy.

RECOMMENDED

2. Tillamook Sharp Cheddar Cheese **$6.99 for 1 pound; aged 9 months**

As the only cheese in the tasting that is annatto-colored (it's orange rather than white), raw Tillamook cheddar stood out not only for its color but for its "tangy" and "piquant" characteristics. Tasters liked this cheese less in the grilled cheese sandwich, where it was criticized for "sweet" and "sour" flavors.

RECOMMENDED

3. Cracker Barrel Sharp White Cheddar Cheese **$3.29 for 10 ounces; aged 2 months**

Called "flavorful and easy," Cracker Barrel won tasters over with its "mellow," "clean" flavor. In the grilled cheese sandwich, it was described as "good and generic," with a "smooth" and "cohesive" texture.

RECOMMENDED

4. Grafton Village Cheese Company Premium Vermont Cheddar Cheese **$3.89 for 8 ounces; aged 1 year**

Grafton uses unpasteurized milk and traditional cheddar-making methods. The crumbly texture and pungent flavor earned top scores among many tasters. Some, however, found it too "pungent."

RECOMMENDED WITH RESERVATIONS

5. Horizon Organic Cheddar Cheese **$3.99 for 8 ounces; aged 6 to 9 months**

Many tasters commented that Horizon Organic cheddar "didn't taste like cheddar"—that it was too potent. While some liked its strength, others called it "stinky" and "barnyardy." Most tasters found the cheese too "runny" when melted.

RECOMMENDED WITH RESERVATIONS

6. Land O Lakes Sharp Cheddar Cheese **$1.99 for 8 ounces; aged 6 to 12 months**

"This cheese is like the kind on a supermarket deli platter," commented one taster, with other tasters agreeing, calling it "bland," "boring," and "rubbery" when eaten out of hand. In the grilled cheese sandwich, some called it "dull," but others liked the "classic grilled cheese" flavor. Called Lake to Lake Cheddar Cheese on the West Coast.

NOT RECOMMENDED

7. Organic Valley Organic Raw Milk Sharp Cheddar **$10.59 for 1 pound; aged 10 months**

Described as "buttermilky" and "sour," this unpasteurized cheddar didn't find many fans. Its texture was described as "rubbery" and "gummy" when raw and "greasy" and "oozy" when melted.

NOT RECOMMENDED

8. Heluva Good Sharp Cheddar Cheese **$2.19 for 8 ounces; aged 2 to 9 months**

"Tastes like mozzarella," said one taster, while another called it "completely one-dimensional." Most found it "tasteless" and "rubbery" both when eaten raw and when melted in a grilled cheese sandwich.

stirred and then pressed against the sides of a large vat to remove the whey. This shortcut changes the texture of the curd slightly, producing a softer, more pliable cheese. Is stirred-curd cheese still technically a cheddar cheese even though it's not cheddared? According to federal standards, it is—as long as it meets the composition requirements for milk fat solids and moisture.

Grafton Village (number four in the tasting) is one of the only companies in the tasting that still hand-cheddars its cheese. This was evident to our tasters, who overwhelmingly described Grafton's cheddar as "flaky" and "crumbly," just like a farmhouse cheddar. Brands made with the stirred-curd method were universally described as even-textured and smooth. To our surprise, tasters did not automatically mark down brands with a smooth texture. In fact, Cabot, Tillamook, and Cracker Barrel, all made using the stirred-curd method, rated higher than Grafton Village's hand-cheddared cheese.

One of the great surprises of our tasting was the success of Cracker Barrel, which, at a mere $3.29 for 10 ounces, outpolled Organic Valley cheddar, which sells for $10.59 per pound and is made with raw milk. Part of the reason for Organic Valley's low rating was its performance in a grilled cheese sandwich. When melted, Organic Valley cheddar became greasy as the fat separated from the milk solids in the cheese. Melted Cracker Barrel, on the other hand, was described by tasters as both "smooth" and "cohesive."

We also had to confront the proclivities of our palates. Because most of us were raised on lower-quality supermarket cheddars, we aren't used to "barnyard" flavors, such as those found in the Horizon Organic and Organic Valley brands. At first, we thought that our rejection of these flavors was merely a lack of sophistication, but this notion was quickly set aside when we tasted authentic farmhouse cheddars that were full-flavored but also sweet, nutty, and herbaceous. All four of the farmhouse cheddars we tasted outpolled Cabot, our top choice among supermarket cheddars. Our favorite farmhouse cheddar comes from England and is produced by a company called Keen's. This cheese is tangy, nutty, and rich. Expect to pay about $18 per pound for this fine cheese.

SCIENCE DESK:
Why Doesn't Evaporated Milk Curdle?

ALL OF THE MACARONI AND CHEESE RECIPES WE TESTED with fresh milk curdled a bit, resulting in a chalky, grainy texture. The one made with evaporated milk remained silky smooth. Why?

Evaporated milk begins as fresh whole milk. In processing, about 60 percent of the water in the milk is removed as the milk is boiled in a vacuum, creating a thickened liquid. This thickened milk is then canned and sterilized. The result is shelf-stable evaporated milk

The process by which the milk is initially heated is called fore-warming. This gentle, controlled heating of the milk helps to condition the proteins to make them more resistant to curdling. The main proteins in question here are large molecules called casein. When exposed to heat, casein molecules tend to clump; these are the chalky bits we saw in the sauce of the macaroni and cheese made with fresh milk. During fore-warming, the big casein molecules are surrounded by smaller molecules of whey protein, and the whey proteins get in the way of the clumping of the casein molecules.

Also interfering with the clumping of the casein molecules are additives in the evaporated milk. Salts, in the form of disodium phosphate and/or sodium citrate, are added to improve the ability of the proteins in the mix to retain water (the release of water is another symptom of curdling). A gum called carrageenan may also be added to prevent fat separation in storage.

How does evaporated milk differ from condensed milk? Evaporated and condensed milk are both made in the same way at the start: by heating milk in a vacuum so that 60 percent or more of the water evaporates. The resulting thick liquid is then either given a high-temperature treatment to sterilize it, making evaporated milk, or heavily sweetened to preserve it, making condensed milk. Both evaporated and condensed milk have about twice the concentration of fat and protein as regular whole milk.

TURKEY TETRAZZINI

WHAT WE WANTED: Turkey Tetrazzini can be an interesting blend of toasted bread crumbs, silky sauce, and a modicum of turkey meat, all bound together by one of our favorite foods: spaghetti. Or it can taste like stale cafeteria food. We wanted the former, not the latter.

The downside of most casseroles—in which the fusion of individual tastes and textures diminishes them—is especially true about turkey Tetrazzini. This dish is often stodgy and heavy, but we wondered if a basic noodle casserole could be reengineered so that this eminently practical American dish could be made worthy of a well-laid table.

A bit of culinary sleuthing solved the most pressing problem: the fact that the ingredients are double-cooked. (Most casserole recipes are two-step affairs: Cook the ingredients, mix them together, and then bake them in a casserole.) In *American Cookery* (Little, Brown & Co., 1972), James Beard suggests using a shallow baking dish rather than a deep casserole. Paired with a very hot (450-degree) oven, this reduces the baking time to a mere 15 minutes, a fraction of the time suggested by most cookbooks. Tasted against casseroles made with longer baking times in slower ovens, those made with this quick method won, hands down; their fresher-tasting vegetables set them leagues apart from the overcooked dullness of cafeteria cuisine.

Next we adjusted the sauce. The traditional choice is béchamel, a sauce in which milk is added to a roux, a paste made from flour and hot fat. We decided to use a velouté, a sauce based on chicken stock rather than dairy. This brightened up both the texture and the flavor, since dairy tends to dampen other flavors. We also played around with the amount of sauce, trying larger and smaller quantities, and found that more sauce overran the taste of the other ingredients. In this case, less was more. It still needed a burst of flavor, however, so we spruced it up with a shot of sherry

and a little lemon juice and nutmeg; a bit of Parmesan cheese provided tang and bite; and a full 2 teaspoons of fresh thyme also helped freshen the flavor.

Most recipes do not toast the bread crumbs before baking. Doing so does add an extra step (in a pinch, you can skip the toasting), but it also adds to the flavor and texture of the dish; it's worth the minimal effort required. Tossing the toasted bread crumbs with a bit of grated Parmesan also helps to boost the flavor.

WHAT WE LEARNED: Pass up the traditional milk-based béchamel sauce and use instead a chicken broth–based velouté sauce, which brightens the flavor of the dish and makes it less heavy. Bake the casserole only briefly in a shallow gratin dish in a hot oven to keep the pasta and vegetables from overcooking.

TURKEY TETRAZZINI serves 8

Tetrazzini is also great when made with leftover chicken. Using a shallow baking dish without a cover and a very hot oven benefits both texture and flavor. Don't skimp on the salt and pepper; this dish needs aggressive seasoning. To make fresh bread crumbs, trim crusts from about 8 slices of good-quality white bread (we like Pepperidge Farm Toasting White) and grind them in the food processor until evenly fine-textured, 20 to 30 seconds.

bread crumb topping

1½ cups fresh bread crumbs (see note)
    Pinch salt
4   tablespoons unsalted butter, melted
¼   cup grated Parmesan cheese

filling

8   tablespoons unsalted butter, plus extra for baking dish
8   ounces white button mushrooms, cleaned and sliced thin (about 3 cups)
2   medium onions, chopped fine (about 1½ cups)
    Salt and ground black pepper
¾   pound spaghetti or other long-strand pasta, strands snapped in half
6   tablespoons unbleached all-purpose flour
3   cups canned low-sodium chicken broth
4   tablespoons dry sherry
¾   cup grated Parmesan cheese
¼   teaspoon grated nutmeg
1   tablespoon juice from 1 lemon
2   teaspoons minced fresh thyme leaves
2   cups frozen peas
4   cups leftover cooked boneless turkey or chicken meat, cut into ¼-inch pieces

1. FOR THE TOPPING: Adjust oven rack to middle position and heat oven to 350 degrees. Mix bread crumbs, salt, and butter in small baking dish; bake until golden brown and crisp, 15 to 20 minutes. Cool to room temperature and mix with ¼ cup Parmesan in small bowl. Set aside.

TECHNIQUE: Breaking Long Pasta Strands Neatly

Though we don't usually recommend breaking strand pasta that we plan to sauce and eat, broken spaghetti or linguine is used in some casseroles, such as turkey Tetrazzini. Here's a neat way to break the spaghetti in half without causing short strands to fly every which way in the kitchen.

1. Roll up the bundle of spaghetti in a kitchen towel that overlaps the pasta by 3 or 4 inches at both ends.

2. Holding both ends firmly, center the rolled bundle over the edge of a counter. Push down with both hands to break the pasta in the middle of the bundle.

3. Holding the bundle vertically over the pot of boiling water, release the bottom of the towel so that the pasta slides neatly into the pot.

2. FOR THE FILLING: Increase oven temperature to 450 degrees. Heat 2 tablespoons butter in large skillet over medium heat until foaming subsides; add mushrooms and onions and sauté, stirring frequently, until liquid from mushrooms evaporates, 12 to 15 minutes. Season with salt and pepper to taste; transfer to medium bowl and set aside. Clean skillet.

3. Meanwhile, bring 4 quarts water to a boil in large pot. Add 1 tablespoon salt and pasta and cook until al dente. Reserve ¼ cup cooking water, drain spaghetti, and return to pot with reserved liquid.

4. Melt remaining 6 tablespoons butter in cleaned skillet over medium heat. When foam subsides, whisk in flour and cook, whisking constantly, until flour turns golden, 1 to 2 minutes. Whisking constantly, gradually add chicken stock. Turn heat to medium-high and simmer until mixture thickens, 3 to 4 minutes. Off heat, whisk in sherry, Parmesan, nutmeg, lemon juice, thyme, and ½ teaspoon salt. Add sauce, sautéed vegetables, peas, and turkey to spaghetti and mix well; adjust seasonings to taste.

5. Turn mixture into buttered 9 by 13-inch gratin dish (or other shallow, ovenproof baking dish of similar size), sprinkle evenly with reserved bread crumbs, and bake until bread crumbs brown and mixture is bubbly, 13 to 15 minutes. Serve immediately.

EQUIPMENT CORNER: Gratin Dishes

WE FOUND THAT A WIDE, SHALLOW DISH IS THE KEY TO good turkey Tetrazzini. A gratin dish (gratin means crust and usually refers to a cheese or bread crumb topping that browns in a hot oven) maximizes the surface area while giving the heat easy access to the crumbs on top. A tour of any kitchen store, however, doesn't limit the possibilities for dishes that fit this bill. We found eight possible options, priced from $7 to $160, including several specifically labeled "gratin dishes" as well as those sold as "casserole dishes" or "oval dishes." We tested these eight dishes to see what differences, if any, we could find.

First and foremost, you must match the surface area of the dish with the recipe. We found that a dish that is too small caused the crumbs to pack on top of one another, creating a layer beneath the surface that never browned. On the other hand, a dish that is too large caused the crumbs to scatter too far apart so that no cohesive layer could form. A dish that is perfect for one recipe might not work in another, so pay attention to sizes in recipes.

We also found the depth of the dish to be important. The 4-inch-high sides of the Corning Ware 4-quart oval roaster ($21.99) cast a shadow over the contents that prevented the edges from browning. Most dishes have shallower sides (we found 2 inches to be ideal) that promote browning.

Another factor is material. Le Creuset's 14-inch oval dish is made of enameled cast-iron, which heats up very slowly. The gratins and casseroles made in this dish were still cool by the time the crust was toasted. We found that lighter, faster-heating materials, such as glass, porcelain, and stainless steel, are better choices for a gratin dish.

Which dish should you buy? We produced hot, nicely browned gratins in several dishes—the Pyrex 2-quart casserole dish ($7), the Emile Henry 13-inch oval dish ($35), the Apilco #14 oval au gratin dish ($68), and the All Clad Stainless oval au gratin dish ($160). All these dishes have shallow sides, between 1¾ and 2 inches high. More money might buy better looks, but it doesn't buy better performance.

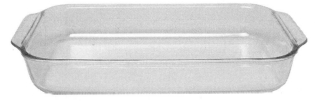

BEST GRATIN DISH
We found that a Pyrex casserole dish, available in any hardware store or kitchen shop, performs well and costs a fraction of the price of other options.

Unlike a fork, tongs won't puncture pork chops and let the juices run out. Tongs are our first choice for turning all meats as they cook.

PORK CHOPS
two ways
CHAPTER 13

We love a juicy, flavorful pork chop. Too bad most pork chops are dry and bland. The pork industry has reduced the fat in pigs by 50 percent since the 1950s. Yes, pork is now the "other white meat," nearly as lean as chicken. But along with all that fat went flavor and juiciness.

Because modern pork is so lean, the home cook has to use new cooking methods to get good results. Well-done pork chops will be tough as shoe leather and won't taste much better. When grilling, this means cooking the chops until they are just a touch rosy in the center. Brining—soaking foods in a solution of water, salt, and sometimes sugar—is another option we wanted to consider.

On the stovetop, we like old-fashioned smothered pork chops in a rich onion gravy. This recipe suffers from twin problems—the pork is tough (not tender, as it should be) and the gravy often starts with canned soup and tastes artificial and pasty. We knew we could do better.

GRILLED PORK CHOPS

WHAT WE WANTED: Thick-cut pork chops that are seared and crispy outside and juicy and perfectly cooked inside.

Burgers and chicken are predictable grilling fare, but throw a thick, juicy pork chop on the fire and you have something exceptional, at least in theory. The reality of many a grilled pork chop is a burnt exterior, raw interior, tough meat, nary a hint of flavor—the list goes on. We were looking for perfection: a plump, Rubenesque chop with a seared crust reminiscent of chiaroscuro and an interior that would be juicy and flavorful all the way to the bone. We wanted a chop that looked and tasted so good that it transcended the far reaches of backyard grilling and became art.

Thick pork chops usually come from the loin of the pig, which runs from the shoulder to the hip (see Getting It Right on page 170). To determine which cut would be best, we conducted a blind taste test with four different chops, starting with the blade chop, which is from the shoulder end, or front, of the loin. Because the shoulder region of the loin has the most fat and is riddled with connective tissue, tasters found the blade chops to be full of flavor but also tough and chewy. At the hip end of the loin are the sirloin chops. These were dry, somewhat tasteless, and a bit tough. Moving on to the center of the loin, we tested the center-cut chop and the rib chop. Although both were tender and flavorful, tasters preferred the rib chops, which were juicy and well marbled with fat.

Although rib chops are flavorful on their own, we wanted to see if we could boost their flavor by using a spice rub, marinade, or brine. We tested two types of rub: dry and wet. The wet rubs, made with spices and a liquid, gave the chops good flavor but also caused their exterior to turn syrupy. Tasters preferred the dry rubs, which combine potent dried spices with sugar to create big flavor and a crisp crust.

Next we tried marinating the chops in an acidic oil mixture flavored with herbs and garlic. While the marinade succeeded in flavoring the exterior of the chops, it did little for the interior. Moreover, the meat took on a slimy texture that prohibited formation of a good crust.

Finally, we tried brining, a method we often turn to here at America's Test Kitchen, in which lean cuts of meat (usually pork or poultry) are soaked in a solution of water and salt and sometimes sugar. (Brining yields moist, well-seasoned meat and poultry that are hard to overcook, an important factor when grilling.) The brined chops were well seasoned throughout, not just on the surface. They were also extremely juicy—each bite was full of moist, seasoned pork flavor, complemented by the warm crunch of the spice rub.

It was now time to grill. As a preliminary test, we pitted hardwood charcoal against the more traditional charcoal briquettes. After grilling a few chops over each, we found we preferred the hardwood for its intensely hot fire and slightly smoky flavor. As for the fire itself, we always begin testing with a single-level fire—that is, a fire of even and generally high heat made by spreading coals evenly across the grill. We threw the chops over the fire and watched as they browned to a beautiful bronze within minutes. But when we pulled the chops off the grill and cut into one, it was rare at the bone. Moderating the temperature of the fire only drew out the cooking time and sacrificed the deep, caramelized crust we had achieved over high heat.

Moving next to a two-level fire, which is achieved by banking more hot coals on one side of the grill than on the other, we tried a multitude of temperature combinations, each time starting the chops over high heat to develop a nicely browned crust. Moving the chops from high to medium, high to low, and high to no heat were all tested, but none of these combinations produced a thoroughly cooked interior in a reasonable amount of time. Throwing the grill lid back on after the initial sear cooked the chops all the way through—a breakthrough to be sure—but the flavor of the meat was adversely affected. (The inside of most charcoal grill covers is coated with a charcoal residue that readily imparts bitter, spent flavors to foods.) Seizing on the notion of covering the chops for part of the cooking time, we turned to a handy disposable aluminum roasting pan to solve the problem. We threw the pan over the chops after searing them over high heat and moving them to the cooler part of the grill. This time we had a crisp crust, juicy meat, and no off flavors.

In our eagerness to serve these perfect chops, we cut into them right off the grill and watched as the juices ran out onto the plate. We allowed the next round of chops to sit covered under the foil pan for five minutes. When we cut into the chops this time, only a little of the juice was expelled. We were surprised, however, to find that these chops were slightly tougher than the chops that did not rest. We took the internal temperature and found that it was now nearly 165 degrees—overcooked in our book. (At 145 degrees, pork is cooked, safe to eat, and still juicy. Temperatures above 150 degrees yield dry, tough meat.) We cooked one more batch of chops and this time took them off the grill earlier, once they had reached an internal temperature of 135 degrees, and let them sit under the foil pan for a good five minutes. Thanks to the residual heat left in the bone, the temperature shot up an average of 10 to 15 degrees, bringing the meat into that desirable range of 145 to 150. Magic. Or perhaps this was art.

WHAT WE LEARNED: **Buy bone-in rib chops, brine them to promote juiciness, sear them quickly, and then allow the interior of the chop to finish cooking over a cooler part of the grill and under a disposable aluminum pan. Pull the chops from the grill when they reach an internal temperature of 135 degrees, cover them with a foil pan, and let the chops rest until the temperature rises 10 to 15 degrees higher and the juices are redistributed in the meat.**

CHARCOAL-GRILLED PORK CHOPS serves 4

Rib loin chops are our top choice for their big flavor and juiciness. Spice rubs add a lot of flavor for very little effort, but the chops can also be seasoned with pepper alone just before grilling. You will need a large disposable aluminum roasting pan to cover the chops and help them finish cooking through to the bone.

¾ cup kosher salt or 6 tablespoons table salt
6 tablespoons sugar
4 bone-in pork loin rib chops or center-cut loin chops, each 1½ inches thick (about 3 pounds total)
1 recipe spice rub (recipes follow) or ground black pepper

1. Dissolve salt and sugar in 3 quarts cold water in 2-gallon zipper-lock plastic bag. Add chops and seal bag, pressing out as much air as possible. (Alternatively, divide brine and chops evenly between two 1-gallon zipper-lock bags.) Refrigerate, turning bag once, until fully seasoned, about 1 hour. Remove chops from brine and dry thoroughly with paper towels. Coat chops with spice rub or season generously with pepper.

2. Ignite large chimney starter filled with hardwood charcoal (about 6 quarts) and burn until covered with thin coating of light gray ash. Build two-level fire by stacking most of coals on one side of grill and arranging remaining coals in single layer on other side. Set cooking grate in place, cover grill with lid, and let grate heat up, about 5 minutes. Use wire brush to scrape cooking grate clean.

3. Cook chops, uncovered, over hotter part of grill until browned on each side, 2½ to 3 minutes per side. Move chops to cooler part of grill and cover with disposable aluminum roasting pan. Continue grilling, turning once, until instant-read thermometer inserted through side of chop and away from bone registers 135 degrees, 7 to 9 minutes longer. Transfer chops to platter; cover with foil pan, and let rest 5 minutes. Internal temperature should rise to 145 degrees. Serve immediately.

VARIATION

GAS-GRILLED PORK CHOPS

Because gas grill lids don't build up a residue that can impart an off flavor to foods (as charcoal grills do), they can be used to concentrate heat to cook the pork chops through; there's no need for a disposable roasting pan.

Follow step 1 of recipe for Charcoal-Grilled Pork Chops. Light grill and turn all burners to high; cover and heat grill 15 minutes. Use wire brush to scrape cooking grate clean. Turn off all but one burner. Place chops over hotter part of grill, cover, and cook until browned on each side, 3 to 4 minutes per side. Move chops to cooler side of grill. Cover and continue cooking, turning once, until instant-read thermometer inserted through side of chop and away from bone registers 135 degrees, 7 to 9 minutes longer. Transfer chops to platter, tent loosely with foil, and let rest 5 minutes. Internal temperature should rise to 145 degrees. Serve immediately.

BASIC SPICE RUB FOR PORK CHOPS

makes ¼ cup, enough for 4 chops

1   tablespoon ground cumin
1   tablespoon chili powder
1   tablespoon curry powder
1   teaspoon ground black pepper
2   teaspoons brown sugar

Combine all ingredients in small bowl.

GETTING IT RIGHT: Shopping for Chops

Pork chops come from the loin of the pig. A whole pork loin weighs 14 to 17 pounds and can be cut into blade chops, rib chops, center-cut chops, and sirloin chops. The loin muscle runs the entire length of the backbone. Starting midway back, the tenderloin muscle runs along the opposite side of the backbone. Center-cut and sirloin chops contain both kinds of muscle. We found that the tenderloin cooks more quickly than the loin and can dry out. This is one reason why we prefer rib chops, which contain only loin meat. Following are tasters' impressions after sampling four different chops cut from the loin. Rib chops were tasters' top choice, followed by center-cut chops.

 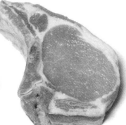 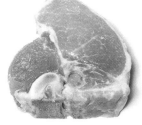 

BLADE CHOP
Fattiest, toughest, juiciest, most flavor

RIB CHOP
Some fat, relatively tender, juicy, great flavor

CENTER-CUT CHOP
Little fat, relatively tender, less juicy, good flavor

SIRLOIN CHOP
Tough, quite dry, little flavor

INDIAN SPICE RUB FOR PORK CHOPS

makes scant ¼ cup, enough for 4 chops

1	tablespoon fennel seeds
1	tablespoon ground cumin
1	teaspoon ground coriander
1	teaspoon ground cardamom
1	teaspoon dry mustard
½	teaspoon ground cinnamon
¼	teaspoon ground cloves
2	teaspoons brown sugar

Grind fennel seeds to powder in spice grinder. Mix with remaining ingredients in small bowl.

EQUIPMENT CORNER: Gas Grills

GAS GRILLS NOW ACCOUNT FOR 6 OUT OF EVERY 10 GRILLS SOLD IN this country. The reasons for their increasing popularity are clear: The fire is easy to light and control. We tested six grills from the leading manufacturers and came to the following conclusions.

In general, we found that you get what you pay for. Inexpensive gas grills, priced at $200 or less, are generally inferior. If you are willing to spend more money (about $350), you can buy a gas grill that works extremely well, with results that can compete with the charcoal grill.

Several features and design elements separate a good gas grill from a poor one. A built-in thermometer that registers real numbers (not just low, medium, and hot) is essential. A gauge that tells you how much gas is left in the tank is also a plus. As you might expect, a large grill offers the cook more possibilities. Unless the cooking surface has an area of at least 400 square inches, you will be able to cook only one slab of ribs at a time. In addition to size, the number of burners is critical. It's not possible to cook by indirect heat on a grill with only one burner because the burner is usually positioned in the center of the grill and the "cool" parts of the grill are too small to accommodate most foods. Indirect cooking requires a grill with at least two burners. With one burner on and one burner off, at least half of the grill will be cool enough for slow cooking.

We found that most gas grills are plenty hot. A bigger problem is that gas grills are often unable to sustain temperatures low enough for barbecuing. Many of the cheaper grills we tested were unable to barbecue a brisket without burning the exterior before the meat was tender. A good grill will maintain a temperature of 250 degrees when the lid is down and just one burner is lit and turned to low.

Perhaps the most shocking conclusion we came to during our testing of gas grills concerned flare-ups. We found that lava rocks soak up dripping fat and will catch fire as

---

TECHNIQUE:
Checking the Fuel Level in a Tank

There's nothing worse than running out of fuel halfway through grilling. If your grill doesn't have a gas gauge, use this technique to estimate how much gas is left in the tank.

1. Bring a cup or so of water to a boil in a small saucepan or glass measuring cup (if using the microwave). Pour the water over the side of the tank.

2. Feel the metal with your hand. Where the water has succeeded in warming the tank, it is empty; where the tank remains cool to the touch, there is still propane inside.

soon as there is some sort of flare-up. Several times we moved flaming chicken parts to the cool side of the grill (without a lit burner), and they still flamed from below for several minutes. It wasn't the chicken that was on fire, it was the lava rocks, which had caught fire even though the burner underneath them was cool.

Lava rocks are not the sole reason for flare-ups. Poor design that traps grease on the bottom of the grill doesn't help either. We consider a drainage system mandatory. The bottom of the cooking chamber should be sloped so that fat runs through an opening in the center and into a drip pan below.

Our favorites among the grills tested, Weber grills, do not have lava rocks. Bars, made from steel coated with porcelain-enamel and shaped like an upside-down V, channel fat down into the bottom of the grill and eventually into a drip pan attached to the underside of the cooking chamber. We find this drainage system to be far superior to other options. For all of these reasons, our favorite grills are the Weber Genesis Silver series, which comes in three different models.

BEST GAS GRILL

We tested grills from leading manufacturers and preferred the Weber Genesis Silver series. The Silver C (seen here) costs $500 and boasts three main grilling burners plus a side burner for heating sauces, beans, or other side dishes. The Silver B ($450) is the same grill minus the side burner. The Silver A ($350) has just two grilling burners. See www.cooksillustrated.com for up-to-date prices and mail-order sources for top-rated products.

GETTING IT RIGHT: Anatomy of a Gas Grill

When shopping for a gas grill, make sure the model you choose has a temperature gauge that registers real numbers, not just low, medium, and high. A fuel gauge, which lets you know when the tank is running low, is another helpful feature.

A warming rack can be useful, but you may want to remove it before grilling for full access to the cooking surface. Weber grills, our top choices, have flavorizer bars—we prefer them to lava rocks—which help direct fat down into the drip pan. To avoid flare-ups, make sure to buy a grill with a good system for draining fat.

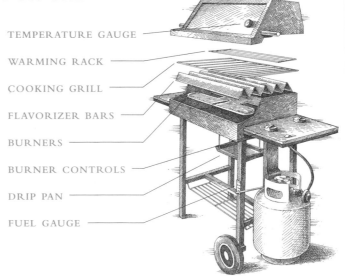

TEMPERATURE GAUGE

WARMING RACK

COOKING GRILL

FLAVORIZER BARS

BURNERS

BURNER CONTROLS

DRIP PAN

FUEL GAUGE

Why Are Bone-In Chops Better?

WE KNEW FROM PAST EXPERIENCE THAT BONE-IN CHOPS taste better than boneless chops, but we wanted to test this notion more systemically. To find out how boneless chops would fare on the grill, we removed the bones from several rib chops, grilled them, and compared them with their bone-in counterparts in a blind taste test. (We took the meat off the grilled bone-in chops and then sliced the meat from both chops so as not to tip off tasters.) The results were clear. Every taster preferred the meat that had been cooked on the bone. It was much more juicy and had more pork flavor than the meat cooked without the bone. We contacted several food scientists, who offered a few explanations.

First, because bone is a poor conductor of heat, the meat located next to the bone doesn't cook as quickly as the rest. Although this factor doesn't alter the cooking time significantly, having a section of the pork chop cook at a slightly slower rate contributes to a juicier end product.

The bone also insulates the muscle closest to it, protecting it from exposure to the air. In a boneless chop, a larger area of muscle is exposed, so more of the flavorful juices evaporate during grilling.

Finally, fat is a crucial source of flavor, and, as it melts during cooking, it also increases the perceived juiciness. In certain cuts, especially ribs and chops, deposits of fat are located next to the bone. When the bone is removed, some fat is removed as well. With less fat, the boneless chops cook up with less pork flavor and seem drier.

TECHNIQUE:
Protecting Gas Grill Controls

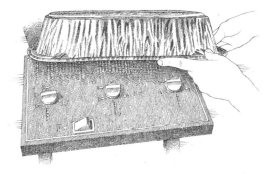

The ignition and burner control knobs on some gas grills can be persnickety if they get wet or dirty from exposure to the elements, especially if the grill is kept outdoors in the snow during the winter. If you don't own a grill cover, try inverting a disposable aluminum roasting pan over the control panel and tape it in place on either end with duct or electrical tape.

TASTING LAB: Enhanced Pork

TODAY'S PORK IS 50 PERCENT LEANER THAN ITS COUNTERpart in the 1950s, and less fat means less flavor and moisture. The industry has addressed this issue by introducing a product called enhanced pork, meat injected with a solution of water, salt, and sodium phosphate. The idea is to both season the pork and keep it from drying out. (The sodium phosphate increases the pH of the meat, which improves its water-retention abilities.) We wondered if we could skip brining and save time by using enhanced pork.

In a side-by-side test, we compared enhanced and unenhanced pork chops as well as brined versions of both. The enhanced pork was salty and had a somewhat artificial flavor. When brined, these chops were extremely salty and inedible. The unenhanced pork that was not brined was dry and bland. The unenhanced pork that had been brined was juicy and well seasoned—it was the clear winner.

As far as we are concerned, the benefits of brining pork are clear. First, you control the salt and avoid any artificial aftertaste. Second, brining guarantees moist meat (as long as you don't overcook pork).

During our research, we found a few supermarkets that carried only enhanced pork. If you must buy enhanced pork, skip the brining step in our grilled pork chop recipe.

SMOTHERED PORK CHOPS

WHAT WE WANTED: Tender, flavorful chops complemented by a heady onion gravy with a satiny, just-thick-enough texture.

Smothered pork chops, a homey dish of chops braised in deeply flavored onion gravy, are folksy, not fancy; denim, not worsted wool. Despite a straightforward cooking process—brown the chops, remove them from the pan, brown the onions, return the chops and cover them with the onions and gravy (hence the term smothered), and braise until tender—initial recipe tests produced bland, dry pork, and near-tasteless gravies with woeful consistencies ranging from pasty to processed to gelatinous to watery.

Poor texture and shallow flavor robs smothered pork chops of their savory-sweet glory. To get it right, we knew we'd have to identify the best chop and the best way to cook it. And the gravy was no less important.

Some of our research recipes specified sirloin chops, which are cut from the rear end of the loin. Our tasters found this cut a little dry and often unavailable. Blade chops, cut from the far front end of the loin, were juicier but suffered the same spotty availability. Of the two remaining types of chops, center-cut loin and rib, we found the latter to be the juiciest and most flavorful because it had a bit more fat (see Getting It Right on page 170).

We tried rib chops as thick as 1½ inches and as thin as ½ inch and were shocked when tasters unanimously chose the thin ½-inch chops. Thick chops overwhelmed the gravy, which we felt should share equal billing with the meat. Thin chops also picked up more onion flavor during cooking. We also tried boneless chops, but they turned out dry so we decided to stick with bone-in for optimum juiciness.

Also in the service of juiciness and thorough seasoning, we indulged our passion for brining by soaking the chops in a simple salt-sugar-water solution before cooking them. It turned out that brining was ill-suited to this dish for two reasons. First, these chops cook in a moist environment provided by the gravy, so why spend time instilling extra moisture to protect them from the harsh, dry heat of grilling, searing, or roasting? Second, no matter how we adjusted the salinity of the brine, the salt-infused meat caused the gravy to become intolerably salty.

Last we tackled the question of cooking time. Although we prefer to slightly undercook pork to ensure tenderness, this is one application where further cooking was necessary because we wanted to infuse the meat with the flavor of the gravy and onions. After their initial browning, the chops registered a rosy 140 degrees on an instant-read thermometer. They were cooked through and tender, but since they had yet to be smothered, they had none of the onion flavor we demanded. Fifteen minutes of braising in the gravy boosted the flavor but toughened the chops, which now registered almost 200 degrees. At that temperature, the meat fibers have contracted and expelled moisture, but the fat and connective tissue between the fibers, called collagen, have not had a chance to melt fully and turn into gelatin. It is this gelatin that makes braised meats especially rich and tender. Another 15 minutes of braising time solved the problem. At this point, the chops registered 210 degrees, and the extra time allowed the fat and collagen to melt completely, so the meat was tender and succulent as well as oniony from the gravy.

It was important that the gravy build on the flavor of the browned pork chops. The canned, condensed soup called for in some recipes produced gravies that tasted processed and glue-like. Water produced a weak, thin gravy, but chicken stock improved the picture, adding much-needed flavor.

For liquid to morph into gravy, it must be thickened. Cornstarch is an easy solution, but it resulted in a gelatinous, translucent sauce that looked and felt wrong. Next we tried adding flour in three different ways. Flouring the chops before browning turned their exteriors gummy and left the

gravy with a chalky mouthfeel. Flouring the onions left the gravy tasting of raw flour. Last, we called upon a roux, a mixture of flour and fat (in this case, vegetable oil) cooked together. This occasioned the need for an extra pan that we'd hoped to avoid, but the results were fantastic. The roux was easy to make, it thickened the sauce reliably without adding the taste of raw flour, and it gave the gravy both a smooth finish and another layer of flavor that was slightly nutty.

The roux was good, but we tried to improve it with two oft-used refinements. First, we fried a couple of slices of bacon and substituted the rendered fat for the vegetable oil in the roux. What a hit! The sweet/salty/smoky bacon flavor underscored and deepened all of the other flavors in the dish. Beyond that, we followed in the footsteps of many a gravymaster who has eked out even more flavor from the roux by browning it for five minutes to the shade of peanut butter. Cooking the flour this way unlocks a rich, toasty flavor that builds as the shade deepens. Both techniques are widespread and justly popular, as they turned out to be huge flavor builders.

The onions play a title role in the gravy. We tried them minced, chopped, and sliced both thick and thin. Thin-sliced onions cooked to a melting texture that was our favorite. We tried different quantities of onions, from one to four, for four pork chops and found that two was best. We tried simply softening the onions until they were translucent versus cooking them for a few more minutes until their edges browned, a winning technique that accentuated their natural sweetness. Perhaps the most important onion test was trying different types, including standard-issue supermarket yellow onions, red onions, and sweet Vidalia onions. The yellow onions triumphed for their "deep brown hue" and "balanced flavor." By comparison, tasters found the red onions to be harsh tasting and ugly and the Vidalias to be "bland" and "wan" looking.

The onions cook in the same pan used to brown the chops. We wanted to make sure that the onions released enough moisture to dissolve (or deglaze) the flavorful, sticky, brown bits (called fond) left in the pan by the chops, so we salted them lightly. The heat and salt worked together to jumpstart the breakdown of the onions' cell walls, which set their juices flowing. We also added 2 tablespoons of water to the pan for insurance.

Our last flavor tweak was an unusual one for us—we eliminated the salt we'd be using to season the chops themselves. Tasters agreed that the salt added to the onions, along with the naturally salty bacon and chicken stock and the garlic, thyme, and bay used to build extra flavor in the gravy, seasoned the dish adequately. These chops were hearty, deeply flavored, and comforting.

WHAT WE LEARNED: For a nice balance with the gravy and to allow for the best absorption of the gravy's flavors, use thin, not thick, rib chops. Brown them well to build the flavor for the gravy, make a nut-brown, bacon-flavored roux to further build flavor, and add thinly sliced yellow onions that will give up their moisture easily. For tender chops, combine the sauce and browned chops and braise for a full 30 minutes.

SMOTHERED PORK CHOPS serves 4

Use low-sodium chicken broth in this recipe; regular chicken broth can result in an overseasoned sauce. Serve smothered chops with a starch to soak up the rich gravy. Simple egg noodles was the test kitchen favorite, but rice or mashed potatoes also taste great.

    3   ounces bacon (about 3 slices), cut into ¼-inch
        pieces
    2   tablespoons all-purpose flour
    1¾ cups canned low-sodium chicken broth
        Vegetable oil
    4   bone-in pork loin rib chops, ½ to ¾ inch thick
        Ground black pepper
    2   medium yellow onions, halved pole to pole and
        sliced thin (about 3½ cups)
        Salt
    2   tablespoons water
    2   medium garlic cloves, pressed through garlic
        press or minced (about 2 teaspoons)
    1   teaspoon minced fresh thyme leaves
    2   bay leaves
    1   tablespoon minced fresh parsley leaves

1. Fry bacon in small saucepan over medium heat, stirring occasionally, until lightly browned and fat is rendered, 8 to 10 minutes. Using slotted spoon, transfer bacon to paper towel–lined plate, leaving fat in saucepan (you should have 2 tablespoons bacon fat; if not, supplement with vegetable oil). Reduce heat to medium-low and gradually whisk flour into fat until smooth. Cook, whisking frequently, until mixture is light brown, about the color of peanut butter, about 5 minutes. Whisk in chicken broth in slow, steady stream; increase heat to medium-high and bring to boil, stirring occasionally; cover and set aside off heat.

2. Heat 1 tablespoon oil in 12-inch skillet over high heat until smoking. Meanwhile, dry pork chops with paper towels and sprinkle with ½ teaspoon pepper. Brown chops in single layer until deep golden on first side, about 3 minutes. Flip chops and cook until browned on second side, about 3 minutes longer. Transfer chops to large plate and set aside.

3. Reduce heat to medium and add 1 tablespoon oil, onions, ¼ teaspoon salt, and water to now-empty skillet. Using wooden spoon, scrape up browned bits on pan bottom; cook, stirring frequently, until onions are softened and browned around edges, about 5 minutes. Stir in garlic and thyme and cook until fragrant, about 30 seconds longer. Return chops to skillet in single layer, covering chops with onions. Pour in warm sauce and any juices collected from pork; add bay leaves. Cover, reduce heat to low, and simmer until pork is tender and paring knife inserted into chops meets very little resistance, about 30 minutes.

4. Transfer chops to warmed serving platter and tent with foil. Increase heat to medium-high and simmer sauce rapidly, stirring frequently, until thickened to gravy-like consistency, about 5 minutes. Discard bay leaves, stir in parsley, and adjust seasonings with salt and pepper. Cover chops with sauce, sprinkle with reserved bacon, and serve immediately.

VARIATIONS
SMOTHERED PORK CHOPS WITH CIDER AND APPLES

Follow recipe for Smothered Pork Chops, substituting apple cider for chicken broth and 1 large or 2 small Granny Smith apples, peeled, cored, and cut into ⅓-inch wedges, for one of the onions, and increasing salt added to onion and apple to ½ teaspoon.

SMOTHERED PORK CHOPS WITH SPICY COLLARD GREENS

Follow recipe for Smothered Pork Chops, increasing oil in step 3 to 2 tablespoons, omitting one onion, and increasing garlic to 4 cloves. Just before returning browned chops to pan in step 3, add 4 cups thinly sliced collard greens and ½ teaspoon crushed red pepper flakes.

SCIENCE DESK: How Braising Works

WHEN YOU GRILL PORK CHOPS YOU WANT TO TAKE THEM off the grill when they are still rosy at the center and the internal temperature registers just 135 degrees. Let the chops stay on the grill any longer (say, until they reach an internal temperature of 160 degrees) and they will be tough and dry. When you braise pork chops, as in the smothered pork chop recipe, you cook them through to an internal temperature of 210 degrees. So how come smothered pork chops are tender but overcooked grilled pork chops are tough and dry?

When you cook pork chops, the bonds between the protein and water rupture. At the same time, the bonds between individual protein molecules become stronger and tighter. In fact, these bonds become so tight that they drive out water from the meat. Eventually, the pork chops become tough and dry.

However, once the internal temperature of the meat reaches about 150 degrees, a second process begins. Pork chops contain a fair amount of collagen, a connective tissue that will begin to melt and become gelatin-like as the temperature climbs. The melted collagen makes the pork chops seem tender and moist. Because collagen won't completely melt until the internal temperature reaches 200 degrees, you must really cook the pork to make full use of this phenomenon.

So braised pork chops cooked to a high internal temperature will seem more moist and more tender than braised chops cooked to a lower internal temperature. That's the magic of collagen.

GETTING IT RIGHT: Develop Flavor in Every Step

Brown is good when it comes to flavor. Cooking each component fully contributes greater flavor to the finished dish.

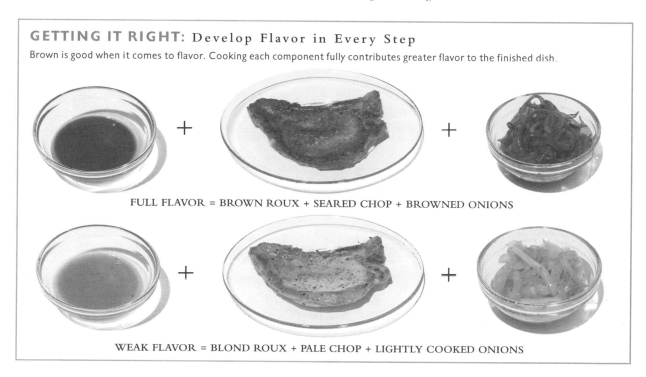

FULL FLAVOR = BROWN ROUX + SEARED CHOP + BROWNED ONIONS

WEAK FLAVOR = BLOND ROUX + PALE CHOP + LIGHTLY COOKED ONIONS

All-American potato salad adds hard-boiled eggs and minced sweet pickles to perfectly cooked potatoes.

BACKYARD bbq

On a hot summer's day, life doesn't get much better than a big, juicy, smoky slab of spicy, mouth-watering ribs. But more often than not, baby back ribs cooked at home come out tasting like dry shoe leather on a bone. Given the expense (two slabs, enough to feed four people, run about $24) and time commitment (many recipes require half a day), bad ribs are a true culinary disaster. Our goal was to produce flavorful, juicy, tender ribs that would be well worth the time, money, and effort.

Potato salad is the natural accompaniment to ribs, and an American version, with mayonnaise, hard-boiled eggs, and sweet pickles, is classic. Potato salad is easy to prepare, but most recipes fail on one of two counts: The potatoes are watery, sloppy-looking, or mushy, or the dressing is dull and heavy. We wanted to fix both problems and create a salad worthy of the finest ribs.

BARBECUED BABY BACK RIBS

WHAT WE WANTED: Ribs barbecued at home can be flavorless and dry. We wanted lots of smoky flavor and moist, tender meat.

Great baby back ribs start at the meat counter. We quickly learned that you have to shop carefully. Unfortunately, labeling of pork ribs can be confusing. Some slabs are labeled "baby back ribs," while other, seemingly identical ribs are labeled "loin back ribs." After a bit of detective work, we learned that the only difference is weight. Both types of ribs are taken from the upper portion of a young hog's rib cage near the backbone (see the illustration on page 181) and should have 11 to 13 bones. A slab (or rack) of loin back ribs generally comes from a larger pig and weighs more than 1¾ pounds; a slab of ribs weighing less is referred to as baby back ribs. (That being said, most restaurants don't follow this rule, using the term baby back no matter what they've got because it sounds better.) During testing, we came to prefer loin back ribs because they are meatier.

There is one other shopping issue to consider. Beware of racks with bare bone peeking through the meat (along the center of the bones). This means that the butcher took off more meat than necessary, robbing you and your guests of full, meaty portions. Once you've purchased the ribs, there remains the question of whether the skin-like membrane located on the "bone side" of the ribs should be left on during cooking. One theory holds that it prevents smoke and spice from penetrating the meat, while some rib experts say that removing it robs the ribs of flavor and moisture. We found that the skin did not interfere with flavor; in fact, it helped to form a spicy, crispy crust.

It was time to start cooking. Our first step was to research the range of grilling times and techniques called for in other recipes. Most recommend a total cooking time of 1½ to 3 hours. Some use a very hot grill, while others use

a moderate grill. We tested all of these recipes and found the resulting ribs to be extremely tough. High-heat cooking was particularly troublesome, as it quickly dried out the meat. Ribs cooked over moderate heat for three hours were better, but they were still too tough.

We realized that the only way to go was the classic "low and slow" method. We built a two-level fire, in which only half of the grill is covered with charcoal, thinking it would be best to smoke the ribs indirectly—on the coal-less side of the grill—to prevent overcooking. (Two full racks of ribs fit on one side of a 22-inch grill.) To add flavor, we placed soaked wood chunks on the bed of coals and then put the cooking grate in place and laid down the spice-rubbed ribs. Finally, we put the grill cover in place, with the vent holes over the ribs to help draw heat and smoke past the meat.

We found that maintaining a temperature between 275

and 300 degrees for four hours produced ribs that were tasty and tender, with meat that fell off the bone. Decent ribs could be had in less time, but they weren't as tender as those cooked for a full four hours. It's easy to tell when the ribs are ready—the meat pulls away from the bone when the ribs are gently twisted.

The problem was that the dry heat of the grill produced ribs that were not as moist as we would have liked. Our next test, then, was to cook the ribs halfway in an oven, using steam, and to finish them on the grill. These ribs were more moist, but now flavor was the problem; these ribs lacked the intense smokiness of ribs cooked entirely on the grill. Hoping to find another way to add moisture, we simmered the ribs in water for two hours. This robbed them of valuable pork flavor.

It then occurred to us that brining the ribs prior to cooking them might be the solution. We used our standard brining formula, which when applied to two 2-pound racks of ribs amounted to a two-hour immersion in 4 quarts of cold water mixed with 2 cups of kosher salt and 2 cups of sugar. This method produced, well, two very highly seasoned racks of ribs. Why? Ribs pack much more bone per pound than other cuts of meat, and all of the meat is right there on the exterior, so the brine doesn't have very far to go. We figured that a 2-pound rack of ribs must soak up the brine much more quickly than an equal-sized roast. We cut back the salt, sugar, and brining time by half, and the results were better, but the meat was still too sweet. We cut back the sugar by half once more, and this time the meat was both moist and perfectly seasoned.

These ribs were so good they didn't even need barbecue sauce, although you certainly could add some if you like. A quick rub with an easy-to-mix spice blend before going on the grill gave them just the right warm and savory touch.

WHAT WE LEARNED: Choose meaty ribs (racks as close to 2 pounds as possible), brine them to add moisture, rub the exterior with spices, and then barbecue over a low fire for four hours for an intense smoky flavor.

BARBECUED BABY BACK RIBS ON A CHARCOAL GRILL serves 4

For a potent spice flavor, brine and dry the ribs as directed, then coat them with the spice rub, wrap tightly in plastic, and refrigerate overnight before grilling. You will need two wood chunks, each about the size of a lemon, for this recipe.

brine

    1   cup kosher salt or ½ cup table salt
    ½   cup sugar
    2   racks (about 2 pounds each) baby back or loin
        back ribs

spice rub

    1   tablespoon plus ½ teaspoon sweet paprika
    1½   teaspoons chili powder
    1¾   teaspoons ground cumin
    1½   teaspoons dark brown sugar
    1½   teaspoons kosher salt or ¾ teaspoon table salt
    ¾   teaspoon dried oregano

GETTING IT RIGHT:
Locating Baby Back Ribs

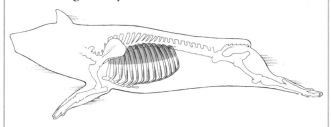

Baby back ribs (also referred to as loin back ribs) are cut from the section of the rib cage closest to the backbone (shaded in the drawing above). Lean center-cut roasts and chops come from the same part of the pig, which explains why baby back ribs can be expensive. Spareribs are cut closer to the belly of the pig, which is also where bacon comes from. Spareribs are larger and much fattier than baby back ribs.

¾ teaspoon ground black pepper
1 teaspoon ground white pepper
½ teaspoon cayenne pepper

1. TO BRINE RIBS: Dissolve salt and sugar in 4 quarts cold water in stockpot or large plastic container. Submerge ribs in brine and refrigerate 1 hour until fully seasoned. Remove ribs from brine and thoroughly pat dry with paper towels.

2. While ribs are brining, cover two 3-inch wood chunks with water in medium bowl; soak wood chunks for 1 hour, then drain and set aside. Combine spice rub ingredients in small bowl. When ribs are out of brine and dried, rub each side of racks with 1 tablespoon spice rub; refrigerate racks 30 minutes.

3. TO BARBECUE RIBS: Open bottom vents on grill. Ignite large chimney starter filled three-quarters with charcoal briquettes (about 4½ quarts, or 65 briquettes) and burn until covered with thin coating of light gray ash. Empty coals into one side of grill, piling them up in mound two or three briquettes high. Place wood chunks on top of charcoal. Put cooking grate in place and cover grill with lid. Let grate heat for 5 minutes, then scrape clean with wire brush.

4. Arrange ribs on cool side of grill parallel to fire; cover, positioning lid so vents are opposite wood chunks to draw smoke through grill (grill temperature should register about 350 degrees on grill thermometer, but will soon start dropping). Cook for 2 hours, until grill temperature drops to about 250 degrees, flipping rib racks, switching their position so that rack that was nearest fire is on outside, and turning racks 180 degrees every 30 minutes; add 10 fresh briquettes to pile of coals. Continue to cook (grill temperature should register 275 to 300 degrees on grill thermometer), flipping, switching, and rotating ribs every 30 minutes, until meat easily pulls away from bone, 1½ to 2 hours longer. Transfer ribs to cutting board, then cut between bones to separate ribs; serve.

BARBECUED BABY BACK RIBS ON A GAS GRILL

If you're using a gas grill, leaving one burner on and the other(s) off mimics the indirect heat method on a charcoal grill. Use wood chips instead of wood chunks and a disposable aluminum pan to hold them.

Follow recipe for Barbecued Baby Back Ribs on a Charcoal Grill through step 2, making following changes: Cover 2 cups wood chips with water and soak 30 minutes, then drain. Place soaked wood chips in small disposable aluminum pan; set pan on burner that will remain on. Turn all burners to high, close lid, and heat grill until chips smoke heavily, about 20 minutes. (If chips ignite, extinguish flames with water from squirt bottle.) Scrape grill grate clean with wire brush; turn off burner(s) without wood chips. Arrange ribs on cool side of grill and cover (grill temperature should

---

TECHNIQUE:
Brushless Grill Rack Cleaning

Food that is being grilled is much less likely to stick to a clean grate. We recommend cleaning the hot grate with a wire brush designed specifically for that purpose. However, if you find yourself without a brush, you can improvise with a pair of tongs and a crumpled wad of aluminum foil.

register about 275 degrees on grill thermometer). Cook for 4 hours, until meat easily pulls away from bone, flipping rib racks, switching their position so that rack that was nearest fire is on outside, and turning racks 180 degrees every 30 minutes. Transfer ribs to cutting board, then cut between bones to separate ribs; serve.

EQUIPMENT CORNER:
Wood Chunks and Chips

WHEN CHOOSING YOUR SMOKING WOOD, CHOICES probably seem limited, as most hardware stores sell only the two most popular types: hickory and mesquite. But many grilling enthusiasts swear by harder-to-find, more exotic woods. We wondered whether it was worth the bother (and expense) to find these woods. We also wondered about the differences between "chips" and "chunks."

It turns out that both wood chips and wood chunks have a place in the world of barbecue. Chunks, because of their larger size, burn considerably longer. More smoke means more flavor, so chunks are our choice for a charcoal grill. We soak the chunks in water for an hour to promote smoking and avoid flaming, and then nestle them into the bed of burning coals.

Unfortunately, when placed on the bottom of a gas grill, wood chunks do not get hot enough to smoke. On a gas grill, you must use wood chips, which should be soaked in water for a minimum of 30 minutes (so they smoke rather than ignite) and then placed in a disposable aluminum pan (to shield them from the lit burner).

With the basics covered, our search for rare wood began. We found a wide selection on Web sites that specialize in barbecuing. We chose nine different types and tested them for flavor differences while barbecuing baby back ribs. The ribs had been brined for 1 hour and were coated with spice rub. We wanted to see how each type of wood smoke would stand up to these big flavors.

We must admit, before testing these woods for differences in flavor, we doubted that we would find much. Isn't wood just

---

TECHNIQUE: Emptying Ashes from a Charcoal Grill

No matter how you do it, emptying a kettle grill of cool ashes is a messy procedure. Here's a neat way to fashion a grill scoop out of a plastic 1-quart or 1/2-gallon milk jug with a handle.

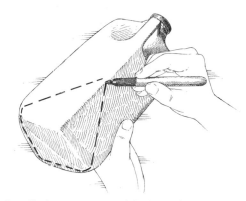

1. Cut off a bottom corner of the jug to form a scoop.

2. The plastic conforms to the curve of the grill bottom, which lets you collect a lot of ashes with a single sweep.

wood? One by one, we were proved wrong. Here are the nine woods we tested with comments about their flavor.

Apple and cherry woods produced slightly sweet and fruity smoke. Peach produced a slightly sweet and very woodsy smoke. Maple, a traditional choice with ham, produced a mellow, sweet smoke, which nicely balanced the spiciness of the ribs. Oak had a very perceptible but not unpleasant acidic note. Hickory produced a strong, pungent, hearty smoke that really stood up to the bold flavors of the spice rub. Pecan, the Southern cousin to hickory, is a bit more mellow but similar to hickory. Alder is the traditional choice with salmon (see page 191), and it has a mild, woodsy flavor. Mesquite is great for grilling because it burns very hot and lends a tangy smoke flavor to food over a short period of time. During the long, slow heat of barbecuing, however, we found the tanginess turned to bitterness. In the end, tasters enjoyed ribs cooked over all of the woods tested, with the exception of mesquite.

BEST WOOD

Wood chunks (left) burn more slowly than wood chips (right) and are our first choice for barbecuing in a charcoal grill. Wood chunks won't work in a gas grill, so use chips and soak them so they smoke rather than ignite.

TASTING LAB: Barbecue Sauce

DESPITE THE BEST OF INTENTIONS, THERE'S NOT ALWAYS time to make barbecue sauce. It's no surprise that many cooks turn to bottled sauces.

We wondered if some brands of bottled barbecue sauce were much better than others. Are the "gourmet" brands worth the extra money, or will a supermarket brand suffice?

We tasted 10 samples to find out. We limited the tasting to tomato-based sauces because they are far and away the most popular and represent what most Americans picture when they think "barbecue sauce."

In general, tasters were not overly impressed with these bottled sauces. Most were much too sweet and had an overly thick, gummy texture. The ingredients responsible were high-fructose corn syrup and food starch. We did find one sauce that everyone agreed was quite good and another three sauces worth considering. Three of these four sauces were more expensive "gourmet," organic offerings, so, at least when it comes to barbecue sauce, more money does buy a better product.

Our favorite sauce is Mad Dog, a boutique brand from Boston. Although the ingredient list is mercifully short (many other sauces have long lists of hard-to-pronounce ingredients), tasters thought this sauce was more complex and balanced than the rest of the pack. It also contained less sugar than most brands and no corn syrup, an ingredient found in all but three of the sauces tested.

Bull's Eye, Sweet Baby Ray's, and Muir Glen received decent scores and mixed comments. Like most supermarket offerings, Bull's Eye is very sweet and has a thick, glossy consistency, but it also delivers a decent hit of smoke, something missing from other mass-market sauces. Tasters liked the strong molasses flavor in the Sweet Baby Ray's and Muir Glen sauces, although neither was an overwhelming favorite. The rest of the sauces were so bad that tasters felt they harmed rather than improved the flavor of plain broiled chicken. With one exception then, this tasting did not uncover products we could get excited about.

As with homemade barbecue sauce, bottled sauces are finishing sauces, not basting sauces. They all contain sweeteners and tomatoes, which will cause foods to burn within minutes after application. Food destined for the grill should not be marinated in barbecue sauce. The food will burn and taste awful. Just brush a little sauce on during the last two or three minutes of the cooking time, and then brush again just before serving.

Rating Barbecue Sauces

WE TASTED 10 BRANDS OF BARBECUE SAUCE, INCLUDING SUPERMARKET BRANDS AS WELL AS SOME "BOUTIQUE" SAUCES sold in upscale markets, dipping broiled chicken in the sauces to evaluate them for flavor and texture. Sauces are listed in order of preference. See www.cooksillustrated.com for up-to-date prices and mail-order sources for top-rated products.

RECOMMENDED
1. Mad Dog Original BBQ Sauce
$5.99 for 19 ounces

The only brand tested without sugar or corn syrup. Molasses delivers modest sweetness. Tasters found this sauce to be "spicy right up front," with smoky, "roasted tomato" flavor.

RECOMMENDED WITH RESERVATIONS
2. Bull's Eye Sweet Hickory Smoke BBQ Sauce
$1.99 for 18 ounces

This "sweet" sauce contains both high-fructose corn syrup (listed first on the label) and molasses (listed fourth). Several tasted complained that "smoke overpowered other flavors," but everyone liked its "glossy" consistency.

RECOMMENDED WITH RESERVATIONS
3. Sweet Baby Ray's Barbecue Sauce
$1.99 for 18 ounces

The first two ingredients are high fructose corn syrup and corn syrup. Not surprisingly, tasters picked up a "strong" corn syrup flavor, but they liked the spice flavors.

RECOMMENDED WITH RESERVATIONS
4. Muir Glen Organic Grill Chef Original Barbecue Sauce
$2.99 for 17 ounces

This sauce is "strong on vinegar and tomato," with a "heavy smoke flavor."

NOT RECOMMENDED
5. Lea and Perrins Original Barbecue Sauce
$2.39 for 18 ounces

Strong, "sweet" tomato flavor could use more "heat" and spices.

NOT RECOMMENDED
6. Gates Original Classic Bar-B-Q Sauce
$5.99 for 18 ounces

"Heavy on the cumin and vinegar" was the verdict about this "thin, loose" sauce.

NOT RECOMMENDED
7. KC Masterpiece Original Barbecue Sauce
$2.29 for 18 ounces

"Big liquid smoke aftertaste," wrote one taster about this smoky-sweet sauce. Others found the sauce is so thick it seemed "more like pudding."

NOT RECOMMENDED
8. Kraft "Slow-Simmered" Original Barbecue Sauce
$1.99 for 18 ounces

This sauce was the only one tested to list vinegar first on the ingredient list. As might be expected, tasters complained about the "sour" flavor.

NOT RECOMMENDED
9. Stubbs Mild Bar-B-Q Sauce
$3.69 for 18 ounces

Tasters did not like the strong hits of vinegar and mustard in this peppery sauce. The "thin, watery" consistency didn't win many fans either.

NOT RECOMMENDED
10. Hunts BBQ Original Recipe Barbecue Sauce
$1.99 for 18 ounces

"Way too sugary" was the overall consensus about this "almost too thick" sauce. Several tasters picked up an "odd maple-cinnamon flavor."

AMERICAN POTATO SALAD

WHAT WE WANTED: A mayonnaise-based potato salad that looks good (no falling-apart, sloppy spuds) and tastes even better.

We decided to focus on a mayonnaise-based salad with hard-boiled eggs, pickles, and celery, the classic accompaniment to any summer picnic or backyard barbecue. We first wanted to know what type of potato to use and how to cook it. Recipe writers seemed split down the middle between starchy potatoes (like russets) and waxy potatoes (like Red Bliss), with starchy praised for being more absorbent and waxy admired for their sturdiness. When making potato salad, we have always just boiled potatoes with the skin on, but steaming, microwaving, roasting, and baking were all options worth trying.

Next, should the potatoes be peeled? If so, when? Some recipes called for cooking potatoes with the skin on, then peeling and seasoning them immediately, working on the assumption that hot potatoes absorb more flavor than cold ones. We wondered if the extra step of seasoning the cooked potatoes with vinegar, salt, and pepper first made any difference. Could we instead just toss all of the ingredients together at the same time?

After boiling, steaming, baking/roasting, and microwaving four different varieties of potatoes—Red Bliss, russets, all-purpose, and Yukon Golds—we found Red Bliss to be the potato of choice and boiling to be the cooking method of choice. Higher-starch potatoes—all-purpose and Yukon Golds as well as russets—are not sturdy enough for salad. They fall apart when cut, making for a sloppy-looking salad.

Next we wanted to see if we could boost flavor at the cooking stage by boiling the potatoes in chicken broth or in water heavily seasoned with bay leaves and garlic cloves. The chicken broth might just as well have been water—there wasn't a hint of evidence that the potatoes had been cooked in broth. The bay leaves and garlic smelled wonderful as the potatoes cooked, but the potatoes were still bland.

The fact that nothing seemed to penetrate the potatoes got us wondering: Does the potato skin act as a barrier? We performed an experiment by cooking two batches of unpeeled potatoes, the first in heavily salted water and the second in unsalted water. We rinsed them quickly under cold running water and tasted. Sure enough, both batches of potatoes tasted exactly the same. We tried boiling peeled potatoes, but they were waterlogged compared with their unpeeled counterparts.

We found the paper-thin skin of the boiled red potato not unpleasant to taste and certainly pleasant to look at in what is often a monochromatic salad. Although this saved the peeling step, we found the skin tended to rip when cutting the potato. Because the skin was particularly susceptible to ripping when the potatoes were very hot, we solved the problem in two ways. First, we cut the potatoes with a serrated knife, which minimized ripping, and second, we let them cool before cutting them.

To find out if the now-cool potatoes would have the capacity to absorb seasoning, we made two salads, letting one cool completely before dressing with vinegar, salt and pepper, and mayonnaise and letting the other cool just till warm and preseasoning with vinegar and salt and pepper well before adding the mayonnaise. (We found the potatoes could still be cut cleanly as long as they were warm but not hot.) The results were clear. The salad made with potatoes seasoned when still warm was zesty and delicious. The other salad was bland in comparison.

WHAT WE LEARNED: For great potato salad, boil unpeeled, low-starch, red-skinned potatoes in unsalted water, cool them slightly, and then cut the potatoes with a serrated knife to minimize tearing of the skin. While the potatoes are still warm, drizzle them with vinegar and season with salt and pepper. When cool, add the mayonnaise and other seasonings.

AMERICAN POTATO SALAD WITH HARD-BOILED EGGS AND SWEET PICKLES serves 4 to 6

Use sweet pickles, not relish, for the best results.

2   pounds red potatoes (about 6 medium or 18 small), scrubbed
¼   cup red wine vinegar
    Salt and ground black pepper
3   hard-boiled eggs (recipe follows), peeled and cut into ½-inch dice
1   medium stalk celery, minced (about ½ cup)
2   tablespoons minced red onion
¼   cup sweet pickles, minced
½   cup mayonnaise
2   teaspoons Dijon mustard
2   tablespoons minced fresh parsley leaves

1. Cover potatoes with 1 inch of water in stockpot or Dutch oven. Bring to simmer over medium-high heat. Reduce heat to medium and simmer, stirring once or twice to ensure even cooking, until potatoes are tender (a thin-bladed paring knife or metal cake tester can be slipped into and out of center of potatoes with no resistance), 25 to 30 minutes for medium potatoes or 15 to 20 minutes for new potatoes.

2. Drain; cool potatoes slightly and peel if you like. Cut potatoes into ¾-inch cubes (use serrated knife if they have skins) while still warm, rinsing knife occasionally in warm water to remove starch.

3. Place warm potato cubes in large bowl. Add vinegar, ½ teaspoon salt, and ¼ teaspoon pepper and toss gently. Cover bowl with plastic wrap and refrigerate until cool, about 20 minutes.

4. When potatoes are cool, toss with remaining ingredients and season with salt and pepper to taste. Serve immediately or cover and refrigerate for up to 1 day.

FOOLPROOF HARD-BOILED EGGS makes 3

You can double or triple this recipe as long as you use a pot large enough to hold the eggs in a single layer, covered by an inch of water.

3   large eggs

1. Place eggs in medium saucepan, cover with 1 inch of water, and bring to a boil over high heat. Remove pan from heat, cover, and let sit for 10 minutes. Meanwhile, fill medium bowl with 1 quart water and 1 tray ice cubes (or equivalent).

2. Transfer eggs to ice bath with slotted spoon and let sit 5 minutes. Tap each egg all over against countertop to crack shell, then roll egg gently back and forth several times. Begin peeling from air-pocket (wider) end. The shell should come off in spiral strips attached to thin membrane. Hard-boiled eggs can be refrigerated for several days.

TECHNIQUE:
Identifying Hard-Boiled Eggs in the Refrigerator

It can be hard to tell which eggs in your refrigerator are raw and which are hard-boiled. To keep them straight, purchase white eggs, and when cooking them add a little balsamic vinegar to the cooking water. This dark brown vinegar will tint the eggshells so you can tell the hard-boiled eggs apart from bright white raw eggs.

BARBECUED salmon

Salmon is America's favorite fish for grilling, but that doesn't mean that it's easy to get it right. Most people who have grilled salmon have had the experience of cooking it to perfection only to lose half of the pieces to the grill. Just as bad are pale salmon steaks with little color or grilled flavor.

We were intrigued with the notion of barbecuing a whole side of salmon. Our goal was to have this large piece of fish spend enough time over the coals to pick up some real wood flavor. Of course, keeping the salmon from drying out would be a big challenge, as would perfecting a method for getting the fish on and off the grill in one piece.

To accompany the salmon, we wanted something more interesting than the raw cucumber garnish that often attends sides of poached salmon at weddings and other fancy parties. For a summer barbecue, we thought a bright cucumber salad would add cool, tart, and creamy flavors to complement the smoky-flavored salmon.

A dozen charcoal and gas grills were used to prepare food for the cameras.

BARBECUED SALMON

WHAT WE WANTED: Smoked salmon flavor achieved on the grill with a whole side of salmon. The texture would be firm but not overly dry, and the fish would be complemented by a strong hit of smoke and wood.

Is it possible to make smoked salmon at home without a smoker? We thought it was worth a try and started off by attempting to make a covered grill act like a cold smoker, which cooks foods at a range of 75 to 110 degrees. We used very few coals, adding them as we went along, often putting out the fire when we added wet wood chunks. The results were disappointing; the salmon was lacking in flavor, and the texture was a bit wet.

Patience is supposed to be a virtue, but in this case impatience turned out to be the key to success. We simply got tired of messing with the process of cold smoking. In fact, at this point we realized that cold smoking, which is used by commercial smokers to make smoked salmon, is simply not practical for home cooks. It takes a very long time, requires both skill and patience, and, because of the low cooking temperatures involved, can be disastrous if health precautions are not followed carefully. We decided to use more briquettes in the initial fire. This eliminated the need to add more coals during the smoking process, and the larger fire was less likely to go out when we added wet wood chunks. This time the results were gratifying. The hotter fire cooked the fish more thoroughly, giving it a more pleasing and flaky texture.

We continued to refine this method over many months of trial and error. Eventually, we perfected a procedure that yields a salmon that has many of the attributes of good smoked salmon but that is crustier and a whole lot easier to make. In fact, the technique is similar to traditional barbecue. The difference between barbecued salmon and cold-smoked salmon is largely one of texture: the cold-smoked salmon is more silky, like lox, whereas barbecued salmon will actually flake.

But the drawback of this method—and the reason why salmon is usually cold-smoked—is that it dries out the fish. We figured that brining in a saltwater solution might help the fish hold onto moisture as it cooked and experimented with various brining times, eventually settling on three to four hours for a fillet weighing 2½ to 3 pounds. Any longer and the flavor of the brine was too intense; any shorter and it didn't produce the desired results as far as texture was concerned. This brined, barbecued salmon definitely had the moist texture we had been longing for, but we were still looking for more flavor to complement its smokiness.

To improve the flavor we added some sugar to the brine. We also experimented with various salt/sugar/water ratios, with different brining times (from two to 24 hours), and with all manner of smoking woods. We eventually settled on the recipe below, which calls for three hours of brining in a solution of 1 cup each of sugar and salt to 7 cups of water and which favors alder wood chunks for the distinctive flavor they give the fish. The salmon this recipe produces has a moist but flaky texture and is just smoky enough, with the natural flavors of the salmon getting a boost from the brining process.

Barbecued salmon can be served warm off the grill as well as chilled, and it works as both a traditional hors d'oeuvre and, somewhat surprisingly, an entrée. For hors d'oeuvres, it is absolutely delicious as is or accompanied with Melba toast (or any other flat bread or cracker), finely chopped white onion, capers, and lemon wedges. If you serve the salmon as an entrée, wedges of lemon will suffice, or you might try one of our sauce recipes.

WHAT WE LEARNED: To protect the fish against the drying effects of the grill, brine it before cooking it. Don't try to cold-smoke salmon at home—use a bit more heat and barbecue it.

BARBECUED SALMON ON A CHARCOAL GRILL serves 4 to 6 as a main course

The grill rack must be hot and thoroughly clean before you place the salmon on it; otherwise the fish might stick. Use foil or the back of a large rimmed baking sheet to get the fish onto the grill. Alder wood is our first choice for this recipe, but hickory works fine, too (see the Equipment Corner on page 183 for more information about the flavors imparted by various types of wood). You will need two wood chunks, each about the size of a lemon, for this recipe.

- 1 cup kosher salt or ½ cup table salt
- 1 cup sugar
- 1 skin-on salmon fillet (about 2½ pounds), pin bones removed (see illustration at right)
- 2 tablespoons vegetable oil
- 1½ teaspoons sweet paprika
- 1 teaspoon ground white pepper

1. Dissolve salt and sugar in 7 cups cold water in gallon-sized zipper-lock plastic bag. Add salmon, seal bag, and refrigerate until fish is fully brined, about 3 hours.

2. Meanwhile, cover two 3-inch wood chunks with water in medium bowl; soak for 1 hour, then drain and set aside.

3. Remove salmon from brine and blot completely dry with paper towels. Place fillet, skin-side down, on 30-inch sheet of heavy-duty foil. Rub both sides of fillet, especially skin side, with oil. Dust flesh side of fillet with paprika and pepper.

4. Meanwhile, open bottom vents on grill. Ignite large chimney starter filled halfway with charcoal briquettes (about 3 quarts, or 45 coals), and burn until covered with thin coating of light gray ash. Empty coals into one side of grill, piling them up in mound two or three briquettes high. Place wood chunks on top of charcoal. Put cooking grate in place, open grill lid vents completely, and cover. Let grate heat for 5 minutes and scrape clean with wire brush.

5. Slide salmon off foil and onto grill rack opposite fire so that long side of fillet is perpendicular to grill rods. Cover, positioning lid so that vents are opposite wood chunks to draw smoke through grill. Barbecue until cooked through and heavily flavored with smoke, 1½ hours. (Temperature will drop from about 350 degrees at start of cooking to about 250 degrees by time salmon is done.)

6. Following illustration 1 on page 192, use two spatulas to remove salmon from grill. Serve either hot or at room temperature, cutting through flesh but not skin to divide salmon into individual portions and sliding spatula between flesh and skin to remove individual pieces, leaving skin behind (see illustrations 2 and 3 on page 192). Serve as is or with one of the sauces that follow.

TECHNIQUE:
Removing Pin Bones from Salmon

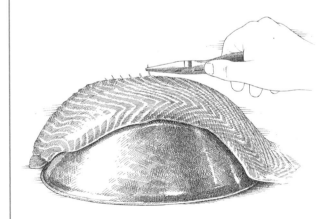

Locating and removing the pinbones from a side of salmon can be tricky. Running your fingers along the flesh is one way to locate them, but we like to drape the salmon over an inverted mixing bowl. The curvature of the bowl forces the pinbones to stick up and out, so they are easier to spot, grasp with needle-nose pliers or tweezers, and remove.

1. Use two spatulas to transfer the cooked fish from the grill to a jelly roll pan or cutting board.

2. Cut through the pink flesh, but not the skin, to divide into individual portions.

3. Slide a spatula between the fillet and the skin to remove individual pieces, leaving the skin behind.

VARIATIONS

BARBECUED SALMON ON A GAS GRILL

If you're using a gas grill, leaving one burner on and turning the other(s) off mimics the indirect heat method on a charcoal grill. Use wood chips instead of wood chunks and a disposable aluminum pan to hold them. Keep a close eye on the grill thermometer to make sure that the temperature remains around 275 degrees.

Follow recipe for Barbecued Salmon on a Charcoal Grill through step 3, making following changes: Cover 2 cups wood chips with water and soak 30 minutes, then drain. Place soaked wood chips in small disposable aluminum pan; set pan on burner that will remain on. Turn all burners to high, close lid, and heat grill until chips smoke heavily, about 20 minutes. (If chips ignite, extinguish flames with water from squirt bottle.) Scrape grill grate clean with wire brush; turn off burner(s) without wood chips. Slide salmon onto grill as directed in step 5 and proceed with recipe.

HORSERADISH CREAM SAUCE makes about I cup

Horseradish and crème fraîche are natural partners to the smoky salmon.

- 1 cup crème fraîche or sour cream
- 2 tablespoons prepared horseradish
- 2 tablespoons minced fresh chives
  Pinch salt

Combine all ingredients in small bowl. (Sauce can be refrigerated in airtight container overnight.)

MUSTARD-DILL SAUCE makes about I cup

Use Dijon, honey, or grainy mustard, as desired. Depending on your choice of mustard, this sauce can be fairly hot.

- 1 cup mustard
- ¼ cup minced fresh dill

Combine all ingredients in small bowl. (Sauce can be refrigerated in airtight container overnight.)

TASTING LAB: Paprika

THE BRILLIANT RED POWDER WE CALL PAPRIKA COMES from the dried pods (fruit) of the plant species *Capsicum annuum L.*, the clan of peppers that ranges from sweet bells to the very hottest chiles. Several varieties of Capsicum annuum L. are used to produce paprika; there is no one specific "paprika pepper." Pods differ in shape and size and vary in degree of potency. Some are round; others are elongated. Some show no pungency; others are fairly hot.

The best paprika is thought to come from Hungary and Spain, with the Hungarian noted for its flavor and the Spanish for its color. In the United States, California and Texas are the main producers. Most European paprika pods are set out to dry naturally in the sun, a process that takes up to 25 days. Domestically grown paprika pods are oven-dried in all of about 30 hours.

Rating Paprika

WE TESTED SIX BRANDS OF PAPRIKA, USING EACH IN CHICKEN PAPRIKASH (A HUNGARIAN STEW MADE WITH A LOT OF paprika). We also tasted each paprika sprinkled over plain white rice. Tasters judged samples on flavor as well as color. Paprikas are listed in order of preference. See www.cooksillustrated.com for up-to-date prices and mail-order sources for top-rated products.

RECOMMENDED
1. Penzeys Hungary Sweet Paprika
$3.39 for 2.4 ounces

The overall favorite, this paprika was hailed for its "roasty," "bold," and "balanced" flavor. The spice did not overpower other ingredients, but it had plenty of depth. Available by mail order.

RECOMMENDED
2. Pendery's Spanish Paprika
$3.25 for 2.72 ounces

This "deeply colored" paprika earned a strong second place in the tasting. It had an "earthy" quality and very rich flavor (though not as rich as our winner), with fruity notes. Available by mail order.

RECOMMENDED
3. McCormick/Schilling Paprika
$3.19 for 2.12 ounces

This California paprika was touted for its "lush," "big red pepper" flavor. Available in supermarkets; sold on the West Coast under the Schilling label.

NOT RECOMMENDED
4. Szeged Hungarian Hot Paprika
$3.49 for 5 ounces

This paprika was deemed intense and slightly bitter. Tasters felt it overwhelmed other flavors in the paprikash. Available in supermarkets.

NOT RECOMMENDED
5. Whole Foods Organic Paprika
$4.79 for 1.68 ounces

This California paprika was judged to be bland and uninteresting. Available in Whole Foods supermarkets.

NOT RECOMMENDED
6. Igo Basque Piment d'Espelette
$12.50 for 1 ounce

This Spanish paprika was so hot that it was hard to detect any flavor; tasters liked this incendiary and extremely expensive paprika the least. Available by mail order.

Paprika can be hot, sweet, or somewhere in between. The differences in pungency, color, and flavor relate to the proportion of *mesocarp* (fruit wall), *placenta* (the white veins), and seeds that are ground together. Sweet paprika is made mostly from peppers' mesocarp, while hot paprika is a product of the placenta and seeds. The latter are ground to yield a spicy powder with an orange-brown color and, some spice experts say, poor flavor. It is almost as pungent as common chile powders and cayenne pepper.

The problem with all of this information is that except for allowing you to choose intelligently between sweet and hot paprika, it does you little practical good at the supermarket when you're trying to figure out which brand of paprika to buy. We came up with six choices: McCormick's (from California), Whole Foods Organic (also California), Penzeys Hungarian Sweet, Szeged Hungarian Hot, Pendery's Spanish Sweet, and Igo Basque Piment d'Espelette (also from Spain).

To test these paprikas, we sprinkled them over plain white rice and used them in a chicken paprikash recipe that called for 3 tablespoons of paprika. (We thought the smoke and fish flavors of the barbecued salmon would make a difficult background against which to taste this delicate spice.)

Penzeys Hungarian Sweet emerged as the overall favorite. The spice did not overpower the stew, but it had plenty of depth. Pendery's Spanish Sweet was the runner-up. It had an "earthy" quality and very rich flavor (though not as rich as our winner), with fruity notes. Although we expected the European brands to do well, we were surprised by the strong third place finish of McCormick's, the leading supermarket brand made with California paprika.

The other three paprikas received less favorable comments. Szeged Hungarian Hot was deemed intense and slightly bitter, the Whole Foods paprika was judged bland and uninteresting, and the Igo Basque Piment d'Espelette was thought to be searingly hot.

Our conclusion? Hungarian sweet paprika in the best choice, but other sweet paprikas (from Spain or California) can deliver good results. Don't use hot paprika.

EQUIPMENT CORNER: Charcoal Grills

FLICKING A SWITCH TO LIGHT A GAS GRILL MAY BE convenient, but for many die-hard grillers nothing beats cooking over a live charcoal fire. The pleasure is utterly visceral—the glowing, red-hot coals, the smoke, the intense sizzle, the interplay of food and flame, and the aroma of searing meat. And, of course, there is the flavor. Charcoal-fueled fires infuse food with characteristic notes of wood and smoke that no gas fire can match.

Yet deciding which charcoal grill to buy is not so straightforward. They come in different shapes and sizes, with different features, and at vastly different prices. We chose six grills from five manufacturers that ran the gamut—from round to rectangular, bare-bones to fully featured, smaller to larger, and less than $50 to more than 10 times that in cost—and pressed them into service in the alley behind the test kitchen for evaluation. A few weeks of grilling steaks, hamburgers, bone-in chicken breasts, and ribs led us to some interesting observations and a couple of decent choices, but not, alas, to a grill that is perfect in all respects.

Grilling a mountain of food over several weeks revealed very little difference in cooking performance among our grills. Each developed fires hot enough to sear the food, which is what charcoal grilling is all about. Each also offered vents to control airflow and thereby the intensity of the fire, but we were not able to detect any advantages or disadvantages based on the number or position of the vents. It was possible, however, to identify two important design factors: the size of the grill and the depth of the grill cover.

A large surface area for grilling is essential if you cook for large groups and is useful even if you don't because it affords the opportunity to grill some extra food alongside tonight's dinner. For instance, we rarely grill a meal without covering every available inch of grill space with vegetables to have on hand for tomorrow's antipasto or pizza or pasta salad. It is also easier to build a two-level fire (hot on one side and cooler on the other) in a large grill. In short, size

Rating Charcoal Grills

WE TESTED SIX GRILLS BY PRESSING THEM INTO DAILY SERVICE IN THE ALLEY OUTSIDE THE TEST KITCHEN. WE JUDGED the grills on size (we preferred larger grills with lids tall enough to accommodate a turkey), attached tables (the bigger, the better), and adjustability of the charcoal or cooking grate. See www.cooksillustrated.com for up-to-date prices and mail-order sources for top-rated products.

BEST BUY

1. New Braunfels Santa Fe, Model 01308725

$99.00

A large, user-friendly grill with better features (built-in thermometer, lower storage shelf) than structural integrity. Huge cooking surface, two wide side tables, and a door into the charcoal area are all great features. We did, however, have to revisit this grill with a wrench to keep it tight and solid.

RECOMMENDED WITH RESERVATIONS

2. Weber Performer

$399.00

The Luxo-version of the classic kettle grill has many nice touches, including a thermometer with real numbers, a large table, hinged cooking rack, lid holder, ash catcher, and overall solid construction. Gas ignition is useful but utterly nonessential. With so many thoughtful features, why didn't Weber make the charcoal or cooking racks adjustable?

RECOMMENDED WITH RESERVATIONS

3. Sunbeam 22-inch Square Portable Charcoal Grill

$49.96

A very nice grill but for three major flaws: relatively small cooking area, a cooking grate that slides around whenever you move the food on it, and a flimsy overall feel.

RECOMMENDED WITH RESERVATIONS

4. The Cajun Grill PG200

$519.00

So heavy and solid it feels like it could weather a cyclone or two intact. Best charcoal rack adjustment system we encountered, yet the rack itself is too narrow to provide even heat over 100 percent of the cooking surface. No way to add charcoal to a fire without removing the cooking rack. Very few features for the money.

RECOMMENDED WITH RESERVATIONS

5. Weber One-Touch Silver

$99.00

Solid and competent but so barebones. The only frill here is the grill rack with handles. The archetypal kettle grill could stand to offer more features for the money.

RECOMMENDED WITH RESERVATIONS

6. Thermos 22½-inch Kettle Grill

$59.99

Thoughtfully featured and fine to grill on, but too small. Because most home cooks have just one charcoal grill, we'd skip this model, which is too shallow to accommodate large cuts for grill-roasting.

does matter. In our group, the New Braunfels Santa Fe was the size champ, with 468 square inches of grilling space.

We generally don't use the cover when grilling over high heat, but it is necessary when grill-roasting large cuts, such as a turkey or prime rib, over lower heat. To trap heat and contain any flavorful smoke generated from wood chunks, the grill cover must fit comfortably over the food and form a tight seal with the grill bottom. We recommend 12 to 14-pound turkeys for grill-roasting (see recipe on page 204), and only the covers on the New Braunfels and Sunbeam grills closed over a 14-pounder (set on a V-rack to promote even cooking). All of the grills in the group except for the Thermos swallowed the 12-pounder.

In some respects, charcoal grills are a little like cars. Any new car will get you from point A to point B, but extra features like traction control or anti-lock brakes make the car easier to drive, and goodies like a sunroof or heated seats help you enjoy the ride more. Likewise, all charcoal grills will cook your food, but there are several features that make the process easier and more enjoyable.

Though we never would have guessed it, the presence of an attached table made a huge difference. After years of precariously balancing trays and platters on deck railings and chair arms, having a secure, accessible place to put dishes and utensils was a welcome relief. The New Braunfels grill doubled the pleasure with two large tables, one on each end of the grill. Score another point for New Braunfels. Among our group, only the Weber One-Touch Silver and the Thermos lacked tables of any kind.

If you plan to barbecue or grill-roast (both methods entail long cooking over a relatively low fire), some means of easily adding charcoal to the fire is useful. Once again, the New Braunfels offered the perfect solution—a small door to the charcoal tray, which made it a breeze to tend the fire and add fuel. The Webers offered a different solution—cooking grates that are either hinged or open at the ends so you can slip charcoal through. If you have to add fuel to any of the other grills, you must endure the hassle of removing the food and the cooking grate to get to the fire.

Another thoughtful feature is some means of adjusting the height of either the charcoal rack or the cooking grate. If given no respite from a hot fire, many foods, such as thick steaks, pork chops, or chicken breasts, will burn on the outside before cooking through on the inside. So they must be finished over a cooler fire. This is easy to accomplish if you can adjust the charcoal tray down away from the cooking grate, as is the case with the New Braunfels, the Cajun, and the Thermos. On the Sunbeam, the charcoal tray is fixed but you can adjust the height of the cooking grate, so the effect is the same. Still, the ability to adjust either the charcoal or cooking grate is not essential. On the Webers, which do not offer such adjustability, you can build a two-level fire that is hot on one side and cool on the other to achieve the same effect. This simply takes a little extra knowledge on the part of the griller. It is easier, though, if you can change the level of the fire with the shift of a lever or the turn of a dial.

Some additional features we encountered were nice but non-essential. Notable among them were the gas ignition on the Weber Performer, which did its job well but added expense and weight. A chimney starter is so easy to use that we could happily forego the gas ignition. Likewise storage racks and bins. On the other hand, an ash catcher, which is simply a container attached to the bottom of the grill to trap ashes—makes life easier when it comes time to clean out the grill. When you barbecue or grill-roast, a built-in thermometer is handy, though if it isn't there you can either use an oven thermometer on the grill rack or put a grill thermometer through lid vents instead.

In the end, value, which we define as the balance of size, features, and price, determined our recommendations. This formula makes the New Braunfels look pretty good, with its impressive size and host of features, all for a modest $99. But it was not perfect. The charcoal tray adjustment system was limited to three positions and it struck us as flimsy, especially compared with the solid, well-designed, seven-position system on the Cajun Grill. Also, the New Braunfels grill did not impress us with awesome structural integrity.

We had to tighten its nuts and bolts several times throughout the testing.

Though the Weber Performer did not offer an adjustment system for moving the charcoal and we viewed its gas ignition system as superfluous, it was solid and extremely well outfitted. The caveat here is price—nearly $400, or four times that of the New Braunfels. (Weber does offer a similar model, the One-Touch Platinum, that comes with an ash catcher and a large attached table, but without the gas ignition system or the thermometer, for about $249. This grill strikes us as a better value than the Performer because it has all of the Performer's important features but none of the bells and whistles that add mightily to the price tag.)

In the end, we'd say the general guideline is to buy the largest, best-outfitted grill your budget will allow. And, silly as it may sound, whatever you do, make sure there is a table attached.

EQUIPMENT CORNER: Charcoal

WOULD YOU EVER HAVE GUESSED THAT HENRY FORD WAS to thank for your charcoal-grilled steak tonight? That's right. Ford pioneered the charcoal briquette industry as a way to profit from the scrap wood generated by manufacturing all those Model T's in the 1920s.

Generally speaking, charcoal is the carbonized remains of wood that has been burned in the absence of oxygen. Without oxygen, resins and moisture in the wood evaporate, leaving behind lightweight, easily lit, combustible charcoal.

Three types of charcoal dominate the market. They are hardwood charcoal (also called charwood, lump charwood, or lump hardwood), which, like the wood used to make it, consists of irregularly shaped pieces and is additive-free; square, pillow-shaped briquettes made from scrap wood and sawdust that is burned and then compacted along with chemicals and other binders that help them both ignite and burn evenly; and a Kingsford product called Match Light, which consists of briquettes that have been permeated with lighter fluid and thereby promise to ignite with the touch of a lit match. (Match Light did live up to its name, quickly producing a spectacular 3-foot column of flame on the windy day we conducted our tests.)

We were anxious to test the common assertion that hardwood charcoal burns hotter and faster than briquettes, so we hooked up a sophisticated, high-range temperature sensor to the cooking grate above fires made from each of the three types of charcoal. We recorded temperatures after five minutes, 15 minutes, and 25 minutes to gauge the drop-off in heat. Sure enough, the hardwood fire was the hottest initially at just above 700 degrees, compared with 660 degrees for the briquettes and 550 degrees for the Match Light; the hardwood also dropped off the most dramatically—by almost 450 degrees—after 25 minutes.

We were also curious to see if we could detect flavor differences in foods grilled with the three types of charcoal, so we sampled steak (because it's hearty) and zucchini (because it's delicate). Though the hardwood charcoal fire formed the thickest, most deeply brown crust on the steaks, tasters did not detect any significant flavor differences in the three steaks. It was another story, however, with the zucchini. The zucchini grilled over hardwood charcoal colored the fastest and tasted the smokiest. The briquette-grilled zucchini had the lightest grilled flavor (but no off flavors), and the Match Light–grilled sample demonstrated a faint but odd bitterness.

So where does this leave us? We'd just as soon avoid any off flavors in delicate foods, so we'll pass on the Match Light charcoal. For grill-roasting over a longer time period at a lower temperature, such as our barbecued salmon recipe, we'd opt for briquettes because they burn a little cooler and a lot longer than hardwood charcoal. But for straight-ahead grilling applications, especially when there's meat on the menu that cries out for a deep sear, we'll take hardwood. Grilling is all about high heat, and we'll take every extra degree that we can get.

CUCUMBER SALAD

WHAT WE WANTED: More often than not, by the time you eat a cucumber salad, the cucumbers have gone soft and watery, losing their appealing texture and diluting the dressing to near tastelessness. This made the primary goal of our testing simple: Maximize the crunch.

Water is the enemy when making cucumber salad. The standing recommendation for ridding watery vegetables such as cucumbers, zucchini, and eggplant of unwanted moisture is to salt them. The salt creates a higher concentration of ions (tiny, charged particles) at the surface of the vegetable than exists deep within its cells. To equalize the concentration levels, the water within the cells is drawn out through permeable cell walls. In the case of cucumbers, this leaves them wilted, yet very crunchy. Of course, some culinary questions remain: How much salt should be used? Should the cucumber slices be weighted, or pressed, to squeeze out the liquid? How long should they drain?

To find out if pressing salted cucumbers really squeezes out more liquid, we trimmed and seeded six cucumbers to 8 ounces each, sliced them on the bias, and tossed each batch with a teaspoon of salt in its own colander set over a bowl. Three of them had zipper-lock freezer bags filled with 1 quart of water placed on top of them; no additional weight was added to the other three. Then we left them all to drain, measuring the liquid each had released after 30 minutes and after 1, 2, 3, and 12 hours. At each time point, the weighted cucumbers had released about 1 tablespoon more liquid than the unweighted cucumbers; 3 versus 2 after 30 minutes, 4 versus 3 after 1 hour, and so on. Interestingly, the weighted cukes gave off

no more liquid after 12 hours than they had after 3 (7 tablespoons at both points). So weighting the cucumbers is worthwhile, but forget about draining the cucumbers overnight; it's not necessary.

At the one-hour mark, we could not detect an appreciable difference in flavor or texture between weighted and unweighted cukes. But we wanted to see how they would perform in salads with different types of dressings. We mixed one batch each of the weighted and unweighted cucumbers with three types of sauce—creamy, oil-based, and water-based—and allowed each to sit at room temperature for one hour. This is where the true value of better-drained cucumbers became obvious; every single taster preferred the salads made with pressed cucumbers for their superior crunch and less diluted dressings.

As for the amount of salt, some cooks recommend simply using the quantity you would normally use to season the cucumbers, while others say you should use more, up to 2 tablespoons per cucumber, and then rinse off the excess before further use. We tried a few cucumbers, prepared exactly as those described above except with 2 tablespoons of salt. The cucumbers with 2 tablespoons did give up about one more tablespoon of liquid within the first hour than those drained with one teaspoon had, but they also required rinsing and blotting dry with paper towels. And despite this extra hassle, they still tasted much too salty in the salads. We advise forgoing the extra salt.

WHAT WE LEARNED: Salt and weight seeded and sliced cucumbers to draw off excess moisture, then rinse, pat dry, and toss the cucumbers with vinaigrette or a creamy dressing made with sour cream or yogurt.

SESAME LEMON CUCUMBER SALAD serves 4

Mild rice vinegar works well in this Asian-inspired dressing.

- ¼   cup rice vinegar
- 1   tablespoon juice from 1 small lemon
- 2   tablespoons Asian sesame oil
- 2   teaspoons sugar
- ⅛   teaspoon hot red pepper flakes, or to taste
- 1   tablespoon sesame seeds, toasted
- 3   medium cucumbers (about 1½ pounds), sliced, salted, and drained (see illustrations, below)

Whisk all ingredients except cucumbers in bowl. Add cucumbers; toss to coat. Serve chilled or at room temperature.

YOGURT MINT CUCUMBER SALAD serves 4

Known as raita, this creamy salad traditionally serves as a cooling contrast with curry dishes.

- 1   cup plain low-fat yogurt
- 2   tablespoons extra-virgin olive oil
- ¼   cup minced fresh mint leaves
- 2   small garlic cloves, minced (about 2 teaspoons)
  Salt and ground black pepper
- 3   medium cucumbers (about 1½ pounds), sliced, salted, and drained (see illustrations, below)

Whisk yogurt, oil, mint, garlic, and salt and pepper to taste in medium bowl. Add cucumbers; toss to coat. Serve chilled, adjusting seasonings if necessary.

CREAMY DILL CUCUMBER SALAD serves 4

Salting and draining the onion along with the cucumbers in this recipe removes the sharp sting of raw onion.

- 1   cup sour cream
- 3   tablespoons cider vinegar
- 1   teaspoon sugar
- ¼   cup minced fresh dill
  Salt and ground black pepper
- 3   medium cucumbers (about 1½ pounds), sliced, salted, and drained (see illustrations, below)
- ½   medium red onion, sliced very thin, salted and drained with cucumbers

Whisk sour cream, vinegar, sugar, dill, and salt and pepper to taste in medium bowl. Add cucumbers and onion; toss to coat. Serve chilled, adjusting seasonings if necessary.

TECHNIQUE: Slicing and Salting Cucumbers

1. Peel and halve each cucumber lengthwise. Use a small spoon to remove the seeds and surrounding liquid from each cucumber half.

2. Lay the cucumber halves flat-side down on a work surface and slice them on the diagonal into ¼-inch-thick pieces.

3. Toss the cucumbers and 1 tablespoon salt in a colander set in a bowl. Weight with a gallon-size plastic bag filled with water. Drain for 1 to 3 hours. Rinse well and pat dry.

Cooking turkey on a grill produces extra-crisp skin, moist meat, and a great smoky flavor.

THANKSGIVING
CHAPTER 16
from the grill

Most cooks don't like to experiment when it comes to holiday foods. In many homes, the Thanksgiving menu is sacrosanct. That said, most cooks would agree that there's plenty of room for improvement. The turkey rarely comes out with both crisp skin and moist meat. It seems that one goal must always be sacrificed to achieve the other. And even if things do go well, the turkey hogs the oven all day, making it difficult to prepare all of the other holiday dishes—the casseroles, the pies—that need to be baked. We wanted to figure out how to use the grill to cook the bird. We hoped to free up oven space and turn out a better-tasting bird.

Sweet potatoes and cranberry sauce are must-haves in most homes at Thanksgiving, but we don't like the overly sweet, marshmallow-topped sweet potato casserole and the stiff cranberry jelly from a can that have become traditional. We wanted to focus on flavor and make the sweet potatoes and cranberry sauce something special while keeping their preparation as simple as possible.

GRILL-ROASTED TURKEY

WHAT WE WANTED: A smoky-tasting turkey with super-crisp skin and juicy, tender meat.

We can still remember the first time we cooked a whole turkey in a covered grill. We lit the charcoal, banked the coals to one side, added some wood chips, and placed a small turkey over the cool part of the grill. Two hours later, we had the best-looking and best-tasting turkey ever—the crispiest skin imaginable coupled with moist meat that had been perfumed with smoke.

Unfortunately, we can also remember the second time we tried this feat. We must have built the fire a little too hot; when we checked the bird after the first hour, the skin had burned. We nonetheless continued grilling, and, before serving, removed the charred skin from the blackened bird. We also served some juicy mango salsa to camouflage the dryness of the overcooked breast.

We have continued to grill-roast turkeys over the years not only because the bird sometimes turns out to be fantastic but also because using the grill for the turkey frees up the oven for all of the other components of a holiday meal. But the results have been consistently inconsistent.

Part of the problem is the inherent unpredictability of grill-roasting over charcoal. Sometimes the fire can be too hot, other times it can be too cool. If the day is particularly windy, the fire will cool down faster than on a hot, sultry night. Because you are cooking with the cover down to conserve fuel (frequent peeking will cause the fire to die down and is a no-no), it's hard to know what's happening inside the grill.

We decided to get serious and figure out what the variables are when grill-roasting a turkey and then devise a method for controlling these variables. Our goal was simple: We wanted a bird with crisp, browned skin, moist meat, and a good smoky flavor—every time.

Because gas grilling involves fewer variables than char-coal grilling, we decided to start with gas. We quickly learned that a small turkey (fewer than 14 pounds) works best when grill-roasting. Even on a really large gas grill, we found that the skin on a large bird burns by the time the meat comes up to temperature. For the same reason, you can't cook a stuffed turkey on the grill. A stuffed bird takes longer to cook through, and this added time almost guarantees that the skin will blacken.

Following the lead of previous turkey recipes developed in the test kitchen, we also confirmed that brining the turkey is a must for a tender, juicy bird. Grilling is even more punishing on delicate breast meat than oven roasting. The bird's proximity to the heat source, coupled with all that smoke (which tends to dehydrate foods), puts brining in the position of making a real difference in the quality of the white meat. If you can't be bothered with brining, buy a kosher bird (the bird is soaked in saltwater during processing, which has an effect similar to brining) or season a regular bird liberally with salt just before grilling and be prepared to serve the white meat with plenty of cranberry sauce.

Next we turned to the question of trussing. Our test kitchen generally ties the legs of the turkey together to keep them from splaying open as they roast. When we tried this, we noticed that the inner thigh cooked more slowly than the rest of the bird. Trussed birds needed an extra 10 to 15 minutes on the grill to get the shielded portion of the thigh up to the correct internal temperature. While this may not sound like much extra time, it translated into overcooked breast meat. Even worse, the skin burned. When we abandoned any trussing or tying of the legs, the temperature in the thighs and breasts was equalized and the skin was extremely crisp and dark brown, but not black.

Our next set of experiments centered on turning the bird. As with oven roasting, we found it best to start the bird breast-side down. After an hour, we flipped the bird breast-side up for the remainder of the cooking time. We noticed that the side (wing and leg) closest to the fire was cooking faster than the other side of the bird. To eliminate this problem, we found it necessary to rotate the bird twice—once when it is turned breast-side up, and once when the cooking is almost completed. Each time, we turned the bird so that the opposite wing and leg faced the heat source.

We next focused on whether to cook the bird right on the grill grate or on a rack. We found that the turkey placed in a nonadjustable V-rack cooked more evenly and with less scorching of the skin than the bird placed right on the grate. But a rack with a sturdy metal base is essential. If the V-rack rests on just two little legs, those legs can fall between the grill grates and the turkey can topple over.

Our last area of investigation on the gas grill concerned temperature. Clearly, we needed to grill-roast the bird over indirect heat, with one burner lit and the other burner(s) turned off. Our question was how to keep the heat on the lit burner. We tested this recipe on three grills—two models with two burners and one model with three burners. We found it best to leave the lit burner turned to high in each case. At lower settings, there was not enough heat to cook the bird properly. The temperature gauges on the three grills we worked with ranged from 300 to 350 degrees during the entire cooking time. Total cooking time for a 12- to 14-pound bird varied from 2 to 2½ hours. (Count on the longer time if the weather is cool or windy.)

Turkey cooked on a gas grill is delicious. The recipe is foolproof, and the skin becomes especially crisp and richly colored. But getting smoke flavor into a gas-grilled bird is not so easy. While adding wood chips before lighting the grill helped some, the resulting smoke flavor was mild. A mildly smoked bird may be fine for some meals, but we think that if you are going to bother with grilling, you might as well get the added benefit of a stronger smoke flavor. The problem with gas grills is that there's no way to add chips once the fire is going. We concluded that removing the turkey, trying to lift off the hot, heavy cooking grate, and then placing more chips over the lit burner was much too dangerous.

Charcoal is another matter. We quickly realized that because we had to add fuel to the fire at the halfway point anyway, we could add more wood at the same time. We came to this conclusion after producing yet another blackened bird. We foolishly thought we could build a really big fire on one side of the grill, put the turkey on the cool side, throw on the cover, and come back two hours later. While it's possible to get the meat up to temperature with this method, the intense initial heat (upward of 425 degrees) causes the skin to burn.

We found it far better to build a moderate fire, bank the coals to one side of the grill, and cook the turkey breast-side down for one hour, just as we had on the gas grill. After an hour, the temperature inside the grill dropped from a high of 350 to 375 degrees to somewhere around 275 degrees. At this point, the grill needed more fuel to finish cooking the turkey. Because we were removing the cooking grate anyway, we decided to add more wood along with a dozen unlit briquettes. (Unlike the very heavy gas grate, you can lift a charcoal grate with heavy-duty tongs. You can also simply toss wood into a pile of charcoal; for gas, you must position the foil tray over the burner, an impossible task when the grill is hot.)

At about this point we began experimenting with chunks of wood versus wood chips. We found that chunks, although not suitable for use with a gas grill, were far superior (they gave off a lot more smoke) and easy to use with a charcoal grill.

So would we cook our next turkey over gas or charcoal? Gas is certainly more convenient and more reliable if the weather is especially cold or windy. However, the extra smoky flavor that only charcoal and wood chunks can deliver makes the kettle grill our first choice for grill-roasting a turkey.

WHAT WE LEARNED: **Brine the bird to keep it moist, and don't bother trussing the turkey; it only serves to slow down the cooking of the dark meat. Grill-roast the turkey over a moderate fire. Use a V-rack to improve air circulation, and turn the bird twice for evenly bronzed skin.**

GRILL-ROASTED TURKEY ON A CHARCOAL GRILL serves 10 to 12

Charcoal gives you the opportunity to add wood twice—at the outset of grilling and when the bird is turned breast-side up at the 1-hour mark—for a stronger smoke flavor. You will need six wood chunks, each about the size of a lemon, for this recipe. (For more information about wood chunks, see the Equipment Corner on page 183.) Hardwood charcoal burns faster and hotter than briquettes, so be sure to use briquettes when grill-roasting turkey. The total cooking time is 2 to 2½ hours, depending on the size of the bird, the ambient conditions (the bird will require more time on a cool, windy day), and the intensity of the fire. Check the internal temperature in the thigh when rotating the bird at the 1-hour-and-45-minute mark. If the thigh is nearly up to temperature (the final temperature should be 175 to 180 degrees), check the temperature again after about 15 minutes. If the thigh is still well below temperature (145 degrees or cooler), don't bother checking the bird again for at least another 30 minutes.

TECHNIQUE: Protecting the Wings

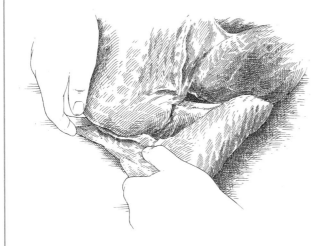

Tucking the wings under the bird will prevent them from burning on the grill.

---

2 cups kosher or 1 cup table salt
1 turkey (12 to 14 pounds), giblets and tail removed, rinsed thoroughly, and wings tucked (see illustration at left)
  Nonstick vegetable cooking spray
2 tablespoons unsalted butter, melted

1. Dissolve salt in 2 gallons of water in large (at least 16-quart) stockpot or clean bucket. Add turkey and refrigerate or set in very cool spot (between 32 and 40 degrees), 12 hours or overnight. (For information about brining outside of the refrigerator, see page 205.)

2. Toward end of brining time, cover six 3-inch wood chunks with water in medium bowl; soak wood chunks for 1 hour, then drain and set aside.

3. Keep bottom vents on grill completely open. Ignite large chimney starter filled three-quarters with charcoal briquettes (about 4½ quarts or 45 coals) and burn until covered with thin coating of light gray ash.

4. Meanwhile, spray V-rack with nonstick cooking spray. Remove turkey from brine and rinse inside and out under cool running water to remove all traces of salt. Pat turkey dry with paper towels; brush both sides with melted butter. Set turkey, breast-side down, in V-rack.

5. Empty coals into one side of grill, piling them up in mound two or three briquettes high. Place 3 wood chunks on top of charcoal. Put cooking grate in place and put V-rack with turkey over cool part of grill. Open grill lid vents halfway and cover, turning lid so that vents are opposite wood chunks to draw smoke through grill. Cover and grill-roast for 1 hour.

6. Remove lid from grill. Using thick potholders, transfer V-rack with turkey to rimmed baking sheet or roasting pan. Remove cooking grate and place 12 new briquettes and 3

remaining wood chunks on top of coals; replace grate. With wad of paper towels in each hand, flip turkey breast-side up in rack. Return V-rack with turkey to cool part of grill so that leg and wing that were facing coals are now facing away. Cover and grill-roast for 45 minutes.

7. Using thick potholders, carefully turn V-rack with turkey (the breast remains up) so that leg and wing that were facing coals are now facing away from coals. Insert instant-read thermometer into each thigh to check temperature and gauge how much longer turkey must cook (see note).

8. Cover and continue grill-roasting until thermometer inserted into thigh registers 175 to 180 degrees, 15 to 45 minutes more.

9. Remove turkey from grill, cover loosely with foil, and let rest 20 to 30 minutes. Carve and serve.

VARIATION

GRILL-ROASTED TURKEY ON A GAS GRILL

If you're using a gas grill, leaving one burner on and turning the other(s) off mimics the indirect heat method on a charcoal grill. Use wood chips instead of wood chunks and a disposable aluminum pan to hold them. The total cooking time is 2 to 2¹/₂ hours, depending on the size of the bird, the ambient conditions (the bird will require more time on a cool, windy day), and the intensity of the fire. Check the internal temperature in the thigh when rotating the bird at the 1-hour-and-45-minute mark. If the thigh is nearly up to temperature (the final temperature should be 175 to 180 degrees), check the temperature again after about 15 minutes. If the thigh is still well below temperature (145 degrees or cooler), don't bother checking the bird again for at least another 30 minutes.

Follow recipe for Grill-Roasted Turkey on a Charcoal Grill through step 4, making following changes: Cover 3 cups wood chips with water and soak 30 minutes, then drain. Place soaked wood chips in small disposable aluminum pan; set pan on burner that will remain on. Turn all burners to high, close lid, and heat grill until chips smoke heavily, about 20 minutes. (If chips ignite, extinguish flames with water from squirt bottle.) Turn off burner(s) without wood chips. Place turkey over cool part of grill and proceed as directed.

TECHNIQUE:
Brining Outside of the Refrigerator

If refrigerator space is at a premium, you may want to brine the bird in a cool spot. Line a 16-quart stockpot, a large bucket, or a cooler with a turkey-sized oven bag. Make the brine and add 4 or 5 frozen gel packs along with the turkey. Tie the bag shut, cover the pot or bucket or close the cooler, and brine as directed, adding more gel packs if necessary.

MASHED SWEET POTATOES

WHAT WE WANTED: A mash with true, earthy, not overly sweet flavor and a flawlessly smooth, creamy texture.

For the holidays, mashed sweet potatoes are often overdressed in a Willie Wonka–style casserole topped with marshmallows and whipped cream. But this candied concoction doesn't hold a candle to an honest, sweet potato mash in terms of flavor. With a deep, natural sweetness that doesn't require much assistance, we knew that the humble sweet potato would taste far better if prepared using a minimum of ingredients.

Still, mashed sweet potatoes have their own set of problems. Nailing a fork-friendly puree every time is like cooking roulette. Mashed sweet potatoes often turn out overly thick and gluey or, to the other extreme, sloppy and loose. We also found that most recipes overload the puree with pumpkin pie seasonings that obscure the potatoes' natural flavor. We wanted to develop a recipe that would bring the deep, earthy sweet potato flavor to the forefront and that would produce a silky puree with enough body to hold its shape while sitting on a fork. Focusing first on the cooking method, we figured we could then test the remaining ingredients, from butter to heavy cream, and finally fiddle with the seasonings.

To determine the best method, we tested a variety of techniques: baking unpeeled potatoes, boiling the potatoes whole and unpeeled, boiling peeled and diced pieces, steaming peeled and diced pieces, and microwaving the potatoes whole and unpeeled. Adding a little butter and salt to the potatoes after they were mashed, we found huge differences in texture, flavor, and ease of preparation. The baked potatoes produced a mash with a deep flavor and bright color, but they took more than an hour to bake through, and handling them right out of the oven was a precarious endeavor. We also found that sweet potatoes range drastically in size, altering their baking times by nearly 30 minutes.

Boiling whole sweet potatoes in their skins turned out a wet puree with a mild flavor. Using a fork to monitor the potatoes as they cooked created holes that seemed to let flavor seep out and excess water in.

Steaming and boiling pieces of peeled potato produced the worst examples, offering zero flavor and loose, applesauce-like texture. The microwave, although fast and easy, was also a disappointment. The rate of cooking was difficult to control, and the difference between an undercooked and overdone potato was about 30 seconds. Over-microwaving the potatoes, even slightly, produced a pasty mouthfeel and an odd plastic flavor. By all accounts, this first round of testing bombed. Yet it did spark an idea.

Focusing on the sorry results, we learned a few things about cooking sweet potatoes. First, their deep, hearty flavor is surprisingly fleeting and easily washed out. Second, the tough and dense flesh reacts much like winter squash when it's cooked, turning wet and sloppy. We also found it safer to peel the sweet potatoes when they were raw and cold rather than cooked and hot. Taking all of this into account, we wondered if braising the sweet potatoes might work. If cut into uniform pieces and cooked over low heat in a covered pan, it seemed plausible that the sweet potatoes would release their own moisture slowly and braise themselves.

Beginning with a little bit of water to get the process going, we found the sweet potatoes were tender in about 40 minutes. We then simply removed the lid and mashed them right in the pot. To our delight, they were full of flavor because they had cooked, essentially, in their own liquid. We tried various pots and heat levels and found that a medium-sized pot (holding two to three layers of potatoes) cooked over low heat worked best. Higher heat levels cooked the potatoes unevenly and in some cases burned them. We also noted that the potatoes cooked quickly when sliced thin rather than cut into chunks. Out of curiosity we tried shredding the potatoes before adding them to the pot, but, as we had expected, the shreds simply oxidized and discolored before they were fully cooked, turning out puree with a pale color and stale flavor.

Up to this point, we had been adding only butter to the puree. We wondered what the typical additions of cream, milk, or half-and-half would do. Making four batches side by side, we tasted mashes made with only butter, with butter and milk, with butter and half-and-half, and with butter and heavy cream. Tasters found the butter-only batch boring, while milk turned the puree bland and watery. The batch with half-and-half came in second, with a heartier flavor and fuller body, but the heavy cream stole the show. Two pounds of potatoes tasted best when blended with 4 tablespoons of unsalted butter reinforced by 2 tablespoons heavy cream. Although this may seem like a miniscule amount of cream, more simply ran over the sweet potato's delicate flavor.

We found that ½ teaspoon of salt was plenty for 2 pounds of potatoes and noted that a bit of sugar did wonders to bolster the flavor. We tried honey, light and dark brown sugar, and molasses but liked the clean, indistinguishable flavor of white sugar for the master recipe. Other common sweet potato seasonings, such as nutmeg, vanilla, allspice, and cinnamon, were simply distracting.

As we had made this recipe many times now, a glaring oversight became obvious. Why didn't we replace the small amount of water used to cook the potatoes with the butter and heavy cream? Curious how the recipe would react without the water, we were gratified when this streamlined technique produced a puree that stood up on a fork with a luxurious texture that was neither loose nor gluey. And having eliminated the water from the mixture, the sweet potato flavor was now more intense than ever. This final twist not only simplified the recipe but also brought the flavor to a higher level.

WHAT WE LEARNED: **Peel the sweet potatoes and slice them thin, then braise in a covered pot with a touch of heavy cream and butter. Don't bother with the typical pumpkin pie seasonings, but do try intriguing complementary flavors from around the world.**

MASHED SWEET POTATOES serves 4

Cutting the sweet potatoes into slices of even thickness is important so that they cook at the same rate. A potato masher (see the Equipment Corner on page 209) will yield slightly lumpy sweet potatoes; a food mill will make a perfectly smooth puree. The potatoes are best served immediately, but they can be covered tightly with plastic wrap and kept relatively hot for 30 minutes. This recipe can be doubled and prepared in a Dutch oven; the cooking time will need to be doubled as well.

  4   tablespoons unsalted butter, cut into 4 pieces
  2   tablespoons heavy cream
  ½   teaspoon salt
  1   teaspoon sugar
  2   pounds sweet potatoes (about 2 large or 3 medium-small potatoes), peeled, quartered lengthwise, and cut crosswise into ¼-inch-thick slices
      Pinch ground black pepper

1. Combine butter, cream, salt, sugar, and sweet potatoes in 3- to 4-quart saucepan; cook, covered, over low heat, stirring occasionally, until potatoes fall apart when poked with fork, 35 to 45 minutes.

2. Off heat, mash sweet potatoes in saucepan with potato masher, or transfer mixture to hopper of food mill and process into warmed serving bowl. Stir in pepper; serve immediately.

VARIATIONS

INDIAN-SPICED MASHED SWEET POTATOES WITH RAISINS AND CASHEWS

Follow recipe for Mashed Sweet Potatoes, substituting dark brown sugar for granulated sugar and adding ¾ teaspoon garam masala to saucepan along with sweet potatoes. Stir ¼ cup golden raisins and ¼ cup roasted unsalted cashews, chopped coarse, into mashed sweet potatoes along with black pepper.

GARLIC-SCENTED MASHED SWEET POTATOES WITH COCONUT MILK AND CILANTRO

Thai flavors provided the inspiration for this variation. Shake the can of coconut milk thoroughly before opening it to combine the coconut cream that rises to the top with the liquid beneath.

Follow recipe for Mashed Sweet Potatoes, substituting ½ cup coconut milk for butter and cream and adding ¼ teaspoon hot red pepper flakes and 1 small garlic clove, minced, to saucepan along with sweet potatoes. Stir in 1 tablespoon minced fresh cilantro along with black pepper.

MAPLE-ORANGE MASHED SWEET POTATOES

Follow recipe for Mashed Sweet Potatoes, stirring in 2 tablespoons maple syrup and ½ teaspoon grated orange zest along with black pepper.

TASTING LAB: Sweet Potatoes

IT'S AN AGE-OLD CULINARY QUESTION: WHAT'S THE difference between a yam and a sweet potato? The answer: it depends on where you live. In American markets, a "yam" is actually a mislabeled sweet potato. If you can get a glimpse of the box they're shipped in, you'll see the words "sweet potato" printed somewhere, as mandated by the U.S. Department of Agriculture. In other parts of the world, the word "yam" refers to a true yam, which is of no relation to the sweet potato. Sold under the label of *ñame* (ny-AH-may) or *igname* here in the United States, a true yam has hairy, off-white or brown skin and white, light yellow, or pink flesh. This tuber is usually sold in log-shaped chunks that weigh several pounds each. Unlike a sweet potato, a true yam is very bland, with an ultra-starchy texture.

So now you know the difference between a sweet potato and a yam. But did you know there are numerous varieties of sweet potatoes available and that they range in

MASHED SWEET POTATOES WITH AFRICAN FLAVORS

Toast ½ teaspoon ground coriander and ⅛ teaspoon cayenne in medium saucepan over medium heat until fragrant, about 30 seconds. Follow recipe for Mashed Sweet Potatoes, cooking butter, cream, salt, sugar, and sweet potatoes in saucepan with toasted spices. Stir in 1 tablespoon chunky peanut butter and 1 tablespoon minced fresh cilantro along with black pepper.

color from pale white to shocking purple? Having developed our recipe for mashed sweet potatoes with the conventional orange-fleshed variety found at our local grocery store, we wondered what difference, if any, these other varieties would make.

Mashing seven varieties of sweet potato side by side, we found the resulting differences in flavor and texture astounding. Of the orange varieties, Beauregard (usually sold as conventional sweet potatoes) was favored for its "standard sweet potato flavor" and perfect texture, while Jewel (sold as a "yam") was "moderately sweet" with a wetter mash, and Red Garnet (sold as a "yam") was downright "savory" and "loose."

In the non-orange category, the white-fleshed Japanese Sweet was "unbelievable," with a "buttery," "chestnut" flavor unlike anything we had ever tasted. By comparison, the similar but less potent flavor of the White Sweet was considered "nice" and "creamy," but the flavor was "fleeting." Ranking at the bottom were the off-white Batata, with its mild flavor and "Play-Doh-like" texture, along with the purple Okinawa, which produced a "dry," nutty-flavored mash with an intense violet hue that was "a bit scary to look at."

EQUIPMENT CORNER: Potato Mashers

THERE ARE TWO CLASSIC STYLES OF POTATO MASHER— wire-looped mashers with a zigzag presser and disk mashers with a perforated round or oval plate. Modern mashers, as it turns out, are simply variations on these two original designs. We tested a total of eight mashers to find those with the most comfortable grip and the most effective mashing mechanism.

When we wrapped up our mash-fest, we concluded that the wire-looped mashers were second-rate, because the space between the loops made it hard to achieve a good, fast mash. Most of the potato pieces escaped between the loops unscathed. Several disk mashers were flimsy and bent under the weight of a few strong mashes. Likewise, steer clear of flat-handled varieties, as they were uncomfortable to grip.

One disk masher, the Exeter ($9.99), is worth mentioning, however, since it is spring-loaded and uses a double-tiered set of wire loops for mashing. It took some muscle to use this masher, but it was the fastest masher tested, turning a pot of boiled potatoes into a smooth puree with just 20 strokes.

In general, the disk mashers outperformed the wire-looped models, and the Profiplus ($15.99) was our favorite. With its small holes, this oval-based masher turned out soft and silky spuds with a reasonable 40 thrusts. Its rounded edges snuggled right into the curves of the saucepan, enhancing its efficacy, and its round handle was easy to grip. The runner-up, the Oxo Good Grips Smooth Masher ($9.99), has an oval metal base and rectangular perforations. The larger perforations allowed a bit more potato through, so it took 50 mashes to do the trick, but the squat device with a cushiony handle was very easy to use. We did not like the all-plastic Oxo Good Grips masher—it has an awkward grip and an ineffective mash—so shop carefully if buying this brand. In any case, avoid disk mashers with perforations larger than ¼ inch.

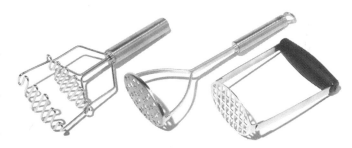

BEST POTATO MASHERS
The disk-style Profiplus Masher (middle) is our favorite because it yielded silky spuds with little effort. The Oxo Good Grips Smooth Masher (right) was the runner-up in our testing. This disk masher was comfortable to use but a bit slower than our top choice. The spring-loaded Exeter Masher (left) was very fast but a bit awkward to use. That said, it was the best wire loop masher tested. See www.cooksillustrated.com for up-to-date prices and mail-order sources for these top-rated products.

CRANBERRY SAUCE

WHAT WE WANTED: A well-balanced sauce—neither too sweet nor too tart—with a soft gel-like texture and some whole berries.

Although cranberry jelly, molded in the shape of the can and sliced into neat disks, is one of the test kitchen's guilty pleasures, it's usually not our first choice for the holiday table. There, a soft, tart-sweet sauce with plenty of whole berries reigns. The best cranberry sauce has a clean, pure cranberry flavor, with enough sweetness to temper the assertively tart fruit but not so much that the sauce is cloying or candylike. The texture should be that of a soft gel, neither too liquidy nor too stiff, cushioning some softened but still intact berries.

Because simple cranberry sauce has only three ingredients—cranberries, sweetener, and liquid—the variables to test were straightforward. Though many of the recipes we researched called for 1 pound of cranberries, we wanted to base ours on 12 ounces of berries simply because all of the bags in stores are that size; we couldn't see the point of opening a second bag to use only a third of it.

Most cranberry sauce recipes use granulated sugar as a sweetener, but we also tried other possibilities, including brown sugar, honey, maple syrup, and corn syrup. Granulated sugar was the tasters' favorite because it balanced the tartness of the berries with a direct sweetness, without adding a strong flavor profile of its own. The corn syrup tasted flat and bland, while the flavors of the maple syrup, brown sugar, and honey were too pronounced, compromising that of the berries. The amount of sugar called for in the recipes we turned up during our research ranged from ⅜ cup to 1½ cups for 12 ounces of berries. In our tests, tasters unanimously favored 1 cup of sugar.

The liquids used to make the sauce ran a wide gamut. We tried batches made with apple juice and cider, white and dark grape juice, orange juice, pineapple juice, cranberry juice cocktail, 7UP, red wine, white wine, port, and champagne. Except for the port and champagne, tasters agreed that none of these liquids—even the orange juice, which is traditional—offered a significant flavor advantage over plain water. In testing different amounts of water, we found that ¾ cup provided the ideal sauce-to-berry ratio once the sauce had reached serving temperature.

Tests of the various cooking times revealed that less is more. About five minutes over medium heat was all it took to achieve a supple, just-firm-enough set in the cooled sauce. Cranberries are high in pectin, a naturally occurring carbohydrate in many fruits. In the presence of sugar and acid (cranberries contain both), the large pectin molecules bond to produce the characteristic jelled consistency. Since pectin molecules are released as the cells of the fruit break down during cooking, the longer the fruit cooks, the more pectin is released (and the more liquid is evaporated), and the stiffer the finished gel becomes. Cooking the sauce for 10 minutes, for instance, resulted in a gel you could slice with a knife. We also tested using a skillet instead of a saucepan and high heat rather than medium heat. We could see no advantage either way and decided to leave well enough alone.

The last round of tests focused on seasoning. Many recipes call simply for cranberries, water, and sugar, while others specify additions such as lemon juice, almond or vanilla extract, and salt. Lemon juice was much too tart, and both extracts left tasters cold, but we were amazed by the dramatic improvement a little salt could make. Just ¼ teaspoon of salt revealed heretofore unknown sweetness in the cranberries and heightened the flavor of the sauce overall, letting loose a full range of high and low flavor notes.

WHAT WE LEARNED: Keep it simple—just water, granulated sugar, and cranberries make the best sauce. Keep it short—simmering for more than five minutes results in a stiff, sliceable gel. And don't forget the salt.

BASIC CRANBERRY SAUCE makes 2¼ cups

The cooking time in this recipe is intended for fresh berries. If you've got frozen cranberries, do not defrost them before use; just pick through them and add about 2 minutes to the simmering time.

¾	cup water
1	cup sugar
¼	teaspoon salt
1	(12-ounce) bag cranberries, picked through

Bring water, sugar, and salt to a boil in medium nonreactive saucepan over high heat, stirring occasionally to dissolve sugar. Stir in cranberries; return to a boil. Reduce heat to medium; simmer until saucy, slightly thickened, and about two-thirds of berries have popped open, about 5 minutes. Transfer to nonreactive bowl, cool to room temperature, and serve. (Can be covered and refrigerated up to 7 days; let stand at room temperature 30 minutes before serving.)

VARIATIONS

CRANBERRY-ORANGE SAUCE

Orange juice adds little flavor, but we found that zest and liqueur pack the orange kick we were looking for in this sauce.

Follow recipe for Basic Cranberry Sauce, heating 1 tablespoon grated orange zest with sugar mixture. Off heat, stir in 2 tablespoons orange liqueur (such as Triple Sec or Grand Marnier).

CRANBERRY SAUCE WITH PEARS AND FRESH GINGER

Peel, core, and cut 2 medium-sized firm, ripe pears into ½-inch chunks; set aside. Follow recipe for Basic Cranberry Sauce, heating 1 tablespoon grated fresh ginger and ¼ teaspoon ground cinnamon with sugar mixture and stirring pears into liquid along with cranberries.

CRANBERRY SAUCE WITH CHAMPAGNE AND CURRANTS

Follow recipe for Basic Cranberry Sauce, substituting champagne for water and adding 3 tablespoons dried currants to liquid along with the cranberries.

A no-cook parsley sauce enlivens our
roast beef tenderloin.

HOLIDAY dinner

CHAPTER 17

America is a land of meat and potato eaters. While the phrase meat and potatoes may seem mundane (it sounds like we are talking about Tuesday-night supper), there's no reason why meat and potatoes can't be special enough for a holiday dinner, especially when the meat is beef tenderloin and the potatoes are scalloped.

Beef tenderloin costs a small fortune, but it is one of the quickest and easiest large cuts to serve to a crowd. The key is to get good color development on the exterior without overcooking the interior. A pale roast won't do, and neither will one that's gray inside.

Betty Crocker may have put scalloped potatoes in a box and thus made them easy enough for everyday cooking, but we think scalloped potatoes should be done right—from scratch—and served with special meals. That said, no one wants to spend hours slicing and layering potatoes into a gratin dish. We were determined to figure out a way to make this dish great while keeping the workload manageable. A thick, gluey sauce (the kind boxed versions yield) wouldn't do, either. We wanted the real thing—creamy, smooth, rich, and cheesy.

ROAST BEEF TENDERLOIN

WHAT WE WANTED: Perfectly cooked meat with a rosy interior and a well-crusted, browned exterior.

For large holiday parties, few cuts can top beef tenderloin. The tenderloin, which comes from the short loin, starts out very tender and can be cooked at a high oven temperature. This elegant roast thus cooks quickly, and its rich, buttery slices are always fork-tender.

Despite its many virtues, however, beef tenderloin is not without its liabilities. Price, of course, is the biggest. Even at a local warehouse-style supermarket, the going rate for a whole beef tenderloin is $7.99 per pound—making for an average sticker price of about $50.

There is good reason for the tenderloin's hefty price. Because it sits up under the spine of the cow, it gets no exercise at all and is therefore the most tender piece of meat. It is one of the two muscles in the ultra-premium steaks known as the porterhouse and the T-bone, so when it is removed from the cow as a whole muscle, it is going to sell for an ultra-premium price. We confirmed this by heading to the supermarket and the local butcher and purchasing $550 worth of beef tenderloin—which bought us just 11 roasts.

A whole beef tenderloin can be purchased "unpeeled," with an incredibly thick layer of exterior fat left attached, but it's usually sold "peeled," or stripped of its fat. Because of our many bad experiences with today's overly lean pork and beef, we purchased six of the 11 roasts unpeeled, determined to leave on as much fat as possible. However, after a quick examination of the unpeeled roasts, we realized that the excessively thick layer of surface fat had to go. Not only would such a large quantity of rendering fat smoke up the kitchen, it would also prohibit a delicious crust from forming on the meat. We dutifully peeled the thick layer of fat from the six tenderloins, but even after removing the sheaths of fat, there were still large pockets of fat on the interior as well as significant surface fat.

Does it make sense to buy an unpeeled roast and trim it yourself? We think not. We paid $6.99 per pound at the butcher for our unpeeled tenderloins, each weighing about 8 pounds. After cleaning them up, the peeled tenderloins weighed about 5 pounds, with a whopping 3 pounds of waste. We purchased peeled tenderloins of similar quality from another source for only $7.99 per pound. Clearly, the unpeeled tenderloins were more expensive with no benefits. And although we don't like tenderloins that have been picked clean, right down to the meat, we recommend buying peeled roasts, with their patches of scattered fat, and letting them be.

The tenderloin's sleek, boneless form makes for quick roasting, but its torpedo-like shape—thick and chunky at one end, gradually tapering at the other end—naturally roasts unevenly. For those looking for a range of doneness, this is not a problem, but for cooks who want a more evenly cooked roast, something must be done.

Folding the tip end of the roast under and tying it bulks up the tenderloin center to almost the same thickness as the more substantial butt end. This ensures that the tenderloin cooks more evenly. (Even so, the tip end is always a little more well-done than the butt.) Tying the roast at approximately 1½-inch intervals further guarantees a more uniformly shaped roast and consequently more even slices of beef. Snipping the silver skin (the translucent sheath that encases certain cuts of beef) at several points also prevents the meat from bowing during cooking. This occurs when the silver skin shrinks more than the meat to which it is attached.

Over the years, we've come to like slow-roasting for large roasts. The lower the heat, we've found, the more evenly the roast cooks. To develop a rich brown crust on these low-roasted larger cuts, we pan-sear them up front or increase the oven temperature for the last few minutes of roasting—or we may do both.

But a beef tenderloin is a different proposition. Though

relatively large, its long, thin shape would seem to dictate a relatively quick cooking time. To determine the ideal roasting temperature, we started at the two extremes, roasting one tenderloin at 200 degrees, the other at 500. As expected, the roast cooked at 500 degrees not only created a very smoky kitchen from the rendering fat, it was also overcooked at each end and around the perimeter. However, the high oven heat had formed a thick, flavorful crust. A good crust is crucial to this rich yet mild-tasting roast, whose flavor is sometimes barely recognizable as beef. Despite the even, rosy pink interior of the beef cooked at 200 degrees, this roast lacked the all-important crust. Neither oven temperature was ideal, so we kept roasting.

Because the higher roasting temperature provided the rich flavor this roast desperately needs, we decided to roast it at as high a temperature as possible. A 450-degree oven still gave us smoke and uneven cooking, so we moved down to 425 degrees. For comparison, we roasted another tenderloin at 200 degrees, this time increasing the oven temperature to 425 degrees at the end of cooking to develop a crust. Both roasts emerged from the oven looking beautiful, and their meat looked and tasted almost identical. Because the tenderloin roasted at 425 degrees was done in just 45 minutes (compared with the slow-roasted tenderloin, which took just about twice as long), we chose the high-heat method.

Although all roasts should rest 15 to 20 minutes after cooking, we found that beef tenderloin improves dramatically if left uncarved even longer. If cut too soon, its slices are soft and flabby. A slightly longer rest—we settled on 30 minutes—allows the meat to firm up into a texture we found much more appealing. Before carving, we preferred removing the big pockets of excess fat, which become more obvious at warm and room temperatures.

WHAT WE LEARNED: **Buy a peeled tenderloin (it's a better value than an unpeeled roast), tie up the tip end to ensure even cooking, roast in a 425-degree oven to create a flavorful crust, and then let the tenderloin rest for 30 minutes so the juices distribute themselves back into the meat.**

ROAST BEEF TENDERLOIN serves 12 to 16

To give the tenderloin a more pronounced pepper crust, increase the amount of pepper to 6 tablespoons and use a mixture of strong black and white and mild pink and green peppercorns. Be sure to crush the peppercorns with a mortar and pestle or with a heavy-bottomed saucepan or skillet. Do not use a coffee or spice grinder, which will grind the softer green and pink peppercorns to a powder before the harder black and white peppercorns begin to break up. See the illustrations on page 216 for more information on preparing the tenderloin.

1   whole peeled beef tenderloin (5 to 6 pounds), thoroughly patted dry
2   tablespoons olive oil
1   tablespoon kosher salt or 2 teaspoons table salt
2   tablespoons coarse-ground black pepper
    Parsley Sauce with Cornichons and Capers (recipe follows)

1. Remove tenderloin from refrigerator 1 hour before roasting to bring meat up to room temperature. Use sharp knife to carefully nick silver skin on side opposite tip with shallow slashes at 1½-inch intervals. Tuck tip end under and tie roast crosswise, knotting at 1½-inch intervals.

2. Adjust oven rack to upper-middle position and heat oven to 425 degrees. Set meat on sheet of plastic wrap and rub all over with oil. Sprinkle with salt and pepper; then lift plastic wrap up and around meat to press on excess.

3. Transfer prepared tenderloin from wrap to wire rack on shallow roasting pan. Roast until instant-read thermometer inserted into thickest part of roast registers about 125 degrees (meat will range from medium-rare to medium in different areas), about 45 minutes. Let stand for about 30 minutes before carving. (Can be wrapped in plastic, refrigerated up to 2 days, sliced, and served chilled.) Cut meat into ½-inch thick slices. Arrange on serving platter and serve with sauce.

TECHNIQUE:
Preparing a Beef Tenderloin

1. To keep the meat from bowing as it cooks, slide a knife under the silver skin and flick the blade upward to cut through the silver skin at five or six spots along the length of the roast.

2. To ensure that the tenderloin roasts more evenly, fold the thin tip end of the roast under about 6 inches.

3. For more even cooking and evenly sized slices, use 12-inch lengths of kitchen twine to tie the roast every 1 1/2 inches.

4. Set the meat on a sheet of plastic wrap and rub it all over with oil. Sprinkle with salt and pepper, then lift the plastic wrap up and around the meat to press on excess. This method guarantees even coverage.

PARSLEY SAUCE WITH CORNICHONS AND CAPERS makes about 1 1/4 cups

Prepare this sauce while the roast rests or several hours in advance and keep it covered at room temperature.

¾	cup minced fresh parsley leaves
12	cornichons, minced (6 tablespoons), plus 1 teaspoon cornichon juice
¼	cup capers, chopped coarse
2	medium scallions, white and light green parts, minced
	Pinch salt
¼	teaspoon ground black pepper
½	cup extra-virgin olive oil

Mix ingredients together in medium bowl.

SCIENCE DESK:
What Happens to Meat as It Rests?

A FINAL BUT VERY IMPORTANT STEP WHEN COOKING tenderloin (and all red meats) is allowing it to rest before slicing. As the proteins in the meat heat up during cooking they coagulate, which basically means they uncoil and then reconnect, or bond, with each other, in a different configuration. When the proteins coagulate, they squeeze out part of the liquid that was trapped in their coiled structures and in the spaces between the individual molecules. The heat from the cooking source drives these freed liquids toward the center of the meat.

This process of coagulation explains why experienced chefs can tell how done a piece of meat is by pushing on it and judging the amount of resistance: the firmer the meat, the more done it is. But the coagulation process is apparently at least partly reversible, so as you allow the meat to rest and return to a lower temperature after cooking, some of the liquid is reabsorbed by the protein molecules as their capacity to hold moisture increases. As a result, if given a

TECHNIQUE:
Learning to Tie Butcher's Knots

Many cooks have trouble tying roasts properly. If that's the case, practice with a roll of paper towels and strands of butcher's twine. It's a lot neater than practicing on a roast.

chance to rest, the meat will lose less juice when you cut into it, which in turn makes for much juicier meat. In the case of beef tenderloin, the texture of the meat also improves, becoming a bit firmer as it rests.

EQUIPMENT CORNER: Boning Knives

THE SLIM, FLEXIBLE BLADE OF A BONING KNIFE MAY LOOK eccentric, but it is perfectly designed to slide nimbly through joints and between bones. It is an essential tool for such tasks as removing cutlets from a whole chicken breast and can also be used to remove fat and silver skin from a beef tenderloin. The slim blade creates less drag through the meat, and the slices made are neater than those possible with the wider blade on a chef's knife.

Because most home cooks are likely to use a boning knife infrequently, we wondered if a cheaper knife would do. To find out, we tested six leading knives with blades between 5 and 7 inches long and prices between $9 and $71. Both large- and small-handed testers used each knife to butcher a whole chicken and to trim beef ribs of fat and silver skin. Each knife was evaluated for handle comfort, slipperiness (hands become very greasy when butchering),

agility (including flexibility), and sharpness.

The winning Forschner (Victorinox) Fibrox boning knife, priced at $17.90, received high marks for its uniquely designed ergonomic handle as well as its slim, highly maneuverable blade and razor-sharp edge. The plastic handle nestled comfortably into both large and small hands, and it stayed there even when our hands became slick with fat. The blade was the narrowest of the lot, which made it very agile. While all the knives arrived with razor-sharp edges, the Forschner seemed exceptionally keen, gliding effortlessly through tough tendon and thick skin.

The J.A. Henckels Professional S boning knife ($49.99) finished a close second. Its blade was nearly as agile as the Forschner, but the handle was somewhat slippery. The Wüsthof-Trident Grand Prix boning knife ($54) was "fiendishly sharp," but the wide blade was not as agile as the top models and the handle became slippery when coated with chicken fat. The textured metal handle of the Global boning knife ($70.99) received mixed reviews, and testers did not like the boxy handle on the Chicago Cutlery boning knife ($14.99) or the flimsy blade on the Farberware Professional boning knife ($8.99).

BEST BONING KNIFE
The Forschner (Victorinox) Fibrox knife boasts a handle that testers found "easy-to-grip" and a narrow blade that shows "great flexibility around bones." Everyone raved about the "amazing" sharpness of this knife out of the box. For an up-to-date price and mail-order source for this top-rated product, see www.cooksillustrated.com.

SCALLOPED POTATOES

WHAT WE WANTED: Layers of thinly sliced, tender potatoes, creamy sauce, and a nicely browned, cheesy crust.

Thinly sliced potatoes layered with cream and baked until they are bubbling and browned are a classic accompaniment to a holiday ham or roast beef. Although the supermarket shelves are lined with "add water, heat, and serve" versions of scalloped potatoes, making them from scratch doesn't have to take much time, and the differences in flavor and texture are tremendous.

To start, we tested three different techniques for "scalloping" potatoes. First, we boiled the potatoes, combined them with a cream sauce thickened with flour (also known as a béchamel), and then finished them in the oven. This method produced a thick, pasty sauce and hollow-flavored potatoes, not to mention several dirty pots.

For our next test we combined raw, sliced potatoes with an unthickened cream sauce, allowing it to cook through and thicken in the oven. While these potatoes had more flavor and the sauce had a better consistency, the cooking time was more than an hour and half.

Wanting to speed up the process a bit, we tried cooking the potatoes in simmering cream for a few minutes before transferring the potatoes and cream to a casserole dish and finishing the potatoes in the oven. This technique allowed the potatoes to get a good head start on cooking and also encouraged them to release some of their starch, which naturally thickened the cream to the consistency of a good sauce. We did find it necessary to cover the pot to prevent the heavy cream and the starch from reducing and thickening too far in advance. By cooking the potatoes in the cream, covered, for about 15 minutes, we were able to reduce the oven time to a mere 20 minutes, resulting in perfectly cooked potatoes and a smooth, lightly thickened cream sauce.

With the technique set, we moved on to the different types of potatoes, testing Yukon Gold, all-purpose, and russet. Although each variety cooked up differently, none was terrible. Yukon Gold and all-purpose potatoes were both a bit too waxy and buttery when mixed with the rich cream. Russet potatoes turned out a bit more tender, and their earthier flavor was the tasters' favorite.

The thickness of the potato slices also made a noticeable difference in the final texture of the casserole. We found that potatoes cut into ⅛-inch-thick slices kept their shape but were still flexible enough to form tight layers that stuck together to create a neat casserole. Thicker slices formed a looser, sloppier casserole, while thinner slices melted together and gave the finished dish the texture of mashed potatoes.

Focusing now on the sauce, we noticed that those made with all heavy cream were overbearingly heavy. We tried half-and-half but found that it wasn't rich enough. Even worse, the sauce made with half-and-half curdled in the oven. Half-and-half simply doesn't have enough fat to keep the dairy proteins from coagulating under high heat, which makes the sauce look curdled. In the end, we simply tempered the heavy cream with a little whole milk, which lightened the rich sauce just enough while keeping its texture smooth.

Scalloped potatoes also contain cheese. We found that a sprinkling of cheese formed a golden crust on the top of the dish while still allowing the cream to bubble up around the edges and thicken. Cheddar is the classic choice, but we got nice results with other cheeses with good melting properties, including Parmesan, Monterey Jack, and Gruyère.

WHAT WE LEARNED: Don't use flour to thicken the sauce (it will be pasty) but instead rely on heavy cream lightened with a little whole milk. To cut the cooking time, simmer the potatoes briefly in the cream and then dump the whole mixture into a baking dish. Use russet potatoes for the best texture and flavor, and slice them thin so they form neat layers.

SCALLOPED POTATOES serves 8 to 10

For the fastest and most consistent results, slice the potatoes in a food processor. See the Equipment Corner on page 165 for information about choosing a gratin dish for this recipe.

  2   tablespoons unsalted butter
  1   small onion, minced
  2   medium garlic cloves, minced
      (about 2 teaspoons)
  3   cups heavy cream
  1   cup whole milk
  4   sprigs fresh thyme
  2   bay leaves
  2   teaspoons salt
  ½   teaspoon ground black pepper
  4   pounds russet potatoes, peeled and cut into
      ⅛-inch-thick slices
  1   cup shredded cheddar cheese (about 4 ounces)

1. Heat oven to 350 degrees. Meanwhile, melt butter in large Dutch oven over medium-high heat until foaming subsides, about 1 minute. Add onion and sauté until it turns soft and begins to brown, about 4 minutes. Add garlic and sauté until fragrant, about 30 seconds. Add cream, milk, thyme, bay leaves, salt, pepper, and potatoes and bring to simmer. Cover, adjusting heat as necessary to maintain light simmer, and cook until potatoes are almost tender (paring knife can be slipped into and out of center of potato slice with some resistance), about 15 minutes.

2. Remove and discard thyme sprigs and bay leaves. Transfer potato mixture to 3-quart gratin dish and sprinkle with cheese. Bake until cream has thickened and is bubbling around sides and top is golden brown, about 20 minutes. Cool for 5 minutes before serving.

VARIATION

SCALLOPED POTATOES WITH WILD MUSHROOMS

Cover ½ ounce dried porcini mushroom pieces with ½ cup hot tap water in small microwave-safe bowl; cover with plastic wrap, cut several steam vents with paring knife, and microwave on high power for 30 seconds. Let stand until mushrooms soften, about 5 minutes. Lift mushrooms from liquid with fork and mince, using chef's knife (you should have about 2 tablespoons). Pour soaking liquid through strainer lined with paper towel and reserve. Follow recipe for Scalloped Potatoes, adding 3½ ounces fresh shiitake mushrooms, sliced ¼ inch thick, and 5 ounces fresh cremini mushrooms, sliced ¼ inch thick, to foaming butter along with onion and cook until mushrooms release their moisture, about 2 minutes. Add minced, rehydrated porcini along with their liquid and cook until all mushrooms are tender and liquid has reduced to about 2 tablespoons, about 3 minutes. Add garlic and proceed as directed, replacing cheddar with Gruyère or Parmesan.

HAM dinner

CHAPTER 18

Ham with green bean casserole makes for a classic American dinner. But a well-stocked supermarket offers many different kinds of ham to choose from, and green bean casserole can be pretty sorry stuff. We wanted to figure out how to make the most of both.

We started by testing all of the major types of hams (as well as brands) available in supermarkets and found that we liked best the spiral-sliced ham with natural juices. It is neither overly pumped up with water nor packed into a cylindrical loaf shape. And for the test kitchen staff, who had to carve all of the hams before the tasting, it was hands-down the most convenient of the bone-in hams.

The green bean casserole of the 1950s was a 1-2-3 recipe consisting of frozen green beans, canned soup, and canned fried onions. It was a testament to convenience at the expense of good taste. We thought we'd be willing to trade some of that convenience for a casserole that tasted really good, starting with fresh green beans instead of frozen and our own simple sauce.

Good green bean casserole begins with fresh beans that are cooked in salted boiling water, shocked in a bowl of ice water, and then drained.

SPIRAL-SLICED HAM

WHAT WE WANTED: The ideal ham is neither dry nor mushy. It should have a nice chew and be accompanied by a complex sauce that's not too sweet. Finally, the ham should be as easy to carve as possible.

We've always been fond of ham. We love its toothy, meaty chew and its unique flavor combination of sweet, salt, and smoke. Despite this devotion to ham, we have to admit that the versions appearing on most holiday tables are far from ideal. Very often they are dry as dust or mushy as a wet paper towel. We decided to find the best possible way to prepare a precooked supermarket ham so that it could live up to its full potential.

Hams vary in terms of the amount of water added during the curing process. A ham that has no added water is labeled just plain "ham." While some manufacturers still make these hams, they are very hard to find in supermarkets. "Ham with natural juices" (as the label would state) has 7 to 8 percent water added; "ham–water added" has 12 to 15 percent water added; and "ham and water product" contains more than 15 percent added water. The more water a ham contains, the less expensive it is per pound. They also vary in terms of bone. They may be boneless, semiboneless, or completely bone-in.

The results of our tasting were pretty predictable: More bone and less water seemed to make for the tastiest hams. Boneless and semiboneless hams had "compressed" textures that we did not like, and the hams with the most water added had the most dilute flavor. Bone-in, spiral-sliced hams with natural juices were the favorite in our tasting. They were neither overly pumped up with water nor packed into a cylindrical loaf shape. They were also the favorite of the test kitchen staff in terms of convenience. After having to carve many of the hams in the testing, we were quite happy to meet up with a ham that had been carved for us. Spiral-sliced hams were hams were hands-down the most convenient of the bone-in choices.

"Cooking" (really, only heating) these fully cooked hams is a no-brainer, which is why, we'll bet, that these hams are so popular around the holidays. The problem is that heating instructions for spiral-sliced hams differ from package to package. To add to the confusion, there are discrepancies in recommended final internal temperatures. Such imprecision wouldn't be such an issue if these hams didn't readily dry out and turn to jerky when improperly heated.

One factor that had to be decided at the outset was the internal temperature to which the ham should be heated. Spiral-sliced hams are fully cooked, and so long as the sell-by date hasn't come and gone, the ham can be served straight out of the package. While most cooks would still elect to heat the ham before serving, there is no consensus as to what temperature it should reach before being brought to the table. The label of one package said 120 degrees. The National Pork Producers Council said 140 degrees. Two manufacturers didn't include a temperature in their heating directions, so we called to inquire and were told 150 degrees by one and 155 degrees by the other. This discrepancy is unfortunate, because heating the ham to the proper internal temperature is critical to helping it retain its juices.

When we heated a ham to 140 degrees it lost a large amount of liquid and was dry. Heating to 130 degrees was an improvement, but we found that taking the ham to only 100 degrees was better yet. The outer inch of the ham registered at about 145 degrees, and residual heat caused the internal temperature to continue rising as the ham rested, covered, after coming out of the oven. After 40 minutes it peaked at 115 to 120 degrees, which had been our original goal. Though this may sound like a low temperature, the ham was warm to the touch and, most important, had remained moist and juicy. And, after all, we are dealing with a precooked cut of meat here.

Having settled on the final temperature, we needed to

figure out exactly how to get there. Our first task was to determine the proper oven temperature. We quickly found that a high (400 degrees) or even a moderate (325 degrees) oven was no good. Though the hams were covered with foil for protection, when subjected to these temperatures they lost an astounding amount of liquid (up to 2 cups); the meat was dry and leathery and the slices torqued and splayed.

We then began experimenting with low oven temperatures. These worked much better, but the cooking time now became an issue. At the low end of the scale, an average 9-pound ham heated in a 225-degree oven was both juicy and moist and held its shape, but it took a grueling 3 ¼ hours to heat up. In a 250-degree oven, the ham was just as good, but it heated in 2¾ hours, shaving 30 minutes off the cooking time.

Although easy, this was still a long process, so we sought means to speed it up. We tried different combinations of high and low temperatures, but they were either detrimental to the moistness of the ham or did nothing to speed its heating.

Someone in the test kitchen then suggested a plastic oven bag instead of the foil cover. Quite to our astonishment, this simple, flimsy looking accouterment trimmed off a few minutes of cooking time per pound. While this may sound insignificant, it can translate into a 20- to 30-minute differential when cooking a piece of meat the size of a ham. How did it work? We posited that the oven bag, wrapped tightly around the ham, eliminated the air space—an insulation of sorts—formed between the foil and the ham, thereby giving the ham direct exposure to heat and speeding its heating. Another step that speeds the heating process is letting the ham stand at room temperature for 90 minutes before putting it in the oven. This, too, takes off a couple of minutes per pound. By using an oven bag and letting the ham stand at room temperature, we had whittled the heating time down to about 2 hours, with a 40-minute rest out of the oven. Protracted though

this process may seem, it's great in that it frees the oven for other last-minute cooking tasks.

With the cooking method in place, we now had two more points to consider: making the sauce and carving the ham. We wanted to come up with something better than the gooey glaze that comes in a packet with many hams. And we wanted to see which of the two cuts of spiral-sliced ham available—the shank or the sirloin—would be easier to carve.

Most spiral-sliced hams come with an enclosed packet of glaze. We tossed them all aside because we have found that glazes, whether prepackaged or homemade, do little to enhance this kind of ham. Instead, they tend to sit on the surface like a layer of gooey candy. Although this may appeal to children, we much prefer to make an interesting, flavorful sauce to accompany the ham. The sauce, since it doesn't use any pan drippings, can be made ahead and reheated. It dresses up the ham, making it look and taste more elegant, and it also adds moisture to carved ham slices, which tend to dry out somewhat as they sit uncovered on a serving platter, waiting for guests to reach for seconds.

We also discovered that the shank end of the ham is substantially easier to carve than the sirloin, or butt, end because of the bone configuration. The packages aren't labeled as such, but the shank can be identified by the tapered, more pointed end opposite the cut side. The sirloin, on the other hand, has a very blunt, rounded end. If you can't find a shank half, however, don't despair; both halves taste equally good. Your knife will just encounter a few more bumps and curves while carving the sirloin half.

WHAT WE LEARNED: **Bake the ham in a 250-degree oven to a low internal temperature to preserve juiciness. Remember that ham is a fully cooked product and that the goal is only to reheat it. To make carving easier, buy a shank-end ham. For grown-up flavor, serve the sauce on the side rather than coating the ham with a sticky glaze.**

SPIRAL-SLICED HAM serves 20 to 30

You can put the ham in the oven cold, bypassing the 90-minute standing time. If you do, add a couple of minutes per pound to the heating time. If using an oven bag, cut slits in the bag so it does not burst. Allow about 3 to 4 servings per pound for a bone-in ham. We recommend buying a shank portion because the bone configuration makes it easier to carve; look for the half ham with a tapered, pointed end (see Getting It Right at right).

1 spiral-sliced half ham (7 to 10 pounds),
    preferably shank end

1. Unwrap ham and remove and discard plastic disk covering bone. Place ham in plastic oven bag, pull tightly for a close fit, tie bag shut, and trim excess plastic (see illustration on page 226). Set ham cut-side down in 13 by 9-inch baking dish and cut four slits in top of bag with paring knife. Alternatively, place unwrapped ham cut-side down in baking dish and cover tightly with foil. Let stand at room temperature 90 minutes.

2. Meanwhile, adjust oven rack to lowest position and heat oven to 250 degrees. Bake until center of ham registers about 100 degrees on instant-read thermometer, 1½ to 2½ hours (about 14 minutes per pound if using plastic oven bag, about 17 minutes per pound if using foil), depending on size of ham.

3. Remove ham from oven and let rest in baking dish in oven bag or with foil cover until internal temperature registers 115 to 120 degrees on instant-read thermometer, 30 to 40 minutes. Cut open oven bag or remove foil, place ham on carving board, and slice according to illustrations on page 225. Serve immediately with one of following sauces, if desired.

GETTING IT RIGHT: Choosing A Ham

SHANK END

BUTT END

For easy carving, look for a shank-end ham (left), which has a tapered, pointed end opposite the cut side. The sirloin, or butt, end (right) has a rounded, blunt end.

DRIED CHERRY AND STOUT SAUCE WITH BROWN SUGAR AND ALLSPICE makes about 4 cups

Stout is a strong, dark beer made from toasted barley. Here it makes a rich, full-bodied sauce with subtle smoky notes and a characteristically bitter finish.

1   cup canned low-sodium chicken broth
2   tablespoons cornstarch
2   tablespoons unsalted butter
3   medium shallots, minced (about 9 tablespoons)
⅛   teaspoon ground allspice
4   cups stout
⅓   cup packed brown sugar
1   cup dried tart cherries (about 5 ounces)
1½   tablespoons balsamic vinegar
      Salt and ground black pepper

1. Whisk together chicken broth and cornstarch in small bowl; set aside. Heat butter in 12-inch skillet over medium heat until foaming; add shallots and sauté until softened, about 3 minutes. Stir in allspice; cook until fragrant, about 30 seconds. Add stout, brown sugar, and dried cherries; increase heat to medium-high, bring to a simmer, and cook until slightly syrupy, about 10 minutes.

2. Whisk broth and cornstarch mixture to recombine, then gradually whisk into simmering liquid; return to simmer to thicken sauce, stirring occasionally. Off heat, stir in balsamic vinegar; season to taste with salt and pepper. (The sauce can be cooled to room temperature and refrigerated up to 2 days. Reheat in medium saucepan over medium-low heat.) Serve with ham.

MUSTARD SAUCE WITH VERMOUTH AND THYME makes about 3 ½ cups

The Dijon mustard lends a creaminess to this sauce, while the whole-grain mustard adds texture and visual appeal.

> 1½ cups canned low-sodium chicken broth
> 2 tablespoons cornstarch
> 2 tablespoons unsalted butter

> 3 medium shallots, minced (about 9 tablespoons)
> 2 cups dry vermouth
> 1 tablespoon packed brown sugar
> ½ cup Dijon mustard
> ¼ cup whole-grain mustard
> 1 tablespoon chopped fresh thyme leaves
> Salt and ground black pepper

1. Whisk together chicken broth and cornstarch in small bowl; set aside. Heat butter in 12-inch skillet over medium heat until foaming; add shallots and sauté until softened, about 3 minutes. Stir in vermouth and sugar; increase heat to medium-high and simmer until alcohol vapors have cooked off, about 4 minutes.

2. Whisk chicken stock and cornstarch mixture to recombine, then gradually whisk into simmering liquid; return sauce to simmer to thicken, stirring occasionally. Off heat, whisk in mustards and thyme; season to taste with salt and pepper. (Sauce can be cooled to room temperature and refrigerated up to 2 days. Reheat in medium saucepan over medium-low heat.) Serve with ham.

TECHNIQUE: Carving a Spiral-Sliced Ham

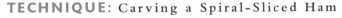

1. With the tip of a paring or carving knife, cut around the bone to loosen the attached slices.

2. Using a long carving knife, slice horizontally above the bone and through the spiral cut slices, toward the back of the ham.

3. Pull the cut portion away from the bone, and cut between the slices to separate them fully.

4. Beginning at the tapered end, slice above the bone to remove the remaining chunk of meat. Flip the ham over and repeat the procedure for the other side.

TECHNIQUE: Trimming the Oven Bag

Use scissors to trim the oven bag, leaving 1 inch above the tie.

TASTING LAB: Spiral-Sliced Hams

SPIRAL-SLICED HAMS OFFER THE BEST COMBINATION OF flavor, texture, and convenience when it comes to slicing, but are all spiral-sliced hams the same? To find out, we rounded up the five most widely available bone-in, spiral-sliced hams. All were heated according to our recipe and served plain (without a sauce or glaze).

We found a wide variety in both flavor and texture. The Cook's Spiral Sliced Hickory Smoked Honey Ham ($2.29 per pound) was the clear winner. Almost all tasters appreciated this ham's clean and meaty flavor, though a few were left wanting stronger sweet, salt, smoke, and spice flavors. Overall, it was declared an "honest ham" that "doesn't seem processed" or "taste like it's pumped full of chemicals."

The Hillshire Farm Spiral Sliced Brown Sugar Cured Ham ($1.79 per pound) also received mostly positive comments. Most tasters noted a pleasant balance of salt and sweet, but others thought the flavor insubstantial and "lacking much assertion." As for the texture, many found it a bit chewy and dry, while a couple of tasters said these qualities made it a "real man's ham."

The other hams in the tasting did not fare as well. Almost every taster remarked on the pock-marked meat of the Hillshire Farm Spiral Sliced Honey Cured Ham ($1.79 per pound). Its appearance, coupled with the rubbery, wet, very "pumped" texture, made this very sweet ham "look and taste like a sponge." Tasters could not get too enthused about the Colonial Spiral Sliced Ham ($2.69), either, finding it spongy and soft. The most expensive ham in the tasting, the Carando Spiral Sliced Hickory Smoked Ham ($3.99 per pound), landed at the bottom of the rankings. Sold under the Farmland label in the Midwest and on the West Coast, this ham elicited comments such as "sour," "acidic," and "musty" from tasters. The meat verged on dry, with a coarse, crumbly, "fall-apart" quality.

EQUIPMENT CORNER:
Timer/Thermometers

A REGULAR TIMER IS FINE FOR REMINDING YOU THAT A certain period of time has elapsed. But it can't tell you precisely when your ham or roast is done. You still need to pull out an instant-read thermometer and check the meat. What if you could combine the timer and thermometer into one handy device? Several companies have done so in making the timer/thermometer, which allows you to use its timing and thermometer functions separately or at the same time. Here's how it works.

Attached to a standard timer-type base is a long wire that ends with a sensor probe that measures temperature. To use this device, you insert the sensor probe into foods before they go into the oven (or on the grill). You place the food in the oven and snake the long wire cord through the oven door opening. The cord attaches to the base unit, which sits on a counter near the oven or attaches to the oven door via a back-mounted magnet. You program the base unit with the desired internal temperature (say 125 degrees for a rare roast beef). Once the sensor probe determines that the meat has reached this temperature, the timer unit will beep. It also provides you with a constant display of the temperature of the food as it rises.

We rounded up six timer/thermometers, ranging in price from $20 to $50, to see which model is the best option for the home cook. We tested each device in beef roasts and set the timer to beep at various temperatures. We doubled-checked these temperatures with a separate thermometer and found that all six models were accurate—they beeped right on cue.

Ease of operation and features, however, revealed some differences. Several models had short wire cords that made them harder to use. Also, the magnet on some timer/thermometers was not strong enough, and we worried that the units would come crashing down onto the floor. A few models were harder to program and read.

In the end, testers agreed that the Polder Cooking Thermometer/Timer ($24.99) was the best choice. It was

the easiest and most intuitive to figure out and use. It also has a long 4-foot cord and the loudest alarm of those tested, making it the best choice to use on the grill. We were intrigued by the Maverick Redi-Check Remote Timer/Oven Thermometer ($49.99), which actually reads the temperature from remote locations using a transmitter in the probe and a receiver in the base unit. However, several minor design flaws (it was less stable than other models and the cord was shorter) and hard-to-follow instructions kept this unusual model from scoring high on our test.

BEST TIMER/THERMOMETER

Among the six models tested, the Polder Cooking Thermometer/Timer was the most stable and sounded the loudest alarm. It also had the longest cord and was the easiest to use. For an up-to-date price and mail-order source for this top-rated product, visit www.cooksillustrated.com.

GREEN BEAN CASSEROLE

WHAT WE WANTED: We wanted to resurrect this dinosaur and transform it by using fresh instead of prepared ingredients to make it taste better. Much better.

Often referred to as the Classic Green Bean Bake, this casserole was developed by Campbell's in 1955 using frozen green beans, canned cream of mushroom soup, and a topping of canned fried onions. The company touted the recipe as "delicious and easy to make, easy to remember, and leaves room for creativity." We thought we would exercise the creativity clause. We started by making the original recipe and then began to experiment.

The frozen beans recommended in the original recipe were certainly easy to use, but they also had a watery taste and a mushy texture in this dish. Fresh beans not only offered more flavor, but we were able to cook them to the appropriate doneness and leave a little bit of crunch. We tried sautéing and steaming the green beans but ended up liking the bright green color and seasoned flavor obtained when they were blanched in boiling, salted water. (Blanching means to submerge briefly in boiling water.) We found the beans tasted best when blanched in 4 quarts of water heavily seasoned with 2 tablespoons of salt for 4 to 5 minutes. We then plunged the beans into ice water (a process called shocking) to stop them from further cooking. Blanching then shocking allowed us maximum control over the cooking process, which meant that the beans were perfectly cooked every time.

Our next concern was the cream-based mushroom sauce. We did not enjoy the thick, pasty texture and lackluster flavor of condensed soup. What we did want was a smooth, velvety sauce filled with potent mushroom flavor. We began by testing two popular methods for making a cream sauce: reducing the cream to the proper consistency, and thickening the cream with flour and butter (also known as a roux). Sauces made by simply reducing cream were too heavy and took too much time for our holiday-size casserole, while sauces thickened with flour tasted pasty and lacked depth of flavor. By combining the methods—using a little flour and reducing the sauce a bit—we got a svelte, flavorful sauce that was neither too rich nor too floury. After testing half-and-half and whole milk, we found neither up to sharing the title ring with lush heavy cream. We tried adding cheese but found the extra flavor to be both overpowering and unnecessary.

Up until now, we had been using white button mushrooms but were disappointed with their lack of flavor. By replacing half of the button mushrooms with cremini and using some dried porcini, we were able to give the sauce a full, earthy, and complex mushroom flavor. While we liked the flavor of portobellos, we found that their meaty texture required more cooking than button mushrooms, making them difficult to incorporate into our otherwise streamlined recipe. Onion, garlic, and fresh thyme were great companion flavors for the mushrooms, while chicken broth helped to pull all of the flavors in the sauce together. We also tried adding bacon, white wine, Madeira, and shallots to the sauce, but found their flavors unwelcome and discordant.

With the green beans and mushroom sauce nailed down, all that was left was the fried onion topping. While deep frying our own onions was out of the question because of the time it takes, we found the canned fried onions simply tasted too commercial to use on their own. By mixing the canned, fried onions with some fresh, seasoned bread crumbs we were able to remove the "from the can taste" of the traditional topping.

WHAT WE LEARNED: Use blanched fresh green beans (not frozen beans), build a sauce with fresh mushrooms, onions, and cream (not canned soup), and mix canned fried onions with fresh bread crumbs to temper their commercial flavor.

GREEN BEAN CASSEROLE serves 8 to 10

All the components of this dish can be cooked ahead of time. The assembled casserole needs only 15 minutes in a 375-degree oven to warm through and brown. A gratin dish works nicely with this recipe. See page 165 for information on our favorite.

topping

- 4 slices sandwich bread with crusts, each slice torn into quarters
- 2 tablespoons unsalted butter, softened
- ¼ teaspoon salt
- ⅛ teaspoon ground black pepper
- 3 cups canned fried onions (about 6 ounces)

beans

- Salt
- 2 pounds green beans, ends trimmed, cut on the diagonal into 2-inch pieces
- ½ ounce dried porcini mushrooms
- 6 tablespoons unsalted butter
- 1 medium onion, minced
- 3 medium garlic cloves, minced (about 1 tablespoon)
- 12 ounces white button mushrooms, wiped clean, stems trimmed, and sliced ¼ inch thick
- 12 ounces cremini mushrooms, wiped clean, stems trimmed, and sliced ¼ inch thick
- 2 tablespoons minced fresh thyme leaves
- ¼ teaspoon ground black pepper
- 2 tablespoons all-purpose flour
- 1 cup canned low-sodium chicken broth
- 2 cups heavy cream

1. FOR THE TOPPING: Pulse bread, butter, salt, and pepper in workbowl of food processor fitted with metal blade until mixture resembles coarse crumbs, about ten 1-second pulses. Transfer to large bowl and toss with onions; set aside.

2. FOR THE BEANS: Heat oven to 375 degrees. Bring 4 quarts water to boil in large pot. Add 2 tablespoons salt and beans. Cook until bright green and slightly crunchy, 4 to 5 minutes. Drain beans and plunge immediately into large bowl filled with ice water to stop cooking. Spread beans out onto paper towel–lined baking sheet to drain.

3. Meanwhile, cover dried porcini with ½ cup hot tap water in small microwave-safe bowl; cover with plastic wrap, cut several steam vents with paring knife, and microwave on high power for 30 seconds. Let stand until mushrooms soften, about 5 minutes. Lift mushrooms from the liquid with fork and mince using chef's knife (you should have about 2 tablespoons). Pour liquid through paper towel–lined sieve and reserve.

4. Melt butter in large nonstick skillet over medium-high heat until foaming subsides, about 1 minute. Add onion, garlic, button mushrooms, and cremini mushrooms and cook until mushrooms release their moisture, about 2 minutes. Add porcini mushrooms along with their strained soaking liquid, thyme, 1 teaspoon salt, and pepper and cook until all mushrooms are tender and liquid has reduced to 2 tablespoons, about 5 minutes. Add flour and cook for about 1 minute. Stir in chicken broth and reduce heat to medium. Stir in cream and simmer gently until sauce has consistency of dense soup, about 15 minutes.

5. Arrange beans in 3-quart gratin dish. Pour mushroom mixture over beans and mix to coat beans evenly. Sprinkle with bread crumb mixture and bake until top is golden brown and sauce is bubbling around edges, about 15 minutes. Serve immediately.

We found that a tube pan produces a better-looking and better-tasting coffee cake than a Bundt pan.

WEEKEND brunch

Coffee cake has left home, abandoning grandma's kitchen for the shelves of ready-made supermarket pastries. Consisting of little more than a flat, dry, rectangular yellow cake topped with hard, pellet-like crumbs and nary a cinnamon swirl in sight, it is a far cry from the coffee cake of yesteryear—the sour cream coffee cake.

That's not to say that there aren't some bad sour cream coffee cakes out there. They're likely to be too dense and wet, too dry and tough, too sweet or too spicy, or just plain bland. The streusel inside the cake may be damp and pasty, and the streusel topping, if any, sometimes melts into the cake, while other times it remains sandy and granular, a world apart from the cake. We wanted the perfect sour cream coffee cake—a weekend indulgence that would be easy enough to make even when company wasn't coming.

Fruit salad is always simple, and when the fruit is good, so is the salad. But how about a great fruit salad with flavor above and beyond the ordinary? That's what we wanted.

Finally, what's brunch without coffee? We investigated grinders, French roast beans, and decaffeination and dispelled some common coffee myths along the way.

SOUR CREAM COFFEE CAKE

WHAT WE WANTED: There are three kinds of coffee cake: the ersatz convenience-store cake, the low-fat variety, and the real thing, packed with sour cream, butter, and sugar. We set out to explore the secrets of the latter, a classic, rich coffee cake that is worth waking up for.

Whether tall and round, loaf-shaped, cake-shaped, or Bundt-shaped, with streusel on the inside, on the outside, or both, sour cream coffee cake is distinguished by two indisputable facts. One: Hardly anyone makes it anymore (and that is a shame). Two: When it is made, it should be an ultra-moist cake, pleasantly rich and dense from the addition of sour cream.

After a first round of testing five different recipes, we came to a few conclusions. First, this is not a lean cake. Made from large amounts of sour cream, eggs, and butter, this cake is decadent. Second, we wanted to find a method of putting this cake together that was simple enough to tackle even before our first cup of coffee. Third, we love crispy, crunchy, yet melt-in-your-mouth streusel so much that we wanted not one but two layers of it on the inside, as well as a sizable amount on the cake top, and we knew that this would require a careful arrangement of sugar, flour, butter, nuts, and spices.

Cake flour is the norm in many sour cream coffee cake recipes, but this is a heavy cake that needs more structure, so we switched to the sturdier all-purpose flour. Brown sugar, a common coffee cake batter ingredient, had too much flavor, so we opted for the lower-profile granulated white sugar. We decided on four eggs, which produced the traditional buttery-yellow cake color and helped to provide for a tight crumb (we didn't want an open crumb, full of gaping, craggy holes). To give the cake tenderness and a capacity to remain moist for days, we relied on butter and, of course, sour cream. One-and-a-half sticks of butter and 1½ cups of sour cream produced the best flavor as well as a velvety mouthfeel.

Quite a few recipes use both baking powder and baking soda to lighten the cake's heavy load, and, after testing a few cakes, we found we didn't disagree. (The baking soda, which reacts with acids to create lift, is necessary because of the quantity of sour cream used.) These recipes, however, used a mere ½ to 1 teaspoon of each, and we disliked the squat, dense cakes that were coming out of our oven. After increasing the amount of leavening bit by bit, we discovered that a hefty 1 tablespoon of baking powder along with ¾ teaspoon of baking soda would lift the cake to a nearly statuesque height.

For the mixing method, we started by creaming the butter and sugar (whipping them to incorporate air), a common cake-making technique. The resulting cake was pleasingly tall, but it also had a crumb that was airy and cakey instead of tight, as we wanted. We then tried a method used in our basic yellow cake recipe, developed several years ago in the test kitchen. This two-stage method starts out by taking slightly softened butter and some of the sour cream and cutting them right into the dry ingredients, as is done for a pie dough. The liquid ingredients—in this case, eggs and more sour cream—are mixed together and then added to the butter/sour cream/dry ingredient mixture. The batter is then beaten until aerated and pale in color. The result was a cake with a tight crumb and a tender texture, and, best of all, it was quick to put together.

The real joy of great sour cream coffee cake is its elegant streusel swirls and crunchy streusel topping. Starting out with the sugar, we tried using solely brown sugar in the streusel, as many recipes dictate. We ended up preferring the appearance and flavor of a streusel made with a combination of granulated and dark brown sugar. What we did not like was the way this streusel melted and congealed into cement-like shards, so we took a cue from several recipes and added flour to prevent this from happening. Cinnamon, nutmeg, allspice, cloves, and even cocoa make regular appearances in

interior layers of streusel pasty and mealy, we reserved it, along with the nuts, for the topping. We also found that we preferred the texture of streusel topping made by cutting cold butter into the dry ingredients; melted butter produced unsightly knobby chunks of streusel. One benefit of this approach is that it eliminated the need to toast the nuts. The pecans in the streusel topping toasted quite nicely on their own during baking. As far as the interior streusel, we liked it to be sweeter than the topping, so we added another ¼ cup of brown sugar.

Now we had the cake, the streusel filling, and the streusel topping. All we had to do was bake the cake. Easier said than done. Time after time we ended up with cakes that seemed underdone. We tried placing the cake in a very hot 475-degree oven, then immediately lowering the temperature. Unfortunately, this blast of heat was enough to burn the sugary streusel topping. We tried adding the streusel 30 minutes into the baking time, but this meant maneuvering a hot pan out of and into the oven—not the safest approach to baking a coffee cake. Noticing that our pan was nearly full of batter, we tried cutting the amount of batter by about a fourth. When combined with baking the cake on the bottom oven rack at a steady 350 degrees for a full hour, this step produced a cake that was cooked all the way through yet was still pleasingly tall. What's more, the streusel was perfectly browned. We found it best to let the cake cool in the pan for at least 30 minutes before unmolding to keep it from cracking. Best of all, if stored well, this cake actually improves with age.

sour cream coffee cake. In the end, we found cinnamon— and a potent 2 tablespoons of it at that—was the only spice needed to lend warmth to the streusel's flavor. Pecans were favored over walnuts, although we found that almonds work equally well, and both tasted better when toasted.

Our coffee cake was now well on the road to success, but some tasters objected to the use of nuts in the streusel to be used as filling. The answer? We blended the basic streusel ingredients—flour, granulated sugar, and brown sugar—together in the food processor, then removed some of the mixture to a bowl to use as filling. Nuts went into the food processor for the topping. Because butter made the

WHAT WE LEARNED: **Use plenty of butter, eggs, and sour cream for a cake that is rich and moist and has a tight crumb. Don't bother with cake flour but do make sure to use plenty of baking powder so this heavy batter rises. Use two layers of streusel and add nuts and butter to the third layer that goes on top.**

SOUR CREAM COFFEE CAKE WITH BROWN SUGAR–PECAN STREUSEL serves 12 to 16

A 10-inch tube pan (with a 10-cup capacity) is best for this recipe (see Getting It Right at right for details).

streusel

¾	cup (3¾ ounces) unbleached all-purpose flour
¾	cup (5¼ ounces) granulated sugar
½	cup (3½ ounces) packed dark brown sugar
2	tablespoons ground cinnamon
2	tablespoons cold unsalted butter, cut into 2 pieces
1	cup pecans, chopped

cake

12	tablespoons (1½ sticks) unsalted butter, softened but still cool, cut into ½-inch cubes, plus 2 tablespoons softened butter for greasing pan
4	large eggs
1½	cups sour cream
1	tablespoon vanilla extract
2¼	cups (11½ ounces) unbleached all-purpose flour
1¼	cups (8¾ ounces) granulated sugar
1	tablespoon baking powder
¾	teaspoon baking soda
¾	teaspoon salt

1. FOR THE STREUSEL: In food processor, process flour, granulated sugar, ¼ cup dark brown sugar, and cinnamon until combined, about 15 seconds. Transfer 1¼ cups of flour/sugar mixture to small bowl; stir in remaining ¼ cup brown sugar and set aside to use for streusel filling. Add butter and pecans to flour sugar mixture in food processor; pulse until nuts and butter resemble small pebbly pieces, about ten 1-second pulses. Set aside to use as streusel topping.

2. FOR THE CAKE: Adjust oven rack to lowest position and heat oven to 350 degrees. Grease 10-inch tube pan (with 10-

cup capacity) with 2 tablespoons softened butter. Whisk eggs, 1 cup sour cream, and vanilla in medium bowl until combined.

3. Combine flour, sugar, baking powder, baking soda, and salt in bowl of standing mixer; mix on low speed for 30 seconds to blend. Add remaining butter and sour cream; mix on low speed until dry ingredients are moistened and mixture resembles wet sand, with few large butter pieces remaining, about 1½ minutes. Increase to medium speed and beat until batter comes together, about 10 seconds; scrape down sides of bowl with rubber spatula. Lower speed to medium-low and gradually add egg mixture in 3 additions, beating for 20 seconds after each addition and scraping down sides of bowl as necessary. Increase speed to medium-high and beat until batter is light and fluffy, about 1 minute.

4. Using rubber spatula, spread 2 cups batter in bottom of prepared pan, smoothing surface. Sprinkle evenly with ¾ cup streusel filling without butter or nuts. Repeat with another 2 cups batter and remaining ¾ cup streusel filling without butter or nuts. Spread remaining batter over, then sprinkle with streusel topping with butter and nuts.

TECHNIQUE: Chopping Nuts Quickly

To make fast work of chopping nuts, place the nuts on a cutting board and hold two chef's knives parallel to each other in one hand and chop. Use the other hand to guide the knives through the nuts.

---

5. Bake until cake feels firm to touch and long toothpick or skewer inserted into center comes out clean (bits of sugar from streusel may cling to tester), 50 to 60 minutes. Cool cake in pan on wire rack for 30 minutes. Invert cake onto rimmed baking sheet (cake will be streusel-side down); remove tube pan, place wire rack on top of cake, and reinvert cake streusel-side up. Cool to room temperature, about 2 hours. Cut into wedges and serve. (Cake can be wrapped in foil and stored at room temperature up to 5 days.)

VARIATIONS

LEMON-BLUEBERRY SOUR CREAM COFFEE CAKE

We prefer frozen wild blueberries for their size and flavor, but frozen cultivated blueberries will work, too.

Toss 1 cup frozen blueberries with 1 teaspoon grated lemon zest in small bowl. Follow recipe for Sour Cream Coffee Cake with Brown Sugar–Pecan Streusel, sprinkling ½ cup blueberries over bottom and middle layers of cake batter before sprinkling with streusel.

SOUR CREAM COFFEE CAKE WITH CHOCOLATE CHIPS

Follow recipe for Sour Cream Coffee Cake with Brown Sugar–Pecan Streusel, sprinkling ½ cup chocolate chips over bottom layer of cake batter and additional ½ cup chocolate chips over middle layer of cake batter before sprinkling with streusel.

APRICOT-ALMOND SOUR CREAM COFFEE CAKE

Follow recipe for Sour Cream Coffee Cake with Brown Sugar–Pecan Streusel, substituting 1 cup slivered almonds for pecans in streusel topping and ½ teaspoon almond extract for vanilla extract in cake batter. Measure ½ cup apricot jam; spoon jam in six 2-teaspoon mounds over bottom and middle layers of cake batter before sprinkling with streusel.

SCIENCE DESK:
How Does Decaffeination Work?

CAFFEINE IS ONE OF HUNDREDS OF DIFFERENT MOLECULES found in a coffee bean. Because its shape and size are different from other molecules, manufacturers can use one of several techniques to filter out the caffeine molecules. Here's how three of the most common techniques work.

One method relies on a direct chemical solvent. The beans are first soaked or steamed in water to soften them. They are then steeped in a solvent—either methylene chloride, a man-made chemical, or ethyl acetate, a naturally occurring chemical in fruit—for up to 12 hours. During this time the solvent binds with the caffeine molecules. When the solvent is removed, the caffeine goes with it. Unfortunately, some of the flavor molecules are also removed and lost in this process.

Another method relies on an indirect chemical solvent. The beans are soaked in water long enough to remove the caffeine and many flavor compounds. The caffeine-and-flavor-packed water is then drained off and solvent is added to the water. The solvent binds with the caffeine molecules, and the solvent, along with the caffeine, is removed from the water, which now contains just flavor molecules. The beans are then soaked in the caffeine-free, flavor-charged water so they will reabsorb the flavor molecules. Unfortunately, not every molecule gets reabsorbed and some flavor is lost in this process.

A third process relies on a charcoal filter to remove the caffeine molecules from the water in which the beans have been soaked. The charcoal filter traps the caffeine molecules but lets the flavor molecules pass through. The water with the flavor molecules is then poured back over the soaked beans. Unfortunately, the charcoal filters traps some flavor compounds and they are lost in the process.

The moral of the story: No matter how coffee is decaffeinated, some flavor is lost.

TASTING LAB: French Roast Coffee

WHEN YOU ORDER A LARGE COFFEE FROM YOUR LOCAL coffee bar on any particular day, you can't be sure just where the beans came from; it may be one of a dozen different countries. But one thing is likely: The beans have been dark-roasted. They may even be French roast beans. Of course, all coffee beans are roasted before being ground and brewed, but a French roast is dark—very dark—and, thanks to Starbucks and other specialty retailers, it is also very popular. It seemed to us, then, that the obvious question for the consumer was, Which brand of French roast beans is best? We tasted nine supermarket brands to find out.

In the first round of tasting Chock Full o' Nuts squeaked by Starbucks for first-place honors, indicating that price (Starbucks costs more than twice as much as Chock Full o' Nuts) is no guarantee of satisfaction. Because the ratings were so close for all brands, we repeated the tasting. The second time around the results were just as close, but the rankings were different. What this second round of tasting made clear, however, was that some tasters consistently preferred a darker roast and others a lighter roast, a key factor that contributed to the odd results. In other words, tasters were not responding to quality per se, they were simply expressing a preference as to what degree the beans were roasted. Is it possible, then, that all French roasts—no matter the type of bean—are not created equal? To try to settle the matter, we decided to turn to some experts and set out for the Excellent Coffee Company, a coffee roaster in Pawtucket, R.I.

We took our nine brands on the road and this time subjected them to an Agtron reading, which measures the amount of light reflected from particles of ground coffee. The darkest roast measured on the scale an Agtron reading of 15, the lightest a reading of 80. According to common industry standards, a French roast usually falls in the range of 20 to 30. Based on their Agtron readings, only four of the nine coffees we tested were true French roasts. Two qualified as Italian roasts, with readings under 20, and three qualified as Viennese roasts, with readings over 30. So brand does make a difference. The beans in brands advertised as French roast are in fact roasted to very different degrees. Coffee drinkers who favor that charred, heavily roasted flavor should go for Starbucks, which has an Agtron reading of 16.9, but if you like a lighter, more subtle cup of coffee, you might choose Chock Full o' Nuts, which has a reading of 31, or Eight O'Clock, with a reading of 38.1.

But what about French roast itself? Despite its popularity, the confusing taste test results made us wonder if the roasting process somehow camouflaged the quality of the beans, thus making brand recognition difficult. We turned to Kevin Knox of Allegro coffee, one-time Starbucks quality-control man and co-author with Julie Sheldon Huffaker of *Coffee Basics* (John Wiley & Sons, 1996). He summed up

French roast by saying, "It's just burnt coffee."

To understand just what Knox means, it's necessary to know a bit about the coffee-roasting process. Beans can be roasted from light (American) to medium (Full City) to dark (Viennese, French, and Italian, the darkest roast). Although these are imprecise terms, the method is simple enough. Beans are roasted by hot air and then cooled. They can be roasted slowly or quickly, and the cooling method can vary as well, and variations in both factors affect flavor. The reason French roast beans are often considered burnt is that they are roasted until many of their carbohydrates (sugar and cellulose) are converted to carbon (that is, incinerated), causing the beans to lose up to 20 percent of their weight in the process. Thus many experts believe French roasting destroys flavors, rendering the differences between high- and low-quality beans meaningless. Forget about the subtle flavor of honeysuckle in Kenyan beans or the bittersweet chocolate taste of Guatemalan Antigua.

To test this theory, we did a tasting at Excellent Coffee of both high-quality and mediocre beans roasted to both light and dark stages. While expert and staff tasters could tell which bean was which when the beans were lightly roasted, the differences between the high-quality and low-quality beans were harder to detect when the beans were darkly roasted; in fact, some tasters preferred the lower-quality dark roast beans to the higher-quality dark roast beans. Knowing that character flaws and nuances in flavor can be masked by dark roasting, professionals "cup," or taste, coffee brewed from very lightly roasted beans.

We also asked the Excellent Coffee experts to blind-taste French roast Starbucks and Chock Full o' Nuts. The result? They preferred the cheaper Chock Full o' Nuts, a lighter roast that they found "mild and sweet," opposed to the dark roast Starbucks, which they found "smoky and sharply acidic." (The tasters did comment, however, that they could discern a higher-quality bean in the Starbucks coffee than in the Chock Full o' Nuts, although they didn't care for the burnt taste of the roasting.)

So the best question to ask when it comes to super-

TECHNIQUE:
Keeping the Remote Control Clean

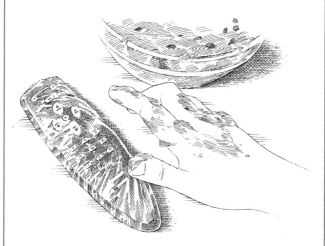

Many cooks enjoy listening to music or watching TV as they cook. Before cooking, wrap the remote control unit in a layer of clear plastic wrap. The buttons remain visible and operable but don't get smeared by sticky hands.

market French roast coffees isn't "Which brand is best?" Even though Starbucks uses high-quality beans, its coffee doesn't have much on Folgers or Eight O'Clock when the beans are French roasted. George Howell, founder of the Coffee Connection, goes so far as to say that "taste can wind up having little to do with quality." What is certain is that for dark roast coffees, the roasting process has a bigger impact on flavor than bean quality.

What is the best question to ask when selecting a French roast coffee? Probably, "How do you like your coffee?" As Howell points out, if given French roast, the person who prefers light roast "will feel like he is walking into a dark room. It's all thickness and no clarity." Meanwhile, someone who favors dark roast but is given light roast "feels like he is being attacked by the corrosive rays of the sun." So forget about beans, price, and country of origin and simply choose the brand of French roast best suited to your palate. If you like a really dark roast, go for something like Starbucks (the beans will be almost black in color). If you like a lighter roast, try Chock Full o' Nuts or Eight O'Clock (the beans will be medium brown). Keep in mind that how you drink your coffee may also influence your choice. Black coffee drinkers may prefer a lighter roast, whereas those who add milk and sugar might find the darker roasts more appealing.

EQUIPMENT CORNER: Coffee Grinders

JUST AS CORN ON THE COB TASTES BEST IF IT'S BOILED within minutes of being picked, coffee tastes best if the beans are ground fresh before they are brewed. With a wide variety of countertop coffee grinders on the market, it is no problem for home cooks to grind beans on demand. The greater challenge is deciding which grinder to buy. Most of the reasonably priced grinders, which generally cost around $20, employ propeller-type blades that work like a blender, literally chopping the beans as they spin. But any coffee enthusiast will quickly allege that blade grinders are rife with problems—namely, that they grind unevenly, they

produce too much superfine coffee dust, and the friction from the spinning blades overheats the coffee grounds. We wondered if any of this would really affect the flavor and body of the brewed coffee or if these allegations barely amounted to a hill of beans.

With a self-imposed price cap of $50, a limit that allowed us to include several low-end burr grinders (a fancier type of machine that works like a motorized pepper mill), we bought 10 popular models from seven manufacturers and 30 pounds of coffee beans. Then we let the grounds fly to determine just how good a grinder $50 (or less, in many cases) would buy.

The first issue we addressed was the evenness of the grind. Michael Kramm, president of Capresso, maker of the Capresso Cool Grind included in our tests, explained that blade grinders actually chop the beans with their furiously spinning blades. In a burr grinder, on the other hand, beans are truly ground a few at a time between two grooved disks, one stationary and the other rotating just above it. The grounds are fed out through a chute into a sealed container. According to Kramm, the disks operate at roughly 7,000 to 9,000 revolutions per minute (RPM), while the motors in most blade grinders spin at 14,000 to 20,000 RPM.

Kramm agreed with other coffee authorities that the blade grinders' rough treatment of the beans often results in unevenly ground coffee, with particles ranging from dust to large chunks in the same batch. Our observations corroborated this, although we found we could improve the evenness of the blade grind either by grinding in short, quick bursts, with stops in between to shake the grinder to redistribute the grounds, or by shaking the grinder as it ground, much as you would a martini in a cocktail shaker (see the illustration on page 240).

The burr grinders produced a more even grind, but tasters did not find that more evenly ground coffee translated into improved flavor. Tasters did prefer the rich body of burr-ground coffee, but they also noticed the tendency of this coffee to taste slightly bitter, owing in part, no doubt, to the more fine and even grind, which made for the coffee's

Rating Coffee Grinders

WE RATED 10 COFFEE GRINDERS, NONE PRICED HIGHER THAN $50, AND EVALUATED THEM ACCORDING TO CAPACITY (more was judged to be better), design, ease of cleaning, and the temperature increase of the coffee (heat can destroy flavor, so the lower the increase during grinding, the better). We tested each unit by grinding 2 ounces of coffee beans (about 8 tablespoons) and using those grounds to brew full, 40-ounce pots of coffee in a new automatic drip coffee maker. The grinders are listed in order of preference. See www.cooksillustrated.com for up-to-date prices and mail-order sources for top-rated products.

RECOMMENDED

1. Capresso Cool Grind, Model 501

$19.95

Has a large capacity and a deep cup, the features we value most in a blade grinder. Some large pieces of bean were left after grinding, however.

RECOMMENDED

2. Krups Fast-Touch Coffee Mill, Model 203

$19.99

No cord wrap, but excellent fit between lid and base. Grinds fine, yet does not create an excessive amount of coffee dust.

RECOMMENDED

3. Mr. Coffee Coffee Grinder, Model IDS55

$14.99

Nice deep lid prevents the (unevenly) ground coffee from spilling. No cord wrap.

RECOMMENDED

4. Braun Aromatic Coffee Grinder, Model KSM 2B

$19.99

Tended to grind on the fine side, rarely leaving large chunks of bean. Did create a noticeable quantity of coffee dust, though.

RECOMMENDED

5. Mr. Coffee Burr Mill, Model BM3

$29.99

Grinds thoroughly and pretty evenly, but not completely without dust. No automatic timer, which is fine. We liked the control offered by a simple on/off toggle.

NOT RECOMMENDED

6. Proctor-Silex Fresh Grind Coffee Grinder, Model E160B

$12.99

So small that you have to grind twice to get enough coffee for one 8-cup pot.

NOT RECOMMENDED

7. Cuisinart Coffee Bar Coffee Grinder, Model DCG-20BK

$19.95

Cord stores in an internal chamber, which makes it difficult to use. Shallow lid spills ground coffee, and there was a loose fit between lid and base.

NOT RECOMMENDED

8. Starbucks Barista Blade Grinder

$19.95

Attractive design, but the lid is so small that coffee spills easily. The coffee is ground evenly, except for the few whole beans usually left behind.

NOT RECOMMENDED

9. Braun Coffee Mill, Model KMM 30

$49.99

We didn't care for the automatic timer because the machine's notion of the proper grind time often did not jibe with our own. Does grind evenly.

NOT RECOMMENDED

10. Capresso Burr Grinder, Model 551

$49.99

Creates more coffee dust than we expected. Also, the power switch is too easy to hit by mistake, an error that sends coffee grounds flying.

greater exposure to and prolonged contact with the water in the coffee maker. These combined forces caused what coffee experts call overextraction, which occurs when too much flavor is extracted from the beans. In our tests, we were less likely to encounter this problem if the coffee was ground coarse, more so than even the coarsest setting on the burr grinders could accomplish.

We were surprised to discover that the coffee brewed with blade-ground beans was less likely to turn out bitter. The tasters did note that coffee from blade-ground beans had less body than coffee from burr-ground beans, but we were happy to sacrifice a little body for the reduced risk of brewing bitter coffee. We also learned that we could improve the body of the coffee somewhat by defying the blade grinders' instructions and grinding the beans a little longer, 20 to 25 seconds, rather than the recommended 10 to 15, without overheating the beans or jeopardizing smooth flavor in the coffee.

Overprocessing the beans into superfine coffee dust was another concern. Experts agree that the best grinders produce minimal dust, which can block waterflow through the filter in many coffee makers. None of the grinders we tested, however, produced enough dust to clog the filter.

The temperature of the coffee grounds was another factor we considered. Ideally, the beans should not heat up too much as they are ground because heat causes the flavorful oils to evaporate, resulting in a loss of flavor. Most experts claim that cheap blade grinders overheat the coffee beans. According to the infrared thermometer we used to measure the temperature of the grounds, this isn't true. The burr grinders actually caused a greater increase in temperature, albeit a slight one. Our tasters, however, were not able to correlate a greater increase in temperature with poorer coffee flavor. The temperature increases we measured seemed to make very little difference.

Any appliance that you use first thing in the morning, while you are half-asleep, had better be well designed and user-friendly. The two design factors that came to matter to us most were capacity and, on blade grinders, depth of the cup. Any grinder should have a capacity large enough to grind in a single batch the beans necessary for a full pot of coffee. Likewise, the cup should be deep enough to contain the grounds without spilling as you remove them from the grinder. All of the burr grinders and the Capresso Cool Grind, Krups Fast Touch, Mr. Coffee Coffee Grinder, and Braun Aromatic blade grinders made the cut here. But the blade grinders offered additional advantages. They were easy to clean, often requiring just a careful wipe of the hopper with a damp paper towel to remove coffee dust, and they were inexpensive, hovering around the $15 to $20 mark. Truth be told, we recommend all of the four blade grinders mentioned above.

That said, we do have one caveat for espresso drinkers. Most manufacturers advise against using a blade grinder—any blade grinder—to grind coffee for use in a pump-driven espresso machine. These grinders simply cannot grind the coffee fine enough. We concur. If this limits your choice to a burr grinder, then we'd go for the Mr. Coffee model because it has a simple on/off switch, which we felt worked better than the timers found on the other two burr models.

TECHNIQUE:
Efficient Coffee Grinding

Many inexpensive blade-type grinders grind coffee beans unevenly, producing some powder as well as some larger pieces of bean. Here's how to even out the grind. With your hand over the hopper, lift the whole unit off the counter and shake it gently as it grinds. (The motion is akin to blending a martini in a cocktail shaker.) By moving the beans around, you help the machine grind more evenly.

FRUIT SALAD

WHAT WE WANTED: Good fruit salads shouldn't taste like sugary desserts. We wanted something both light and flavorful, with a clear emphasis on the fruit.

Making a good, fresh fruit salad is not that hard when good fruit is available. Nor is it very hard, we found, to make a truly great fruit salad, complemented by a simple, sweet-tart dressing that enhances the fruit and adds layers of interest and flavor.

That said, most of the recipes we tested failed to deliver on this promise. Fruit salads are traditionally dressed with yogurt or sugar syrup or simply served plain. We felt that yogurt dressings fell short because they mask the colors, shapes, and jewel-like beauty of cut fruit. And the inescapable truth is that no matter what sort of flavoring you add, yogurt dressing always tastes like, well, yogurt. The fruit almost falls by the wayside. Sugar syrup can be insipidly sweet, and plain cut-up fruit can be boring.

So we chose another route, adapting a classic French dressing called *gastrique*. The definition of gastrique varies from cookbook to cookbook, but we agree with the renowned culinary encyclopedia *Larousse Gastronomique*, which says that a gastrique is a reduction of an acidic liquid, usually vinegar, and sugar; it typically accompanies savory dishes made with fruit, such as duck à l'orange. The process of reducing the liquid over high heat couldn't be simpler, and, after some experimentation, we found that 1 cup of acidic liquid reduced with ¼ cup of sugar produced just the right balance of tart and sweet. The mixture complemented all the fresh fruits we wanted to use.

This technique worked beautifully with citrus, wine, and spirits, allowing us to introduce complex flavors beyond the traditional vinegar. We also got great results from infusing the gastriques with additional flavors, such as cinnamon in the brandy mixture for plums and figs or lemon zest and cardamom in the champagne mixture for

nectarines and berries. Our last step was to add some high, bright flavor notes with both lemon juice and zest. With that, we achieved a complex layering of flavors in 16 minutes flat.

WHAT WE LEARNED: A reduction of something acidic (like wine, citrus juice, or vinegar) and sugar is the perfect "sauce" for fruit salad. This reduction complements the fruit and can be flavored with spices, extracts, or citrus zests.

STRAWBERRIES AND GRAPES WITH BALSAMIC AND RED WINE REDUCTION

makes about 6 cups

An inexpensive balsamic vinegar is fine for use in this recipe. Save high-quality vinegar for other preparations in which the vinegar is not cooked.

- ¾ cup balsamic vinegar
- ¼ cup dry red wine
- ¼ cup sugar
  Pinch salt
- 3 whole cloves
- 1 tablespoon grated zest plus 1 tablespoon juice from 1 lemon
- ¼ teaspoon vanilla extract
- 1 quart strawberries, hulled and halved lengthwise (about 4 cups)
- 9 ounces large seedless red or black grapes, each grape halved pole to pole (about 2 cups)

1. Simmer vinegar, wine, sugar, and salt in small, heavy-bottomed nonreactive saucepan over high heat until syrupy and reduced to ¼ cup, about 15 minutes. Off heat, stir in cloves, lemon zest and juice, and vanilla; steep 1 minute to blend flavors, and strain.

2. Combine strawberries and grapes in medium bowl; pour warm dressing over fruit and toss to coat. Serve immediately at room temperature or cover with plastic wrap, refrigerate up to 4 hours, and serve chilled.

NECTARINES, BLUEBERRIES, AND RASPBERRIES WITH CHAMPAGNE-CARDAMOM REDUCTION makes about 6 cups

Dry white wine can be substituted for the champagne.

- 1 cup champagne
- ¼ cup sugar
  Pinch salt

TECHNIQUE: Handling a Mango

Mangoes are notoriously hard to peel, owing to their shape and slippery texture. Here's how we handle this tough kitchen task.

1. Start by removing a thin slice from one end of the mango so that it sits flat on a work surface.

2. Hold the mango cut-side down and remove the skin with a sharp paring knife in thin strips, working from top to bottom.

3. Once the peel has been removed, cut down along the side of the flat pit to remove the flesh from one side of the mango. Do the same thing on the other side of pit.

4. Trim around the pit to remove any remaining flesh. The flesh can now be chopped or sliced as desired.

---

1 tablespoon grated zest plus 1 tablespoon juice from 1 lemon
5 cardamom pods, crushed
3 medium nectarines (about 18 ounces), cut into ½-inch wedges (about 3 cups)
1 pint blueberries
½ pint raspberries

1. Simmer champagne, sugar, and salt in small, heavy-bottomed nonreactive saucepan over high heat until syrupy, honey-colored, and reduced to ¼ cup, about 15 minutes. Off heat, stir in lemon zest and juice and cardamom; steep 1 minute to blend flavors, and strain.

2. Combine nectarines, blueberries, and raspberries in medium bowl; pour warm dressing over fruit and toss to coat. Serve immediately at room temperature or cover with plastic wrap, refrigerate up to 4 hours, and serve chilled.

HONEYDEW, MANGO, AND BLUEBERRIES WITH LIME-GINGER REDUCTION

makes about 6 cups

Cantaloupe can be used in place of honeydew although the color contrast with the mango won't be as vivid.

1 cup juice plus 1 tablespoon grated zest from 4 limes (zest limes before juicing)
¼ cup sugar
Pinch salt
1 (1-inch) piece fresh ginger, peeled and minced (about 1 tablespoon)
1 tablespoon juice from 1 lemon
½ small honeydew melon, seeds and rind removed, cut into 1-inch pieces (about 2 cups)
1 mango (about 10 ounces), peeled and cut into ½-inch pieces (about 1½ cups)
1 pint blueberries

1. Simmer lime juice, sugar, and salt in small, heavy-bottomed nonreactive saucepan over high heat until syrupy, honey-colored, and reduced to ¼ cup, about 15 minutes. Off heat, stir in lime zest, ginger, and lemon juice; steep 1 minute to blend flavors, and strain.

2. Combine melon, mango, and blueberries in medium bowl; pour warm dressing over fruit and toss to coat. Serve immediately at room temperature or cover with plastic wrap, refrigerate up to 4 hours, and serve chilled.

RED PLUMS AND FIGS WITH BRANDY-CINNAMON REDUCTION makes about 6 cups

Red plums make the best visual contrast with the dark-colored figs.

1 cup brandy
¼ cup sugar
Pinch salt
1 (3-inch) stick cinnamon
1 tablespoon grated zest plus 1 tablespoon juice from 1 lemon
4 red plums (about 1¼ pounds), pitted and cut into ½-inch-thick wedges (about 4 cups)
12 fresh black mission figs (about 12 ounces), quartered lengthwise (about 2 cups)

1. Simmer brandy, sugar, and salt in small, heavy-bottomed nonreactive saucepan over high heat until syrupy, honey-colored, and reduced to ¼ cup, about 15 minutes. Off heat, stir in cinnamon and lemon zest and juice; steep 1 minute to blend flavors, and strain.

2. Combine plums and figs in medium bowl; pour warm dressing over fruit and toss to coat. Serve immediately at room temperature or cover with plastic wrap, refrigerate up to 4 hours, and serve chilled.

QUICK breads

Quick breads are leavened chemically with baking powder and/or baking soda rather than yeast. Most quick breads are easy to prepare and ready to bake in a matter of minutes. The appeal of quick breads, such as cinnamon buns and banana bread, is clear. They are quick, sweet, and . . . did we say, quick? Of course, just because something is quick doesn't mean you want to eat it.

Supermarket cinnamon buns (the kind that come in a tube) are quick, but in a kitchen tasting we found that they all have an odd, artificial flavor and sponge-like texture that no one liked. Real cinnamon buns are a day-long affair that require a yeasted dough. We figured there had to a better way—a fast recipe that relied on baking powder but still delivered the tender, light crumb of the real thing.

Banana bread sounds so thrifty. Unfortunately, many banana breads are dry on the inside and sticky on the outside. Just because this recipe starts with over-the-hill bananas doesn't mean it should taste like leftovers. We knew there had to be a way to make a tender, moist loaf with real banana flavor without becoming spendthrifts.

We prefer metal measuring cups over plastic ones. The metal cups are sturdy enough to withstand constant use in the test kitchen.

CINNAMON BUNS

WHAT WE WANTED: Yeasted cinnamon buns take hours to make, and store-bought buns are dreadful. Could we transform a recipe for baking-powder biscuits into quick, high-rise cinnamon buns?

Cinnamon buns are quick to please: You bite into one, and you're happy. The bun is tender and fluffy, the filling is sweet and spicy, and the glaze is sinful, encouraging even the well-bred to lick the gooey remnants from their fingers. It's a shame, then, that making cinnamon buns at home can try the patience of the most devoted cooks. Most recipes call for yeast, which means they also call for a lot of time and skill as well as a standing mixer (or powerful biceps). The alternative is to make cinnamon buns from a tube or a box, options that produce inferior buns whose flavor lies somewhere between chemicals and cardboard. Our aim was to put cinnamon buns back in the home kitchen in good time, sacrificing neither flavor nor fluffiness for speed. In short, we wanted great buns without the hassle.

We started with a tasting of our favorite yeasted cinnamon buns. With a soft and resilient texture and a bready, open crumb, the texture of these buns was top-notch, and the combination of cinnamon and yeast produced a grown-up flavor. Unfortunately, the start-to-finish time was nearly five hours. Now we knew what texture and flavor we wanted from cinnamon buns. We just wanted it quicker and easier.

Toward this end, the first decision we made was to work from recipes leavened with baking powder rather than yeast. The next step was to determine the best method for incorporating the fat into the other ingredients. First we tried the classic mixing method of cutting cold butter into dry ingredients, as is done for pie dough. This method turned out cinnamon buns that were dense, flaky, and craggy rather than tender, light, and fluffy.

The next mixing method we tried called for combining melted butter with the liquid ingredients in a food processor, then adding the dry ingredients. While we hoped that the food processor would make the mixing process easier, these baked-off buns weren't worth the effort. The dough was very sticky, making it difficult to work with.

The last method we tried was a quick cream biscuit method, in which heavy cream is added to flour, sugar, baking powder, and salt. What makes this dough unique is its complete lack of butter. The dough relies entirely on the heavy cream for tenderness and flavor. Still better, the dough can be mixed in a minute using just one bowl. This process was by far the fastest and easiest, and we wanted to go with it, but a few refinements would be required before it produced really good cinnamon buns.

To make the dough more tender, our first thought was to replace the all-purpose flour with more delicate, lower-protein cake flour. But low-protein cake flour turned the dough into a sticky mess that was hard to roll out.

Our next inclination was to test whole or skim milk in place of heavy cream, but whole milk made the buns too heavy, and skim milk made them tough and bland. We increased the amount of baking powder to achieve lightness but ended up with metallic-tasting buns. We then tested buttermilk, a common ingredient in biscuit doughs, and had some success. (We also added ½ teaspoon of baking soda to balance the acidity of the buttermilk. Baking soda reacts with the acid in buttermilk to produce carbon dioxide gas, which causes lift.) The acid in the buttermilk gave the buns a more complex flavor and tenderized the gluten in the dough, making the interior airy and light.

But now the dough was too lean for our taste (owing to the buttermilk, most of which is made by adding acidic cultures to skim or partially skimmed milk—see the Science Desk on page 249). We arrived at the solution when we added 2 tablespoons of melted butter to the buttermilk. Just as we had hoped, the dough was tender, complex, and rich.

Whereas most recipes instruct bakers to roll out the dough, we found it easier to pat the dough into a rough-shaped rectangle, thus making the recipe even simpler. For the cinnamon-sugar filling we decided on a union of brown sugar, white sugar, cinnamon, cloves, and salt. Before sprinkling the filling on the dough, we brushed it with 2 tablespoons of melted butter to help the filling cling to the dough. Because the cinnamon mixture was loose and dry, however, it was still apt to fall away from the dough when the buns were cut and transferred to the baking pan. The easy solution was to add 1 tablespoon of melted butter to the dry ingredients, which made the mixture the consistency of wet sand, allowing us to press it into the dough easily. This time the filling stayed put.

Next we tackled the rolls' appearance. Instead of rising to the occasion in the oven, they were slouching in their seats. We reviewed the quick cream biscuit recipe to see if we might find the source of the problem there. Sure enough, the recipe stated that if the dough wasn't kneaded before being shaped, it didn't rise nicely in the oven. We made two batches of dough, kneading one and not the other, and were surprised to find that just a quick 30-second

knead solved the problem. Contrary to what one might think, the short knead didn't toughen the buns; it just provided the dough with enough strength to take in a big breath and hold it.

To finish the buns, we tried a host of different glazes, all based on a quick confectioners' sugar and water glaze, which is inherently pasty and grainy. After a few trials, we found a way to sufficiently mask the graininess and pasty flavor by combining buttermilk and cream cheese, then sifting the confectioners' sugar over the paste (if the sugar is not sifted, the glaze will be lumpy). This glaze was smooth, thick, and pleasantly tangy, although it does add one more ingredient to the shopping list for the buns: cream cheese.

As for what to bake the buns in, we tried muffin tins, pie plates, cookie sheets, springform pans, glass baking dishes, and cake pans. With its straight sides, round shape, and perfect size, we chose a 9-inch nonstick cake pan. We started baking at 425 degrees and got lucky the first time out. The buns baked in 25 minutes, rose and browned nicely, and were cooked all the way through.

Now the moment of truth had come. It was time for a blind tasting of our quick cinnamon buns head-to-head with our yeasted cinnamon buns. The quick buns got a quick nod of approval, with many tasters even preferring them to the more sophisticated and elegantly flavored yeasted buns. Best of all, these shortcut cinnamon buns can be on the table in an hour—a fact you may very well choose to keep to yourself.

WHAT WE LEARNED : **Whisk buttermilk and melted butter into the dry ingredients to create a light, tender dough with plenty of flavor. Don't bother rolling out the dough— just pat it into a rectangle, cover with the spiced brown sugar filling, roll it up into a log, and cut into individual buns. Cream cheese masks the chalkiness in a quick buttermilk and powdered sugar glaze.**

QUICK CINNAMON BUNS WITH BUTTERMILK ICING makes 8 buns

Melted butter is used in both the filling and the dough and to grease the pan; melt the total amount (8 tablespoons) at once and measure it out as you need it. The buns are best eaten warm, but they hold up reasonably well for up to 2 hours.

1 tablespoon unsalted butter, melted, for pan

cinnamon-sugar filling

¾ cup (5¼ ounces) packed dark brown sugar
¼ cup (1¾ ounces) granulated sugar
2 teaspoons ground cinnamon
⅛ teaspoon ground cloves
⅛ teaspoon salt
1 tablespoon unsalted butter, melted

biscuit dough

2½ cups (12½ ounces) unbleached all-purpose flour, plus additional flour for work surface
2 tablespoons granulated sugar
1¼ teaspoons baking powder
½ teaspoon baking soda
½ teaspoon salt
1¼ cups buttermilk
6 tablespoons unsalted butter, melted

icing

2 tablespoons cream cheese, softened
2 tablespoons buttermilk
1 cup (4 ounces) confectioners' sugar

1. Adjust oven rack to upper-middle position and heat oven to 425 degrees. Pour 1 tablespoon melted butter into 9-inch nonstick cake pan; brush to coat pan. Spray wire cooling rack with nonstick cooking spray; set aside.

2. TO MAKE CINNAMON-SUGAR FILLING: Combine sugars, spices, and salt in small bowl. Add 1 tablespoon melted butter and stir with fork or fingers until mixture resembles wet sand; set filling mixture aside.

3. TO MAKE BISCUIT DOUGH: Whisk flour, sugar, baking powder, baking soda, and salt in large bowl. Whisk buttermilk and 2 tablespoons melted butter in measuring cup or small bowl. Add liquid to dry ingredients and stir with wooden spoon until liquid is absorbed (dough will look very shaggy), about 30 seconds. Transfer dough to lightly floured work surface and knead until just smooth and no longer shaggy.

4. Pat dough with hands into 12 by 9-inch rectangle. Brush dough with 2 tablespoons melted butter. Sprinkle evenly with filling, leaving ½-inch border of plain dough around edges. Press filling firmly into dough. Using bench scraper or metal spatula, loosen dough from work surface. Starting at long side, roll dough, pressing lightly, to form tight log. Pinch seam to seal. Roll log seam-side down and cut evenly into eight pieces. With hand, slightly flatten each piece of dough to seal open edges and keep filling in place. Place one roll in center of prepared nonstick pan, then place remaining seven rolls around perimeter of pan. Brush with 2 tablespoons remaining melted butter.

5. Bake until edges are golden brown, 23 to 25 minutes. Use offset metal spatula to loosen buns from pan. Wearing oven mitt, place large plate over pan and invert buns onto plate. Place greased cooling rack over plate and invert buns onto rack. Cool about 5 minutes before icing.

6. TO MAKE ICING AND FINISH BUNS: While buns are cooling, line rimmed baking sheet with parchment paper (for easy cleanup); set rack with buns over baking sheet. Whisk cream cheese and buttermilk in large nonreactive bowl until thick and smooth (mixture will look like cottage cheese at first). Sift confectioners' sugar over; whisk until smooth glaze forms, about 30 seconds. Spoon glaze evenly over buns; serve immediately.

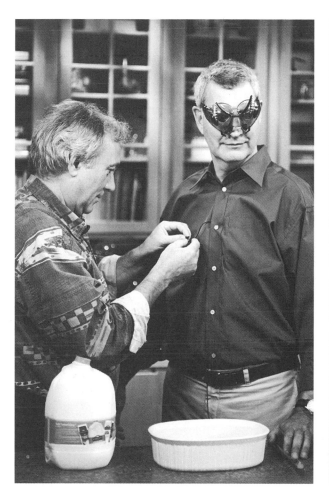

SCIENCE DESK:
The Magic of Buttermilk

BUTTERMILK IS THE SECRET INGREDIENT IN OUR CINNAMON bun recipe. What gives this dairy product its magical powers? Originally, buttermilk was the liquid left after churning milk to make butter. All the fat went into the butter and the liquid that was leftover—a thin, watery, somewhat sour liquid with occasional little dots of yellow butter floating in it—was called buttermilk because of the little pieces of butter.

This is how buttermilk was made on the farm. Today, buttermilk is something quite different. In fact, modern buttermilk should really be called butterless milk. It is a fermented dairy product, like yogurt or sour cream. Fermentation creates deep, complex flavors in foods. Think of beer, cheese, coffee, and chocolate—all of which are products of fermentation. In the fermentation of skim milk to make buttermilk, citric acid and a buttery tasting compound called diacetyl are produced. Together, the citric acid and diacetyl create a tangy, slightly sour milk with a bit of butter flavor. That's why quick breads made with buttermilk are so tasty.

BANANA BREAD

WHAT WE WANTED: A soft, moist, and tender bread for snacking or toasting, with real banana flavor.

Overripe bananas on the kitchen counter are an excellent excuse to make banana bread. However, many banana breads are flat, gritty, or heavy. Worse, some loaves taste only remotely of bananas. Good banana bread is soft and tender, with plenty of banana flavor and crunchy toasted walnuts. It should be moist and light, something so delicious that you look forward to the bananas on the counter turning soft and mushy.

In our testing, we found it very important to pay close attention to the condition of the bananas. Sweet, older, darkly speckled bananas infused the bread with both moisture and flavor, which meant that the bread, whether still warm or day-old, succeeded with less butter (just 6 tablespoons) than the amount used in most recipes (8 tablespoons).

We also experimented with the way we prepared the bananas for the batter: slightly mashed, mashed well, and pureed. Loaves with slightly mashed bananas left chunks of fruit. We preferred a smoother texture, but pureeing the bananas turned out to be a bad idea, because the batter did not rise as well. Leavener probably escaped before the thin batter developed enough structure to trap gases. Bananas that we mashed well by hand kept the batter thick but lump-free.

We still wanted more moisture in the bread, so we tried mixing in milk, buttermilk, sour cream, and plain yogurt. Sour cream added richness, but it also made for a heavy texture and an unattractive, pebbly crust. Milk added little flavor and created a slick crust. Buttermilk added a delightful tang, but yogurt let the banana flavor stand out. And because yogurt has more solids than buttermilk, it made for a more solid loaf, which we preferred.

While the yogurt softened the bread's crumb, we still sought a more delicate, open grain. So we decided to experiment with various mixing methods to see how they affected the final texture. We considered the quick bread method (dry ingredients mixed in one bowl, liquids in another, with the two then gently stirred together) and the creaming method (butter and sugar creamed together, dry and wet ingredients then alternately mixed in).

The creaming method created a soft texture (reminiscent of butter cake) and good volume from the whipped sugar and butter. However, its lighter color looked less appetizing next to the golden-brown loaf achieved with the quick bread method. The quick bread method produced a delicate texture, too, and the less consistent crumb looked hearty and delicious. It also rose more than the creamed loaf. All in all, it was a better choice.

Take caution when mixing, though. When we stirred the wet and the dry ingredients into a smooth batter, the loaves turned out small and tough. Flour contains protein, and when protein mixes with water, gluten develops. The more you stir with a spoon, the more the gluten proteins arrange into long, orderly bundles. These bundles create an elastic batter that resists changing shape and cannot rise as well. To minimize gluten development, fold together the wet and dry ingredients gently, just until the dry ingredients are moistened. The batter should still be thick and chunky, but without any streaks of unincorporated flour.

Although we liked the simple flavors of bananas and toasted walnuts for the master recipe, we also found that banana bread works well with more adventurous flavors, including chocolate, macadamia nuts, orange zest, cinnamon, and nutmeg.

WHAT WE LEARNED: Ripe bananas are the key to proper texture and flavor in this bread. Yogurt adds a nice tang to the loaf and keeps the bread moist. Don't bother with creaming the butter and sugar—just melt the butter and fold all of the wet ingredients into the dry ingredients for a delicate but sturdy crumb.

BANANA BREAD makes one 9-inch loaf

For this recipe, use a loaf pan that measures 9 inches long, 5 inches across, and 3 inches deep. See the Equipment Corner on page 252 for more information about buying loaf pans. To toast walnuts, place them in a dry skillet over medium heat and toast, shaking pan occasionally, until they are fragrant.

2	cups (10 ounces) unbleached all-purpose flour
¾	cup (5¼ ounces) sugar
¾	teaspoon baking soda
½	teaspoon salt
3	very ripe, soft, darkly speckled large bananas, mashed well (about 1½ cups)
¼	cup plain yogurt
2	large eggs, beaten lightly
6	tablespoons butter, melted and cooled
1	teaspoon vanilla extract
1¼	cups walnuts, toasted and chopped coarse

1. Adjust oven rack to lower-middle position and heat oven to 350 degrees. Grease and flour 9 by 5-inch loaf pan; set aside.

2. Whisk flour, sugar, baking soda, and salt together in large bowl; set aside.

3. Mix mashed bananas, yogurt, eggs, butter, and vanilla with wooden spoon in medium bowl. Lightly fold banana mixture into dry ingredients with rubber spatula until just combined and batter looks thick and chunky. Fold in walnuts. Scrape batter into prepared loaf pan and smooth surface with rubber spatula.

4. Bake until loaf is golden brown and toothpick inserted in center comes out clean, about 55 minutes. Cool in pan for 5 minutes, then transfer to wire rack. Serve warm or at room temperature.

VARIATIONS

BANANA-CHOCOLATE BREAD

Follow recipe for Banana Bread, reducing sugar to 10 tablespoons and mixing 2½ ounces grated bittersweet chocolate (heaping ½ cup) into dry ingredients.

BANANA-COCONUT BREAD WITH MACADAMIA NUTS

Adjust oven rack to middle position and heat oven to 350 degrees. Toast ½ cup flaked, sweetened coconut and 1 cup chopped macadamia nuts on small baking sheet, stirring every 2 minutes, until golden brown, about 6 minutes. Follow recipe for Banana Bread, substituting toasted macadamias and coconut for walnuts.

ORANGE-SPICE BANANA BREAD

Follow recipe for Banana Bread, adding 1 teaspoon ground cinnamon, ¼ teaspoon grated nutmeg, and 2 tablespoons grated orange zest to dry ingredients.

TECHNIQUE: Freezing Bananas

Rather than throwing away one or two overripe bananas, they can be saved until you have enough to make banana bread. Place the overripe bananas in a zipper-lock plastic bag and freeze. As needed, add more bananas to the bag. When you are ready to make bread, thaw the bananas on the counter until softened.

BANANA BREADS
FOR UNMOLDING
+ EATING
(SCENE 3)

EQUIPMENT CORNER: Loaf Pans

A GOOD LOAF PAN WILL EVENLY BROWN BANANA BREAD and other quick breads (as well as yeast breads, such as sandwich bread). In addition, the pan should release loaves cleanly and it should be easy to get the pan in and out of the oven, with little chance of sticking an oven mitt into the batter or baked bread.

We tested 10 loaf pans made from a variety of materials, including metal, glass, and stoneware. Some of the pans were nonstick-coated and others were not. Several pans were "professional grade" and quite heavy, others were light. Prices ranged from $3 to $16. We baked two quick breads and one yeasted white bread in each pan and focused on browning, release of the loaf, and ease of handling the pan.

We found that dark-colored metal loaf pans browned breads more evenly than light-colored metal pans. Most of the dark metal pans were lined with a nonstick coating that also made the release of baked breads especially easy. We found that sweet breads, such as banana bread, were especially prone to burning in glass loaf pans. Sticking was also a problem in these pans. Stoneware loaf pans did a decent job of browning, but we had trouble removing loaves from these pans. Pans with handles at either end were easier to work with because they kept us from sticking an oven mitt into the edge of a baked loaf.

In the end, we recommend that you buy a metal loaf pan with a nonstick coating. Although there's no harm in spending more money on heavier pans, one of the cheapest, lightest pans in our testing (Ekco Baker's Secret, $3.99) was the favorite. One final piece of advice: Even with the nonstick coating, we recommend greasing and flouring your loaf pan to ensure easy release.

Rating Loaf Pans

WE TESTED 10 STANDARD-SIZE LOAF PANS BY BAKING AT LEAST THREE LOAVES, ONE EACH OF WHITE SANDWICH BREAD, cornbread, and lemon loaf cake, all baked to the same internal temperature. Pans were greased with nonstick cooking spray. Depth and evenness of browning, loaf release, and design factors such as the presence of handles and the width of the pan (as it affected the loaves' appearance) were equally important criteria. Performance differences between the recommended pans were so minor that we've arranged them in order of price, from cheapest to most expensive. See www.cooksillustrated.com for up-to-date prices and mail-order sources for top-rated products.

RECOMMENDED

1. Ekco Baker's Secret Non-Stick Large Loaf Pan

$3.99

Handles on both ends made this pan easy to move in and out of the oven. Browning was excellent, and release was a breeze, as was cleaning.

RECOMMENDED

2. Chicago Metallic SilverStone Bakeware Medium Loaf Pan

$5.99

Handles made it easy to work with and performance was fine, though the crust on white bread was just a tad light.

RECOMMENDED

3. Kaiser Backform Loaf Pan

$10.99

Exemplary browning, great release, and handles add up to a great pan.

RECOMMENDED

4. Chicago Metallic Professional Loaf Pan

$13.99

Slightly better browning of the white bread than with the less expensive Chicago Metallic SilverStone pan, but has no handles.

RECOMMENDED

5. Calphalon Nonstick Professional Bakeware Medium Loaf Pan

$15.99

Heavy pan with a high-quality feel. Produced beautifully shaped, beautifully browned loaves but for a hefty price.

NOT RECOMMENDED

6. Mirro Comet Loaf Pan

$2.99

Neither depth nor evenness of browning was up to our standards in loaves baked in this shiny pan.

NOT RECOMMENDED

7. Corning Pyrex Original Loaf Dish

$3.99

Handles make it easy to grab and move, but it took a fair amount of gentle shaking to release the sweet lemon loaf cake. Also did not brown as well as top-rated pans.

NOT RECOMMENDED

8. Wilton Enterprises Performance Loaf Pan

$4.99

Corners and edges of white bread loaves were noticeably light in color. Also, loaves had a wide, squat shape.

NOT RECOMMENDED

9. Stoneware Loaf Pan

$14.95

Browning was fine, but bottom crusts of lemon loaf cake and cornbread stuck to the pan, causing loaves to break.

NOT RECOMMENDED

10. WearEver CushionAire Nonstick Insulated Bakeware Loaf Pan

$15.99

Browned poorly, felt bulky to handle, and produced square, unattractive loaves. Sweet breads tended to stick.

TASTING LAB: Yogurt

PLAIN YOGURT MAY NOT BE THE WORLD'S SEXIEST FOOD, but there is plenty of mystique surrounding this refrigerator staple, perhaps owing to that ad campaign featuring centenarian Georgians (the Soviet variety) who ate yogurt every day. Once consumed mainly by hippies, yogurt is now a mainstream product, available in countless flavors, including cotton candy and kiwi. We were interested in plain yogurt, which bakers often use to add moistness to quick breads and muffins.

We had three questions at the outset of our research. First, does the inclusion of certain bacteria (the "active cultures" in yogurt) affect flavor? Second, does fat content make a difference in flavor and/or texture? You can buy nonfat, low fat, or whole milk yogurt, and we wanted to taste all three. Third, are the leading supermarket brands just fine, or is it worth seeking out specialty brands, especially those found in natural foods stores?

Yogurt was probably first made by chance when milk was accidentally fermented by wild bacteria. Today, the process is controlled. Milk (whole, low fat, or skim) is pasteurized and usually homogenized. (Some companies leave whole milk unhomogenized to retain a separate cream layer in their yogurt.) Active bacteria cultures are then added to the milk, and the milk is poured directly into cups and kept in a warm environment for several hours. The bacteria convert the milk sugar (called lactose) into lactic acid, causing the proteins in the milk to coagulate and thicken. Lactic acid also gives yogurt its characteristic tang. Finally, the yogurt is cooled and refrigerated.

We rounded up 10 leading brands of yogurt, including four made with whole milk, two with low fat milk, and four with skim milk, and tasted them straight from the container. We quickly determined that the type of bacteria used to culture the milk had no discernible effect on our tasters' ratings. Fat content was more complicated. Yogurts made with low fat milk and whole milk took the top four spots. However, two whole milk yogurts fared poorly. Yes, our

tasters appreciated the richness and flavor contributed by the extra fat, but in the end other considerations took precedence.

In terms of flavor, a happy medium between tart and bland carried the day. Yogurts that were extremely tart landed at the bottom of the rankings.

In terms of texture, our tasters spoke loud and clear. They preferred smooth, creamy yogurts to those that were lumpy, chalky, grainy, watery, or curdlike. In fact, tasters put such a high premium on smoothness that two nonfat brands with decent textures finished a respectable fifth and sixth in our tasting.

Our ideal yogurt is creamy and smooth and has some tang without being sour or acidic. Some milk fat is a plus. While it's easy to pick out the yogurt that meets these criteria on a spoon, what about when baking? Would the higher-fat products make better banana bread?

To find out, we baked loaves with nonfat, low fat and whole milk yogurt. Tasters had a hard time detecting differences, and all of the loaves were enjoyed. The texture of the yogurt didn't matter (watery and smooth yogurt baked up the same), nor did the flavor (the other ingredients in the recipe masked the sourness of even the most sour samples). Given the small amount of yogurt in this recipe, this result is not surprising. We also tried a corn muffin recipe that calls for 1 cup of yogurt and found that the muffins made with whole milk yogurt were both more moist and more tender than muffins made with low fat or nonfat yogurt.

Rating Plain Yogurts

WE PURCHASED 10 BRANDS OF PLAIN YOGURT AVAILABLE AT SUPERMARKETS AND NATURAL FOODS STORES. EACH yogurt was sampled straight from the container, although we did mix the yogurts just prior to the tasting to incorporate any separated liquid or cream. Tasters were asked to evaluate each yogurt on both texture and flavor. The yogurts are listed in order of preference.

HIGHLY RECOMMENDED
1. Colombo Low Fat Plain Yogurt
$2.69 for 32 ounces

Tasters gave this brand a big thumbs up, praising the "clean taste" and "mild tang" of this "creamy," "silky" yogurt.

RECOMMENDED
2. Brown Cow Organic Whole Milk Plain Yogurt
$2.39 for 24 ounces

Tasters liked this "rich," "buttery" yogurt, which was described as "slightly sweet, slightly lemony." A couple of tasters noticed a pleasant "goaty" quality to this "creamy" and "smooth" yogurt.

RECOMMENDED
3. Stonyfield Farm Organic Low Fat Plain Yogurt
$3.39 for 32 ounces

Tasters thought this yogurt was a bit "mild" and some went so far as to call it "bland." However, its "velvety" texture assured high scores.

RECOMMENDED
4. Stonyfield Farm Organic Cream on Top Whole Milk Plain Yogurt
$3.19 for 32 ounces

This yogurt was pretty "sour" and "acidic." Although "smooth," the consistency was thinner than other top brands.

RECOMMENDED WITH RESERVATIONS
5. Dannon Fat Free Plain Yogurt
$2.69 for 32 ounces

Tasters liked the "mildly tangy" flavor of this yogurt. Several panelists detected a "mineral taste." Others detected a "grainy," "chalky" consistency.

RECOMMENDED WITH RESERVATIONS
6. Colombo Fat Free Plain Yogurt
$2.99 for 32 ounces

Several tasters noted an "unpleasant" aftertaste in this "acidic" yogurt. The texture was slightly "gelatinous" but not objectionable.

RECOMMENDED WITH RESERVATIONS
7. Brown Cow Cream Top Whole Milk Plain Yogurt
$2.99 for 32 ounces

Unlike the other Brown Cow product made with whole milk, this one was not a clear winner. Several tasters picked up the same "goat-like" flavor, but the texture was "watery," "mealy," and "lumpy."

NOT RECOMMENDED
8. Stonyfield Farm Nonfat Plain Yogurt
$3.19 for 32 ounces

This "bland" yogurt had a "watery," "lumpy" texture that was a real turn-off for tasters.

NOT RECOMMENDED
9. Brown Cow Nonfat Plain Yogurt
$2.89 for 32 ounces

"Very sour," with a "bitter aftertaste." "Grainy," "lumpy" texture assured a low finish.

NOT RECOMMENDED
10. Erivan Acidophilus Yogurt
$1.99 for 16 ounces

This whole milk yogurt was so sour and acidic that one taster complained that it "hurts the back of the throat." The "lumpy," "watery" texture did not help.

RUSTIC BREAD
at home

Real country bread, the kind made by an artisan and never found at the supermarket, is a thing of beauty. The crust is shatteringly crisp, the crumb is chewy and filled with plenty of holes. The flavor is hearty and rugged. This loaf can be slathered with butter or used to build a sandwich with personality. We wanted to develop a recipe that was every bit as good as the best country loaves baked in a hearth at the finest bakeries but that was still doable for the home cook baking in a home oven. After baking hundreds of loaves, we think you'll agree that our loaf meets this challenge.

A loaf of rustic country bread sliced and ready for a close-up.

RUSTIC COUNTRY BREAD

WHAT WE WANTED: A large, crusty European-style country loaf with great flavor and chew.

Flour, water, yeast, and salt. That's about as simple as it gets in the kitchen, or so we thought when we set out to develop a reliable home recipe for a crusty, full-textured, European-style country bread. This is the kind of bread that is a main course all by itself; the first bite hits you with a heady burst of crackle and chew, an inspired whiff of yeast, and a hint of sourness.

We expected that a sponge starter (a "sponge" of flour, water, and yeast is left to ferment, then additional flour, water, and other ingredients are added in) would produce more flavor than a quick rise using a greater amount of yeast, and this turned out to be true. In fact, we only used ½ teaspoon of instant yeast (most recipes call for up to a tablespoon) for 6 cups of flour. We also varied the sponge recipe by using equal amounts of whole wheat and white flour for added flavor and texture.

The next element to consider was water. Professional bakers know that a high water content produces more texture and chew. To figure out the percentage of water in a bread recipe (as a percentage of the flour weight), you calculate the weight, in grams, of water in the recipe (each cup of water weighs 237.5 grams) and divide that by the weight of the flour (1 cup of flour weighs 130 grams). After some research, we figured that a water content of 68 percent would be about right. The theory was that the higher percentage of water—most bread recipes run around 60 percent—would improve the chew. We tried this formula and got mediocre results. It was good bread, but without the big-league chew we wanted.

We then visited Iggy's Bakery just outside of Boston. The bread made there has a big chew, a big crust, and big flavor. The chief baker told us we needed to push the water level even higher. He pointed to the plastic vats filled with rising dough—a sticky mass that would just about pour. This was a breakthrough. Our idea of bread dough had been a nonstick satin ball, easy to handle and more solid than liquid. But this stuff puddled and pulled, shimmered and shook. At Iggy's, they use a mixture of three flours—high protein, whole wheat, and rye—for optimum flavor and texture.

Back in the test kitchen, we increased the water percentage to near-dangerous levels. The revised recipe now had 2½ cups of water to 6 cups of flour, which brought the percentage of water to flour up to a whopping 76 percent, a percentage so high it borders on heresy. However, this high percentage was slightly counteracted by the fact that almost 30 percent of the total flour used was whole wheat and rye. We chose these flours for flavor, but they also absorb more water than white flour does.

Professional bakers use giant mixers and special shaping machines that handle moist dough easily. In our test kitchen we use the same equipment that home cooks use, and the bread stuck to our hands, the wooden counter, the mixer bowl, the damp dish towel, and even the heavily floured peel (the shovel-like tool used to get breads in and out of the oven). We tried to knead the dough by hand, but this was almost impossible without adding lots of flour. Still, at the end of the day, the bread was vastly improved. Although a bit sticky, the inside had cavernous air holes and some real chew.

We now turned our attention more closely to the flour. Up until now, we had been using a professional baker's bread flour, which has a very high level of protein (about 14 percent). We decided to try both a regular bread flour and an all-purpose flour to see if protein content would have a noticeable affect on the finished product. The all-purpose flour yielded an extremely wet, unworkable dough; the dough made with regular bread flour was wetter than the high-protein loaf but still workable. Of most interest, however, was the fact that these lower-protein flours produced a chewier, crustier loaf, although we felt that the loaf made with all-purpose flour was a little too tough. After additional testing, it became clear that we had to adjust the recipe to accommodate the lower-protein flours, which can't absorb as much water as higher-protein flour. When we reduced the amount of water used in our regular bread flour dough to 2⅓ cups, the results were even better. Because this flour is sold in supermarkets, we decided to use it in our recipe.

We also wanted to try varying the amount of the other ingredients we were using: salt and honey. Most recipes with 6 cups of flour use 2 teaspoons of salt, and this amount was just right. Honey is often added to boost flavor and promote browning of the crust (sugar promotes browning). When we added 2 tablespoons of honey, the flavor was a bit deeper and the crust turned a rich nut-brown.

Kneading by hand was not our first choice (it can be done, however). We tried using a food processor with a metal blade, which worked fine except that our $250 machine sounded like a lawnmower in a dense patch of weeds; all that was missing was a curl of blue smoke and the smell of burning rubber. The machine simply could not handle 6 cups of quicksand. We tried the recipe in two half-batches, which worked pretty well. We found that leaving the metal blade in the processor between batches is best (you won't get absolutely all of the first batch out of the processor bowl); otherwise your hands will get sticky and dough may ooze out around the center core of the bowl when the second batch is mixed. We recommend that you process for no more than 30 seconds, which is enough time to knead the dough, and we recommend this method only for home cooks with a good heavy-duty processor.

The best solution was a heavy-duty standing mixer with a dough hook. We simply threw in the ingredients, mixed them briefly with a large, stiff rubber spatula, and then turned the machine on at the lowest setting for 15 minutes. We then transferred the dough to an oiled bowl to rise for about 2 hours, or until tripled in volume. Allowing the dough to triple in volume both improves flavor and helps the dough to develop more "muscle," which helps the bread maintain its shape when baked.

Even after 15 minutes of kneading, the dough was difficult to handle. After a few tries with various methods, we came up with the following, which was the least messy. For the first rise, simply use a rubber spatula to transfer the wet dough to the oiled bowl (a plastic tub is fine, too). After letting the bread rise for about 2 hours, use the same spatula to transfer the dough onto a lightly floured surface. Now flour both your hands and the dough (the latter lightly). Press the dough very gently into a round and then fold it into a ball. Note that you should handle the dough as little as possible at this point both because it is still a little sticky (you'll be tempted to add extra flour) and because excessive handling is bad for rustic bread—you want an irregular texture with lots of air holes. This point goes for all bread making: Strong kneading after the first rise will harm the delicate structure of the dough.

The best way to move the dough from here on in is to use a large dough scraper, two metal spatulas, or a thin floured baking sheet. Transfer the dough smooth-side down into a colander or a basket that has been lined with a piece of muslin or linen that has been well floured. The flour should be rubbed into the fabric so the dough will not stick. A banneton is a cloth-lined woven basket designed just for this purpose. You can purchase one or try making your own, as we did. Muslin, which is cheaper than linen, works well and comes in different grades from fine (the most expensive) to coarse (the least expensive). Use the cheaper variety to line your basket, and make sure that it is 100 percent unbleached cotton. A real banneton has the linen or muslin sewn right into the basket, an optional refinement. The basket we used was 4 inches high, 7 inches wide across the bottom, and 12 inches wide across the top. A colander is also a perfectly good option. It works well because it allows for air flow (the dough is more likely to stick to the muslin when sitting in a bowl).

For its second rise the dough needs to be covered directly. We tried a damp dish towel, but it stuck to the dough. It was like unwrapping a piece of saltwater taffy on a hot day. Aluminum foil proved more effective because the dough is less likely to stick to it and it allows the dough to breathe, keeping the dough from rising too much. If the dough rises too much at this point you will end up with a fluffy texture (plastic wrap, for example, will cause too much rising). The foil gives the dough shape and allows you to transfer it easily to the peel when the second rise is completed.

The last major issue was the crust. The key, according to most experts, is steam. Just to test this theory, we baked one loaf with no steam at all, and the crust was thin and unappealing. This bread does need steam, but there are many ways in which to provide it. For convenience' sake, we chose to spray the loaf before putting it in the oven.

We also tested starting oven temperatures. We began testing with 500-degree oven and then immediately turned the heat down to 400 degrees, working under the assumption that the higher temperature would offset the drop in temperature caused by opening the oven door and adding the dough (the dough absorbs a great deal of heat quickly). The resulting crust was thin and disappointing. Next we tried baking the bread at 500 degrees for the first 15 minutes and then reducing the temperature to 400. The crust was scorched. It cooked so fast that the interior had no time to cook properly. The best baking temperature turned out to be a constant 450 degrees.

WHAT WE LEARNED: For good flavor, use very little yeast and let it ferment in a sponge before adding most of the flour and water. Use some rye and whole wheat flours for flavor, and add a lot of water for good chew. Let the dough rise twice (the second time in a muslin-lined basket), and bake until the crust is deeply browned and the internal temperature reaches 210 degrees.

RUSTIC COUNTRY BREAD makes I large round loaf

Whole wheat and rye flours contribute to this bread's full flavor, and extra oven time gives the bread its thick crust. Because of its high water content, the bread will be gummy if pulled from the oven too soon. To ensure the bread's doneness, make sure its internal temperature reads 210 degrees by inserting an instant-read thermometer into the bottom of the loaf. Also look at the crust—it should be very dark brown, almost black. Because the dough is so sticky, a heavy-duty standing mixer is best for kneading, but food processor and hand-kneading instructions follow this recipe. Keep in mind that rising times vary depending on kitchen temperature (the times listed below are minimums). You can vary the texture by increasing or decreasing the flour. For bread with a finer crumb and less chewy texture, increase the flour by $1/4$ cup increments. For coarser, chewier bread, decrease the flour by the same increments. To develop a crisp crust, you need to bake the bread on tiles or a stone. To vary flavors, add 1 tablespoon minced hearty herbs, such as rosemary or thyme, with the salt, or mix in $1/2$ cup chopped toasted walnuts or pecans just before kneading ends.

sponge

$1/2$ teaspoon instant dry yeast (see Tasting Lab on page 262)

1 cup water (room temperature)

1 cup ($5\frac{1}{2}$ ounces) bread flour

1 cup (5 ounces) whole wheat flour

dough

$3\frac{1}{2}$ cups ($19\frac{1}{4}$ ounces) bread flour, plus more as needed to lightly dust work surface, hands, and dough

$1/2$ cup ($2\frac{1}{2}$ ounces) rye flour

$1\frac{1}{3}$ cups water (room temperature), or more as needed

2 tablespoons honey

2 teaspoons salt

1. FOR THE SPONGE: Stir yeast into water in medium bowl until dissolved. Mix in flours with rubber spatula to create stiff, wet dough. Cover with plastic wrap; let sit at room temperature for at least 5 hours, preferably overnight. (Can be refrigerated up to 24 hours; return to room temperature before continuing with recipe.)

2. FOR THE DOUGH: Mix flours, water, honey, and sponge in bowl of standing mixer with rubber spatula. Knead dough, using dough hook attachment, on lowest speed until dough is smooth, about 15 minutes, adding salt during final 3 minutes. If dough looks dry after salt is added, add water in 1-tablespoon increments every 30 seconds until smooth consistency is reached. Transfer dough to large, lightly oiled container or bowl. Cover with plastic wrap; let rise until tripled in size, at least 2 hours.

3. Turn dough onto lightly floured surface. Dust dough top and hands with flour. Lightly press dough into round by folding edges of dough into middle from top, right, bottom, and left, sequentially, then gathering it loosely together. Transfer dough, smooth-side down, to colander or basket lined with heavily floured muslin or linen. Cover loosely with large sheet of aluminum foil; let dough rise until almost doubled in size, at least 45 minutes.

4. Meanwhile, adjust oven rack to low-center position and arrange baking tiles to form surface that is at least 18 by 12 inches or place large baking stone on rack. Heat oven to 450 degrees.

5. Cover peel or back of large baking sheet with large piece of parchment. Invert dough onto peel and remove muslin. Use scissors or serrated knife to cut three slashes on dough top. With scissors, trim excess parchment around dough. Fill spray bottle with water and spritz dough four or five times.

6. Slide dough, still on parchment, from peel onto tiles or stone; remove peel with quick backward jerk. Bake until

instant-read thermometer inserted in bread bottom registers 210 degrees (see illustration below) and crust is very dark brown, 35 to 40 minutes, turning bread around after 25 minutes if not browning evenly. Turn oven off, open door, and let bread remain in oven 10 minutes longer. Remove, then let cool to room temperature before slicing, about 2 hours. To crisp crust, place cooled bread in 450-degree oven for 10 minutes.

VARIATIONS

RUSTIC COUNTRY BREAD KNEADED IN A FOOD PROCESSOR

Make sponge as directed in recipe for Rustic Country Bread. Mix half of sponge and half of flours and honey in food processor fitted with metal blade. Pulse until roughly

---

TECHNIQUE:
Taking the Temperature of Bread

Professional bread recipes often suggest taking the internal temperature of a loaf to gauge when it's done.

A. For bread that is baked free-form, tip the loaf up with a hand shielded by an oven mitt or potholder and insert the probe through the bottom crust into the center of the loaf.

B. For bread that is baked in a loaf pan, insert the probe from the side, just above the edge of the loaf pan, directing the probe at a downward angle toward the center of the loaf.

blended, 3 to 4 one-second pulses. With machine running, add half of water (⅔ cup) slowly through feed tube; process until dough forms ball. Let sit for 3 minutes, then add half of salt and process to form smooth dough, about 30 seconds longer. Transfer dough to large, lightly oiled container or bowl, leaving metal blade in processor (some dough will remain under blade). Repeat process with remaining half of ingredients. Proceed with recipe as directed.

RUSTIC COUNTRY BREAD KNEADED BY HAND

Make sponge as directed in recipe for Rustic Country Bread. Place sponge and all dough ingredients, except 2 cups of bread flour, in large bowl. Stir mixture with wooden spoon until smooth, about 5 minutes. Work in reserved flour and then turn out onto floured board. Knead by hand for 5 minutes, incorporating no more than additional ¼ cup flour as you work. Dough will be very wet and sticky. Proceed with recipe.

TASTING LAB: Yeast

ALONG WITH FLOUR AND WATER, YEAST IS AN ESSENTIAL ingredient in bread recipes. Several kinds are available to home cooks. All yeast begins as a small, cultured, purified sample that feeds and multiplies continuously in a liquid medium until it reaches the desired volume and stage of development. This liquid yeast is sold by the tankerful to commercial food manufacturers. For bakeries, yeast companies remove some of the moisture from liquid yeast to create a product called "crumbled yeast," which is sold in 50-pound bags. The next processing step extrudes the yeast to make a product that remains fully hydrated yet fine enough to press into the small cakes you see for sale on supermarket shelves and labeled cake yeast, fresh yeast, or compressed yeast. Further processing yields dried, powdered yeast, called active dry yeast. The same process is used to make other dry yeasts, including instant yeast (also called

rapid-rise or quick-rise yeast), although this product starts with different strains of yeast.

We wondered whether the type or brand of yeast made a difference when making bread. To find out, we tested several different brands as well as the three major categories of yeast—cake, active dry, and instant. We prepared three recipes with each yeast—an American sandwich bread (with a small amount of butter, sugar, and milk), a baguette (without sugar or dairy), and a kuchen (with substantial amounts of butter, sugar, and dairy). We placed the doughs made with instant yeast in a warmed oven for just 40 minutes, whereas breads made with the cake and regular active dry yeast took about two hours when left to rise on the counter. We followed the general recommendations regarding the strength of cake yeast and used twice as much cake yeast as dry active or instant yeast.

Although we expected slower-rising active dry and cake yeasts to promote more flavor in the finished loaves, this was not the case. Our tasters actually preferred the breads made with instant yeast. The faster rise, in fact, yielded more flavor and produced a noticeably sweeter bread. One theory is that a rapid rise provides less time for the creation of the acidic byproducts of fermentation, hence a sweeter loaf. It is also true that instant yeast has superior enzyme activity, which converts starches to sugar faster (and so perhaps more completely) than regular-rise varieties.

Even more to the point, though, is the fact that instant yeast is not necessarily an inferior product. Yeast is a plant, and different varieties have quite different qualities, as do different varieties of, say, roses. Instant yeast has been genetically engineered to reproduce the best characteristics of yeasts from around the world. Although genetic engineering often results in loss of flavor, our blind taste tests confirmed that in this case it produced an excellent product.

As for why this yeast works faster, there are two primary reasons. In addition to the more rapid enzyme activity described above, instant yeast also has an open, porous structure, which means that it can absorb liquid instantly. When this yeast was introduced for home use, consumers

had some difficulty with it because they continued to follow their habit of "proofing" the yeast—dissolving it in water to see if it bubbled, which was "proof" that the yeast was alive and could do its work—rather than mixing it directly into the flour, as instructed by the manufacturer. Because of its efficiency, this new yeast dissolved in water rapidly and ran out of food (starch) and died before the rising process was complete. To correct this problem, scientists went back and added more starch to the mix, giving the yeast enough food to survive proofing.

Today, however, most yeast does not need to be dissolved in water before being used in a recipe. For one thing, yeast is now marked with an expiration date for freshness, so there's no need to proof, or test, the yeast as long as the

expiration date hasn't passed. (Note that these expiration dates should be taken seriously. We tried baking a loaf with yeast that was one month past expiration, and the rising times were double those experienced with fresh yeast. The resulting loaf was more dense, with a smaller rise.)

Keep in mind that whether you dissolve yeast directly in liquid or add it to the flour, the temperature of the water or milk used is crucial. Dry yeast will die in ice water or in liquids at 125 degrees or higher.

We rely on instant yeast in our recipes. If you want to use active dry yeast, you can use an equal amount, but note that rising times will be longer. If you want to use cake yeast, you'll need twice as much yeast as recommended in the recipe. Note that cake yeast is highly perishable and must be refrigerated.

EQUIPMENT CORNER:
Dry Measuring Cups

MEASURING CUPS ARE BASIC NECESSITIES IN THE kitchen; without them, even the simplest cookie recipe would be compromised. Kitchen stores offer a wide range of measuring cups, from those with rubber comfort grips on their handles to heavy-gauge aluminum and stainless steel. We wondered if one kind of cup would be easier or more efficient to use than another. To find out, we put eight readily available measuring-cup sets to the test and came up with clear guidelines for your next purchase. Prices ranged from $2.99 to $19.99.

We tested every individual measuring cup by measuring flour and sugar with our favored "dip and sweep" method (dipping the cup into the bin, scooping out a heaping cupful, then leveling the cup with the straight side of a knife or icing spatula). While dipping and sweeping, we paid particular attention to cup construction—our measuring cups need to stand up to hundreds of repeated dips in the flour or sugar bin. Given the uncompromising nature of baking, accuracy was also important, so we weighed each cup of flour to make sure they all maintained the standard weight of 5 ounces of flour per cup.

Across the board, measured weights were remarkably consistent. We found that the precision of the measurements depended more on the consistency of the measuring method than on the construction of the cups themselves.

We did find, however, that a sturdy handle is critical to successful dipping and sweeping. Some plastic handles actually bent when the cup was full. (They seemed likely to snap under extra pressure—say, when measuring shortening.) Other handles were simply too short, forcing the hand to snuggle close to the cup and get covered in flour. More than one set was so heavy-handled that the cups tipped over when sitting on the counter—annoying when cups are empty and a disaster when full. Sturdy, riveted stainless steel handles were highly rated and preferred.

Material played a dual role in the usefulness of a cup, affecting both sturdiness and ease of cleaning. Plastic failed to impress on both counts. It's more likely to melt if you inadvertently place it near a heat source or to warp in a particularly hot dishwasher. Plastic models were also troublesome when it came to cleaning. They are more likely to scratch, creating rough surfaces that cause bits of sugar or flour to stick. Our testers universally preferred heavy-gauge metal. It stood up to heavy dipping and resisted any type of scratch or ding.

If you're looking for a measuring cup that offers ease of use and longevity, choose one with a long, sturdy handle and a heavy, well-constructed base. The cup will make measuring a breeze and give you years of use.

Rating Dry Measuring Cups

WE RATED EIGHT SETS OF MEASURING CUPS BY REPEATING "DIP AND SWEEP" MEASUREMENTS OF FLOUR AND SUGAR hundreds of times. (We dipped the cup into a bin of flour or sugar, scooped up a heaping cupful, then leveled the contents with the straight edge of an icing spatula.) The cups are listed in order of preference. See www.cooksillustrated.com for up-to-date prices and mail-order sources for top-rated products.

RECOMMENDED

1. Amco Stainless Steel Measuring Cups

$12.99

Heavy and sturdy; downgraded only for the handle, which meets the cup below the top, making leveling more difficult.

RECOMMENDED WITH RESERVATIONS

2. Oxo Good Grips Stainless Steel Measuring Cups

$19.99

Sturdy but heavy comfort-grip handles cause the cups to tip over when empty and balance precariously when full. They do not nestle together well and must be wrestled apart.

RECOMMENDED WITH RESERVATIONS

3. Fox Run Stainless Steel Measuring Cups

$6.99

Good set for infrequent use; the metal is thinner than in other models and the handles less securely riveted, imparting a flimsy feel and an occasional tip-over.

NOT RECOMMENDED

4. Oneida 18/8 Stainless Steel Measuring Cups

$19.99

Shiny, sturdy, and an interesting design, but not very functional—downgraded for small handles and measurement marks printed on the bottom of the bowl instead of the sides of the cup or the handles.

NOT RECOMMENDED

5. Oneida Colour Grip Measuring Cups

$7.99

Nice grip, good leveling, and heat-resistant plastic material, but the color-coded handles bent while scooping flour from a bin.

NOT RECOMMENDED

6. Oxo Good Grips Measuring Cups

$4.99

Very light and flimsy feeling, with easily scratched black plastic. The cups tip over when empty and they are not easy to level because the rim edge is too thick.

NOT RECOMMENDED

7. Pyrex Accessories Measuring Cups

$2.99

Very short, awkward handles are hard to grip, especially when scooping flour from a bin. Easily scratched plastic surface is difficult to clean.

NOT RECOMMENDED

8. Pyrex Accessories Professional Clear Measuring Cups

Price: $9.99

Lexan plastic cups tipped over from heavy, long handles. The cups do not nestle together cleanly, but they are easy to level.

No peeking. Jack makes Chris wear a blindfold for the tasting of cookies made with light, dark, and blackstrap molasses.

COOKIE JAR favorites

Cookies are so simple, so basic, so American, so easy. How is it then that most Americans buy bad supermarket cookies? Except for the sweetness of sugar, these cookies are devoid of flavor (close your eyes and you can't tell whether the cookie is made with chocolate or molasses), and the texture is either dry and crumbly or unnaturally gooey and soft. There is a better way, and it's not as difficult as you might think.

The test kitchen has taken two classics—soft, fudgy chocolate cookies and spiced molasses cookies—and made them great again. We've figured out the secrets to superior flavor as well as an irresistible chewy texture. Best of all, these recipes are easy. Yes, they demand some attention to detail—two or three minutes in the oven can make the difference between a chewy cookie and a dry one—but the techniques are so easy that even the novice baker will succeed the first time out.

CHOCOLATE COOKIES

WHAT WE WANTED: A chocolate cookie so fudgy and so flavorful it would be unforgettable.

Obsessions often begin with chance encounters, a wry, fetching smile glanced out of the corner of an eye or perhaps one's first taste of a home-grown tomato. One of our greatest obsessions has been the first transcendent bite of the perfect chocolate cookie, still warm out of the oven. That first bite would reveal a center of hot fudge sauce, and the texture would call to mind chocolate bread pudding with a deep, complex chocolate flavor. This would be the sort of confection that creates intense focus while it is consumed, sights and sounds subordinate to taste, overloading the other senses to the point of dysfunction.

The problem is that we have, for years, been trying to perfect this cookie. We have created large, dense cookies that were rich and decadent, but the chocolate flavor was dull. We have also experimented with thin, crisp cookies (nice but not intense), chewy cookies (good but not showstoppers), and cakelike chocolate cookies, which tend to be dry and uninspiring. The test kitchen also made a half-dozen recipes from various cookbooks and discovered a world of difference in texture, flavor, and appearance, from soft mocha-colored disks to thick mounds of pure fudge. This panoply of outcomes gave us pause, since the ingredient lists seemed to have more in common than the cookies themselves. Figuring out what makes a chocolate cookie tick was going to require weeks of testing and a great deal of detective work.

Our first step was to strip the recipes down to their basics to understand the fundamentals. A chocolate cookie is a mixture of melted chocolate, sugar, eggs, butter, flour, baking soda or powder, and salt. Vanilla, coffee, and nuts are extras.

The key issues were how to handle the butter and eggs.

The butter can be melted or creamed, and the eggs can be beaten or just whisked into the batter. For the first test batch, we melted the butter and whipped the eggs. The results were good, but the cookies were a bit cakey and loose, without any chew. For the next batch we melted the butter and did not beat the eggs. These cookies were a bit dry and cakey. When we started creaming the butter and beating the eggs into it after creaming, we noticed an immediate improvement. However, we finally settled on a modified creaming method with minimal beating to produce moist cookies that were not cakey.

The next issue was one of proportions, that is, the ratio

of flour to butter to eggs to sugar to chocolate. This was going to be crucial to the thickness of the cookie, its texture, and the degree to which the taste of chocolate would dominate. Looking over the recipes we had tested, we saw so many permutations that we felt like the British trying to crack the German secret code in World War II.

To organize the facts, we made a chart of the various ratios of eggs, sugar, chocolate, and butter to flour, with related comments on the taste, texture, and shape of each cookie we had tested. We quickly noted that the ratio of eggs and butter to flour was less important than the ratio of sugar and chocolate to flour. The driest cookie used less than ½ cup of sugar per cup of flour; the richest, wettest cookie used 3 cups. The cookie with the faintest chocolate flavor and a relatively firm, dry texture used only 2 ounces of chocolate per cup of flour, whereas other recipes used up to a pound of chocolate with only ½ cup of flour. After many tests designed to balance sweetness and moisture, we settled on 1 cup of sugar and 8 ounces of chocolate to 1 cup of flour. Finally, we had a moist cookie with good chocolate flavor. Nonetheless, we thought the flavor and texture could be still better, so we moved on to other ingredients.

We started with all white granulated sugar and then tested a mixture of brown sugar and granulated, which seemed to improve the flavor and added just a bit more moisture. We also tried corn syrup, which had little effect. A small amount of vanilla extract and instant coffee powder rounded out the flavors. Throughout the testing, we had been using all-purpose flour. We decided to try cake flour, but the resulting cookies were a bit too delicate. We also varied the quantity of flour throughout the testing process, starting at 3 cups and eventually working our way down to 2 cups. To create a thicker, more stable cookie, we tried replacing some of the butter with vegetable shortening (Crisco), but this created an unattractive, greasy-looking cookie with a pale white sheen. We thought that the choice

of leavener might be important, so we tested baking powder against baking soda and found that the cookies with the powder were slightly thicker.

At this point our cookie was thick and very good, but still not the sort of thing that would reduce the average adult to tears of joy. The flavor was remained a bit dull, and the texture was moist but monochromatic. We wondered if we could solve this problem by varying the type of chocolate. We found that unsweetened chocolate, an ingredient often called for in chocolate cookie recipes, added intensity to the flavor. Unfortunately, we also discovered an aggressive sour note in these cookies, even when the sugar level was adjusted for the bitterness of the chocolate. Semisweet and bittersweet chocolate turned out to be better choices owing to their rounder, less potent flavors. These chocolates undergo more processing than unsweetened, and they also get other flavorings; this no doubt gives them a smoother, richer flavor overall. (For more information on types of chocolate, see the Science Desk on page 271.)

Our hunt was almost over, but now we wondered if a bit of cocoa powder might add more depth of flavor to our cookie. One-half cup of Dutch-processed cocoa was substituted for the same amount of flour, and the chocolate flavor became both smoother and deeper. (We also tried a batch of cookies made only with cocoa powder and no chocolate and they were disappointing, having just a faint chocolate flavor.) At last, we had brought our fantasy to life: a double-chocolate cookie that was both rich and soft, with an intense chocolatey center that would drive anyone to distraction.

WHAT WE LEARNED: **For smooth, rich chocolate flavor, use a combination of semisweet chocolate and Dutch-processed cocoa powder. Add enough flour to give the cookies structure; any more flour only makes the cookies drier and cakier.**

THICK AND CHEWY DOUBLE-CHOCOLATE COOKIES
makes about 3½ dozen cookies

To melt the chocolate in a microwave, heat at 50 percent power for 2 minutes, stir, then continue heating at 50 percent power for 1 more minute. If not completely melted, heat an additional 30 to 45 seconds at 50 percent power. We recommend using a spring-loaded ice cream scoop to scoop the dough. Resist the urge to bake the cookies longer than indicated; they may appear underbaked at first but will firm up as they cool.

The balls of raw dough should be about the size of a golf ball. Don't skimp or the cookies won't be moist and fudgy.

2	cups (10 ounces) unbleached all-purpose flour
½	cup Dutch-processed cocoa powder
2	teaspoons baking powder
½	teaspoon salt
16	ounces semisweet chocolate, chopped
4	large eggs
2	teaspoons vanilla extract
2	teaspoons instant coffee or espresso powder
10	tablespoons (1¼ sticks) unsalted butter, softened
1½	cups packed (10½ ounces) light brown sugar
½	cup (3½ ounces) granulated sugar

1. Sift together flour, cocoa, baking powder, and salt in medium bowl; set aside.

2. Melt chocolate in medium heatproof bowl set over pan of almost-simmering water, stirring once or twice, until smooth; remove from heat. Beat eggs and vanilla lightly with fork, sprinkle coffee powder over to dissolve, and set aside.

3. In bowl of standing mixer fitted with paddle attachment, beat butter at medium speed until smooth and creamy, about 5 seconds. Beat in sugars until combined, about 45 seconds; mixture will look granular. Reduce speed to low and gradually beat in egg mixture until incorporated, about 45 seconds. Add chocolate in steady stream and beat until combined, about 40 seconds. Scrape bottom and sides of bowl with rubber spatula. With mixer at low speed, add dry ingredients and mix until just combined. Do not overbeat. Cover with plastic wrap and let stand at room temperature until consistency is scoopable and fudgelike, about 30 minutes.

4. Meanwhile, adjust oven racks to upper-middle and lower-middle positions and heat oven to 350 degrees. Line two baking sheets with parchment paper. Leaving about 1½ inches between each ball, scoop dough onto parchment-lined cookie sheets with 1¾-inch ice cream scoop.

5. Bake, reversing position of baking sheets halfway through baking (from top to bottom and front to back), until edges of cookies have just begun to set but centers are still very soft, about 10 minutes. Cool cookies on sheets about 10 minutes, slide parchment with cookies onto wire racks, and cool to room temperature. Cover one baking sheet with new piece of parchment paper. Scoop remaining dough onto parchment-lined sheet, bake, and cool as directed. Remove cooled cookies from parchment with wide metal spatula and serve.

THICK AND CHEWY TRIPLE-CHOCOLATE COOKIES

If you like bursts of warm melted chocolate in your cookies, include chocolate chips in the batter. The addition of chips will slightly increase the yield of the cookies.

Follow recipe for Thick and Chewy Double-Chocolate Cookies, adding 12 ounces (about 2 cups) semisweet chocolate chips to batter after dry ingredients are incorporated in step 3.

SCIENCE DESK: Types of Chocolate

THERE ARE MANY OPTIONS WHEN IT COMES TO CHOCO-late: unsweetened, bittersweet, semisweet, cocoa powder, and chips. The question is, how are they different?

Unsweetened chocolate, often called baking chocolate or chocolate liquor, is made from roasted cocoa beans and contains about 50 percent solids from the beans and 50 percent cocoa butter. Bittersweet and semisweet chocolates (also called dark chocolates) are made from unsweetened chocolate that is ground with sugar and then further refined. Because bittersweet and semisweet chocolates are about 50 percent sugar, they have less chocolate flavor than unsweetened, which has no added sugar. (Although individual brands may vary, bittersweet averages around 46 percent sugar by weight; semisweet is about 57 percent sugar.) The chocolate flavor they do have, however, is less bitter and more complex, features appreciated by many bakers.

Chocolate chips are made from chocolate with relatively little cocoa butter, about 30 percent or even less. (Dark chocolates, by comparison, must have at least 35 percent cocoa butter.) This is because the chips will not hold their shape with more fat. This lower percentage of cocoa butter makes for a less buttery flavor and a grainier texture.

Cocoa powder is made from unsweetened chocolate. Much of the fat is removed by pressing, leaving behind the solids. These leftover solids are then fluffed up and packaged. Dutch-processed cocoa is less acidic than regular cocoa, and many people feel that this results in a stronger, more interesting chocolate flavor.

Another factor that affects the quality of one brand of chocolate over another is the use of additives. Most processed dark chocolates include vanilla, lecithin (which makes chocolate smoother when poured), and other flavorings, often including soy. In addition, some manufacturers roast their beans for a shorter time on the theory that when the chocolate is baked by consumers it will undergo additional processing.

As for which type of semisweet chocolate is best for a chocolate cookie, we tested four major brands head to head:

GETTING IT RIGHT:
The Secret to Evenly Baked Cookies

Does your oven turn out trays of baked cookies that vary in color and texture as in the photo above? Are some cookies burnt around the edges, while others on the same baking sheet are not quite done? Most ovens do this because the temperature varies from back to front, side to side, and top to bottom. The solution is simple. At the halfway mark in the baking time, rotate the cookie sheet so that the back side now faces front. If there are two cookie sheets in the oven, switch their position so that top goes to bottom and bottom goes to top. Follow this regimen and the result will be batch after batch of evenly baked cookies.

Nestlé, Baker's, Ghirardelli, and Callebaut. The Baker's turned out a gritty cookie that received low marks, Nestlé had an off, somewhat fruity taste, and the Ghirardelli had a muted but pure chocolate flavor that was quite pleasant. Callebaut was our favorite, with a big chocolate flavor that was clean, direct, and full of punch.

EQUIPMENT CORNER:
Measuring Spoons

MEASURING SPOONS DON'T USUALLY GET A LOT OF CON-sideration: bought once and done. But have you ever wondered if your set of spoons is accurate? Would an expensive set do a better job? To find out, the test kitchen purchased 10 different sets of measuring spoons, made from both plastic and stainless steel, ranging in price from $1.99 to $14.99.

First we wanted to determine whether the spoons measured accurately. According to the Office of Weights and Measures, a division of the National Institute of Standards and Technology, a true tablespoon of water should weigh precisely 14.742 grams. We filled each of the spoons with water and then weighed the water to see how close the measurement came to the official standard.

We also assessed each set of measuring spoons for durability. Would the spoons break under pressure? Melt? Dent? And we looked at usability, too. Was it easy to level the spoons when measuring dry ingredients? Was it easy to fill the spoons with liquid?

We were prepared for large differences in degree of accuracy but found none. All of the spoons weighed in within a few hundredths of grams of the official standard—not enough to compromise even the most exacting recipe. But technical accuracy does not always beget accurate measurement. If a spoon cannot be leveled easily, for instance, or if it is dented, accuracy is compromised. Usability and durability are therefore the determinants of accuracy when it comes to most measuring spoons.

In terms of usability, testers preferred spoons with

deeper bowls as opposed to those with narrow and elongated or wide and shallow bowls. Shallow bowls allowed more liquid to spill as the result of a slight misstep or unsteady hand. The narrow, elongated bowls made dipping and scooping into anything but a very deep container impossible. Many spoons were difficult to level cleanly. Some had bumps along the rim of the bowl, and others had handles that did not meet the bowl neatly. (To level, we used the back of a dinner knife or icing spatula, sliding along the base of the handle, onto the bowl.)

In terms of durability, all testers preferred stainless steel spoons—plastic models, no matter how thick, felt flimsy and more likely to break, bend, crack, or melt. Heavier stainless steel models were sturdier and therefore less likely to become dented or scratched. In the end, we found a heavy-duty stainless steel set of spoons that fit the bill and cost just $4.

Rating Measuring Spoons

WE TESTED 10 SETS OF MEASURING SPOONS MADE FROM A VARIETY OF MATERIALS. WE ASSESSED DURABILITY AND usability (how easy is it to measure and level dry ingredients? are liquid ingredients more or less likely to spill over the edge?). Spoon sets are listed in order of preference. See www.cooksillustrated.com for up-to-date prices and mail-order sources for top-rated products.

RECOMMENDED

1. Progressive International Stainless Steel Measuring Spoon Set

$3.99

The easiest to level and fill, so they also proved to be the most consistent in terms of accuracy. Sturdy and firm.

RECOMMENDED WITH RESERVATIONS

2. Oneida 18/8 Stainless Steel Measuring Spoon Set

$14.99

Easy to level and extremely sturdy. Spoons could not be linked together, and the measurement label are on the underside of the handles.

RECOMMENDED WITH RESERVATIONS

3. Rowoco Long Handle Measuring Spoons

$5.99

Long handles were useful when reaching into deep or narrow containers. However, the handle curved down before meeting the bowl, which made leveling more difficult.

RECOMMENDED WITH RESERVATIONS

4. Progressive International Stainless Steel Measuring Spoons with Colored Handles

$2.99

The wide, shallow bowls made measuring difficult, as did the handles, which curved down to meet the bowl.

RECOMMENDED WITH RESERVATIONS

5. Oneida Plastic Heat Resistant Colourgrip Measuring Spoons

$5.99

Best of the plastic models because of the spoons' good grip and deep bowls.

RECOMMENDED WITH RESERVATIONS

6. Pyrex Plastic Measuring Spoon Set

$1.99

Firmer plastic than most models, with a 25-year guarantee—second best among the plastic models.

RECOMMENDED WITH RESERVATIONS

7. Good Cook's Collection Stainless Measuring Spoons

$2.49

Our least favorite stainless spoons. A slight misstep and most of the contents were lost from the extra-wide, shallow bowls. Thin steel makes the spoons easy to bend or dent.

RECOMMENDED WITH RESERVATIONS

8. Oxo Good Grips Plastic Measuring Spoon Set

$2.99

These plastic spoons were flimsy and light with bowls that scratched quickly.

NOT RECOMMENDED

9. Pyrex Professional Clear Spice Jar Measuring Spoon Set

$4.99

These clear plastic spoons with extra-long, narrow bowls were unusually difficult to work with. Bumpy, uneven plastic ridge on bowl rims made leveling very difficult.

NOT RECOMMENDED

10. Kitchen Art Adjust-a-Spoon Measuring Spoon

$3.99

This single plastic spoon has a sliding level for each measurement. Dry and wet ingredients became trapped inside the hollow base, and the pushing mechanism was sticky and slow.

MOLASSES SPICE COOKIES

WHAT WE WANTED: An uncommonly moist, soft, yet chewy, tooth-sinking texture and a warm, tingling spiciness paired with the dark, bittersweet flavor of molasses.

Molasses cookies are the cookie pariahs, the dowdy group in the cookie crowd—permanently out of style and hopelessly old-fashioned. But we've come to appreciate good molasses cookies for their honesty and simplicity. On the outside, their cracks and crinkles give them a humble, charming countenance. Unfortunately, molasses spice cookies are often miserable specimens, no more than flat, tasteless cardboard rounds of gingerbread. They can be dry and cakey without the requisite chew; others are timidly flavored with molasses and are either recklessly or vacantly spiced.

We started by testing a half-dozen different recipes, using a variety of fats, flours, and mixing methods. Although these early experiments yielded vastly different cookies in terms of both flavor and appearance, a few things were clear. The full, rich flavor of butter was in, flat-tasting shortening was out. Flour required no fussing over—unbleached all-purpose flour was perfectly suited to the task. The mixing technique was a standard one: Cream the butter and sugar, add any eggs, then the molasses, and, finally, stir in the dry ingredients.

Molasses is at the core of these cookies. Enough must be used to give them a dark, smoky, bittersweet flavor, but we found that a surfeit of molasses creates a sticky, unworkable dough. For the amount of butter (12 tablespoons) and flour (2¼ cups) we were using, the molasses ceiling was ½ cup. We had been using mild (also called light) molasses up to this point, but in an attempt to boost flavor, we baked batches with dark and blackstrap molasses. Cookies made with dark molasses were filled with bold flavor and rich color, and they garnered much praise. Those made with blackstrap molasses had a few fans, but, for most of us, the wicked brew overtook the spices and embittered the cookies.

Molasses alone cannot supply the cookies with enough sweetness, so either granulated or brown sugar would be required. Dark brown sugar (we chose dark over light for its stronger molasses flavor) yielded cookies that were surprisingly puffy and cakey, and they spread too little on the baking sheet. Granulated sugar yielded cookies that were pale both in color and flavor. A combination of granulated and brown sugars was the ticket. The brown sugar fortified the molasses flavor while the granulated sugar, a spreading agent, allowed the cookies to attain a good, even thickness in the oven without much puff. After some fiddling, we found equal amounts of brown and granulated sugar to be ideal.

Most molasses cookie recipes call for no more than a single egg to bind things together. The white of a whole egg—harmless as it may seem—made the dough sticky. The difference was subtle, but the white also caused the baked cookie to have a slightly cakelike crumb and a firmer, drier feel than we cared for. A lone yolk was all the cookies wanted or needed.

Molasses is a mildly acidic ingredient, so baking soda, an alkali that reacts with the acidity of the molasses to provide lift, is the logical leavener for these cookies. In our testing, cookies with too little baking soda were flat and failed to develop those attractive fault lines. The proper amount of baking soda (1 teaspoon) gave the cookies nice height—a pleasure to sink your teeth into—and a winsome appearance, with large, meandering fissures.

It was time to refine the flavor of the cookies. A teaspoon of vanilla extract complemented generous amounts of sharp, spicy ground ginger and warm, soothing cinnamon. Cloves, rich and fragrant, and allspice, sweet and mysterious, were added, but in more judicious quantities. Nutmeg was pedestrian and had little to offer. Finely and freshly ground black pepper, however, added some intrigue—a soupçon of heat against the deep, bittersweet flavor of the molasses.

To shape the molasses cookies, we rolled generous heaping tablespoons of dough into balls, coating them with granulated sugar, which, after baking, gave the cookies a frosted

sparkle. Out of a 375-degree oven, the cookies were perfect—the edges were slightly crisped and the interiors soft and chewy. We determined that the cookies must be baked one sheet at a time since cookies baked on the lower rack inevitably baked up puffed and smooth rather than craggy and cracked.

Most important, we noted that the cookies must come out of the oven when they appear substantially underdone, otherwise their soft, moist, chewy texture will harden upon cooling. Whisk them out when the edges are hardly set, the centers are still soft and puffy, and the dough looks shiny and raw between the cracks. The cookies finish baking with residual heat, so don't shortchange them of a five-minute repose on the baking sheet before removal to the cooling rack.

While the spicy aroma lingers in the kitchen, bite into a warm, soft, chewy molasses spice cookie. These cookies may be out of style, but they are definitely not out of favor.

WHAT WE LEARNED: Use a blend of molasses, light brown sugar, and granulated sugar for good flavor and proper spreading of the dough in the oven. Use only a single egg yolk to keep the cookies from puffing up as they bake. Finally, bake just one cookie sheet at a time and take the cookies out of the oven when they still look underdone to guarantee a moist, chewy texture.

MOLASSES SPICE COOKIES makes about 22 cookies

For best flavor, make sure that your spices are fresh. Light or mild molasses gives the cookies a milder flavor; for a stronger flavor, use dark molasses. (See the Tasting Lab on page 277 for more information about molasses.) Either way, measure molasses in a liquid measure. If you find that the dough sticks to your palms as you shape the balls, moisten your hands occasionally in a bowl filled with cold tap water and shake off the excess. Bake the cookies one sheet at a time; if baked two at a time, the cookies started on the bottom rack won't develop the attractive cracks. Remove the cookies from the oven when they still look slightly raw and underbaked. If you plan to glaze the cookies (see recipe below), save the parchment paper used to line the cookie sheet during baking.

⅓   cup (about 2½ ounces) granulated sugar, plus
     ½ cup for dipping
2¼ cups (11¼ ounces) unbleached all-purpose
     flour
1   teaspoon baking soda
1½   teaspoons ground cinnamon
1½   teaspoons ground ginger
½   teaspoon ground cloves
¼   teaspoon ground allspice
¼   teaspoon finely ground black pepper
¼   teaspoon salt
12   tablespoons (1½ sticks) unsalted
     butter, softened
⅓   cup packed (2¾ ounces) dark brown sugar
1   large egg yolk
1   teaspoon vanilla extract
½   cup light or dark molasses

1. Adjust oven rack to middle position and heat oven to 375 degrees. Line two baking sheets with parchment paper. Place ½ cup sugar for dipping in 8- or 9-inch cake pan.

2. Whisk flour, baking soda, spices, and salt in medium bowl until thoroughly combined; set aside.

3. In standing mixer fitted with paddle attachment, beat butter with brown sugar and remaining ⅓ cup granulated sugar at medium-high speed until light and fluffy, about 3 minutes. Reduce speed to medium-low and add yolk and vanilla; increase speed to medium and beat until incorporated, about 20 seconds. Reduce speed to medium-low and add molasses; beat until fully incorporated, about 20 seconds, scraping bottom and sides of bowl once with rubber spatula. Reduce speed to lowest setting; add flour mixture and beat until just incorporated, about 30 seconds, scraping down bowl once. Give dough a final stir by hand to ensure that no pockets of flour remain at bottom. Dough will be soft.

4. Using tablespoon measure, scoop heaping tablespoon of dough and roll it between your palms into 1¼- to 1½-inch ball; drop ball into cake pan with sugar and repeat to form about 4 balls. Toss balls in sugar to coat and set on prepared baking sheet, spacing them about 2 inches apart. Repeat with remaining dough.

5. Bake, one sheet at a time and reversing position of baking sheet from front to back halfway through baking, until cookies are browned, still puffy, and edges have begun to set but centers are still soft (cookies will look raw between the cracks and seem underdone), about 11 minutes. Do not overbake.

6. Cool the cookies on baking sheet for 5 minutes, then use wide metal spatula to transfer cookies to wire rack; cool cookies to room temperature and serve.

VARIATIONS

MOLASSES SPICE COOKIES WITH DARK RUM GLAZE

For the glaze, start by adding the smaller amount of rum; if the glaze is too thick to drizzle, whisk in up to an additional ½ tablespoon rum.

Follow recipe for Molasses Spice Cookies. When completely cool, return rack with cookies to cooled parchment-lined baking sheets. Whisk 1 cup confectioners' sugar (about 4 ounces) and 2½ to 3 tablespoons dark rum in medium bowl until smooth. Drizzle glaze over cookies with soup spoon (see illustration below), dipping spoon into glaze as necessary. Transfer cookies to wire rack and allow glaze to dry, 10 to 15 minutes.

MOLASSES SPICE COOKIES WITH ORANGE ESSENCE

The orange zest in the sugar coating causes the sugar to become sticky and take on a light orange hue, giving the baked cookies a unique frosty look.

In workbowl of food processor, process ⅔ cup granulated sugar and 2 teaspoons grated orange zest until pale orange, about 10 seconds; transfer sugar to 8- or 9-inch cake pan and set aside. Follow recipe for Molasses-Spice cookies, adding 1 teaspoon grated orange zest to dough along with molasses and substituting orange sugar for granulated sugar when coating dough balls in step 4.

TECHNIQUE: Glazing Cookies

Once the cookies are completely cool, return them to the parchment-lined baking sheets. Dip a spoon into the glaze, then move the spoon over the cookies so that glaze drizzles down onto them.

TASTING LAB: Molasses

MOLASSES, A BYPRODUCT OF THE CANE SUGAR–REFINING process, is the liquid that is drawn off after the cane juice has been boiled and undergone crystallization. The resultant molasses is then subjected to subsequent boilings; with each boiling, the molasses grows increasingly dark, bitter, and potent, as more sugar is extracted from it.

There are three types of molasses. Light molasses comes from the first boiling, dark molasses from the second, and blackstrap from the third. In the past, sulfur dioxide was often added to molasses to clarify it. Although this process made molasses more attractive, it also added an unappealing flavor. Today, most molasses, including all major brands, is unsulfured.

Grocery store shelves are not packed with molasses options. Grandma's is the baseline offering, and Brer Rabbit brand can be found in well-stocked supermarkets nationwide. Blackstrap molasses is commonly available in natural foods stores. We made cookies with five different bottles of molasses. Tasters liked both brands of light and dark molasses but found blackstrap molasses too overpowering in a cookie. The moral of the story: Use either light or dark molasses based on your preference for a mellow or intense molasses flavor.

Rating Molasses

WE TESTED FIVE BRANDS OF MOLASSES IN OUR molasses spice cookies. Tasters evaluated the cookies on both color and flavor. All of the brands, except one, were highly rated and received similar scores. All brands are available in supermarkets and/or natural foods stores.

RECOMMENDED
1. Grandma's Original Molasses
$2.39 for 12 ounces

Cookies made with this light molasses had a warm bronze color. The molasses flavor was solid, decently rich, and "nicely balanced." Good choice for those who like molasses but not its bitterness.

RECOMMENDED
2. Grandma's Robust Molasses
$2.39 for 12 ounces

This dark molasses filled the cookies with both dark color (akin to a chocolate cookie) and deep flavor. They were criticized as "too strong" by one taster but touted as "spicy and rich" by another.

RECOMMENDED
3. Brer Rabbit Mild Flavor Molasses
$3.75 for 12 ounces

Cookies made with this molasses turned a lovely sepia color. The cookies garnered comments such as "complex and nuanced" and "fruity" with a "clean finish."

RECOMMENDED
4. Brer Rabbit Full Flavor Molasses
$3.75 for 12 ounces

These cookies had an even richer sepia color than those made with mild Brer Rabbit. "Straight-up" and "smooth" molasses flavor without even so much as a trace of bitterness.

NOT RECOMMENDED
5. Plantation Blackstrap Molasses
$2.99 for 15 ounces

A couple of tasters admired the potent molasses flavor, but most others remarked that the molasses was so overwhelming that the spices could hardly be tasted. User discretion advised.

LEMON meringue pie

Lemon meringue pie is a three-component recipe:
crust, lemon filling, and meringue. Each part of this recipe can be
tricky to prepare. Without the weight of a filling to keep it in place, the
pie shell can shrink or balloon in the oven as it prebakes. The lemon
filling can be too loose, too gluey, too bland, or too puckery. And the
meringue topping can exude liquid and break down, ruining the filling
and crust underneath.

Our challenge was to take each component of this recipe and perfect it. We started with the crust and developed a method for blind-
baking a pie shell that works every time. A secret ingredient helps this
crust remain crisp when filled. The filling proved to be rather simple. It
requires a careful balance of ingredients to get the right texture and flavor, but the technique is straightforward. The meringue was another
story. We tested it nearly 30 times before we hit upon a method that
ensures the underside (next to the filling) is fully cooked without causing the top of the meringue to burn.

THE RECIPES
Lemon Meringue Pie

EQUIPMENT CORNER
Rolling Pins

TASTING LAB
Store-Bought Pie Crusts

278 HERE IN AMERICA'S TEST KITCHEN

Real pie weights (made from either metal or ceramic) are heavier than the usual stand-ins (rice or dried beans) and do a better job of preventing empty pie shells from ballooning in the oven.

LEMON MERINGUE PIE

WHAT WE WANTED: The ideal lemon meringue pie has a rich filling that balances the airy meringue without detracting from the flavor of lemon. The lemon filling should be soft but not runny, firm enough to cut but not stiff and gelatinous. The meringue itself should not break down and puddle on the bottom or "weep" on top, not even on rainy days. Finally, the crust must be crisp, not soggy.

Lemon meringue pie begins with a fully baked pie shell. Baking an unfilled pie pastry, called blind baking, can be the ultimate culinary nightmare. Without the weight of a filling, a pastry shell placed in a hot oven can shrink dramatically, fill with air pockets, and puff up like a linoleum floor after a flood. The result? A shrunken, uneven shell that can hold only part of the filling intended for it.

We started with our favorite pie dough recipe and began to investigate the effects of resting the dough (in the refrigerator or the freezer), docking it (pricking the dough before it bakes), and weighting the crust as it bakes to keep it anchored in place. All three tricks are used by professional bakers to prevent common problems encountered when blind-baking a crust.

We found that refrigeration does the best job of preventing shrinkage. Pastry shrinkage is caused by gluten. Simply put, when you mix flour with water, the proteins in the flour react to form elastic strands of gluten. The strands of gluten in the dough get stretched during the rolling process, and if they are not allowed to relax after rolling, the pastry will snap back like a rubber band when baked, resulting in a shrunken, misshapen shell. Resting allows the tension in the taut strands of dough to ease so that they remain stretched and do not shrink back when heated.

This process does not occur, however, if the dough is immediately placed in the freezer to rest after rolling. When frozen, the water in the crust solidifies, freezing the gluten

in place so it is not free to relax. When the dough is baked, the tense, stretched strands of gluten snap back, causing the crust to shrink.

We might have concluded that pie dough should be refrigerated and not frozen if we hadn't noticed that the frozen crusts, although shrunken, were much flakier than the refrigerated crusts. Pastry is made up of layers of dough (protein and starch from the flour combined with water) and fat. Dough and fat have different heat capacities. When you place the pastry in the oven after freezing it (rather than just refrigerating it), the dough heats up and starts to set relatively quickly in comparison with the time it takes for the butter to melt and then vaporize, as butter has a much higher proportion of water than the dough. As a result, by the time the water in the butter starts to turn to steam, the dough is well into its setting phase. The air spaces occupied by the frozen butter, now that it has largely turned to steam, hold their shape because the dough is far along in the baking process. And this makes for a very flaky pie crust.

Dough that has been refrigerated, on the other hand, is not as well set by the time the butter vaporizes. The air pockets disappear as the soft dough sinks into the spaces left by the butter. We came to a simple conclusion: First refrigerate the pie shell to relax the gluten, thus solving the problem of shrinkage during baking, then pop the dough in the freezer to improve flakiness.

This bit of science led us to yet another discovery. It is common knowledge that lard or vegetable shortening such as Crisco produces very flaky doughs. In fact, we use a combination of butter and shortening in our recipe because of the improvement in texture over an all-butter crust (the butter is what gives the crust its flavor). The explanation for this phenomenon is simple. Lard and Crisco don't melt as quickly as butter when heated. Therefore, they retain their shape as the dough sets up, keeping the layers of pastry separate.

While this combination chilling method prevents

are also better heat conductors and promote more thorough browning of the pastry.

We got the most consistent results and even browning by baking the crust in the middle rack at a constant 375 degrees. At higher temperatures the pastry was prone to overbrowning and burned in spots, while lower temperatures caused the edges to brown well before the bottom did. More important than temperature and placement, though, was cooking time.

There are two stages in prebaking. In the first stage, the dough is baked with a lining and weights. This stage usually takes about 25 minutes; the objective is to cook the dough until it sets, at which point it can hold its shape without assistance. When the dough loses its wet look, turns off-white from its original pale yellow, and the edges just start to take on a very light brown color, the dough is set. If you have any doubts, you can carefully (the dough is hot) touch the side of the shell to make sure the crust is firm. If you remove the pie weights too soon, the sides of the dough will slip down, ruining the pie shell. For the second stage, the foil and weights are removed, and the baking continues until the crust is deep golden brown.

We discovered one final trick when baking the pie shell. The lemon filling tends to make even a fully baked, golden brown crust a bit soggy. We discovered that coating the dough with graham cracker crumbs while rolling it out helps counter any ill effects from the filling and the crust remains crisp longer.

With the pie shell baked, we focused next on the filling. The standard ingredients in lemon meringue pie were established some time ago: sugar, water (or sometimes milk), cornstarch (sometimes mixed with flour), egg yolks, lemon juice (and usually zest), and a little butter. To our tastes, the straightforward lemon flavor of the water-based filling is pleasant, but it is also one-dimensional, lacking depth. Milk, however, subdues the lemon flavor. The solution is to rely

shrinkage, ballooning can occur when air pockets form beneath the crust. Typically, bakers dock (or prick) the dough with the tines of a fork before it goes into the oven. However, we found that docking was not necessary as long as the dough is weighted. Because weighting is a must—it not only prevents ballooning but keeps the shell, especially the sides, in place as it bakes—we do not bother to dock pastry dough. Some professional bakers swear by "official" pie weights, while others make do with rice or dried beans. We found that metal or ceramic pie weights do a better job than rice or beans. They are heavier and therefore more effective at preventing the pastry from puffing. Pie weights primarily on water and a lot of egg yolks (we use six rather than the more conventional three), eliminating the milk altogether. This has another benefit: The extra yolks allow you to cut back on cornstarch and still achieve a firm filling.

The meringue is much more tricky. On any given day it can shrink, bead, puddle, deflate, burn, sweat, break down, or turn rubbery. Most cookbooks don't even attempt to deal with the problems of meringue. They follow the standard recipe—granulated sugar and cream of tartar beaten slowly into the egg whites—assuming, apparently, that there is no way around the flaws. After making 30-something lemon meringue pies, we're not sure we blame anyone for skirting the issue. For as easy as it was to figure out the perfect lemon filling, the meringue remains, finally, only a manageable mystery.

The puddling underneath the meringue is from undercooking. Undercooked whites break down and return to their liquid state. The beading on top of the pie is from overcooking. This near-the-surface overcooking of the meringue causes the proteins in the egg white to coagulate, squeezing out moisture, which then surfaces as tears or beads. This double dilemma might seem insurmountable, but we hit upon a solution.

If the filling is piping hot when the meringue is applied, the underside of the meringue will not undercook; if the oven temperature is relatively low, the top of the meringue won't overcook. Baking the pie in a relatively cool oven also produces the best-looking, most evenly browned meringue. To stabilize the meringue further, we like to beat in a tiny bit of cornstarch; if you do this, the meringue will not weep, even on hot, humid days.

WHAT WE LEARNED: Apply graham cracker crumbs to keep the crust crisp. Refrigerate and freeze the pie dough before baking for a crust that won't shrink and is extra flaky. Use water rather than milk in the filling to keep the focus on the lemon juice and zest. Apply the meringue to piping-hot filling and bake the pie in a cool oven for perfectly cooked meringue that won't puddle or weep.

LEMON MERINGUE PIE serves 8

Make the pie shell, let it cool, and then begin work on the filling. As soon as the filling is made, cover it with plastic wrap to keep it hot and then start working on the meringue topping. You want to add hot filling to the pie shell, apply the meringue topping, and then quickly get the pie into the oven.

graham cracker–coated pie shell

1¼	cups (6¼ ounces) unbleached all-purpose flour
½	teaspoon salt
1	tablespoon sugar
3	tablespoons all-vegetable shortening, chilled
4	tablespoons unsalted butter, chilled, cut into ¼-inch pieces
4–5	tablespoons ice water
½	cup graham cracker crumbs

lemon filling

1	cup (7 ounces) sugar
⅛	teaspoon salt
1½	cups water
½	cup juice from 2 or 3 lemons (see illustrations on page 283)
6	large egg yolks
¼	cup cornstarch
1	tablespoon grated zest from 1 lemon
2	tablespoons unsalted butter

meringue topping

1	tablespoon cornstarch
⅓	cup water
¼	teaspoon cream of tartar
½	cup (3½ ounces) sugar
4	large egg whites
½	teaspoon vanilla extract

1. FOR THE PIE SHELL: Pulse flour, salt, and sugar in food processor fitted with steel blade until combined. Add shortening and process until mixture has texture of coarse sand, about 10 seconds. Scatter butter pieces over flour mixture; cut butter into flour until mixture is pale yellow and resembles coarse crumbs, with butter bits no larger than small peas, about ten 1-second pulses. Turn mixture into medium bowl.

2. Sprinkle 4 tablespoons ice water over mixture. With blade of rubber spatula, use folding motion to mix. Press down on dough with broad side of spatula until dough sticks together, adding up to 1 tablespoon more ice water if it will not come together. Flatten dough into 4-inch disk. Wrap in plastic and refrigerate at least 1 hour, or up to 2 days, before rolling.

3. If dough has been refrigerated longer than 1 hour, let stand at room temperature until malleable. Generously sprinkle work area with 2 tablespoons graham cracker crumbs. Place dough on work surface and scatter more crumbs over dough. Roll dough to 12-inch disk, sprinkling remaining crumbs underneath and on top of dough as it is rolled. Dough should be heavily coated with crumbs. Transfer dough to pie plate by rolling dough around rolling pin and unrolling it over 9-inch pie plate or by folding dough in quarters, then placing dough point in center of pie plate and unfolding. Working around circumference of pie plate, ease dough into pan corners by gently lifting dough edges with one hand while pressing around pan bottom with other hand. Trim dough edges to extend about ½ inch beyond rim of pan. Fold overhang under itself; flute dough or press tines of fork against dough to it flatten it against rim of pie plate. Refrigerate dough-lined pie plate until firm, about 40 minutes, then freeze until very cold, about 20 minutes.

4. Adjust oven rack to lower-middle position and heat oven to 375 degrees. Remove dough-lined pie plate from freezer and press doubled 12-inch piece of heavy-duty foil inside pie shell and fold edges of foil to shield fluted edge; distribute 2 cups ceramic or metal pie weights over foil. Bake, leaving foil and weights in place until dough looks dry and is light in color, 25 to 30 minutes. Carefully remove foil and weights by gathering corners of foil and pulling up and out.

Continue baking until deep golden brown, about 12 minutes more. Transfer pie shell to wire rack.

5. FOR THE FILLING: Bring ¾ cup sugar, salt, water, and lemon juice to simmer over medium-high heat in medium, nonreactive saucepan, stirring occasionally with wooden spoon to ensure sugar dissolves. Meanwhile, whisk yolks, remaining ¼ cup sugar, cornstarch, and lemon zest in medium bowl until thick and combined. Gradually whisk simmering liquid into egg mixture to temper, then return mixture to saucepan and bring to boil over medium heat, stirring constantly; boil until thickened, 1 to 2 minutes. Off heat, whisk in butter. Place plastic wrap directly on surface of filling to keep hot and prevent skin from forming.

6. FOR THE MERINGUE: Mix cornstarch with water in small saucepan; bring to simmer, whisking occasionally at beginning and more frequently as mixture thickens. When mixture starts to simmer and turn translucent, remove from heat. Let cool while beating egg whites.

7. Heat oven to 325 degrees. Mix cream of tartar and sugar together in small bowl. Beat egg whites and vanilla in bowl of standing mixer until frothy. Beat in sugar mixture, 1 tablespoon at a time; until sugar is incorporated and mixture forms soft peaks. Add cornstarch mixture, 1 tablespoon at a time; continue to beat meringue to stiff peaks. Remove plastic from filling and return to very low heat during last minute or so of beating meringue (to ensure filling is hot).

8. Pour filling into pie shell. Using rubber spatula, immediately distribute meringue evenly around edge and then center of pie to keep it from sinking into filling (see illustration 1, at left). Make sure meringue attaches to pie crust to prevent shrinking (see illustration 2, at left). Use spoon to create peaks all over meringue. Bake pie until meringue is golden brown, about 20 minutes. Transfer to wire rack and cool to room temperature. Serve.

EQUIPMENT CORNER: Rolling Pins

A GOOD ROLLING PIN CAN QUALIFY AS A FAMILY heirloom. But if your grandmother's tried-and-true pin has not been passed down to your kitchen and you want to buy one, you have quite an array of choices. Should you buy a pin with a nonstick coating, one that is made of marble, or one with ergonomic handles? Could any one pin really make a difference in your baking? We tested eight models readily found in kitchen and hardware stores and decided on a definite favorite.

We purchased two wooden pins without handles—one with tapered ends, and one that was straight. Three other wooden pins had standard dowel-type handles with ball bearings and represented three different sizes: the largest weighed in at 3½ pounds and was 15 inches long, another was a quite small 1½ pounds and 10½ inches long, and the last was in between these two, at 2½ pounds and 11 ½ inches long. We purchased three novelty pins—one marble, one nonstick-coated aluminum, and one wooden model with

TECHNIQUE:
Applying Meringue Topping

1. Start by placing dabs of meringue evenly around the edge of the pie. Once the edge of the pie is covered, fill in the center with the remaining meringue.

2. Use a rubber spatula to anchor the meringue to the edge of the crust or it may pull away and shrink in the oven.

ergonomic comfort grips. The grips on this last model were made of molded plastic and had the feel of a steering wheel, with thumbs placed on top and wrists straight. Prices ranged from $6.99 to $35.99.

We decided to test the pins on three kinds of dough: a standard pie dough, a delicate sugar cookie dough, and a resilient yeasted coffee cake dough. We were particularly interested in the versatility of these pins—whether they could perform equally well in all tasks. No one wants more than one pin in the kitchen. For all three doughs, we were looking for a fast, easy roll—one that allowed us to feel the dough and did not require application of too much pressure.

Almost immediately a favorite and a least favorite became evident. The tapered wood pin without handles took first place. Testers could easily turn and pivot the tapered pin and apply pressure as needed across the dough. In addition, this pin measured 20 inches long, making it suitable for any task. Many of the other wooden pins were too short (some just 10 or 11 inches in length) and could not be used to roll out large pieces of dough.

The marble pin was a bit heavy over delicate sugar cookie dough, but this pin could be refrigerated before handling buttery doughs, which was a plus. It landed in second place. The ergonomic pin landed near the bottom of the ratings, as did the nonstick model, which was much too light and most definitely not stickfree.

TASTING LAB: Store-Bought Pie Crusts

EVERYONE KNOWS THAT HOMEMADE PIE CRUST OFFERS the best combination of buttery flavor and flaky texture. The ingredient list couldn't be shorter—just flour, fat, sugar, salt, and ice water—and making the dough takes just seconds in a food processor. However, few tasks inspire as much fear, even among seasoned cooks, as does rolling out pie pastry. It's no surprise then that many cooks turn to store-bought frozen or refrigerated pie crust. We wondered if any of these products could compete with the real thing made at home.

Rating Rolling Pins

WE SELECTED EIGHT PINS AND USED THEM TO ROLL OUT TENDER SUGAR COOKIE DOUGH, STANDARD PIE DOUGH, AND stiff yeasted coffee cake dough. The rolling pins are listed in order of preference. See www.cooksillustrated.com for up-to-date prices and mail-order sources for top-rated products.

RECOMMENDED

1. Thorpe Solid French Pie Rolling Pin

$6.99

This 20-inch tapered wooden pin was a joy to work with. Testers could easily turn and pivot this pin and apply pressure as they liked all across the dough. This pin is also great for whacking cold, rested doughs to soften them up for rolling.

RECOMMENDED WITH RESERVATIONS

2. Himark Classic White Marble Rolling Pin

$8.99

This marble pin was a little too short (just 10 inches long) and ran a bit heavy over delicate dough (it weighed in at a whopping 4 1/2 pounds), but it was a smooth performer in all other areas. A bonus is that it stays cold after refrigeration for working with particularly buttery doughs.

RECOMMENDED WITH RESERVATIONS

3. Thorpe Hardwood Rolling Pin

$31.99

This standard wood rolling pin with handles had good speed, but we needed to use a bit more pressure than expected, as it is so much larger (3 inches in diameter) and heavier than the other pins tested. It always felt a bit out of control.

RECOMMENDED WITH RESERVATIONS

4. Williams-Sonoma Straight Baker's Pin

$14.00

Some testers (with larger hands) liked this solid, straight wooden pin, but most felt that it was too thick. This pin was awkward to use, and it was hard to get a sense of how the dough was responding.

NOT RECOMMENDED

5. Williams-Sonoma Maple Rolling Pin

$32.99

This pin was shorter than most other wooden models tested and therefore less useful for rolling out medium or large pieces of dough. Testers found it necessary to exert a fair amount of pressure on the handles of this lightweight pin.

NOT RECOMMENDED

6. Foley Rolling Pin

$11.99

This small pin (just 10 1/2 inches long) was not a good performer. It was both too light and too short, which necessitated putting a lot of pressure on the handles. It was good for neither the doughs nor testers' wrists.

NOT RECOMMENDED

7. Comprep Comfort Pin

$35.99

The plastic ergonomic handles on this wooden pin not only looked silly, but they were difficult to work with and offered no benefit whatsoever. If this pin was used by someone with long fingernails, the grip would be both painful and unworkable.

NOT RECOMMENDED

8. Fox Run Non-Stick Rolling Pin

$9.99

All three doughs stuck to this aluminum pin with a nonstick coating. The pin was ineffective at all tasks. Light and flimsy, it could also be dented or easily nicked.

We also wondered (especially given the fact that some cooks will never make their own pie crust) if some of these products are better (or less terrible) than others.

To find out, we purchased five pie crusts, baked them according to package directions, and compared them with our homemade pie shell, which we prebaked according to our recipe. (We omitted the dusting of graham cracker crumbs so as not to confuse matters.)

As expected, tasters had no trouble picking out the homemade pie crust. The texture was flaky and the flavor was buttery and natural. None of the store-bought crusts came close in terms of texture, and only one was deemed to have decent flavor.

The Whole Foods crust was too crumbly, tender, and moist, but tasters commented on the "buttery flavor" of this crust. Just as important, tasters did not complain about odd, chemical flavors, which plagued the other crusts. Not surprisingly, the Whole Foods crust is the only one to have an ingredient list close to that for homemade pie dough—just flour, butter, and water.

The four other store-bought pie crusts were made with either partially hydrogenated vegetable shortening or partially hydrogenated lard. As might be expected, tasters found these crusts to be lacking in flavor. Perhaps because these crusts are made without butter, manufacturers add other ingredients to compensate, including corn syrup and food colorings. Our tasters disliked these crusts, describing them with terms such as "chemical aftertaste," "plastic," "stale," "rancid," and "fake."

None of the store-bought crusts, including our "winner," wowed tasters with their texture. None came close to our flaky ideal. Tasters used terms like "greasy," "brittle," "tough," and "mushy" when describing the texture of the store-bought crusts.

For the best flavor and texture, we recommend making your own pie dough. If that's not an option, look for an all-butter crust at an upscale supermarket or gourmet store. Based on our experience, this crust may not have the best texture, but it probably will taste pretty good.

Rating Store-Bought Pie Crusts

WE PURCHASED FIVE STORE-BOUGHT PIE CRUSTS (four frozen, one refrigerated) and baked them according to the package directions. Tasters were asked to evaluate each crust in terms of both flavor and texture. The crusts are listed in order of preference and are available in supermarkets.

RECOMMENDED IN A PINCH
1. Whole Foods Pie Shells

$3.99 for two 9-inch crusts

Tasters praised the "buttery flavor" in this supermarket brand. Made with just flour, butter, and water, this crust is free of chemical flavors that plagued the rest of the field.

NOT RECOMMENDED
2. Oronoque Orchards Regular Pie Crusts

$2.59 for three 9-inch crusts

This crust made with vegetable shortening was faulted for its "bland," "dull," "starchy" flavor and chemical aftertaste.

NOT RECOMMENDED
3. Pillsbury Pie Crusts

$2.50 for two 9-inch crusts

Unlike the other crusts tested, this one is sold in the refrigerator case. The crust is folded in quarters—you unfold the crust and fit it into your own pie plate. Tasters thought this well-known crust was "sweet," "greasy," and "stale."

NOT RECOMMENDED
4. Pillsbury Pet-Ritz Deep-Dish Pie Crusts

$1.25 for two 9-inch crusts

A few tasters faulted this crust for being "bland;" most were more harsh, complaining about "bad shortening taste."

NOT RECOMMENDED
5. Mrs. Smith's 9" Deep Dish Pie Crusts

$2.50 for three 9-inch crusts

Tasters detected unusual flavors here, which they described as "fake sour taste," "strange aftertaste," and "uncooked sweet flavor."

Mashed Sweet Potatoes **page 207**

Pan-Roasted Chicken **page 107**

American Potato Salad with Hard-Boiled Eggs and Sweet Pickles **page 187**

Basic Cranberry Sauce **page 211**

Grill-Roasted Turkey **page 204**

Red Plums and Figs with Brandy-Cinnamon Reduction **page 243**

Banana Bread **page 251**

Sour Cream Coffee Cake with Brown Sugar–Pecan Streusel **page 234**

Quick Cinnamon Buns with Buttermilk Icing **page 248**

Flourless Chocolate Cake **page 326**

298

Sour Cherry Cobbler **page 311**

Thick and Chewy Double-Chocolate Cookies **page 270**

Lemon Meringue Pie **page 282**

New York–Style Cheesecake with Strawberry Topping **page 332**

Individual Hot Fudge Pudding Cakes **page 321**

We went through crates of strawberries
before hitting on the best way to
prepare them for shortcake.

SHORTCAKE & cobbler

CHAPTER 24

What could be more all-American than strawberry shortcake? But when the "cake" consists of store-bought spongy rounds with no flavor and the berries are rock-hard specimens trucked in from thousands of miles away, strawberry shortcake can go very wrong. Luckily, it's easy to fix these problems. Start with a homemade shortcake and use only ripe, juicy berries. We'll show you how.

Cherry cobbler can be trickier. At least with strawberries, you know that any fruit that tastes good will make a decent dessert. But with cherries, the home cook has no such luck. Sweet Bing cherries become insipid when baked. Sour cherries are a must. But where do you get sour cherries? The season seems to last only about three weeks in many parts of the country. Is there an acceptable jarred or canned alternative to fresh fruit?

To answer these questions, we made cherry cobblers in the dead of winter. We had crates of frozen berries shipped to the test kitchen. We talked to experts who had traveled behind the Iron Curtain in the 1980s searching for new cherry cultivars. We're happy to report that our efforts paid off.

STRAWBERRY SHORTCAKE

WHAT WE WANTED: A rich, cakey biscuit offset by juicy, sweet berries and mounds of whipped cream.

Shortcakes may seem similar to crisps and cobblers, but there is one important difference—the fruit is not cooked. For a true shortcake, sweetened fruit, usually strawberries, is spread between a split biscuit. A dollop or two of whipped cream is also added. The contrast of the cool fruit, warm and cakey biscuit halves, and chilled whipped cream places this dessert in a category by itself.

Because the fruit is not cooked, frozen fruit is not an option. The fruit must be ripe as well. Half-ripe berries will bake up fine in a pandowdy but will make a second-rate shortcake. Also, because the fruit is not baked, only softer fruits are appropriate. A pear or apple shortcake does not make sense. Strawberries are soft enough and have enough flavor to be used uncooked.

We don't like quartered or sliced strawberries in shortcake—they often slide off the split biscuit—but we don't like the look of a crushed fruit shortcake either. So we found a happy compromise by slicing most of the strawberries and then crushing the remaining portion of the berry mixture to unify the sliced fruit. The thick puree anchors the remaining whole or sliced fruit so that it won't slip off the split biscuit.

The rest of our testing for this recipe revolved mostly around the biscuit. Strawberry shortcake requires something different from the biscuit topping used in our cherry cobbler recipe. There, the fruit is so juicy and sweet that a light, tender biscuit works best. Shortcake, on the other hand, must be substantial enough to withstand splitting and layering with juicy fruit and whipped cream. It should be more dense and cakey. We assumed that a richer biscuit—that is, one made with eggs—would work best.

To make sure, we tried four very different recipes for sweetened biscuits—a baking powder version, with fat cut into flour, baking powder, salt, and sugar and then moistened with milk; a buttermilk biscuit, with buttermilk in place of milk and baking soda substituted for part of the baking powder; a cream biscuit, with heavy cream standing in for the milk and some of the fat; and an egg-enriched cream biscuit, with an egg and half-and-half replacing the milk. After sampling each, we felt that the egg-enriched biscuits had the advantage. The baking powder and buttermilk biscuits weren't rich enough. The cream biscuits were good looking but gummy inside. The egg and half-and-half biscuits were finer-textured and more cakelike.

With our general direction settled, we began to test individual ingredients. Because biscuits should be tender, we assumed that low-protein cake flour would deliver the best results. Defying our predictions, the cake flour biscuit came in last, with a meltingly tender but powdery and dry texture that was too much like shortbread. There was not enough gluten in this flour to support all the fat. Shortcake made with all-purpose flour were tender, moist, and cakey. They were our clear favorites, besting a combination of cake and all-purpose flours as well as the plain cake flour.

We then experimented with liquids, figuring that the egg might be crucial but maybe not the half-and-half, which had won in our initial test. Buttermilk made the biscuits too savory, while heavy cream made them squat and dense. Milk was fine, but the richer flavor of half-and-half made it our first choice.

The food processor is foolproof and is our preferred method for mixing biscuits. For cooks without a food processor, we suggest freezing the butter and then using a box grater to shave the butter into bits before cutting it into the flour.

When testing dough shaping, we made an interesting discovery. Although hand-formed biscuits look attractive, we found they were fairly easy to overwork, since warm hands can cause the dough's surface butter to melt. A biscuit cutter

requires less handling, and dough rounds cut this way develop a natural crack around the circumference during baking, making them easy to split by hand. We also realized we didn't need a rolling pin. Patting the dough to a thickness of ¾ inch on a floured work surface was fast and easy.

After cutting six perfect rounds of dough, we found that the scraps could be pulled together, kneaded, and cut to get one or two more rounds. These shortcakes, however, will be a little tougher and less attractive than those from the first cutting.

WHAT WE LEARNED: Mash some of the berries and slice the rest for a chunky puree that won't slide off the biscuits. Add an egg and half-and-half to make a biscuit rich enough and cakey enough for dessert.

STRAWBERRY SHORTCAKE serves 6

Start the recipe by preparing the fruit, then set the fruit aside while preparing the biscuits to allow the juices to become syrupy. We find that pasteurized cream has a better flavor than ultrapasteurized cream. Many organic brands are pasteurized.

fruit

8	cups hulled strawberries
6	tablespoons (2⅔ ounces) sugar

shortcake

2	cups (10 ounces) unbleached all-purpose flour, plus more for work surface and biscuit cutter
5	tablespoons (about 2¼ ounces) sugar
1	tablespoon baking powder
½	teaspoon salt
8	tablespoons unsalted butter, chilled, cut into ½-inch cubes
1	large egg, lightly beaten
½	cup plus 1 tablespoon half-and-half or milk
1	large egg white, lightly beaten

whipped cream

1	cup chilled heavy cream, preferably pasteurized or pasteurized organic
1	tablespoon granulated sugar
1	teaspoon vanilla extract

1. FOR THE FRUIT: Place 3 cups hulled berries in large bowl and crush with potato masher. Slice remaining 5 cups berries and stir into crushed berries along with sugar. Set fruit aside to macerate for at least 30 minutes and up to 2 hours.

2. FOR THE SHORTCAKE: Adjust oven rack to lower-middle position and heat oven to 425 degrees. In workbowl of food processor fitted with metal blade, pulse flour, 3 tablespoons sugar, baking powder, and salt to combine. Scatter butter pieces over and process until mixture resembles coarse meal, about fifteen 1-second pulses. Transfer to medium bowl.

3. Mix beaten egg with half-and-half in measuring cup. Pour egg mixture into bowl with flour mixture. Combine with rubber spatula until large clumps form. Turn mixture onto floured work surface and lightly knead until it comes together.

4. Use your fingertips to pat dough into 9 by 6-inch rectangle about ¾ inch thick, being careful not to overwork dough. Flour 2¾-inch biscuit cutter and cut out 6 dough rounds. Place rounds 1 inch apart on small baking sheet, brush tops with egg white, and sprinkle with remaining 2 tablespoons sugar. (Biscuits can be covered and refrigerated for up to 2 hours before baking.)

5. Bake until shortcakes are golden brown, 12 to 14 minutes. Place baking sheet on wire rack and cool cakes until warm, about 10 minutes.

6. FOR THE WHIPPED CREAM: As soon as shortcakes go into oven, place nonreactive, deep bowl and beaters of electric mixer in freezer for 20 minutes. (If freezer is too crowded to accommodate bowl, place beaters in bowl, fill with ice water, and chill on counter. When bowl and beaters are well chilled, dump out ice water and dry thoroughly.)

7. While biscuits are cooling, remove bowl from freezer and add cream, sugar, and vanilla. Beat on low speed until small bubbles form, about 30 seconds. Increase speed to medium and continue beating until beaters leave a trail, about 30 seconds. Increase speed to high and continue beating until cream is smooth, thick, and nearly doubled in volume, about 20 seconds for soft peaks.

8. TO ASSEMBLE: When shortcakes have cooled slightly, split them in half crosswise (see illustration below). Place each cake bottom on individual serving plate. Spoon portion of fruit and then dollop of whipped cream over each cake bottom. Cap with cake top and serve immediately.

TECHNIQUE: Hulling Strawberries

If you don't own a huller, you can improvise with a melon baller or ¼ teaspoon measure. We also use a plastic drinking straw for this job. Just push the straw through the bottom of the berry and up to the leafy stem. The straw will remove the core as well as the leafy top in one motion.

TECHNIQUE: Splitting Shortcake

When the shortcakes have cooled, look for a natural crack around the circumference. Gently insert your fingers into the crack and split the shortcake in half.

CHERRY COBBLER

WHAT WE WANTED: **Real cherry flavor paired with a tender, feather-light, deeply browned biscuit topping.**

A fleet of tender biscuits on a sea of sweet fruit, good cobblers hold their own against fancy fruit desserts. But unlike fancy fruit desserts, cobblers come together in a couple of quick steps and can be dished up hot, ready to hit the dance floor with a scoop of vanilla ice cream. Sour cherries have sufficient acidity to cook up well and become truly expressive with a touch of sugar and some heat. (Sweet eating cherries, like Bings, lose their flavor when cooked.) Because fresh sour cherries are so hard to find (their season lasts just a few weeks in summer), we tested a half-dozen alternatives (see the Tasting Lab on page 312 for details). Jarred sour cherries (specifically the Morello variety) beat out canned and frozen sour cherries as well as fresh cherries in various forms.

A cobbler should be juicy, but not swimming in juice, and it should taste like the fruit whose name it bears. Jarred cherries come awash in juices, which we would use to produce the sauce. Because jarred cherries have already been processed, they are already cooked: the less heat they're exposed to thereafter, the better. Straining off the juice, we dumped the drained contents of four 24-ounce jars of Morellos into a 13 by 9-inch baking dish, then thickened and sweetened 3 cups of the juice. The resulting flavor was a bit flat. We replaced 1 cup of the cherry juice with red wine and added a cinnamon stick, a pinch of salt, and a whiff of almond extract. Much better. Red wine and sour cherries have a natural affinity; the cinnamon stick added a fragrant woody depth; and, as with all fruits, salt performed its usual minor miracle. The almond extract brought the entire flavor experience up a couple of notches. For thickener we resolved to go with cornstarch, which could be mixed in with the sugar. The cherry juices were then brought to a simmer and poured over the waiting cherries and baked. Lightly thickened fruit is best; a cobbler shouldn't be thick enough to spread on toast.

We also had some requirements for the cobbles. We wanted them feather-light but deeply browned and crisp. This said a number of things to us. The first was: No eggs. Eggs would make our biscuits too heavy and substantial. (After working for years with the test kitchen's scone recipe, a light and tender English biscuit that uses no eggs, we felt supported in that expectation.) The second thing it said was buttermilk. Buttermilk biscuits are famously light and tender. The third precept came by way of a number of Southern recipes, which said a wet dough made a nice light biscuit. We baked several biscuit variations to confirm these notions, settling on all-purpose flour, a moderate amount of butter, small amounts of baking powder and soda, a touch of sugar (plus more on top for crunch), a wave of buttermilk, and a nice hot oven. Dispensing with rolling altogether, we simply dropped the biscuits onto the fruit with an ice cream scoop. The biscuits had a buttery lightness, a mild tang, and a crunchy, sugary top.

Not quite satisfied with their pale bellies touching the fruit, we undertook to bake the biscuits for 15 minutes on a baking sheet while the filling was coming together on the stove. We then wedded them to the fruit for only 10 minutes in the oven. By then the fruit (already hot from the cooked sauce) was bubbling around the biscuits, which were deeply browned on top and baked through underneath. Heaven in about a half-hour.

Jarred Morellos made a fine cobbler. But we were anxious to try fresh, and then summer finally came. Fresh sour cherries, we learned, are classified in two groups, amarelles and griottes. The former have lighter flesh—tan on the inside—and clear juices; the latter are dark—even black—with deep red juice. The best known examples of each group are Montmorency (an amarelle) and Morello (a griotte). Most tart cherries grown in the United States are Montmorency.

Those from Eastern Europe are Morello. However, as we researched this subject, we made an exciting discovery: Morello cherries had made their way to the United States.

In 1984, well before unrestricted travel and commerce in Eastern Bloc countries became commonplace, Dr. Amy Iezzoni, professor of horticulture at Michigan State University, traveled extensively throughout Hungary to locate a vigorous sour cherry cultivar she could bring home to Michigan. Having spent years hybridizing local sour cherry seedlings, Hungarian breeders were prepared to release new cultivars with improved characteristics.

Sure enough, Iezzoni returned home with a dazzling Morello cultivar, which she named Balaton (after a lake in its native environs). She enlisted it in her breeding program, currently the only sour cherry breeding program in the United States. Under her care, the Balaton has thrived in its new climate. Cherry trees prefer long winters, Iezzoni told us, as well as cooler spring and summer temperatures, which favor normal fruit and flower development and lower the incidence of disease. The moderating winds of Lake Michigan reduce the probability that cherry flowers will be killed by an early freeze, much as Europe's continental climate buffers harsh weather.

Unlike the fragile and perishable Montmorency (a 400-year-old cultivar that has not been subject to cross-breeding to make it more vigorous), Balaton cherries are robust enough once harvested to endure shipping well. Not only are they larger and plumper than Montmorency cherries, but their dark juices are beautiful and mysterious.

With this knowledge and some fresh cherries, we got to work in the test kitchen. To test available varieties, we used both Morellos and the more delicate Montmorencies.

And how were the cobblers with fresh cherries? Both varieties of fresh cherries graced the recipe, yielding cobblers with plump, gorgeous, deeply flavorful fruit. The Montmorency cherries bore a candy apple red and a flavor resonant with almond accents; the fresh Morellos were transcendent, with a smooth richness and complex flavor notes. If you can get your hands on fresh sour cherries

during their brief season in July, buy them—quickly—and start baking. And take heart. When the brief sour cherry season is over, jarred Morello cherries will create a cobbler that is almost as wonderful.

WHAT WE LEARNED: Jarred Morello cherries are the best year-round choice for a cobbler. Spike the cherry juices with red wine and cinnamon and thicken them with cornstarch. For really crisp biscuits, bake them separately for 15 minutes, then slide the biscuits over the warm cherry filling and bake just 10 minutes longer.

SOUR CHERRY COBBLER serves 12

Use the smaller amount of sugar in the filling if you prefer your fruit desserts on the tart side and the larger amount if you like them sweet. Serve with vanilla ice cream or lightly sweetened whipped cream.

biscuit topping

2	cups (10 ounces) unbleached all-purpose flour
6	tablespoons (2½ ounces) sugar plus additional 2 tablespoons for sprinkling
½	teaspoon baking powder
½	teaspoon baking soda
½	teaspoon salt
6	tablespoons cold unsalted butter, cut into ½-inch cubes
1	cup buttermilk

cherry filling

4	(24-ounce) jars Morello cherries, drained (about 8 cups drained cherries), 2 cups juice reserved
¾–1	cup (5¼ to 7 ounces) sugar
3	tablespoons plus 1 teaspoon cornstarch
	Pinch salt
1	cup dry red wine
1	(3-inch) stick cinnamon
¼	teaspoon almond extract

1. Adjust oven rack to middle position and heat oven to 425 degrees. Line baking sheet with parchment paper.

2. FOR THE BISCUIT TOPPING: In workbowl of food processor fitted with steel blade, pulse flour, 6 tablespoons sugar, baking powder, baking soda, and salt to combine. Scatter butter pieces over and process until mixture resembles coarse meal, about fifteen 1-second pulses. Transfer to medium bowl; add buttermilk and toss with rubber spatula to combine. Using a 1½- to 1¾-inch spring-loaded ice cream scoop, scoop 12 biscuits onto baking sheet, spacing them 1½ to 2 inches apart. Sprinkle biscuits evenly with 2 tablespoons sugar and bake until lightly browned on tops and bottoms, about 15 minutes. (Do not turn off oven.)

3. FOR THE CHERRY FILLING: Meanwhile, spread drained cherries in even layer in 13 by 9-inch glass baking dish. Stir sugar, cornstarch, and salt together in medium nonreactive saucepan. Whisk in reserved cherry juice and wine, and add cinnamon stick; set saucepan over medium-high heat, and cook, whisking frequently, until mixture simmers and thickens, about 5 minutes. Discard cinnamon stick, stir in almond extract, and pour hot liquid over cherries in baking dish.

4. TO ASSEMBLE: Arrange hot biscuits in 3 rows of 4 over warm filling. Bake cobbler until filling is bubbling and biscuits are deep golden brown, about 10 minutes. Cool on wire rack 10 minutes; serve.

VARIATION

FRESH SOUR CHERRY COBBLER

Morello or Montmorency cherries can be used in this cobbler made with fresh sour cherries. Do not use sweet Bing cherries. If the cherries do not release enough juice after macerating for 30 minutes, cranberry juice makes up the difference.

cherry filling

1¼	cups (8¾ ounces) sugar
3	tablespoons plus 1 teaspoon cornstarch
	Pinch salt
4	pounds fresh sour cherries, pitted (about 8 cups), juices reserved
1	cup dry red wine
	Cranberry juice (if needed)
1	(3-inch) cinnamon stick
¼	teaspoon almond extract
1	recipe Biscuit Topping (see preceding recipe)

1. Stir together sugar, cornstarch, and salt in large bowl; add cherries and toss well to combine. Pour wine over cherries;

let stand 30 minutes. Drain cherries in colander set over medium bowl. Combine drained and reserved juices (from pitting cherries); you should have 3 cups. If not, add enough cranberry juice to equal 3 cups.

2. While cherries macerate, prepare and bake biscuit topping.

3. Spread drained cherries in even layer in 13 by 9-inch glass baking dish. Bring juices and cinnamon stick to simmer in medium nonreactive saucepan over medium-high heat, whisking frequently, until mixture thickens, about 5 minutes. Discard cinnamon stick, stir in almond extract, and pour hot juices over cherries in baking dish.

4. Arrange hot biscuits in 3 rows of 4 over warm filling. Bake cobbler until filling is bubbling and biscuits are deep golden brown, about 10 minutes. Cool on wire rack 10 minutes; serve.

TASTING LAB: Cherries

FRESH SOUR CHERRIES MAY BE THE BEST CHOICE FOR baking, but they are available only for a few weeks during the summer. What's the best option at other times of the year when making cherry cobbler? Should you use fresh sweet cherries? What about processed sour cherries? We rounded up six contenders—fresh sweet cherries, frozen sweet cherries, canned sweet cherries, jarred sour cherries, frozen sour cherries, and canned sour cherries—and made cobbler fillings with each one.

Although most of these cherry products made a cobbler filling that looked good, only one—jarred Morello

---

TECHNIQUE: Pitting Cherries

A cherry pitter (sold in most kitchenware stores) is the best tool for removing pits from fresh sour cherries. If you don't own this gadget, you can improvise as follows. With any of these methods, work over a bowl to catch the cherry juices.

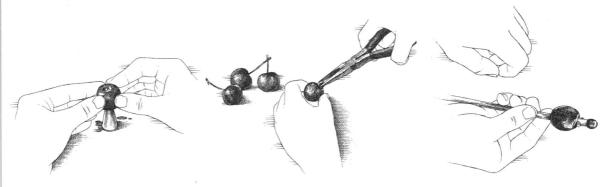

A. Push the bottom of a cherry down onto the pointed, jagged end of a pastry bag tip. The pastry tip will push the pit out the top. Take care not cut your fingers on the points as they pierce the fruit.

B. Pierce the skin at the stem with a pair of needle-nose pliers, spread the pliers just enough to grasp the pit, and pull it straight out.

C. Push a drinking straw through the bottom of the cherry, forcing the pit up and out the top.

Rating Cherry Products

WE TESTED SIX ALTERNATIVES TO FRESH SOUR CHERRIES IN OUR COBBLER FILLING RECIPE. TASTERS EVALUATED THE cooked cherries in terms of flavor, color, and texture. They also rated the "sauce" made by each cherry product when cooked with the other filling ingredients. For varieties without packing liquid, we substituted cranberry juice. Cherries are listed in order of preference. All of these products are widely available in supermarkets, with the exception of our winner, which is available in Trader Joe's markets. See www.cooksillustrated.com for an up-to-date price and mail-order source for jarred Morello cherries.

RECOMMENDED

1. Trader's Joe Dark Morello Cherries in Light Syrup

$2.29 for 24.7 ounces

These jarred sour cherries from Germany are packed in water and sugar. Tasters praised their "true, fruity" flavor and remarked that the cherries were "plump" and "still had some chew." They made a sauce that was "complex," with "winey notes" and "good body."

NOT RECOMMENDED

2. Fresh Bing Cherries

$6.98 per pound

Sweet Bing cherries are the variety you find in supermarkets. They were deemed "mildly fresh" and "sweet." Their texture was "very, very firm," and they seemed "undercooked." The sauce they made was "too sweet" and "thin."

NOT RECOMMENDED

3. Cascadian Farm Frozen Sweet Cherries

$3.79 for 10 ounces

These organic sweet cherries come from Chile and cooked up with a "mushy," "jamlike" texture. Their flavor was "sweet" and "winey." The sauce they made tasted more like other fruits (tasters mentioned plums and blueberries), and it was extremely thick.

NOT RECOMMENDED

4. Comstock Canned Dark Sweet Pitted Cherries

$2.99 for 15 ounces

These sweet cherries are packed in heavy syrup and were judged to be "bland," "flavorless," and "stale." Their texture was described as "limp" and "mushy." The "runny" sauce they made was "sour" and "like cough syrup."

NOT RECOMMENDED

5. Comstock Canned Tart Red Pitted Cherries

$1.99 for 14.5 ounces

These sour cherries are packed in water, which may explain their very poor finish. They were "flat tasting" and "flavorless," with a "strange gummy texture." They made a "watery" sauce that "burned the throat" with its tartness.

NOT RECOMMENDED

6. Friske Orchards Frozen Red Tart Cherries

$7.50 for 24 ounces

The individually quick frozen (IQF) cherries from northern Michigan were a real disappointment. They tasted "sour" and "harsh," and panelists complained about their "spongy," "rubbery" texture. The sauce they made was deemed "dull" and "medicinal."

cherries from Trader Joe's—made a filling that tasted good. We loved their deep ruby red color, tart flavor, and plump and meaty texture. In fact, these cherries delivered bracing flavor and a great chew right out of the jar.

The other sour cherries (canned and frozen) landed at the bottom of the rankings. None of the three sweet cherry products (fresh, frozen, and canned) scored all that well either, although tasters felt that fresh Bing cherries were the best sweet option. In the end, tasters concluded that jarred Morello cherries were the only product worth using—cobblers made with the other cherry products were lackluster and bland.

Why did the jarred sour cherries sweep the tasting while the frozen and canned sour cherries couldn't even beat mediocre sweet cherry products? We have two explanations for these curious findings. First, the jarred sour cherries that we tested were Morellos, an especially flavorful variety. Second, these cherries (unlike the frozen or canned sour cherries) were packed in sugar syrup. The canned sour cherries we tested were packed in water, which seemed to wash away their flavor. The frozen cherries were frozen as is, and this delicate fruit just doesn't freeze all that well. The lightly sweetened packing liquid from the jarred cherries added flavor to the cobbler filling and helped give it a pleasing, slightly thickened texture.

SCIENCE DESK:
Browning and Baking Soda

THE BAKING SODA AND THE BAKING POWDER IN THE biscuits for our cherry cobbler recipe provide leavening. But did you know that the baking soda also serves another function? It enhances browning. In fact, many pastry chefs add a little baking soda to baked goods to promote browning rather than to cause lift.

Browning is an extremely important phenomenon in cooking because browned food tastes better. When carbohydrates and proteins are heated together, the sugar (from the carbohydrates) and the amino acids (from the proteins) combine to form hundreds of new, distinct flavor compounds in a process called the Maillard reaction. These newly formed compounds are what makes browned food taste so much more complex and interesting than food that is not browned. So increasing browning is a good thing.

Why does baking soda increase browning? Because browning occurs best in an alkaline environment. Here's how it works. An amino acid molecule has two ends—one is the amino end and one is the acid end. As you might guess, the acid end is acidic, but (as you might not guess) the amino end is alkaline. It's the alkaline end that has to react with the sugar molecules for browning to occur. In an acidic solution, the alkaline ends are destroyed. In an alkaline environment, the amino ends thrive and are free to react with the sugar to create browning.

The biscuit portion of our cobbler recipe contains buttermilk, which is very acidic. Baking soda, being an alkaline itself, reacts with the buttermilk to create a rise in the dough, but it also creates an alkaline environment, thus permitting the amino ends of the amino acid molecules to react with the sugar and produce browning. A biscuit recipe with buttermilk and baking powder alone may or may not rise (depending on how much you use), but it certainly won't brown very well.

Doc dons his conquistador outfit to help illustrate the dramatic history of chocolate.

TWO CHOCOLATE cakes

Who can resist a chocolate cake? No one in the test kitchen, that's for sure. The words "chocolate cake" can mean different things to different people. It might be a lopsided layer cake that you've spent hours making, baking, and frosting. Or it might be a flavorless sheet cake from the supermarket. We have two requirements for chocolate cake: It has to taste great, and it should be easy to prepare. We also have two recipes—one plain looking, one fancy looking—that meet both of these requirements.

A hot fudge pudding cake is an old-fashioned American cake straight from the pages of community cookbooks. Although this two-layer concoction, with cake and sauce baked together in one pan, will never win any beauty contests, its flavor is pure chocolate and the gooey texture is addictive, especially if served warm with ice cream on top. Unfortunately, many versions of this recipe fail to deliver the right balance of cake to sauce.

A flourless chocolate cake is a thing of beauty. Like a chocolate cheesecake, only with more flavor and a better texture, this mousse-like cake whispers elegance (and chocolate) with every bite. Yes, this recipe requires a springform pan and a water bath, but there are only three ingredients—chocolate, butter, and eggs—so the batter goes together in a flash. Our goal was to figure out the right proportions of these ingredients and the best baking method in order to turn out a cake that was neither too light nor too heavy.

HOT FUDGE PUDDING CAKE

WHAT WE WANTED: A homey, no-fuss chocolate cake with hot fudge sauce—baked together in one dish.

Hot fudge pudding cake has several aliases: Denver pudding cake, chocolate upside-down cake, brownie pudding cake, or sometimes simply chocolate pudding cake. This 1950s community cookbook recipe may be a bit dated, but it's a boon to the cook looking for a simple baked dessert that requires no creaming or whipping. Hot fudge pudding cake is definitely not a dessert for entertaining; it does not impress with its looks. It's a humble, homely dessert with bumps, lumps, and cracks, an easy one to turn up your nose at. But those who have eaten hot fudge pudding cake know its charms: unpretentious, moist, brownie-like chocolate cake sitting on a pool of a chocolate sauce so thick it's reminiscent of pudding, with both miraculously baked at the same time in the same dish. Served warm with vanilla ice cream, this cake more than makes up for its lack of looks.

In the matter of pudding cakes, there are two distinct styles. The fussier version requires beaten egg whites rather than chemical leaveners for lift and a hot water bath to produce a soufflé-like cake above a custard-like sauce. Then there's the absurdly simple hot fudge pudding cake that resembles a chemically leavened brownie and can be made by a rookie baker equipped with only a few bowls and a whisk. It was the latter style that we were pursuing, so we gathered a few recipes and tried them. All were disappointing. Instead of deep and chocolatey, they tasted dull and mild. Instead of providing enough spoon-coating sauce to accompany the cake, some were dry, with a disproportionate amount of cake, while the others were soupy, with a wet, sticky, underdone cake.

For those who aren't familiar with the magic of pudding cakes, here's how they work. The batter is made in the manner of a brownie batter, but with milk added. After the batter goes in the baking dish, things take an unusual turn. A mixture of sugar and cocoa is sprinkled over the batter, then liquid is poured on top, and the mess goes into the oven. (Depending on the recipe, the cocoa and sugar may first be dissolved in hot water, then poured over.) The step of pouring liquid over the batter is so odd that the cook making a hot fudge pudding cake for the first time quickly becomes skeptical. With baking, however, what looks to be a mistake is transformed into a dessert. The cake rises to the surface, and the liquid that started out on top sinks to the bottom, taking the sugar and cocoa with it, becoming the "hot fudge" part of the dessert.

With a working recipe cobbled together, our first goal was to pump up the chocolate flavor, suspecting that the problem was that most recipes call for cocoa rather than chocolate. In our experience, cocoa alone carries potent—sometimes acrid—chocolate flavor, but it cannot deliver the complexity or richness of chocolate. We tried adding different amounts of bittersweet chocolate to the pudding cake. Two ounces in addition to the ⅓ cup of cocoa was the ideal amount to obtain fuller flavor. More chocolate and the cake was too wicked with chocolate and its texture became sodden.

We also thought to try regular "natural" cocoa versus Dutch-processed cocoa. The former is lighter in color and more acidic than the latter. In a side-by-side tasting, we were stunned by the difference. The "natural" cocoa version tasted sharp and harsh, but the one made with Dutch-processed cocoa (we used Droste, a brand widely available in supermarkets) tasted smooth, round, and full. It was unanimous. Every person who tasted the two cakes vastly preferred the one made with Dutch-processed cocoa. To sweeten the cake and counter the bitterness of even the Dutch-processed cocoa, ⅔ cup of sugar was required. We tried substituting some brown sugar for granulated but found it a nuisance because of the way it clumps (not a problem if the butter and sugar were being creamed

together, but this cake was too easy for that). Besides, the brown sugar added no significant flavor benefit.

The next issue to settle was that of eggs, and there seemed to be two choices: recipes that contained an egg and those that didn't. The eggless cakes were mushy and crumbly. Their crumb lacked structural integrity, and, because they were soft and mushy, there seemed to be little distinction between what was supposed to be cake and what was supposed to be hot fudge. We tried as many as two whole eggs, but our preference was for a pudding cake made with just one yolk. It was brownie-like, with a nice, tooth-sinking crumb. Cakes made with whole eggs were drier and slightly rubbery.

So far, we had been using 1 cup of unbleached all-purpose flour, but the cake layer was a tad too thick. We tried smaller amounts of flour, hoping that the texture wouldn't suffer as a consequence. We ended up preferring the cake with ¾ cup of flour. It tasted more richly of chocolate and had a moist, brownie-like texture. It had a little less height, but this made it a better match for the amount of sauce.

The butter in hot fudge pudding cake is always melted,

never creamed. (This cake requires a heavy-duty leavener, such as baking powder, to force the cake layer up through the sludge that becomes the sauce. Although creaming is one way to provide lift, in this case we found that the contribution made by aerated butter was minimal and not worth the effort.) With only 4 tablespoons of melted butter, the cake tasted lean and dry. With 8, it was leaden and greasy. Six tablespoons was the ideal amount. Like most other cakes, hot fudge pudding cake contains some dairy, usually milk. We tried heavy cream and half-and-half to see if either had desirable effects. Heavy cream made a slick, greasy, fat-laden cake. With half-and-half, the cake was somewhat greasy and a little too rich. Milk was the way to go.

For lift, we relied on baking powder. One recipe called for 2 tablespoons per cup of flour ("chemical warfare" was one taster's term for this mixture). Two teaspoons of baking powder was just fine. To heighten flavor, we added ¼ teaspoon salt and 1 tablespoon vanilla (there was a lot of chocolate flavor to contend with).

As mentioned above, there are two ways to add the ingredients destined to become the fudge sauce. A mixture of cocoa and sugar can be sprinkled on the batter and water then poured over it, creating what looks like a pan-full of river sludge. Alternatively, the cocoa and sugar can first be dissolved in boiling water. We compared two such pudding cakes. The one with the sprinkled cocoa/sugar mixture baked up with crisp edges and a faintly crisp crust that we preferred over the uniformly soft, cakey surface of the other. It was as if some of the sugar, moistened by the water, remained at the surface even after the liquid seeped to the bottom, and then caramelized to form a pleasing crust.

We tried different amounts of cocoa in the sauce-to-be and landed at ⅓ cup, the same amount we put in the cake. A mixture made with all granulated sugar resulted in a toffee-like crust, rather sticky and tough, with one-dimensional sweetness. We preferred a mix of granulated and brown sugar, with the molasses flavor of the latter producing a full, round taste.

The amount of water poured over the cake determines the amount of sauce at the bottom. One and one-half cups—a little more than what most recipes call for—was ideal, yielding an ample amount of sauce with the right consistency. Some hot fudge pudding cake recipes suggest using coffee instead of water. Indeed, we thought the coffee was a nice addition. It didn't interfere with the chocolate flavor but nicely complemented it, cutting through some of the cake's cloying qualities and enriching the flavor. For ease, we took to using 2 teaspoons of instant coffee mixed into the water, but cold, brewed coffee cut with a little water works as well.

We tested different oven temperatures and baking times. While most recipes indicated 350 degrees for about 35 minutes, we preferred 325 degrees for 45 minutes. The lower temperature helped keep the sauce from rapidly bubbling, a phenomenon that can cause spillage if left unchecked. In addition, the slightly longer baking time promoted a nicer crust. We noted that this cake combined lots of pleasing textures: a silky sauce, a moist, cakey crumb, and a thin, brittle crust, especially around the edges.

When attacked with a spoon straight from the oven, the hot fudge pudding cake revealed a thin, blistering-hot sauce and a sodden cake. If allowed to cool for 20 to 30 minutes, the sauce became pudding-like and the cake brownie-like. The warm cake cries out to be served with vanilla or coffee ice cream (whipped cream just isn't serious enough). For serving to guests, we adapted the recipe to bake in individual ramekins so that apologies for the cake's dowdy appearance need not be made so profusely. Leftovers reheat well in the zap of a microwave, but don't count on having any.

WHAT WE LEARNED: **For the best flavor and texture, use a combination of Dutch-processed cocoa and melted bittersweet chocolate in the cake layer. For the sauce, sprinkle the cake batter with a mixture of cocoa, brown sugar, and granulated sugar and then cover with coffee.**

HOT FUDGE PUDDING CAKE serves 8

If you have cold, brewed coffee on hand, it can be used in place of the instant coffee and water, but to make sure it isn't too strong, use 1 cup of cold coffee mixed with $1/2$ cup of water. Serve the cake warm with vanilla or coffee ice cream. Leftovers can be reheated, covered with plastic wrap, in a microwave oven.

2	teaspoons instant coffee
1½	cups water
⅔	cup (2½ ounces) Dutch-processed cocoa
⅓	cup packed (1¾ ounces) brown sugar
1	cup (7 ounces) granulated sugar
6	tablespoons unsalted butter
2	ounces bittersweet or semisweet chocolate, chopped
¾	cup (3¾ ounces) unbleached all-purpose flour
2	teaspoons baking powder
1	tablespoon vanilla extract
⅓	cup whole milk
¼	teaspoon salt
1	large egg yolk

1. Adjust oven rack to lower-middle position and heat oven to 325 degrees. Lightly spray 8-inch square glass or ceramic baking dish with nonstick cooking spray (see illustration on page 321). Stir instant coffee into water; set aside to dissolve. Stir together ⅓ cup cocoa, brown sugar, and ⅓ cup granulated sugar in small bowl, breaking up large clumps with fingers; set aside. Melt butter, remaining ⅓ cup cocoa, and chocolate in small bowl set over saucepan of barely simmering water; whisk until smooth and set aside to cool slightly. Whisk flour and baking powder in small bowl to combine; set aside. Whisk remaining ⅔ cup sugar, vanilla, milk, and salt in medium bowl until combined; whisk in yolk. Add chocolate mixture and whisk to combine. Add flour mixture and whisk until batter is evenly moistened.

2. Pour batter into prepared baking dish and spread evenly to sides and corners. Sprinkle cocoa/sugar mixture evenly over batter (cocoa mixture should cover entire surface of batter); pour coffee mixture gently over cocoa mixture. Bake until cake is puffed and bubbling and just beginning to pull away from sides of baking dish, about 45 minutes. (Do not overbake.) Cool cake in dish on wire rack about 25 minutes before serving.

VARIATION

INDIVIDUAL HOT FUDGE PUDDING CAKES

Follow recipe for Hot Fudge Pudding Cake, heating oven to 400 degrees and lightly spraying eight 6- to 8-ounce ramekins with nonstick cooking spray; set ramekins on baking sheet. Divide batter evenly among ramekins (about ¼ cup per ramekin) and level with back of spoon; sprinkle about 2 tablespoons cocoa/sugar mixture over batter in each ramekin. Pour 3 tablespoons coffee mixture over cocoa/sugar mixture in each ramekin. Bake until puffed and bubbling, about 20 minutes. (Do not overbake.) Cool ramekins about 15 minutes before serving (cakes will fall).

TECHNIQUE: No-Mess Spraying

To keep cooking spray from covering your counters with an oily film, try this trick. Open the dishwasher door, place the item to be greased on the door, and spray away. Any excess spray will be cleaned off the door the next time you run the dishwasher.

TASTING LAB: Vanilla Extract

ALMOST TWO-THIRDS OF THE WORLD'S SUPPLY OF VANILLA beans comes from Madagascar, an island off the eastern coast of Africa. Significant amounts of vanilla beans are also grown in Mexico and Tahiti. Tahitian beans are a hybrid that originated spontaneously on several islands in the South Pacific. Beans grown everywhere else in the world, including Mexico and Madagascar, are from the same species.

Although vanilla beans are convenient to use in custards (the pods are split lengthwise, the seeds scraped into the liquid, and the pods usually added to infuse more flavor), extracts make the most sense for baking, including cakes and cookies. (You could make vanilla sugar by nestling a split bean in some sugar, but this process takes about a week.)

When shopping for extracts, you have two basic choices: pure extract and imitation. Pure vanilla extract is made by steeping chopped vanilla beans in an alcohol and water solution. Imitation vanilla extract is made from vanillin, a product extracted from conifer wood pulp that has been chemically rinsed.

We figured that tasters would have no trouble picking out pure vanilla extract from imitation products. We also expected the gourmet brands available in upscale markets and by mail to outpoll supermarket offerings. Well, we sure were wrong.

We tried nine extracts (seven pure, two imitation) in a basic sugar cookie with just flour, butter, and sugar. It turns out that most people, including pastry chefs, can't even tell the difference between a cookie made with vanilla extract and a cookie made with the imitation stuff, let alone the differences between brands of real vanilla. In a cookie (as well as in chocolate cake, or any cake for that matter), the quantities of extract are so small and the other ingredients so flavorful that these differences are hard to detect.

We decided to try our pure and imitation extracts in an eggless custard. We choose a panna cotta recipe that calls for just cream, milk, sugar, and gelatin. We also followed a standard tasting protocol in the vanilla business and mixed each extract with milk at a ratio of 1 part extract to 8 parts milk. Although you would never use so much extract in a real application, this high concentration makes it easier to detect specific characteristics in extracts.

The results of this tasting were so shocking that we repeated it, only to come up with similarly surprising findings. Tasters couldn't tell the difference between real and imitation vanilla. In fact, in the panna cotta tasting, the imitation extracts took first and third place, with two "premium" brands, Nielsen-Massey and Penzeys, leading the pack among real extracts. In the milk tasting, the imitation extracts took the top two spots, followed by real extracts from Nielsen-Massey and Penzeys. Although we are loath to recommend an imitation product, it seems that most people don't mind imitation extract and, in fact, many tasters actually like its flavor. Note that you won't save money by choosing an imitation extract—it costs about the same as pure vanilla extract.

EQUIPMENT CORNER: Digital Scales

IN OUR TEST KITCHEN, WE WEIGH MOST BAKING INGREDIENTS as well as meats, fruits, and vegetables for cooking. An apple pie, for example, would look uninspiring if it were filled with only 2½ pounds of apples instead of 4 pounds, which is why making a recipe that simply calls for "X" number of medium apples without a specific weight can be risky. If you were to choose apples that were smaller than those intended by the recipe writer, you'd end up with a flat pie.

This is why we reviewed 13 kitchen scales some seven years ago. Testers preferred electronic models with digital readouts because they were easier to read and seemed more accurate than the mechanical models with dial displays. The natural question then was, which electronic scale is best? To find out how things look now, we recently scrutinized eight popular models, ranging in price from just over $25 to $125, and discovered a few differences that made some units easier to use than others.

Perhaps the biggest advantage of digital scales over dial-face models is readability. Some digitals, however, are easier to read than others. We found that readability depends equally on the design of the scale and the size of the display. Scales with large displays that were angled steeply and set far away from the weighing platform were the easiest to read because the display was not hidden beneath the rim or in the shadow of the vessel on the platform, be it a dinner plate, cake pan, or mixing bowl. For these reasons, and because its weighing platform was elevated far above the scale base, the Soehnle Cyber was the exemplar in terms of design and readability. The Cuisinart and the Salter were also particularly easy to read.

A few other features made some scales easier to use than others. For instance, the two Soehnles tested had the largest weighing platforms, at roughly 7 inches, which could accommodate a large portion of ground meat or a raw chicken without letting anything spill onto the base. That feat would be much less likely on the Measurement Specialties and Terraillon scales, with their comparatively small 5-inch platforms. For the sake of comparison, the platform on the professional electronic scale in our test kitchen measures a full 11 inches wide.

Large capacity was another feature we valued highly. The Soehnle Cyber, Salter, Cuisinart, and EKS were the best of the lot, all with 11-pound capacities, which meant they could easily weigh a large roast. The Sunbeam and the Terraillon, on the other hand, could handle weights up to only 4½ pounds, and the Measurement Specialties was designed to hold only 2 pounds, so you couldn't even weigh a large chicken on it.

All of the scales but one, the Measurement Specialties, offered a metric conversion feature, and every single scale offered something called a tare feature, which allows you to set the scale back to zero with a container such as a mixing bowl on the platform, thus giving you a reading on the weight of the food alone. All of the scales also had an automatic shut-off feature. While this is certainly a good way to preserve battery life, we found it annoying when the scale shut itself off after a short cycle of less than two minutes, often before we were

Rating Digital Kitchen Scales

WE TESTED EIGHT DIGITAL KITCHEN SCALES AND RATED THEM ACCORDING TO DISPLAY VISIBILITY, CAPACITY (THE HIGHER, the better), platform size (the larger, the better), ease of use, accuracy, and measuring increments. Display visibility was the most important criterion, followed by capacity and the size of the measuring platform. The scales are listed in order of preference. See www.cooksillustrated.com for up-to-date prices and mail-order sources for top-rated products.

HIGHLY RECOMMENDED

1. Soehnle Cyber Electronic Kitchen Scale, Model 8048

$124.95

Detachable glass platform was large and especially easy to clean. Easy-to-read display and high capacity were also pluses.

RECOMMENDED

2. Salter Electronic Aquatronic The Baker's Dream, Model 3007

$59.95

Well liked for its long 5-minute automatic shut-off time, fluid weight feature, and rubber feet, which prevent sliding. On the downside, the ridge between the weighing platform and the base can trap food particles.

RECOMMENDED

3. Cuisinart Precision Electronic Scale, Model SA-110A

$69.95

Good display and long 6-minute automatic shut-off time; rubber feet help prevent sliding. The ridge between the weighing platform and the base can trap food particles.

RECOMMENDED WITH RESERVATIONS

4. Soehnle Magnum Electronic Baking & Domestic Scale, Model 8038 63

$64.95

Good accuracy, generous weighing platform, and decimal weighing increments were pluses, but scale slides around on the countertop and the flat display can be hard to read.

RECOMMENDED WITH RESERVATIONS

5. EKS Electronic Scale

$69.00

Very accurate, but the textured weighing platform is hard to clean. The display starts in metric and must be changed to the U.S. standard every time, which is irritating, as is the short automatic shut-off time.

NOT RECOMMENDED

6. Sunbeam Deluxe Digital Scale, Model 6025

$49.95

Good accuracy, but low capacity (less than 5 pounds) will pose problem for some kitchen tasks. The scale often did not return to zero when the weight was removed.

NOT RECOMMENDED

7. Measurement Specialties Thinner Electronic Food/Diet Scale, Model MS-11

$26.92

Intended for dieting, so display reads out in ounces only, not pounds. Despite 2-pound capacity claim, we found actual capacity to be 10 pounds.

NOT RECOMMENDED

8. Terraillon Electronic Food Scale, Model BE225-T

$44.95

Good accuracy, but low capacity (less than 5 pounds) and a small weighing platform held it back. Also, unimpressive automatic shut-off time, and did not always return to zero when weight was removed.

finished adding ingredients to the bowl. Guilty on this count were the Measurement Specialties, the Terraillon, and the EKS. The Soehnle Cyber, Salter, and Cuisinart scales provided a reliable margin of five or six minutes.

Last, we preferred scales that displayed weight increments in decimals, including both Soehnles, the Sunbeam, and the Measurement Specialties. Decimals were easier to work with when scaling recipes up or down, and they had a minor advantage in terms of accuracy because they measured in increments of one tenth of an ounce, or 0.1, in the lower weight ranges. The scales that displayed fractions—the Salter, Cuisinart, EKS, and Terraillon—measured in increments of one-quarter ounce, or 0.25, in those ranges.

Philosophically, we feel that every scale should be perfectly accurate all of the time. Realistically, we found otherwise. In fact, after extensive testing with calibrated laboratory weights, only one of the scales tested, the EKS, proved to be absolutely accurate every time. Up through 4 pounds, the scale with the largest average inaccuracy, just a hair over 0.25 ounce, was the Cuisinart. The others were off by about 0.2 ounce, or even less. In the higher weight ranges of 8 pounds or more, the margins of inaccuracy increased to just above 0.5 ounce for both Soehnles and to a full ounce for both the Salter and the Cuisinart. We noted with all of the scales that placing them on a very flat, solid surface helped produce a sure reading. If the surface was at all unstable or wobbly, the readings would fluctuate from one increment to the next.

Philosophy aside, all of our scales were accurate enough in the lower weight ranges for most home cooks, particularly when making savory dishes. No one would be able to tell, for instance, if your meatloaf contained 7.75 ounces of ground pork rather than 8 ounces. Even in baking, inaccuracy of 0.25 ounce would be all right in the vast majority of recipes.

For its sleek and thoughtful design, good accuracy, and superior readability, the handsome but expensive Soehnle Cyber was the star of this show. Understandably, though, many cooks may be reluctant to drop $125 on a scale. In that case, both the Salter and the Cuisinart offer optimal readability and 11-pound capacities for about $70 or less.

FLOURLESS CHOCOLATE CAKE

WHAT WE WANTED: **A dense, moist, ultra-chocolate cake with a texture somewhere between an airy mousse and a heavy cheesecake.**

To our knowledge, flourless chocolate cake is the only dessert that is named for a missing ingredient. Besides this, the word cake stretches the point in describing this very popular dessert; although some recipes replace flour or crumbs with ground nuts, the quintessence of the genre contains only chocolate, butter, and eggs—nothing that could conceivably be called a dry ingredient. The result is more confection than cake, like a dense baked mousse or chocolate cheesecake, with butter replacing cheese.

Although the ingredient choices are limited—chocolate, butter, and eggs, sometimes sugar, and sometimes liquid such as water, coffee, or liqueur—the proportions as well as mixing and baking methods differed considerably in the recipes we researched.

We selected and baked six recipes that represented the array of choices. The results were staggering in their variety. One cake resembled a flourless fudge brownie, one was more like an ultra-dense, creamy custard, and one was a pouffy, fallen soufflé-like affair.

Although nearly all of the desserts were enticing in their own way, we were quickly able to define our criteria for the ultimate flourless chocolate cake. We wanted something dense, moist, and ultra-chocolatey, but with some textural finesse. We wanted a mouthfeel and texture somewhere between a substantial marquise au chocolat—that dense, buttery, and just slightly aerated chocolate mousse with a characteristically dry yet creamy texture—and a heavy New York–style cheesecake, which requires the mouth to work for just a second before the stuff melts and dissolves with sublime flavor. We wanted the flavor and character of good, eating-quality chocolate to reign supreme, with no unnecessary sweetness and not even the slightest grain of sugar on the palate. In short, we wanted an intense, bittersweet "adult" dessert, not a piece of fudge or a brownie or a thick chocolate pudding, and certainly nothing fluffy.

Some recipes used unsweetened chocolate instead of semisweet or bittersweet, but we rejected this idea after tasting just one cake made with unsweetened chocolate. Neither flavor nor texture was smooth or silky enough for us, and there was a slight chalky sensation on the palate. This made perfect sense. Unsweetened chocolate is coarse and needs high heat to blend perfectly with the sugar required to sweeten it. It is most successful in desserts with a cakey or fudgy texture, when perfect smoothness is unnecessary. Hot fudge sauce made with unsweetened chocolate is smooth because it is cooked to a temperature high enough to melt the sugar and change the physical properties of the chocolate. But our flourless chocolate cake is more like chocolate mousse, chocolate truffles, or ganache—ingredients are few, cooked very gently, and the results must be perfectly smooth. Made to be nibbled, semisweet and bittersweet chocolates are incomparably smooth, refined so that chocolate and sugar are intimately married and every particle is smaller than the human palate can detect.

The next decision had to do with the baking temperature and whether or not a water bath was indicated. The original recipe for this now-popular dessert was flawed by hard, crumbly edges—surely caused by baking for a short time at a high temperature without a water bath. We tried a similar recipe baked at a high temperature for a short time but in a water bath. It was creamier by far, but we could taste raw egg. We guessed that, like cheesecake, this dessert required a longer baking time at a lower temperature in a water bath to allow the interior to reach a safe temperature without overcooking the edges. We found that 325 degrees in a water bath produced a successful sample.

The trick in baking this cake, however, was knowing when to stop. Just like cheesecake, our flourless chocolate cake must be taken from the oven when the center still jiggles and looks quite underdone, as it continues to cook after it comes out of the oven. The center of the cake should register 140 degrees on an instant-read thermometer.

Before determining the perfect quantities of butter and eggs for a pound of chocolate, we decided to test textures. We were pretty sure that the ultimate cake would need some form of aeration from beaten eggs to achieve the texture that we wanted. In the first test, we whisked the eggs over gentle heat to warm them (as for a génoise, or very light sponge cake without leavening), and then beat them until about triple in volume and the consistency of soft whipped cream. We then folded the whipped eggs into the warm chocolate and butter in three parts. In the second test, we separated the eggs and whisked the yolks into the warm chocolate and butter and then beat the whites to a meringue before folding them in. In the third test, we simply whisked the eggs, one by one, into the warm chocolate and butter, as though making a custard.

The sample made with eggs simply whisked into the melted chocolate and butter was dense and smooth like a very rich custard or crème brûlée. Our definition of the ultimate flourless chocolate cake ruled this version out. The cake with beaten whole eggs differed from the one with yolks and meringue more than we expected. Surprisingly, the difference in flavor was greater than the difference in texture. Whole beaten eggs produced a dessert with nicely blended flavors, while the cake with separated eggs tasted as if the ingredients had not been completely integrated. Along the way, we realized that we could eliminate the step of warming the eggs before beating them, since cold eggs produce a denser foam with smaller bubbles, which in turn gave the cake a more velvety texture.

WHAT WE LEARNED: **Just three ingredients—whipped whole eggs, a good-quality bittersweet or semisweet chocolate, and butter—will yield a dense, rich texture and true chocolate flavor. Make sure not to overbake this cake or the texture will be ruined.**

FLOURLESS CHOCOLATE CAKE serves 12 to 16
Even though the cake may not look done, pull it from the oven when an instant-read thermometer registers 140 degrees. (Make sure not to let tip of thermometer hit the bottom of the pan.) It will continue to firm up as it cools. If you use a 9-inch springform pan instead of the preferred 8-inch, reduce the baking time to 18 to 20 minutes. We like the pure flavor of chocolate. However, coffee or liqueur (choose something that tastes like nuts, coffee, or oranges) can added if desired. In any case, choose a high-quality chocolate that you enjoy eating out of hand.

8   large eggs, cold
1   pound bittersweet or semisweet chocolate, chopped
½   pound (2 sticks) unsalted butter, cut into ½-inch chunks
¼   cup strong coffee or liqueur (optional)
    Confectioners' sugar or cocoa powder for decoration

1. Adjust oven rack to lower-middle position and heat oven to 325 degrees. Line bottom of 8-inch springform pan with parchment and grease pan sides. Cover pan underneath and along sides with sheet of heavy-duty aluminum foil and set wrapped pan in large roasting pan. Bring kettle of water to boil.

2. Beat eggs with handheld mixer at high speed until volume doubles to approximately 1 quart, about 5 minutes. Alternately, beat in bowl of electric mixer fitted with wire whip attachment at medium speed to achieve same result, about 5 minutes.

3. Meanwhile, melt chocolate and butter (adding coffee or liqueur, if using) in large heatproof bowl set over pan of almost simmering water, until smooth and very warm (about 115 degrees on an instant-read thermometer), stirring once or twice. (To use microwave, melt chocolate at 50 percent power for 2 minutes, stir, add butter, and continue heating at 50 percent power, stirring every minute, until chocolate and butter have melted and are smooth, another 2 to 3 minutes total.) Using large rubber spatula, fold ⅓ of egg foam into chocolate mixture until only a few streaks of egg are visible; fold in half of remaining foam, then last of remaining foam, until mixture is totally homogenous.

4. Scrape batter into prepared springform pan and smooth surface with rubber spatula. Set roasting pan on oven rack and pour enough boiling water to come about halfway up side of springform pan. Bake until cake has risen slightly, edges are just beginning to set, thin glazed crust (like a brownie) has formed on surface, and instant-read thermometer inserted halfway through center of cake registers 140 degrees, 22 to 25 minutes. Remove springform pan from water bath and set on wire rack; cool to room temperature. Cover and refrigerate overnight to mellow flavors. (Cake can be covered and refrigerated for up to 4 days).

5. About 30 minutes before serving, remove springform pan sides, invert cake on sheet of waxed paper, peel off parchment pan liner, and turn cake right-side up on serving platter. Sieve light sprinkling of confectioners' sugar or unsweetened cocoa powder over cake to decorate, if desired.

SCIENCE DESK:
The Allure of Chocolate

SINCE THE DAYS OF THE ANCIENT AZTECS, WHO BELIEVED that chocolate conferred sexual prowess on those who consumed it, chocolate has been not just a food but a passion. Many have attempted to deter chocolate fanatics from the object of their obsession, but to little avail. When a sixteenth-century Spanish priest tried to prevent his New World parishioners from drinking chocolate during mass, swords were drawn to protect the coveted drink. The next day the priest was found dead of poisoning.

As it turns out, there may be a scientific reason for our intense desire for chocolate. Researchers have recently discovered that chocolate contains unusually large amounts of phenylethylamine, a stimulant similar to chemicals released by the human body during sex. Other scientists say that the caffeine in chocolate causes the craving. Still other experts attribute chocolate's addictive properties to chemicals called cannabinoids, which are in the same family as certain molecules found in marijuana.

But do these explanations make sense? To get the same amount of caffeine that's in an 8-ounce cup of coffee, you'd have to eat one pound of chocolate. To get any pharmacological effect from the cannabinoids, you'd have to eat 27 pounds of chocolate.

As these numbers suggest, it may be the chocolate itself—in its entirety—that satisfies one's cravings, not any single compound it contains. A recent study supports this theory. In this experiment, one group of people was given white chocolate, which doesn't contain the pharmacologically active components in chocolate, and another group was given capsules with the chemical components in chocolate that some scientists believe are responsible for its addictive power. The white chocolate, without the chemical compounds, did a better job of satisfying cravings than the capsules with the compounds.

So it seems that the flavor and mouthfeel of chocolate is what people crave. But there is a bit of science to mouthfeel—the almost otherworldly silken texture that cocoa butter gives to a bar of chocolate. Unlike other fats, which melt at room temperature, cocoa butter stays firm up to 92 degrees. As a result, chocolate stays solid until you put it into your mouth. The temperature inside the human mouth is a couple of degrees higher than the melting point of cocoa butter, so the chocolate melts very slowly. In fact, it seems to melt into—rather than just in—your mouth. Now, that's a source of passion all by itself.

Cheesecake ingredients come together quickly in a standing mixer.

NEW YORK cheesecake

CHAPTER 26

IN THIS CHAPTER

Cheesecake has taken a tawdry twist these days, sullied by ice cream–style flavors such as Irish coffee, cappuccino crunch, and Key lime. We all know that the only true cheesecake—the one with unimpeachable credentials—is the New York cheesecake. It is a subtle orchestration of different textures made sublime by a rare and welcome exercise in restraint. Rejecting the Ben and Jerry school of everything-but-the-kitchen-sink concoctions, the ideal New York cheesecake is timeless in its adherence to simplicity.

It should be a tall, bronze-skinned, and dense affair. At the core, it should be cool, thick, smooth, satiny, and creamy. Radiating outward, it goes gradually from velvet to suede, then, finally, around the edges, it becomes cake-like and fine-pored. The flavor should be pure and minimalist, sweet and tangy, and rich to boot.

A New York cheesecake should not taste citrusy or vanilla-laden, nor should it be fluffy, mousse-like, leaden, gummy, chewy, or starchy. It should not be so dry as to make you gag, and it definitely should not bake up with a fault line as large as the San Andreas (we're talking New York, after all).

If we met all these goals, our cheesecake would be good enough to be named after New York.

NEW YORK–STYLE CHEESECAKE

WHAT WE WANTED: A tall, bronze-skinned, dense cheesecake that would be creamy in the middle and cake-like around the edges. The flavors should be pure and minimalist.

There is no shortage of New York cheesecake recipes in cookbooks or magazines or on the Internet. We began our recipe testing by baking up five promising recipes. One turned out looking and tasting more like a gargantuan round of goat cheese than a cheesecake. The other four were good, but tasters cited each for some sort of infraction—an overabundance of orange zest, a taste of raw flour, a pasty mouthfeel, or a texture too light for New York cheesecake that compromised every one of them. We wanted a cheesecake far simpler and purer in flavor, with a flawless texture. With this lucid vision of New York cheesecake and a fierce appetite, we embarked on a long journey.

Some recipes claim that a pastry crust was the crust of choice for the original New York cheesecake, so we tried one. That effort, though, resulted only in a crust that became soggy beneath the filling. Most recipes forgo the pastry crust for a crumb crust—cookie or cracker crumbs are tasty and more practical options. Every taster considered a mere dusting of crumbs on the bottom of the cheesecake insufficient. We wanted a crust with more presence.

A graham cracker crust—made with 1 cup of crumbs, some sugar, and melted butter, pressed into the bottom of a springform pan, and prebaked until fragrant and browning around the edges—was ideal at a thickness of about ⅜ inch. If served within a day of being baked, it retained its crispness. (When held for a couple of days, the crust softened, but tasters still appreciated its sweet toasty flavor, and the texture was superior to a gummy pastry crust.) Brown sugar and ground cinnamon did not improve the crust. We also tried substituting gingersnaps and then chocolate wafers for the graham crackers. Although the former were overpowering,

the latter worked well, remaining crisp even longer than the graham cracker crumbs. Nonetheless, most tasters preferred graham crackers, so we decided to include the chocolate wafers as an alternative.

A great New York cheesecake should be of great stature. One made with 2 pounds (four bars) of cream cheese was not tall enough. We threw in another half pound, reaching the springform pan's maximum capacity, and the cheesecake stood tall. The amount of sugar was quickly settled at 1½ cups. The cheesecake struck a perfect balance of sweet and tangy.

Cheesecakes require a dairy supplement to the cream cheese, such as heavy cream, sour cream, or sometimes both. We made a cheesecake without additional dairy and quickly discovered why it is necessary. Cream cheese on its own produces a pasty cake, akin to mortar—much like a bar of cream cheese straight out of its wrapper. Additional dairy loosens up the texture of the cream cheese, giving the cake a smoother, more luxurious texture. Although some recipes call for as much as 1½ cups of sour cream per 8 ounces of cream cheese, we found that ⅓ cup sour cream combined with 2½ pounds cream cheese was ideal. (Too much sour cream makes cheesecake taste sour and acidic.) As for heavy cream, another common addition, we found that amounts large enough to improve the texture of the cheesecake also dulled the flavor. So it was cream cheese and sour cream—and, once again, restraint was key.

Eggs help bind the cheesecake, make it cohesive, and give it structure. They also help create a smooth, creamy texture. Whole eggs alone are often called for in softer, airier cheesecakes of non–New York persuasions. Recipes for New York cheesecake, however, agree that a few yolks in addition to whole eggs help to produce the velvety, lush texture of a proper New York cheesecake. After much testing, we settled on 6 whole eggs plus 2 yolks, a combination that produced an agreeable texture: dense but not heavy, firm but not rigid, and perfectly rich.

Starch—usually either flour or cornstarch—helps to thicken cheesecake, but, as evidenced by the half-dozen or so starch-laced cakes we made, even in amounts as small as a tablespoon, a gummy, starchy presence can be detected. Tasters much preferred the meltingly luxurious quality of a completely starch-free cheesecake.

Perfecting the flavor was a weighty issue, but an easy one to work through. Tasters moaned that orange zest made cheesecake that tastes like a Creamsicle, so it was out of there in a New York minute. Next to go was lemon zest because its flavor was distracting. A couple teaspoons of lemon juice, however, perked things up without adding a distinctively lemon flavor. Just a bit of salt (sodium is already part of cream cheese) and a couple of teaspoons of vanilla extract rounded out the flavors. Thankfully, all of the tasters in the kitchen were on the same page. We all appreciated a minimalist cheesecake.

One reason cheesecake is well loved by cooks is that it goes together easily. Even so, we noted that care must be used when mixing the ingredients lest the batter end up with small nodules of unmixed cream cheese that mar the smoothness of the baked cake. Frequent and thorough scraping of the bowl during mixing is key to ensuring that every bit of cream cheese is incorporated. It's also helpful to start with semisoftened cream cheese. It doesn't need to be at room temperature, and it definitely doesn't need to be microwaved. Simply cutting the cream cheese into chunks and letting it stand while preparing the crust and assembling the other ingredients—30 to 45 minutes—makes mixing easier. (When icebox-cold, the cream cheese resists being mixed. It clings to the beaters and bowl in firm, waxy chunks and requires much scraping and beating before it will cooperate.)

There are many ways to bake a cheesecake—in a moderate oven, in a low oven, in a water bath, or in the New York fashion, in which the cake bakes at 500 degrees for

about 10 minutes and then at 200 degrees for about an hour. We tried them all, but the New York method was the only one that yielded the attractive nut-brown surface we were after. This supersimple, no-water-bath (no leaking pans, layers of foil prophylactics, or boiling water), dual-temperature baking method also produced a lovely graded texture—soft and creamy at the center and firm and dry at the periphery.

The New York baking method was not without flaws, however. After an hour at 200 degrees, the very center of the cheesecake—even after chilling—was loose and slurpy, the result of underbaking. Some recipes leave the cheesecake in the still-warm, turned-off, propped-open oven for about 30 minutes to finish setting up. When we tried this, the cheesecake was marginally better but still insufficiently baked.

Next we extended the hour-long oven time to 90 minutes, baking the cheesecake to an internal temperature of about 150 degrees. Once chilled, it was cheesecake perfection. With a cleanly set center rather than a wet and sloppy one, it sliced into neat slabs. And though each slice kept its shape, every bite was satiny on the tongue. Because all ovens bake differently, it's important to guard against overbaking the cheesecake. Taken to internal temperatures of more than 160 degrees, our test cheesecakes were hopelessly cracked (see the Science Desk on page 334 for details). To avoid this problem, use an instant-read thermometer. It is the most reliable means of judging the doneness of the cheesecake.

Cheesecake is also well loved (by the sweet tooth, not the waistline) because it lasts longer in the refrigerator than a dessert should. After a day or two, the crust is a little soggy, but the cake tastes every bit as good. For breakfast, forget the bagel. Go for the cheesecake.

WHAT WE LEARNED: The secret to the perfect New York cheesecake is a character trait that most New Yorkers would never admit to—restraint. Don't add extraneous flavor or use flour, which mars the texture. And don't overbake. Once the center is cleanly set (or reaches 150 degrees on an instant-read thermometer), the cheesecake is done.

NEW YORK–STYLE CHEESECAKE
makes one 9-inch cheesecake, serving 12 to 16

For the crust, chocolate wafers (Nabisco Famous) can be substituted for graham crackers; you will need about 14 wafers. The flavor and texture of the cheesecake is best if the cake is allowed to stand at room temperature for 30 minutes before serving. When cutting the cake, have a pitcher of hot tap water nearby; dipping the blade of the knife into the water and wiping it clean with a kitchen towel after each cut helps make neat slices.

graham cracker crust
- 1 cup (4 ounces) graham cracker crumbs (8 whole crackers, broken into rough pieces and processed in food processor until uniformly fine)
- 1 tablespoon sugar
- 5 tablespoons unsalted butter, melted, plus additional 1 tablespoon melted butter for greasing pan

cheesecake filling
- 2½ pounds cream cheese, cut into rough 1-inch chunks and left to stand at room temperature for 30 to 45 minutes
- ⅛ teaspoon salt
- 1½ cups (10½ ounces) sugar
- ⅓ cup (2½ ounces) sour cream
- 2 teaspoons juice from 1 lemon
- 2 teaspoons vanilla extract
- 2 large egg yolks plus 6 large whole eggs

1. FOR THE CRUST: Adjust oven rack to lower-middle position and heat oven to 325 degrees. Combine graham cracker crumbs and sugar in medium bowl; add 5 tablespoons melted butter and toss with fork until evenly moistened. Brush bottom and sides of 9-inch springform pan with most of remaining melted butter, making sure to leave enough butter to brush pan in step 3. Empty crumbs into springform pan and press evenly into pan bottom (see illustration on page 334). Bake until fragrant and beginning to brown around edges, about 13 minutes. Cool on wire rack while making filling.

2. FOR THE CHEESECAKE FILLING: Increase oven temperature to 500 degrees. In standing mixer fitted with paddle attachment, beat cream cheese at medium-low speed to break up and soften slightly, about 1 minute. Scrape beater and bottom and sides of bowl well with rubber spatula; add salt and about half of sugar and beat at medium-low speed until combined, about 1 minute. Scrape bowl; beat in remaining sugar until combined, about 1 minute. Scrape bowl; add sour cream, lemon juice, and vanilla, and beat at low speed until combined, about 1 minute. Scrape bowl; add yolks and beat at medium-low speed until thoroughly combined, about 1 minute. Scrape bowl; add whole eggs two at a time, beating until thoroughly combined, about 1 minute, and scraping bowl between additions.

3. Brush sides of springform pan with remaining melted butter. Set springform pan on rimmed baking sheet (to

GETTING IT RIGHT:
Preventing a Cracked Cheesecake

Overbaking will cause an unsightly crack to develop, as will cooling the baked cheesecake without first freeing the sides of the cake from the pan.

catch any spills if springform pan leaks). Pour filling into cooled crust and bake 10 minutes; without opening oven door, reduce oven temperature to 200 degrees and continue to bake until instant-read thermometer inserted into center of cheesecake registers about 150 degrees, about 1½ hours. Transfer cake to wire rack and run paring knife between cake and side of springform pan. Cool until barely warm, 2½ to 3 hours. Wrap tightly in plastic wrap and refrigerate until cold, at least 3 hours. (Cake can be refrigerated up to 4 days.)

4. To unmold cheesecake, remove sides of pan. Slide thin metal spatula between crust and pan bottom to loosen, then slide cake onto serving plate. Let cheesecake stand at room temperature about 30 minutes, then cut into wedges and serve.

FRESH STRAWBERRY TOPPING
makes about 1½ quarts

The dense, creamy richness of a New York cheesecake makes it the perfect candidate for some kind of fruity foil. A ruby-colored, glazed strawberry topping is the classic fruit accompaniment to New York cheesecake. This topping is best served the same day it is made.

  2   pounds strawberries, cleaned, hulled, and cut lengthwise into ⅛ to ¼-inch slices
½   cup (3½ ounces) sugar
     Pinch salt
  1   cup (about 11 ounces) strawberry jam
  2   tablespoons juice from 1 lemon

1. Toss berries, sugar, and salt in medium bowl; let stand until berries have released juice and sugar has dissolved, about 30 minutes, tossing occasionally to combine.

2. Process jam in food processor until smooth, about 8 seconds; transfer to small saucepan. Bring jam to simmer over medium-high heat; simmer, stirring frequently, until dark and no longer frothy, about 3 minutes. Stir in lemon juice; pour warm liquid over strawberries and stir to combine. Let cool, then cover with plastic wrap and refrigerate until cold, at least 2 hours or up to 12 hours. To serve, spoon a portion of topping over each slice of cheesecake.

SCIENCE DESK:
Why Do Cheesecakes Crack?

SOME COOKS USE THE CRACK TO GAUGE WHEN A cheesecake is done. We say if it's cracked, it's overdone, not to mention unsightly. Exactly what happens, you may ask, that causes the cheesecake to form a fault line?

What we learned from two months of baking was that when the internal temperature of a cheesecake rose beyond 160 degrees, it almost always cracked. The best way to prevent cheesecake from cracking is to use an instant-read thermometer to test its doneness. Take it out of the oven when it reaches 150 degrees at the center to avoid overbaking.

That said, there is a second opportunity for the cheesecake to crack, this time outside of the oven. During testing, a perfectly good-looking cake cracked as it sat on the cooling rack. Evidently, the cake shrank during cooling and clung to the sides of the springform pan. If the cake clings tenaciously enough, it splits at its weakest point, the center. To avoid this type of late cracking, free the cheesecake from the sides of the pan with a paring knife as soon as it comes out of the oven.

TASTING LAB: Store-Bought Cheesecakes

COULD IT BE POSSIBLE THAT EVEN GOOD COOKS MIGHT be better off simply defrosting a store-bought frozen cheesecake instead of baking a fresh one at home? We wanted to make sure our efforts (and possibly yours) weren't in vain, so we thawed four commercial cheesecakes and conducted a blind taste test, adding our homemade version

as one of the contenders.

The contestants were Sara Lee Classic New York Style Cheesecake ($6.29 for 32 ounces); The Ultimate New York Cheesecake ($8.99 for 15 ounces), made by David Glass, a gourmet dessert company; Original Cheesecake from The Cheesecake Factory ($16.95 for 38 ounces), a chain of eateries featuring more than 30 flavors of cheesecake; and Trader Joe's New York Style Cheesecake ($3.69 for 18 ounces), sold by the discount natural foods grocery chain.

TECHNIQUE:
Patting the Crust into Place

1. Use bottom of ramekin or drinking glass to press crumbs into bottom of buttered springform pan. Press crumbs as far as possible into edges of pan.

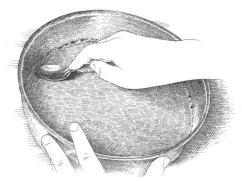

2. Use teaspoon to neatly press crumbs into circumference of pan to create clean edge.

It was a landslide, with our homemade cheesecake winning easily. Tasters prized its "fresh," "tangy" flavor and "crisp" crust with "true graham flavor." To our surprise, Sara Lee earned second place for its "soft," "smooth" texture, though a few tasters remarked that it left a "burning sensation" in the back of their throats. Sara Lee easily beat out more expensive "gourmet" cheesecakes made by David Glass and The Cheesecake Factory. Tasters described the David Glass entry as "artificially vanilla," with an "overly cinnamony crust." The Cheesecake Factory cake was deemed "acidic and sour." Each and every taster put the Trader Joe's cheesecake in last place, uniformly rejecting it as "pasty," "floury," and "absolutely tasteless."

The lesson here is clear: Don't be lured by the ease of store-bought cheesecake. Take the time to make it at home, and you won't be disappointed. If you simply don't have the time to make your own cheesecake, don't waste money on "gourmet" brands. Sara Lee is just fine.

EQUIPMENT CORNER: Kitchen Timers

A KITCHEN TIMER IS ONE OF THOSE PIECES OF EQUIPMENT to which most home cooks don't give much thought. In a professional test kitchen, however, a good timer is essential. We use the same models available to home cooks, but we rely on them dozens of times every day. Each test cook has his or her own timer, and we decided to find out which model is best.

We gathered eight digital kitchen timers, ranging in price from $7 to $30. (We don't see the point of using an old-fashioned dial timer that you turn and set. It's impossible to measure short periods with these timers and hard to tell the difference between six minutes and seven.) Although it seems obvious that a timer will be accurate, we checked all eight digital timers to make sure. As expected, each one kept time accurately.

Because each of the timers were accurate, we focused on other features that would we thought would appeal to the home cook. Among the most important were the ability to count in seconds (good for delicate foods such as eggs); maximum time (we preferred timers that could cover at least 10 hours—enough to tackle an all-day barbecue project or overnight bread rising); more than one built-in timer (for timing several dishes at once); and continued count-up after the alarm sounds (so you know how long a dish has been cooking past the desired time). Important ease-of-use considerations included size and readability of the display (the bigger, the better), and the design of the buttons (large, raised buttons were preferred).

One timer had all these features and more, and it quickly emerged as the winner. As the name suggests, the West Bend Clock/Triple Timer model 40053 ($29.99) has 3 separate timers. It measures in seconds, counts up to 24 hours, and counts up after the alarm sounds. It also includes interrupt, memory, and stopwatch features. The large displays and buttons are exceptionally easy to read and use.

The Pyrex Professional Programmable Timer/Clock Model #17105 and the Polder Triple Kitchen Timer/Clock Model 891, both $19.99, were also well liked but neither was as easy to use as the winning West Bend model. The other five models tested lacked one or more of the above-mentioned features (most did not record seconds) and failed to impress our testers.

BEST KITCHEN TIMER

The West Bend Clock/Triple Timer does it all and was the clear winner in our tests. See www.cooksillustrated.com for up-to-date prices and a mail-order source for this product.

PHOTO CREDITS

Keller + Keller

xii, xiv (lower-middle right, bottom right), 17, 18, 30, 36, 84, 86, 94, 109, 110, 123, 132, 145, 146, 160, 177 (top), 212, 227 (top), 245, 249, 257, 263, 264, 279, 280, 285, 304, 315, 316, 324, 328

Bill Miles

iv

Elisabeth O'Donnell

viii, xiv (top left & right, upper-middle left & right, lower-middle left, bottom left), xv, 2, 13, 16, 25, 39, 41, 44, 50, 52, 55, 59, 64, 102 (left), 118, 127 (top), 154, 157, 166, 178, 189, 200, 205, 211, 219, 221, 230, 252, 254, 266, 272, 277 (left), 286, 314

Carl Tremblay

15, 23, 34, 37, 62, 80, 91, 92, 103, 108, 112, 124, 129, 135, 148, 163, 175, 180, 208, 226, 233, 241, 246, 268, 275, 307, 310, 319, 331

Daniel van Ackere

9, 14, 26, 29, 33, 35, 42, 48, 53, 58, 60, 63, 87, 89, 101, 102 (right), 113, 114, 115, 117, 127 (bottom), 131, 139, 143, 152, 155, 161, 165, 170, 172, 177 (bottom), 184, 185, 193, 195, 209, 217, 224, 227 (bottom), 234, 239, 253, 255, 265, 270, 271, 273, 277 (right), 287, 288, 313, 323, 333, 335